Baker's
Bible Study
Guide

Derek Prime

Baker Book House
Grand Rapids, Michigan 49506

Formerly published under the titles, *Questions on the Christian Faith,* © 1967, and *Bible Guidelines,* © 1967 by Derek Prime.

Combined edition issued 1982 by Baker Book House with permission of copyright owner

ISBN: 0-8010-7076-7

First printing, July 1982
Second printing, June 1984

Printed in the United States of America

Contents

Questions on the Christian Faith

Bible Guidelines

The Ten Commandments

Subjects arising, directly or indirectly, from the Ten Commandments

Desires and works of man's sinful flesh
("The seven deadly sins")

Christian character
("The fruit of the Spirit")

Commitment to Christ and the gospel

THE ANSWERS

Using the Book

This book should be studied or referred to *with the Bible at hand*. The concern throughout has been to state what the Bible has to say in answer to each question. Where possible every statement has a Bible reference which should substantiate or illustrate it in some way.

The material has been set out in sections and sub-sections, both numerically and alphabetically, to make it easy for the book to be studied by sections, rather than read through hurriedly.

Read without the Bible this book will appear heavy and solid. Read with the Bible it should become alive through the power of Bible-truth.

Bible Definitions

The endeavour has been made to avoid words which would not be familiar to the reader who is only just becoming acquainted with Biblical language and phraseology. But this is not always possible and the attempt sometimes means that the full force of an idea is lost. Where a word is unusual or has a particular significance in the Bible, a brief explanation of the word and its use will be found at the end of the book in the section entitled "Bible Definitions".

BIBLE REFERENCES

(Alphabetical list of the books of the Bible and the abbreviations used)

Acts	Acts	*Esth.*	Esther
Amos	Amos	*Ex.*	Exodus
I Chron.	I Chronicles	*Ezek.*	Ezekiel
II Chron.	II Chronicles	*Ezra*	Ezra
Col.	Colossians	*Gal.*	Galatians
I Cor.	I Corinthians	*Gen.*	Genesis
II Cor.	II Corinthians	*Hab.*	Habakkuk
Dan.	Daniel	*Hag.*	Haggai
Deut.	Deuteronomy	*Heb.*	Hebrews
Eccl.	Ecclesiastes	*Hos.*	Hosea
Eph.	Ephesians	*Isa.*	Isaiah

Jas.	James	*Num.*	Numbers
Jer.	Jeremiah	*Obad.*	Obadiah
Job	Job	*I Pet.*	I Peter
Joel	Joel	*II Pet.*	II Peter
John	John	*Philem.*	Philemon
I John	I John	*Phil.*	Philippians
II John	II John	*Prov.*	Proverbs
III John	III John	*Ps.*	Psalms
Jonah	Jonah	*Rev.*	Revelation
Josh.	Joshua	*Rom.*	Romans
Jude	Jude	*Ruth*	Ruth
Judg.	Judges	*I Sam.*	I Samuel
I Kings	I Kings	*II Sam.*	II Samuel
II Kings	II Kings	*S. of Songs*	Song of Solomon (Song of Songs)
Lam.	Lamentations		
Lev.	Leviticus	*I Thess.*	I Thessalonians
Luke	Luke	*II Thess.*	II Thessalonians
Mal.	Malachi	*I Tim.*	I Timothy
Mark	Mark	*II Tim.*	II Timothy
Matt.	Matthew	*Tit.*	Titus
Micah	Micah	*Zech.*	Zechariah
Nahum	Nahum	*Zeph.*	Zephaniah
Neh.	Nehemiah		

Finding References

A few hints may be helpful for those not used to finding references in the Bible.

An example: I Thessalonians 2: 13.

The name "Thessalonians" refers to the book in the Bible. All Bibles have a list of books in the front and some have an alphabetical list as well. Look up "Thessalonians" in this list and you will find the page number. The "I" before the name indicates that there is more than one book of this name. "Thessalonians" has books "I" and "II".

The figure immediately after the name is the number of the chapter in that book and the last figure is the number of the verse.

In the Authorised or King James' Version the verses are all separated, but in the Revised Version or the New English Bible the chapters are in paragraphs but the equivalent verse number is placed in the margin. A little practice will soon make you familiar with the lay-out of the Bible.

Questions on the Christian Faith

I. DEFINING CHRISTIANITY

Question: What is Christianity?

Answer: It is the only way of knowing God aright, and of living for Him.

1. There is but one God.

(a) There have been, and are, many so-called gods; but they are false (*I Cor.* 8: 4–6).

(b) There is one God (*Eph.* 4: 6).

(c) Although God is revealed to us as a Trinity, the Lord our God is one Lord (*Deut.* 6: 4).

(d) He is the Creator (*Gen.* 1: 1 ff).

(e) He is supreme (*Rom.* 11: 36; *Rev.* 19: 6).

(f) He is the Judge of all men (*Gen.* 18: 25; *Rom.* 2: 16).

2. Men and women are not in a right relationship with God.

(a) When first created, man was in a right relationship with God; he possessed true knowledge, righteousness and holiness, for God made all things perfect (*Gen.* 1: 27, 31; *Eccl.* 7: 29).

(b) In such a condition, man enjoyed fellowship with God (*Gen.* 3: 8).

(c) The right relationship was exchanged for a wrong relationship through the fall of man, i.e. man's disobedience (*Gen.* 3).

(d) Sin came into the world through Adam, and death through sin (*Rom.* 5: 12); all men share in sin (*Rom.* 3: 23).

(e) Human sin constitutes a barrier to man's fellowship with God who is holy and righteous (*Isa.* 59: 2; *I John* 1: 5).

(f) Men are strangers to the life of God, estranged and hostile in mind to God (*Eph.* 4: 18; *Col.* 1: 21).

(g) In such a position man is incapable of knowing God and of living righteously (*Ps.* 14: 1–4; *Isa.* 64: 6; *Rom.* 7: 18).

3. Christianity proclaims what God has done through Jesus Christ to make possible man's reconciliation to God.

(a) God has no pleasure in the death of the wicked (*Ezek.* 33: 11).

(b) He loves the world (*John* 3: 16).

(c) He sent His Son into the world to save sinners (*I Tim.* 1: 15); this purpose involved His bearing the sin of sinners, and experiencing the death due to sinners (*I Pet.* 2: 24; *Isa.* 53: 5, 6).

(d) Through Christ God has made possible reconciliation, and men may be urged to be reconciled to God (*II Cor.* 5: 18, 19, 20).

(e) On repentance and faith men may enter into the benefits of this reconciliation (*Mark* 1: 15; *Acts* 17: 30; *Rom.* 5: 1 ff).

4. Having been reconciled to God, a man may know God.

(a) God then gives to the reconciled man such an understanding of Christ that he realises that to know Christ is to know God (*II Cor.* 4: 6).

(b) Christ came to reveal the Father (*John* 14: 8, 9).

(c) Christ delivered to men the words of God (*John* 14: 24).

(d) Christ is the way for us to God (*John* 14: 6).

(e) The Spirit of Christ is sent

into our hearts when we are reconciled to God that we may know God (*John* 14: 16, 17; *Rom.* 8: 15, 16; *Eph.* 1: 17).

(f) This experience of knowing God was promised when the new covenant which God would make with men was made known through the prophets (*Jer.* 31: 34).

(g) Knowing God means:

(i) A growing appreciation of the character of God (*Eph.* 1: 17; *Col.* 1: 10; *II Pet.* 3: 18; *I John* 1: 5; *I John* 4: 8).

(ii) Liberty and confidence to enter into God's presence (*Heb.* 10: 19 f).

(iii) Fellowship with the Father and with His Son Jesus Christ (*I John* 1: 3).

5. Having been reconciled to God, a man may live for God.

(a) He feels a constant urge to do so (*II Cor.* 5: 15; *Rom.* 12: 1).

(b) He possesses a new dynamic which encourages him in this new direction (*II Cor.* 5: 17; *Gal.* 2: 19, 20; *Phil.* 2: 13).

(c) The Holy Spirit who dwells within makes possible a new way of life (*Rom.* 8: 9; *Gal.* 5: 22–24).

(d) Living for God means:

(i) Negatively, not to go on sinning (*Rom.* 6: 11, 13).

(ii) But positively, to devote one's life to God (*Rom.* 6: 11, 13).

(iii) To make it one's ambition to please Him (*II Cor.* 5: 9).

(iv) To live a life of simple and straightforward obedience to the commandments of God (*I John* 2: 4, 5).

(v) To strive after holiness more and more (*I Thess.* 4: 1–4).

6. Men who know God and who live for Him find themselves re- stored, in some measure, to the original condition of man before the fall.

(a) Before the fall, man knew God and was righteous (*Gen.* 1: 27; 2: 15).

(b) When a man is "in Christ" there is a new creation (*II Cor.* 5: 17).

(c) That man is brought to a true knowledge of God (*Col.* 3: 10).

(d) Righteousness and holiness then become the pattern of his life (*Eph.* 4: 24).

7. The knowledge of God and the possibility of living for Him are possible through Jesus Christ alone.

(a) The key statement is *John* 14: 6: "Jesus saith . . . I am the Way, the Truth, and the Life; no man cometh unto the Father, but by me."

(b) Although there may be many ways to Christ, there is but one way to the Father.

(c) Knowledge about God may be gained by observing nature, providence and history; but all such knowledge is incomplete and insufficient (*Rom.* 1: 19, 20), and is quite different from knowing God in personal intimacy.

(d) Life lived by men without Christ is not pleasing to God (*John* 15: 5; *Eph.* 2: 3, 12).

(e) Only through Jesus Christ is possible the right relationship we so desperately need (*Acts* 4: 12).

(f) To Christ alone can we turn for the knowledge of God and for eternal life (*Matt.* 11: 27; *John* 6: 68; 17: 3).

8. It is easy to appreciate why true Christianity is so aggressive.

12

(a) Without saving faith in Christ, men are dead towards God, having no hope and without God in the world, lost and condemned (*Eph.* 2: 1, 12; *John* 3: 18).

(b) Christianity is unique (*John* 14: 6). The Incarnation, the perfect Life of Christ, the "once-for-all" nature of His death as a sacrifice for sins, His Resurrection, His Ascension, and His promised return are all unique facts. They are unique not only in history but also in their continuing consequences (*Acts* 2: 39). Nowhere are higher conceptions of God to be found. No one is a more sufficient Saviour than Christ.

(c) Whilst Christians should not be intolerant of the adherents of other religions, they cannot accept that these religions are in any way approved by God or properly satisfying to men (*I Thess.* 1: 9; *I John* 4: 1–3).

(d) By reason of men's desperate need and the compelling love of God Christianity must be aggressive (*Matt.* 9: 36–38; *Mark* 16: 15, 16): truth opposes error; holiness cannot compromise with sin; the love of God in the hearts of reconciled men compels them to proclaim the Christian gospel (*II Cor.* 5: 14, 20).

(e) Christianity is worth dying for (*Acts* 20: 24; *II Tim.* 1: 8–12).

2. LEARNING THE TRUTH ABOUT CHRISTIANITY

Question: Where are we to learn the truth about Christianity?

Answer: From the Bible alone.

1. **Christianity presents us with particular historical facts and spiritual truths which are to be understood and believed (*I John* 1: 1–4).**

For example:

(a) The deity of Christ (*John* 20: 31);

(b) His Incarnation (*I John* 4: 2, 3; *II John* 7; *John* 1: 14);

(c) His unique death for our sins (*I Cor.* 15: 3; *I John* 2: 2; 4: 10);

(d) His resurrection (*John* 20: 29; *I Cor.* 15: 4; *Acts* 2: 32);

(e) His ascension (*Acts* 7: 55, 56; *Heb.* 1: 3; 2: 9);

(f) His second coming (*I Thess.* 1: 10).

2. **The record of these historical facts and the witness to these spiritual truths are found in the Bible (*Luke* 1: 1–4).**

For example:

(a) The deity of Christ (*John* 1: 1–14; *Matt.* 16: 13–20);

(b) His Incarnation (*Matt.* 1: 18–25; *Luke* 1: 26–38; 2: 1–7);

(c) His death for our sins (*Matt.* 27: 26–61; *Mark* 15: 15–41; *Luke* 23: 27–49; *John* 19: 13–37);

(d) His resurrection (*Matt.* 28: 1–10; *Mark* 16: 1–13; *Luke* 24: 1–48; *John* 20: 1–29; *I Cor.* 15: 4–8);

(e) His ascension (*Mark* 16: 19; *Luke* 24: 51; *Acts* 1: 9–11);

(f) His second coming (*Matt* 24: 3–31; *I Thess.* 5: 1–3; *II Thess.* 1: 7–10).

3. **The distinctive significance or interpretation of any fact or truth of Christianity is that which the Bible gives (*John* 20: 30, 31; *I Cor.* 10: 11).**

(a) Many of the truths of Christianity need explanation in detail (*Luke* 24: 27; *Acts* 18: 26).

(b) Human understanding, unaided, cannot provide the satisfactory explanation (*Matt.* 16: 17; *I Cor.* 2: 14).

(c) The Scriptures were given by God to provide us with the illumination and instruction we need (*Ps.* 119: 130; *Matt.* 21: 42; *Rom.* 15: 4)—the basis on which the gospel is preached is the statements of the Scriptures (*Luke* 24: 44–47; *Acts* 10: 43; 17: 2; 18: 28; *I Cor.* 15: 3, 4).

(d) The Holy Spirit uses the Scriptures to make plain truths to which we would otherwise be blind (*Luke* 24: 27).

(e) When we fail to understand what the Scriptures say on a subject, we soon err in our judgment on spiritual matters (*Mark* 12: 24; *Matt.* 22: 29).

4. **The Bible alone must be our authority in all matters of faith and conduct.**

(a) The Bible is authoritative (*Matt.* 22: 31).

(b) It is inspired by God (*II Tim.* 3: 16; *II Pet.* 1: 19–21).

(c) The revelation the Bible provides is final—anything which goes against it is false (*Isa.* 8: 20; *Gal.* 1: 8, 9).

(d) The revelation God has given in the Bible—through prophets, apostles and through Christ—is at the foundation of the Church (*Eph.* 2: 20).

(e) Every opinion must be examined in the light of what the Bible says (*Acts* 17: 11).

(f) What the Bible says must be the deciding factor in any decision that has to be made (*Matt.* 4: 1–11; *Acts* 15: 14, 15).

(g) The Bible provides all that a man needs to know and tells him all he ought to be to please God (*II Tim.* 3: 15–17).

(h) If we fail to recognise the Bible's supreme authority in matters of faith and conduct, we shall find ourselves breaking God's commandments through attention to lesser authorities (*Matt.* 15: 2, 3, 6).

(i) Hollow and delusive speculations based upon traditions of man-made teaching quickly capture our attention if we neglect the Bible's authority (*Col.* 2: 8).

5. **Everything points logically to the supreme authority of the Bible whenever Christianity is under consideration.**

(a) Christ came to fulfil the promises made by God in the Old Testament Scriptures (*Luke* 24: 27, 44).

(b) The New Testament came into being because of the saving work of Christ (*I Cor.* 11: 25; *Luke* 1: 1–4; *Mark* 1: 1; *Rev.* 1: 19).

(c) The Spirit of Christ who caused the Old Testament Scriptures to be written caused also the New Testament Scriptures to be written (*I Pet.* 1: 11; *John* 14: 26; *Heb.* 2: 4).

3. THE BIBLE

Question: What is the Bible?

Answer: The Books of the Old and New Testaments, given by inspiration from God, containing everything which we are to believe and do, that our souls may be saved and God served.

1. The Bible is a collection of books —a library.

(a) The Old Testament is made up of the Law of Moses, the prophets, and the Book of Psalms (*Luke* 24: 44).

(b) What we call historical books the Jews reckoned among their prophetic or inspired writings: "the Psalms", as the first and longest item, was a way of referring to the final section of these inspired "Writings". The historical books record the dealings of God with His people, and provide the contemporary background of the prophets' ministries.

(c) God's messages were entrusted to the Jews in the Old Testament Scriptures (*Rom.* 3: 2).

(d) The New Testament is made up of the four gospels, which record the earthly ministry of Jesus, the Acts of the Apostles, which describes the establishment and growth of the early Church, the epistles which reveal the teaching of the apostles to the early churches, and the Book of the Revelation (sometimes called "the Apocalypse" meaning "an unveiling") which is a prophetic book, looking very much into the future.

(e) The Books of the Bible should be read as books rather than as collections of verses or texts.

(f) The Books of the Bible have come together from a variety of backgrounds:

(i) They were written by kings (e.g. David wrote many of the Psalms), prophets (e.g. Isaiah), apostles (e.g. Paul), historians (e.g. The Books of Kings), and others (e.g. Luke and his gospel and the Acts).

(ii) They were written in one of three languages, although mainly in Hebrew (the Old Testament) and Greek (the New Testament).

(iii) They were written over a period of more than a thousand years.

(iv) They originated from places as far apart as Babylon and Rome.

(v) They were written by as many as forty different individuals.

2. The books of the Bible have to do with either the Old or the New Covenant, or Testament.

(a) The books of the Old Testament may be said to have to do in general with the covenant God made with the children of Israel in the wilderness before they entered the promised land.

(b) The essential message of the Old Testament, if we have in mind the demand the covenant made for obedience, was "This do and thou shalt live" (*Lev.* 18: 5; *Luke* 10: 28)—although this manner of expressing it is a limited simplification.

(c) The books of the New Testament may be said to deal with the new covenant promised in the Old Testament (*Jer.* 31: 31–34) and fulfilled in Christ (*Matt.* 26: 28; *Heb.* 13: 20).

(d) The essential message of the New Testament is "Believe on the Lord Jesus Christ, and thou shalt be saved" (*Acts* 16: 31).

3. The Books of the Old and New Testaments share a common inspiration—the inspiration of the Holy Spirit.

(a) The New Testament speaks often of the Scriptures as a product of the creative activity of the Spirit of God. He is their primary author (*II Pet.* 1: 21; *II Tim.* 3: 16).

(b) More than 500 times in the Pentateuch alone is divine authority claimed (e.g. statements such as those found in *Deut.* 4: 5 and *Ex.* 20: 1).

(c) Christ promised the Holy Spirit's inspiration to His apostles (*John* 14: 26; 15: 26, 27; 16: 13).

(d) The apostles claimed to have His inspiration (*Acts* 2: 33; 15: 28; *I Thess.* 1: 5; 4: 8; *I Cor.* 4: 1).

(e) The apostolic writings were put on the same level as other inspired writings, i.e. the Old Testament Scriptures (*II Pet.* 3: 15; *I Thess.* 5: 27).

4. **The inspiration of the Bible by the Holy Spirit accounts for the authority it is recognised to have.**

(a) It does not look to the Christian Church for its authority, for it has its own authority (*I Thess.* 1: 5).

(b) The Bible is consequently worthy of our closest attention (*II Pet.* 1: 19, 21; *Josh.* 1: 7, 8).

5. **Everything which God requires us to believe is found in the Bible** (*Acts* 8: 26–38; *I Cor.* 15: 1–4; *John* 5: 39). Its words are not to be added to or impaired (*Deut.* 4: 2; *Rev.* 22: 18, 19).

6. **Every principle which is to govern our life and conduct is to be found in the Bible** (e.g. The Sermon on the Mount, *Matt.* 5: 1–7, 29; Paul's practical instructions to the Thessalonians, *I Thess.* 4: 1–12; 5: 12–22).

7. **Through the good news of Christ which the Bible contains, our souls may be saved** (*John* 5: 39; *II Tim.* 3: 15; *John* 20: 31).

8. **By means of the Bible's instruction a man may be perfectly equipped for God's service** (*Ps.* 19: 7, 8; *II Tim.* 3: 16, 17).

4. THE INSPIRATION OF THE BIBLE

Question: How do we know that the Bible is the Word of God?

Answer: The Holy Spirit endorses it as the Word of God, causing us to accept its message and to prove its power in our lives. (To this "internal" evidence there may be added many "external" evidences which give supporting testimony to the endorsement of the Holy Spirit.)

1. **The Holy Spirit is connected very intimately with the Bible.**

(a) All the books of the Bible owe their origin to Him (*Matt.* 22: 43 f, R.V.; *Heb.* 3: 7; *Acts* 28: 25).

(b) The writers were "borne along" by the Holy Spirit's influence (*II Pet.* 1: 21). The exercise of their natural faculties was not interfered with, yet spontaneously they produced what God planned —so perfectly so that what they said, God said (*Dan.* 9: 10).

2. **As the Bible is either read or preached it is the Holy Spirit's particular right to endorse its truth to individual readers or hearers, according to His will.**

(a) When the Holy Spirit chooses so to act, the message of the Bible comes over with power behind it— the Holy Spirit's power—which results in conviction (*I Thess.* 1: 5).

(b) The message of the Bible is recognised to be then what it is— the Word of God and not the word of men (*I Thess.* 2: 13).

(c) When such power is known, the call of God to the individual through the Bible, by the working of the Holy Spirit, is answered— that is to say, the message is received, and acted upon. That the promises of the gospel then become real in a person's life confirms the truth of the Bible (*I Thess.* 1: 6, 7, 8; *Ps.* 34: 4, 6, 8).

(d) The Bible finds a primary place in the individual's life as a consequence, changing it for good (*I Thess.* 1: 9, 10; 2: 14; *Ps.* 119: 9, 11).

3. The Christian's conviction that the Bible is the Word of God grows as his experience of God increases.

(a) Every promise he claims rightfully is fulfilled (*II Cor.* 1: 20).

(b) The more he learns of the Scriptures the more he finds them suitable to his need (*Ps.* 119: 49–56).

(c) He finds that the Holy Spirit speaks to him through the Bible, whether he reads in the Old or the New Testament (*Ps.* 95: 7–11; compare *Heb.* 3: 7–11, noticing verse 7—"as the Holy Ghost saith, Today if ye will hear his voice . . .").

(d) The Bible becomes more and more of a power in his life (*I Thess.* 2: 13; *Heb.* 5: 14).

4. As the Christian considers the "external" evidences that the Bible is the Word of God his conviction is strengthened.

There are many such evidences and each is worthy of thought:

(a) The Bible's age.

(b) Its preservation in spite of many attacks.

(c) Its amazing unity, although made up of 66 different books, written by over 40 authors, over a great period of time.

(d) The prophecies made in the Bible which have been fulfilled (*Deut.* 28: 64; cf. *Jer.* 30: 11;

Micah 5: 2; *Zech.* 9: 9; 11: 12, 13).

(e) Its knowledge of human nature.

(f) Its frankness and honesty when dealing with its heroes.

(g) Its superb moral teaching: it never falls short of the highest even in the darkest hours of human history.

(h) Its power to change men's lives.

(i) The testimony of much of modern science. The evidence which science gives concerning the creation of the universe, the evidence of geology, archaeology and geography all add confirmation to the fact that the Bible is the Word of God.

(j) Most important of all the "external" evidences is Christ's repeated testimony to the Old Testament as the Word of God (e.g. *Mark* 12: 36; *Matt.* 5: 18).

5. The essential conviction that the Bible is the Word of God comes not from these "external" evidences, however, but from the Holy Spirit.

(a) Spiritual insight is given to the Christian believer (*I John* 2: 20, 27).

(b) The Holy Spirit guides the Christian into everything which is true (*John* 16: 13, 14).

(c) Christians are given an understanding which is not natural to man (*I Cor.* 2: 10–12): this fact explains the growing conviction they possess that the Bible is the Word of God.

5. THE EXISTENCE OF GOD

Question: What proof is there of the existence of God?

Answer: God is not visible to the

17

human eye: thus there can be no "direct" proof of God. But He has given clues to His existence and His nature both in creation and in the nature of man; and a glorious revelation of Himself in the Person of His Son, Jesus Christ. Added to these evidences, there is the witness of the Bible, and of those who have found God.

1. That men should ask this question is proof of man's sinfulness and corruption.

(a) The question demonstrates man's folly and corruption through sin (*Ps.* 14: 1).

(b) The question results from man's sinful pride and rebellion (*Ps.* 10: 4).

(c) When men do not want to be convinced of God's existence, God gives them up to their depraved reason (*Rom.* 1: 28).

(d) Their thinking ends in futility and their wisdom becomes foolishness (*Rom.* 1: 21, 22).

2. The Bible does not endeavour to answer this question—i.e. to prove God's existence—but always assumes God's existence.

(a) All the wonders of creation are recognised to be expressions of His power (*Ps.* 19: 1).

(b) All that is good is accepted as coming from Him (*Jas.* 1: 17).

3. The Bible makes plain that no one has ever seen God the Father: thus visible proof of His existence is not provided for men.

(a) No one has ever seen God (*John* 1: 18).

(b) God is not visible to the human eye (*I Tim.* 1: 17; 6: 16).

4. Although men may gain a real knowledge of God, that knowledge can be only partial in this life.

(a) Man can never fully comprehend God (*Isa.* 55: 8, 9).

(b) Man's knowledge of God in this life can be partial only (*I Cor.* 13: 9, 10, 12).

5. Nevertheless God has provided many impressive indirect proofs of His existence: He has not left Himself without witness (*Acts* 14: 17).

6. First, there is the witness of creation.

(a) Reason points to the need of a first cause, i.e. the world could not make itself: the Bible names that First Cause—God (*Gen.* 1: 1; *John* 1: 1; *Acts* 17: 24; *Ps.* 100: 3).

(b) For example, in creation we see thought (*Ps.* 139: 14), forethought (*Gen.* 2: 6), laws (*Ps.* 19: 4–6), and life (*Gen.* 7: 15; 26: 12–14). Behind such there must be a Thinker (*Gen.* 1: 3, 31; *Isa.* 55: 8, 9), an overruling Providence (*Eph.* 1: 11), a Law-Giver (*Isa.* 33: 22; *Jas.* 4: 12), and a Life-Giver (*Acts* 17: 25).

(c) God has disclosed from the beginning His everlasting power and deity in His creation: the eye of reason discerns God's characteristics in the things He has made (*Rom.* 1: 18–20).

(d) The heavens declare the glory of God, and the firmament proclaims His handiwork (*Ps.* 19: 1; *Ps.* 8: 1, 3; *Isa.* 40: 25, 26; *Jer.* 10: 10–13).

(e) In creation, God gives clues to His nature, in the kindness He shows (*Acts* 14: 17; *Matt.* 5: 45).

7. Secondly, there is the witness of man himself.

(a) The wonder of man's own

creation points to a Creator (*Ps.* 139: 14).

(b) The idea of God is written on men's hearts since man was made in God's image (*Gen.* 1: 26, 27).

(c) Man has a natural intuition that there is a God: this is seen in a natural religiousness in men, mistaken and polluted as it may become (*Acts* 17: 22, 23).

(d) Man's conscience witnesses to a law within him by nature—and where there is law there is a Law-Giver (*Rom.* 2: 14, 15).

(e) It is the fool—the corrupt man lacking understanding—who says, "There is no God" (*Ps.* 14: 1).

8. The witness of creation and of man himself makes up what we may describe as "general revelation", that is to say, facts and understanding given to all men at all times to observe in the world, and from which they may draw logical conclusions as to God's existence. We now come to what we may describe as "special revelation", that is to say, revelation which could not have come to man by his study of nature or by the use of his own reason.

9. Thirdly, and most important of all the witnesses we shall mention, there is the witness of Jesus Christ.

(a) God has revealed Himself to us in Jesus Christ His Son (*II Cor.* 4: 6).

(b) Christ made known the Father (*John* 1: 18).

(c) He is the visible image of the invisible God (*Col.* 1: 15–17).

(d) As Jesus Christ dwelt amongst men, men saw His glory, such glory as belongs to God only (*John* 1: 14).

(e) The human Jesus who could be seen, looked upon and felt, was seen to be the Son of God (*I John* 1: 1–3). The apostles and disciples needed no more proof of God's existence: through the Son they knew the Father also (*John* 14: 7).

(f) His miracles bore witness similarly to His deity (*John* 20: 30, 31).

(g) To have seen Jesus was to have seen the Father (*John* 14: 9).

10. Fourthly, there is the witness of the Bible.

(a) The Bible claims to be a revelation from the invisible God (*II Tim.* 3: 16). As we consider the evidences which demonstrate its divine origin so we are convinced of the existence of God.

(b) Some of the predictions it makes, claiming to come from God, are proved true. The good He promises and the evil He threatens (*Rom.* 1: 18), are found to happen in men's experience (*Isa.* 41: 23, 24). God challenges the so-called gods of the heathen to do likewise (*Isa.* 41: 22, 23).

11. The general revelation provided by creation and the nature of man himself, and the special revelation provided by the Incarnation of Jesus Christ and the Bible are confirmed also by the witness of the Church of Jesus Christ and by the experience of individual members.

(a) The confirming witness of the Church of Jesus Christ.

(i) The early Church had its testimony confirmed by God by means of signs, miracles and many different works of power (*Heb.* 2: 4).

(ii) The amazing growth of the Church is accounted for satisfactorily only by the power of God (*Acts* 16: 5; *Matt.* 13: 31, 32).

(iii) Its amazing life and continuance is explained by the fact that it is the Church of the living God (*I Tim.* 3: 15).

(iv) Its preservation finds a satisfactory explanation only in the promise of Christ (*Matt.* 16: 18; *Acts* 5: 38, 39).

(b) The confirming witness of individual members.

(i) They have found their search for God rewarded (*Heb.* 11: 6).

(ii) In knowing Jesus Christ they know God (*I John* 1: 1–2).

(iii) They know that the Son of God has come and given them an understanding to know God as a reality in personal experience (*I John* 5: 20).

(iv) They feel God's presence (*Acts* 23: 11; *Matt.* 28: 20; *Heb.* 13: 5).

(v) Their lives know transformation (*II Cor.* 5: 17; 3: 18).

(vi) An irrepressible testimony is theirs (*Acts* 4: 20).

12. Conclusion.

(a) If men's asking of this question —what proof is there of the existence of God?—is sincere, God will provide the answer in a manner which will leave them in no doubt (*Isa.* 55: 6; *Jer.* 29: 13; *Matt.* 7: 8).

(b) That which convinces a man is his personal experience of God through Christ and by the Spirit (*John* 20: 28; *II Tim.* 1: 12).

6. THE BEING OF GOD

Question: What is God in Himself?

Answer: God is Spirit: invisible, without body, personal, great beyond human estimation, life-giving, and supremely powerful.

1. God is Spirit.

(a) *John* 4: 24—"God is a Spirit: and they that worship Him must worship Him in spirit and in truth"—is the nearest approach we get to a definition of the Being of God.

(b) Being Spirit, God has no body; a spirit has not flesh and bones (*Luke* 24: 39).

2. He is invisible.

(a) Being Spirit, God is invisible: no man has ever seen Him or can see Him (*I Tim.* 6: 15, 16).

(b) God is not discernible by our physical senses (*John* 1: 18).

(c) It was on the grounds of the fact that the people saw no form of God on the day that He spoke to them at Horeb that they were instructed not to make any graven image of God for themselves (*Deut.* 4: 15).

3. He is personal.

(a) He is a Personal Spirit, revealing Himself to Moses, for example, as "I AM THAT I AM" (*Ex.* 3: 14).

(b) Personal fellowship may be enjoyed with Him:

(i) He spoke to Adam (*Gen.* 2: 16; 3: 9 ff);

(ii) He revealed Himself to Noah (*Gen.* 6: 13 ff);

(iii) He entered into covenant with Abraham (*Gen.* 12: 1–3);

(iv) He conversed with Moses, as a friend with friend (*Ex.* 33: 11);

(v) He makes His abode with believing men and women (*John* 14: 23);

(vi) The Christian enjoys fellowship with Him (*I John* 1: 3).

4. He is very great.

(a) As the Lord, He is unique (*Isa.* 45: 6).

(b) He speaks with supreme authority (*Heb.* 1: 2).

(c) He alone has immortality inherent in Himself (*I Tim.* 6: 16)—see 6 (a) below.

(d) He is infinite: heaven and the highest heaven cannot contain Him (*I Kings* 7: 27).

(e) There is no one to whom He may be likened or compared (*Isa.* 40: 18).

(f) There are no limits or bounds to be fixed to any of His characteristics, for example:

(i) So far as space is concerned, He is everywhere (*Jer.* 23: 24; *Ps.* 139: 7–10);

(ii) So far as time is concerned, He is eternal (*Ps.* 90: 2, 4; *Isa.* 40: 28; *Hab.* 1: 12);

(iii) So far as knowledge is concerned, He knows all things (*Ps.* 139: 2–5; 147: 5; *I John* 3: 20).

(g) In the light of His greatness, we can see the relevance of the second commandment: "Thou shalt not make unto thee any graven image, or any likeness of any thing that is in heaven above, or that is in the earth beneath, or that is in the water under the earth" (*Ex.* 20: 4).

5. God is clearly beyond our complete understanding.

(a) He dwells in the high and holy place (*Isa.* 57: 15).

(b) His judgments are unsearchable, His ways are untraceable, and His knowledge is beyond our estimation (*Rom.* 11: 33–34; *I Cor.* 2: 16).

(c) He dwells in unapproachable light (*I Tim.* 6: 16).

(d) We do not know God here as He is; we are like people seeing a reflection in a mirror dimly (*I Cor.* 13: 12).

6. He has life-giving power in Himself.

(a) Being the source of all being and life, all things trace their beginning from Him (*Gen.* 1: 1).

(b) God's existence depends upon no one besides Himself; He said to Moses, "I AM THAT I AM" (*Ex.* 3: 14).

(c) He has life-giving power in Himself (*John* 5: 26).

(d) He gives to all men life and breath and everything (*Acts* 17: 25).

7. He does what He pleases.

(a) He does whatever He pleases everywhere (*Ps.* 115: 3; 135: 6; *Dan.* 4: 35).

(b) His will always prevails; His purposes are always fulfilled (*Isa.* 46: 10).

(c) None can resist His will, or say to Him, "What doest Thou?" (*Rom.* 9: 19; *Dan.* 4: 35).

(d) He does with His creatures whatever He pleases: the nations are as nothing before His power (*Isa.* 40: 15, 17).

(e) His dominion is an everlasting dominion, and His kingdom endures from generation to generation (*Dan.* 4: 34).

7. THE ATTRIBUTES OF GOD

Question: What is God like?

Answer: He is holy, righteous, loving, good, wise, all-knowing, eternal, unchanging, and independent of all His creation.

1. God is holy.

(a) The holiness of God is His most outstanding characteristic because it marks Him as quite different and distinct from all His creatures (*Ps.* 99: 3; *Isa.* 40: 25; *Hos.* 11: 9).

(b) Each Person of the Godhead is said to be holy (*John* 14: 26; 17: 11; *Acts* 4: 30).

(c) Holiness is the initial feature of God's character with which men are confronted (*Ps.* 24: 3; *Isa.* 6: 3).

(d) He is majestic in holiness (*Ex.* 15: 11); there is none holy like Him (*I Sam.* 2: 2).

(e) His holiness is such that He cannot overlook wickedness and dishonesty (*Micah* 6: 10–13); He is of purer eyes than to behold evil and cannot look on wrong (*Hab.* 1: 13).

(f) He desires that His spiritual children should share His holiness (*Heb.* 12: 10; *I Pet.* 1: 15, 16).

2. God is righteous.

(a) He is righteous, and His righteousness is always the same (*John* 17: 25; *Zeph.* 3: 5).

(b) He is just and righteous in all that He does (*Isa.* 30: 18)—even in the bringing of calamity upon His people (*Dan.* 9: 14).

(c) Righteousness and justice are at the foundation of His government (*Ps.* 97: 2).

(d) He is the righteous Judge (*Ps.* 7: 11), who always does right (*Gen.* 18: 25), and who will judge the world with righteousness (*Ps.* 96: 13).

(e) He is justified in His sentence and blameless in His judgment (*Ps.* 51: 4).

(f) He does not overlook anything His children do for Him and the love they show to Him (*Heb.* 6: 10).

3. God is loving.

(a) Everything about God displays His love (*Ps.* 25: 10): indeed He is love (*I John* 4: 8, 16).

(b) He has revealed Himself as a God merciful and gracious, slow to anger and abounding in steadfast love and faithfulness (*Ex.* 34: 6; *Ps.* 51: 1; *Joel* 2: 13; *Jonah* 4: 2; *Micah* 7: 18).

(c) His love is so great that it is said to extend to the heavens (*Ps.* 36: 5).

(d) His love for His people cannot be brought to an end; where human love would end, His continues (*Hos.* 11: 8–9).

(e) His love is the basis of the redemption He provides (*Hos.* 3: 1, 2).

(f) His love is seen supremely in His sending of His Son into the world to be the propitiation for our sins (*I John* 4: 8, 9, 10).

4. God is good—by which we mean that He is in every way all that He as God should be; He is absolutely perfect.

(a) He is good (*II Chron.* 30: 18; *Ps.* 86: 5; 106: 1; 107: 1; 118: 1), and alone so (*Mark* 10: 18).

(b) His goodness is seen in His creation (*Gen.* 1: 4, 10, 12, 18, 21, 25, 31; *I Tim.* 4: 4).

(c) His goodness is seen in what He does (*Ps.* 119: 68; 104: 24–31).

(d) His goodness is seen in His gifts (*Jas.* 1: 17; *Ps.* 85: 12; 145: 9; *Neh.* 9: 20; *Acts* 14: 17).

(e) The commandments and the directions He gives to men are good (*Rom.* 7: 12; *Ps.* 119: 39; *Heb.* 6: 5).

(f) The promises He gives are good (*I Kings* 8: 56).

(g) The will and purpose He gives for our life is good (*Rom.* 12: 2), and no good thing does He withhold from those who walk uprightly (*Ps.* 84: 11).

(h) The work which He begins in Christians' lives at their regeneration is a good work (*Phil.* 1: 6).

(i) Even when God needs to discipline Christians it is always for their good (*Ps.* 119: 67, 71; *Heb.* 12: 10).

(j) There is no limit to the good He gives to His children in Christ (*Rom.* 8: 32; *Eph.* 1: 3).

5. God is wise.

(a) He is the source of wisdom (*Dan.* 2: 22, 23; *Isa.* 31: 2; *Job* 12: 13); it belongs to Him (*Dan.* 2: 20).

(b) His wisdom is seen in creation (*Prov.* 3: 19, 20; *Jer.* 10: 12; *Ps.* 104: 24).

(c) His wisdom is seen in the natural processes of the earth (*Isa.* 28: 23–26).

(d) His wisdom is seen in the working out of human history (*Isa.* 28: 29; 31: 2).

(e) He gives wisdom to the wise and knowledge to those who have understanding (*Dan.* 2: 21).

(f) His wisdom and understanding are beyond measurement, and certainly beyond man's power to investigate and understand (*Ps.* 147: 5; *Job* 28: 12–21; *Rom.* 11: 33).

6. God knows all things.

(a) Knowing all things, none can offer advice to Him (*I Cor.* 2: 16).

(b) He knows all things and nothing is hid from Him (*Hos.* 5: 3).

(c) No creature is hidden from His scrutiny (*Heb.* 4: 13; *Prov.* 15: 3; 5: 21); He is acquainted with all our ways (*Ps.* 139: 3).

(d) Everything lies naked and exposed to God (*Heb.* 4: 13).

(e) If hell and destruction are before the Lord, how much then are the hearts of men before Him (*Prov.* 15: 11).

7. God is eternal.

(a) His years have no end (*Heb.* 1: 11, 12); He is the living God (*Rev.* 7: 2).

(b) He is the eternal "I AM" (*Ex.* 3: 14), the first and the last (*Isa.* 44: 6).

(c) From everlasting to everlasting He is God (*Ps.* 90: 2), and He inhabits eternity (*Isa.* 57: 15).

(d) With Him one day is like a thousand years, and a thousand years like one day (*II Pet.* 3: 8; *Ps.* 90: 4).

(e) When the everlasting hills and eternal mountains disappear He remains (*Hab.* 3: 6).

8. God is unchanging.

(a) He does not change (*Mal.* 3: 6).

(b) In the midst of change, He is the same (*Heb.* 1: 12).

(c) With Him there is no variation or shadow of inconsistency (*Jas.* 1: 17).

(d) He is unchangeable in His purposes and promises (*Heb.* 6: 17); once He has spoken, He does what He has said (*Num.* 23: 19).

(e) His purposes stand for ever, and His plans last from age to age (*Ps.* 33: 11).

9. God is independent of all His creation.

(a) He made Himself known to Moses as "I AM WHO I AM" (*Ex.* 3: 14).

(b) He makes His decisions independently of anyone (*Dan.* 4: 35; *Rom.* 9: 19, 20; 11: 33, 34; *Ps.* 115: 3).

(c) He is independent in all His qualities and abilities (*Isa.* 40: 18–23).

8. THE TRINITY

Question: What is meant by saying that God is a Trinity?

Answer: The one true God is one in every way, in nature, will and being; but one in three distinct Persons—Father, Son and Holy Spirit.

(The word 'Trinity' is not found in the Bible. Nevertheless it sums up what the Bible teaches throughout concerning the mystery of God's Being. The term was first used to preserve the truth concerning the Being of God against the false teaching of heretics.)

1. There is one God.

(a) There is but one living and true God, or divine Being (*Deut.* 6: 4; *Mark* 12: 29; *Rom.* 3: 30; *I Tim.* 2: 5; *Jas.* 2: 19).

(b) Before Him was no god formed; nor shall there be any after Him (*Isa.* 43: 10). He is the first and the last (*Isa.* 44: 6).

(c) There is none besides Him (*Deut.* 4: 35; *Isa.* 44: 6).

2. God exists in three Persons: the Father, the Son and the Holy Spirit.

(a) Since the beginnings of human history God has revealed Himself as a Trinity: indications of the truth of the Trinity are found in the Old Testament, and in the earliest books.

(b) On occasions God speaks using the first person plural (*Gen.* 1: 26; 11: 7; *Isa.* 6: 8).

(c) The form of God's blessing is threefold (*Num.* 6: 24–26).

(d) A distinction is made between the Lord and the angel of the Lord, who Himself is God, to whom all divine titles are given and divine worship offered (*Gen.* 16: 10–13; 18: 13–14, 19, 25, 33; 22: 11 ff; 48: 15, 16; *Ex.* 3: 2, 6, 14; 13: 21; 14: 19; 23: 20, 21; *Josh.* 5: 13–15; *Judg.* 6: 11 ff; 13: 3 ff).

(e) As the revelation of the Old Testament is continued, the distinction between the Lord and the angel of the Lord becomes clearer. This messenger of the Lord (*Mal.* 3: 1) is called the Son of God (*Dan.* 3: 25). His personality and divinity are clearly revealed (*Zech.* 3: 1). He is of old, even from everlasting (*Micah* 5: 2), the Mighty God (*Isa.* 9: 6), the Lord of David (*Ps.* 110: 1), who was to be born of a virgin (*Isa.* 7: 14), and bear the sins of many (*Isa.* 53).

(f) With regard to the Holy Spirit, He is represented in the first chapter of Genesis as the source of order and life in the created universe (*Gen.* 1: 2). In the books that follow in the Old Testament, He is represented as inspiring the prophets (*Micah* 3: 8; cf. *II Pet.* 1: 21), giving wisdom, strength and goodness to statesmen and warriors, and to the people of God (*Ex.* 31: 3; *Num.* 11: 17, 25; *Deut.* 34: 9; *Judg.* 3: 10; 11: 29; *I Sam.* 10: 6; 16: 13).

(g) And then, of course, there is the ample evidence of the fact of the Trinity throughout the New Testament, and the particular evidence of the baptismal formula (*Matt.* 28: 19) and the apostolic benediction (*II Cor.* 13: 14).

3. The Father, the Son and the Holy Spirit are three distinct Persons: that is to say, these Persons are not simply different modes of appearance God uses in His relationship to us.

(a) The Father says "I" (*John* 12: 28); the Son says "I" (*John* 17: 4); the Spirit says "I" (*Acts* 13: 2).

(b) The Father says "Thou" to the Son (*Mark* 1: 11); the Son says "Thou" to the Father (*John* 17: 2); the Father and the Son use the words "He" and "Him" in reference to the Spirit (*John* 14: 26; 15: 26).

(c) Although the work of the Father and the Son is one, Jesus said, "My Father worketh hitherto, and I work" (John 5: 17), implying that their being—in some mysterious way beyond our understanding—is distinct.

(d) The Father loves the Son (*John* 3: 35); the Son loves the Father (*John* 14: 31); the Spirit testifies of the Son (*John* 15: 26).

(e) Some acts are referred to the Father, Son and Spirit: for example, creation and preservation. The Father created the world (*Isa.* 40: 28); the Son created the world (*John* 1: 3); the Spirit created the world (*Gen.* 1: 2; *Job* 33: 4). The Father preserves all things (*Neh.* 9: 6); the Son upholds all things (*Heb.* 1: 3); the Spirit is the source of all life (*Ps.* 104: 30).

(f) Other acts are mainly referred to the Father, others to the Son, and others to the Spirit: for

example, the work and plan of redemption. The Father elects and calls, the Son redeems by His blood, and the Spirit sanctifies (*I Pet.* 1: 2).

4. There is a particular order of relationship between the Persons of the Trinity.

(a) The Father is first (*John* 5: 26, 27; *Eph.* 1: 3).

(b) The Son is second: He is begotten of the Father and is sent by Him (*Ps.* 2: 7; *John* 3: 16; *Heb.* 1: 5; *I John* 4: 14).

(c) The Spirit is third: He proceeds from the Father and the Son (*John* 14: 17; 15: 26; 20: 22).

5. The order of relationship does not imply that the Father, the Son and the Holy Spirit do not possess true and equal divinity: their true and equal divinity is insisted upon.

(a) The Father is God (*I Cor.* 8: 6; *Eph.* 4: 6).

(b) The Son is God (*John* 1: 14, 18; 20: 28, 31; *Phil.* 2: 6; *Tit.* 2: 13).

(c) The Holy Spirit is God (*Acts* 5: 3, 4; *II Cor.* 3: 18).

(d) In the Bible all the divine characteristics are considered as belonging to the Father, Son and Holy Spirit: for example, holiness (*Ex.* 15: 11; *Acts* 2: 27; 1: 5); love (*John* 3: 16; *Eph.* 3: 19; *Gal.* 5: 22); omnipotence (*Job* 42: 2; *Isa.* 9: 6; *I Cor.* 2: 4 and *Rom.* 1: 4); omniscience (*Heb.* 4: 13; *John* 21: 17; *I Cor.* 2: 10); omnipresence (*Jer.* 23: 23, 24; *Matt.* 28: 20; *Ps.* 139: 7–10).

6. The Trinity is a mystery—quite beyond our comprehension—to be accepted and believed.

(a) We cannot delve into God's secrets which He has not chosen to reveal (*Rom.* 11: 33–36; *I Tim.* 6: 16).

(b) Nor can the angels of heaven fathom the mystery of His being (*Isa.* 6: 2, 3).

(c) By means of the Scriptures we are given sufficient understanding of the work of the Trinity, in creation, redemption, and sanctification to be saved and to be brought to eternal glory (*II Tim.* 3: 15–17; *Col.* 1: 11–14).

9. THE CREATION

Question: What is the Christian explanation of creation?

Answer: The God and Father of our Lord Jesus Christ is the creator of all things. God the Son and God the Holy Ghost were active in the creation; and God has ordained that all creation shall ultimately belong to the Son. In the final analysis, acceptance of the truth of the absolute creation of all things by God is a matter for faith rather than scientific proof.

1. Genesis 1 is the foundation of any Christian explanation of creation.

(a) Many of the problems people have about creation are resolved when it is realised that Genesis 1 is an account of God's creation in poetic rather than scientific terms, an account which is concerned with the fact of creation rather than with providing scientific explanation.

(b) The emphasis is upon what God accomplished in a period of six days by successive creative acts:

Day One: Light (*Gen.* 1: 3–5);

Day Two: Firmament and division of the waters (*Gen.* 1: 6–8);
Day Three: Dry land and vegetation (*Gen.* 1: 9–13);
Day Four: The light-giving bodies (*Gen.* 1: 14–19);
Day Five: Birds and fishes (*Gen.* 1: 20–23);
Day Six: Animals and man (*Gen.* 1: 24–31).

(c) We cannot state dogmatically what is meant by the word "day", as used in Genesis 1—it is sometimes used of an indefinite period (*Ps.* 105: 8) or of a very long period of time (*II Pet.* 3: 8).

(d) The Genesis account of creation is clearly designed to be simple, to be intelligible for men at all stages in human history, describing the truth of God's complex creation in but few words.

2. God is the Creator.

(a) The Lord created all things (*Ps.* 33: 6; 102: 25; *Isa.* 40: 26; 44: 24; 45: 12; *Acts* 17: 24; *Rev.* 4: 11; 10: 6).

(b) He created the heavens (*Neh.* 9: 6; *Isa.* 42: 5; 45: 18).

(c) He created the earth and all that is on it (*Neh.* 9: 6; *Ps.* 90: 2; *Isa.* 42: 5; 45: 18).

(d) All being comes from God (*I Cor.* 8: 6): He gives life and breath to all things (*Isa.* 42: 5; *Acts* 17: 24, 25).

(e) From one forefather He has created every race of men to live over the face of the whole earth (*Acts* 17: 26).

(f) He sustains all that He has made (*Neh.* 9: 6; *Isa.* 40: 26, 28), for the entire creation is dependent upon His power for its existence (*Acts* 17: 28; *Col.* 1: 17).

3. The work of creation is said to have belonged both to the Son and the Holy Spirit.

(a) During the creative period, it was the Holy Spirit who moved upon "the face of the waters", bringing forth the order God purposed (*Gen.* 1: 2; *Job* 26: 13).

(b) It was, however, through Christ that everything was made, whether spiritual or material, seen or unseen (*John* 1: 3; 1: 10; *Col.* 1: 16; *Heb.* 1: 2).

(c) For Christ is both the First Principle and the Upholding Principle of the whole scheme of creation (*Col.* 1: 17; *Heb.* 1: 3).

(d) God the Father has ordained that to the Son the whole of creation shall ultimately belong (*Heb.* 1: 2).

4. Essential facts about God's creation.

(a) The implication throughout is that God's creation was from nothing by the power of His Word (*Gen.* 1: 1; *Ps.* 33: 6, 9; *Heb.* 11: 3).

(b) God performed His work of creation independently of any creature (*Job* 38: 4 ff; *Isa.* 44: 24), and God remains independent of His creation (*Rom.* 9: 5).

(c) God did not need to create the world or man; it was an act of His free and sovereign will (*Prov.* 16: 4; *Acts* 17: 25; *Rev.* 4: 11).

(d) God created the world for the display of His own glory (*Col.* 1: 16; *Rev.* 4: 11); and thus His eternal power and divinity have been plainly discernible through the things which He has made from the very beginning (*Rom.* 1: 20).

(e) The Bible makes no attempt to reveal or to explain how God performed the creation: the absolute creation of all things by God is, in the final analysis, something which we believe because we accept the revelation of God (*Heb.* 11: 3).

(f) The God of creation is the God of redemption (*II Cor.* 4: 6).

10. THE PROVIDENCE OF GOD

Question: Is God in control of everything?

Answer: God controls all things, working out everything in agreement with the counsel and design of His own will.

1. God's control extends to the whole universe.

(a) He is the only Sovereign, King of kings, and Lord of lords (*I Tim.* 6: 15): His throne is in the heavens, and His kingdom rules over all (*Ps.* 103: 19).

(b) He keeps in being the whole universe by His word of power (*Neh.* 9: 6; *Heb.* 1: 3).

(c) The government of the entire universe is with Him (*Deut.* 10: 14; *Ps.* 135: 6; *Dan.* 4: 35).

2. God's control of nature follows.

(a) All natural forces are in His control (*Ps.* 29).

(b) The elements are at His command (*Ps.* 68: 9; *Jonah* 1: 4).

(c) All the processes of nature are at His direction (*Gen.* 8: 22; *Ps.* 107: 33, 34, 38; *Jer.* 31: 35).

3. God's control of His creatures follows.

(a) His care, for example, extends to the smallest of His creatures:

He gives the beasts their food (*Ps.* 147: 9).

(b) Not a single sparrow falls to the ground without His knowledge (*Matt.* 10: 29).

(c) He can appoint all His creatures to perform His will (*Jonah* 1: 17; 2: 10): even for ravens to convey bread and meat to His servants (*I Kings* 17: 6).

4. God's control of men—and of evil men—follows.

(a) There are occasions when God, desiring to show His wrath and to make known His power, has put up with evil men due for destruction, in order to make known the riches of His glory to those whom He has purposed to save (*Rom.* 9: 22, 23).

(b) Sometimes God sees to it that the worst of men are allowed to be exalted in order that they may work for God without their knowing it (*Isa.* 10: 5, 7).

(c) He uses even the enemies of His people to discipline them in their disobedience (*Judg.* 2: 14, 15, 21–23; 3: 12).

(d) On the other hand, He can harden the hearts of His people's enemies so that either they fall into His people's hands or even destroy themselves (*Josh.* 11: 20; *Judg.* 7: 22).

5. God's control of nations follows.

(a) God fixed the bounds of the peoples of the earth (*Deut.* 32: 8).

(b) He can make a nation large or small (*Obad.* 2).

(c) In the affairs of the world, and its rulers, the Lord puts down one leader and lifts up another (*Ps.* 75: 7; *I Sam.* 16: 1).

(d) He uses heathen nations to accomplish the disciplining of His disobedient people (*Isa.* 5: 26; *Amos* 3: 9–11; 6: 14; *Hab.* 1: 12).

(e) So far as it has suited His purposes, He has allowed nations to walk in their own ways (*Acts* 14: 16).

(f) Behind the strange, gracious actions of unbelieving rulers towards God's people at various times is the working of God in their hearts without their knowledge (*Ezra* 1: 1): for example, Tiglath-pileser (*Isa.* 10: 6, 7); Cyrus (*Isa.* 41: 2–4); Artaxerxes (*Ezra* 7: 21)—each pursuing his own chosen course, served the furtherance of God's will, though in their personal living they were disobedient, self-willed and sinful.

6. God's control of history follows.

(a) His dominion is everlasting and His kingdom endures from generation to generation (*Dan.* 4: 34): thus all the events of human history are under His direct control (*Rev.* 9: 15).

(b) He fixes the epochs of human history and the limits of men's territory (*Acts* 17: 26).

(c) God is at work in unrecognised events and processes to bring about His purposes of blessing: it was the Lord who sent Joseph ahead of his brothers to Egypt (*Ps.* 105: 16–22); it was the Lord who turned the hearts of the Egyptians to hate God's people (*Ps.* 105: 25); it was the Lord who called Cyrus, a heathen ruler, "His anointed" because He was going to use him to do His will for His people (*Isa.* 44: 28–45: 4).

(d) The outstanding example of God at work in an event—unrecognised at first—to do His will was the Cross (*Acts* 4: 28; cf. 2: 23).

(e) In all the events of history God is working out His purpose of calling into one body, the Church, men and women of every nation and people, saved through Christ (*Eph.* 3: 3–11).

7. God's control of all circumstances follows.

(a) God, not chance, decides what happens in the affairs of men (*Prov.* 16: 33; cf. *Jonah* 1: 7).

(b) Behind every circumstance is the Lord (*Amos* 3: 6).

(c) He can shorten life or lengthen it (*Ps.* 102: 23; *Job* 1: 21).

(d) The Lord brings both happiness and calamity (*Isa.* 45: 7); success and victory in battle (*I Sam.* 11: 13) and the power to get wealth (*Deut.* 8: 18) are from Him, as too is the power to bring illness or to remove it (*Deut.* 7: 15).

(e) Ordinary daily needs are within His concern and control (*Matt.* 6: 30, 33).

(f) The will of God may be worked out in what appears to be a complete accident (*I Kings* 22: 28, 34).

8. God's special control of affairs on behalf of His people follows.

(a) God's care extends to all individuals, and especially to His people (*I Pet.* 5: 7).

(b) He delivers His people from trouble (*Ps.* 23: 5; 34: 7; 107: 2).

(c) He can hand His people over to their enemies for a period to discipline them if need be (*Judg.* 3: 8; 4: 2; 6: 1).

(d) God is in complete control when His people are persecuted (*Acts* 8: 1, 4; *Phil.* 1: 28, 29).

(e) He gives a sure footing in life to the righteous (*Ps.* 33: 18, 19).

(f) He supplies every need of His children according to His riches in glory by Christ Jesus (*Phil.* 4: 19), guaranteeing that everything in life will be worked out for the spiritual and eternal good which God has in view (*Rom.* 8: 28).

9. God's control of Satan is clearly involved, and is taught.

(a) The Lord can put a restraint upon Satan as He will (*Job* 1: 12).

(b) He gives Satan, at times, power to do his wicked worst, but God is always in control (*Rev.* 9: 1; 20: 7).

II. WAR AND SUFFERING

Question: If God controls all things, why are there wars and suffering?

Answer: Wars, suffering, and such like, are permitted by God insofar as they may serve to fulfil His purposes; His final and sure purpose is that they shall cease.

1. God's control does not conflict with human responsibility.

(a) His control does not involve Him in human sin: men remain free agents, morally responsible for their decisions (*Deut.* 30: 15–20).

(b) God is unchanging in His holiness, justice and goodness: it is inconceivable that in anything that He does He could do anything other than that which is right (*Gen.* 18: 25)—He is eternally self-consistent (*Mal.* 3: 6).

(c) The blame for evil belongs completely to the sinner (*Luke* 22: 22; *Acts* 2: 23).

29

2. God's control in relation to wars.

(a) War is assumed to be a necessary human experience in this evil world (*Judg.* 3: 1, 2; *Luke* 21: 9; *Matt.* 24: 6).

(b) Wars are the result of men forsaking the Lord and pursuing false gods (*Judg.* 5: 8).

(c) The Lord permits nations to labour for no good purpose, making their scheme profitless as it suits His purposes (*Hab.* 2: 13).

(d) He permits wars in order to call men to repentance, for wars can be a punishment and a warning voice to unbelievers (*Rev.* 9: 13–21), although men and women in general refuse to learn the lessons of war, and repent (*Rev.* 9: 18 ff).

(e) Wars shall cease after the coming of the Day of the Lord and the ushering in of His kingdom (*Isa.* 2: 4; *Micah* 4: 1–8).

3. God's control in relation to suffering.

(a) In the sufferings of the righteous, who have no immunity from suffering (*Eccl.* 9: 2), the mysterious purposes of God are worked out perfectly (*Job*).

(b) Tragedy, accident, suffering are not automatically to be assumed to be the consequences of the individual sufferer's sin (*Luke* 13: 2, 4; *John* 9: 2, 3).

(c) Suffering of some sort or another is clearly taught to be an indispensable part of discipleship of Christ (*Acts* 9: 16; *II Tim.* 4: 5; *Heb.* 11: 33–38; *Rev.* 1: 9).

(d) Suffering has a place in God's loving discipline of His children (*Prov.* 3: 11, 12; *Heb.* 12: 5–11).

(e) While impenitent men are not

sanctified through suffering (*Rev.* 16: 8, 9), believers are restored to the Lord by means of it often after straying from Him (*Ps.* 119: 67).

(f) Suffering is to be patiently endured by the Christian for very good reasons (*II Cor.* 1: 6):

(i) Suffering accepted submissively, though not understood, glorifies God and brings blessing in the end (*Job* 1: 21, 22; 2: 10; 42: 1–6, 10);

(ii) Christ is able to help us in our suffering (*Heb.* 2: 18);

(iii) Suffering is temporary, and is tempered by the Lord's mercy (*Lam.* 3: 31–33);

(iv) God sets a limit on the suffering, knowing how much we can endure (*I Cor.* 10: 13);

(v) No kind of suffering or difficulty can separate the believer from Christ (*Rom.* 8: 35–39).

(g) The Christian may even rejoice in his sufferings because of the confidence he has of the benefits which shall come from them (*Rom.* 5: 3–5):

(i) Proof of the genuineness of his faith (*I Pet.* 1: 7);

(ii) Improvement in Christian character (*Jas.* 1: 2–4);

(iii) Knowledge that fellowship with God is his greatest possession (*Ps.* 73: 14, 23–26; *Hab.* 3: 17–19);

(iv) The discovery of God's comfort (*II Cor.* 1: 7);

(v) The encouragement of others through our own experience of God's comfort (*II Cor.* 1: 4);

(vi) A deeper understanding of life and its meaning (*Eccl.* 7: 3);

(vii) Preparation for the glory to come (*I Pet.* 4: 13);

(viii) Good to others spiritually (*Phil.* 1: 12–14; *Gal.* 4: 13).

(h) The Lord can use suffering so

much to a person's good that he comes to look back upon it with tremendous thanksgiving (*Ps.* 119: 71).

4. Thus the completeness of God's control is plain.

(a) God accomplishes all things according to the counsel of His will (*Eph.* 1: 11).

(b) The control of God over everything is really beyond our minds to comprehend (*Ps.* 92: 5–9).

(c) It is so complete that He can laugh at all His enemies would seek to do (*Ps.* 2: 4; *Mal.* 1: 4, 5).

(d) He does what He pleases, and He does not have to answer to His creatures for what He does (*Ps.* 115: 3; *Dan.* 4: 35; *Rom.* 9: 20).

5. The completeness of God's control will be demonstrated at the Day of Judgment.

(a) The judgment of the wicked is certain: the Lord is on high for ever (*Ps.* 92: 7–9).

(b) God will adequately punish evildoers and vindicate the righteous on the day of judgment (*Rom.* 2: 4–11; 12: 19; cf. *Ps.* 37: 14, 15; *Mal.* 3: 13–4: 1).

(c) Evil is not punished as quickly as we anticipate, only because God is patient and gives many opportunities to men for repentance (*Rom.* 2: 4; *II Pet.* 3: 8, 9; *Rev.* 2: 21).

(d) The seeming prosperity of the wicked, therefore, is a temporary thing; they are not to be envied (*Ps.* 37: 1, 2, 9, 10).

6. The Christian's reaction to God's control of all things.

(a) Our response should be to declare, "Great is the Lord" (*Mal.* 1: 5).

(b) No matter how desperate the circumstances, we should consider God's love and say, "If God be for us, who can be against us?" (*Ps.* 107: 43; *Rom.* 8: 31).

(c) The basis for all fear is removed (*Isa.* 10: 24–27; *Matt.* 10: 31).

(d) We may look to God for vindication in His time (*Ps.* 40: 13–15; cf. *I Pet.* 2: 23).

(e) We should submit to all circumstances, ready to learn what God is going to teach through them (*Ps.* 39: 9), learning at least contentment in them (*Phil.* 4: 11): because we always have Him (*Heb.* 13: 5).

(f) We should pray for those in authority, being in subjection to them, as ordained of God (*I Tim.* 2: 1–3; *Rom.* 13: 1).

(g) When we do not understand God's seeming delays to remedy wrong, we should say, "I will quietly wait" (*Hab.* 3: 16; *Jas.* 5: 7–8).

12. SIN

Question: What is sin?

Answer: Sin is basically rebellion against God. Arising from the corruption of the human heart, it is the cause of our separation from God, and the reason for our deserving God's wrath. Sin is man's greatest problem.

1. Sin is basically rebellion against God.

(a) Sin is doing wrong (*Dan.* 9: 5).

(b) Sin is acting wickedly (*Dan.* 9: 5); it is doing evil in the sight of the Lord (*Ps.* 51: 4).

(c) Sin is turning aside from God's commandments and ordinances (*Dan.* 9: 5)—what the Bible calls "transgression" (*Ps.* 51: 1).

(d) Sin is falling short of God's glory (*Rom.* 3: 23).

(e) Sin is ignoring God's Word as it has come to us through the messengers He has provided (*Dan.* 9: 6; *Heb.* 3: 13).

(f) Sin is lawlessness (*Hos.* 4: 2; *I John* 3: 4).

(g) Sin is rebellion (*Dan.* 9: 5)—the result of hostility to God (*Rom.* 8: 7).

(h) The essence of sin is to be against God (*Ps.* 51: 4).

(i) Sin entered the world by man wanting things which belong to God alone (*Gen.* 3: 5).

(j) Sin ignores God's authority (*Gen.* 2: 16, 17; 3: 6).

(k) Sin casts doubts upon God's character (*Gen.* 3: 4).

(l) Sin does not accept the wisdom of God (*Gen.* 3: 4, 5).

2. Sin is the result of the corruption of the human heart.

(a) From the heart flows the springs of life (*Prov.* 4: 23), e.g. as a man thinks in his heart so is he (*Prov.* 23: 7).

(b) Sin begins in the heart (*Matt.* 5: 28).

(c) All the evil things in men's lives come from within (*Mark* 7: 21, 22, 23).

(d) God, who searches the mind and tries the heart, declares that the human heart is deceitful above all things, and desperately wicked (*Jer.* 17: 9, 10).

3. Sin is the cause of our separation from God.

(a) Our sin is known to God when it is hidden perhaps from everyone else (*Ps.* 51: 4).

(b) Sin brings confusion of face before God (*Dan.* 9: 7).

(c) Sin separates us from God (*Deut.* 31: 17, 18; *Ps.* 78: 59–61; *Isa.* 59: 1–2; *Amos* 3: 2, 3; *Micah* 3: 4).

(d) Sin makes impossible, therefore, the enjoyment of fellowship with God (*Gen.* 3: 8; *I John* 1: 6), for it puts us at a distance from God (*Ps.* 51: 11).

4. Sin is that which brings down God's wrath upon us.

(a) We gain an understanding of sin when we appreciate God's holiness (*Isa.* 6: 3, 5).

(b) God knows the precise extent of our sin (*Amos* 5: 12).

(c) Living according to the passions of our flesh, and following the desires of our body and mind, we are by nature the children of wrath (*Eph.* 2: 3).

(d) Sin draws forth God's wrath (*Rom.* 1: 18; 3: 5); the wrath of God rests on the sinner by reason of his sin (*John* 3: 36).

(e) God's wrath against sin will be revealed on the Day of Judgment—the Day of His wrath (*Rom.* 2: 5, 6).

(f) Sin leads to destruction (*Matt.* 7: 13).

5. Sin is man's greatest problem.

(a) Sin's pathway is all too easy to tread (*Matt.* 7: 13).

(b) Sin can so deceive us that we flatter ourselves that it will never be found out (*Ps.* 36: 2); but sin surely finds us out (*Ex.* 2: 12 ff).

(c) Sin is like leaven: it spreads its corruption (*I Cor.* 5: 6).

(d) All the time sin is persisted in, there can be no restoration to God (*Hos.* 5: 4).

(e) We need to be delivered from the wrath to come (*Rom.* 5: 9; *I Thess.* 1: 10).

(f) Sin must be dealt with if men are to have fellowship with God (*Heb.* 2: 17; *I Pet.* 3: 18).

13. THE FALL

Question: What is meant by the fall of man?

Answer: By the fall of man we mean that event in history by which sin came into the world through one man and death through sin.

1. The fall was preceded by temptation.

(a) Yielding to deception Eve fell into sin (*I Tim.* 2: 14).

(b) By the devil's cunning, man's thoughts were corrupted and he lost his single-hearted devotion to God (*II Cor.* 11: 3).

(c) Our first parents were tempted to doubt God's Word (*Gen.* 3: 6).

(d) They became proud and independent, willing to accept the temptation expressed in the words "Ye shall be as gods" (*Gen.* 3: 5).

2. Disobedience was the cause of the fall.

(a) Having doubted God's Word, our first parents disbelieved it (*Gen.* 3: 4).

(b) Having disbelieved God's Word, they disobeyed it (*Gen.* 3: 6).

(c) They disobeyed God's clear command by eating the fruit of the tree of the knowledge of good and evil (*Gen.* 2: 16, 17; 3: 6).

(d) This act constituted rebellion against God's authority (*Gen.* 2: 17).

3. The immediate consequence of the fall.

(a) Man's attitude to God immediately changed: Adam and Eve hid themselves from the presence of the Lord God (*Gen.* 3: 8)—an awareness of guilt and separation from God had come.

(b) Man ceased to be a spiritual being in the way in which he had been previous to his disobedience: he is unspiritual (*Jude* 19); he cannot understand spiritual things (*I Cor.* 2: 14); he is naturally earth-bound and sensual (*Jas.* 3: 15); he is without God (*Eph.* 2: 12).

(c) Man's sin brought the penalty of death upon all (*Gen.* 2: 17; 3: 19).

(d) Man's experience of the wonder of God's creation was immediately spoiled: childbearing became associated with pain (*Gen.* 3: 16); daily work became a matter of toil (*Gen.* 3: 17, 18).

(e) Man's sin had immediate effect on all the creation over which he had been given charge (*Gen.* 1: 28; 3: 17).

(f) Continuing trouble came to all who followed after our first parents:
  (i) Murder (*Gen.* 4: 8, 23);
  (ii) Polygamy (*Gen.* 4: 19);
  (iii) Revenge (*Gen.* 4: 24);
  (iv) Immorality (*Gen.* 6: 2);
  (v) Increasing wickedness (*Gen.* 6: 5).

4. The continuing consequences of the fall.

(a) All the immediate consequences

of the fall listed above continue.

(b) As a result of the fall, man is astray from God and has lost his purpose in living (*Isa.* 53: 6).

(c) He loves darkness rather than light, because his deeds are evil (*John* 3: 19, 20).

(d) He no longer does God's will, although he was made for this purpose (*Rom.* 3: 23).

(e) He loses the dignity which was his by his original creation the more he moves away from God (*Rom.* 1: 22, 23).

(f) Instead of being glad at what truth he still knows about God, man suppresses it because it makes him too uncomfortable (*Rom.* 1: 18, 20, 21).

14. ORIGINAL SIN

Question: What is original sin?

Answer: Adam was the responsible head of the human race, and thus his sin is imputed to all. We are born fallen creatures, and we go astray from God from birth.

1. Adam represented all men and so his sin is imputed to us all.

(a) Adam represented all mankind (*Rom.* 5: 12–19; *I Cor.* 15: 22, 45–49).

(b) It was through Adam that sin entered the world (*Rom.* 5: 12).

(c) The wrongdoing of Adam brought death upon all men (*Rom.* 5: 15).

(d) The wrongdoing of Adam established the reign of death (*Rom.* 5: 17).

(e) The result of Adam's sin was condemnation for all men (*Rom.* 5: 18).

(f) By the disobedience of Adam —one man—the many were made sinners (*Rom.* 5: 19): his sin is reckoned to us all.

(g) The basis on which God deals with us with regard to Adam is the basis on which He deals with us with regard to Christ: just as through Adam we were made sinners, so through Christ we may be made righteous (*I Cor.* 15: 22, 45–49).

2. Being born fallen creatures, we go astray from birth.

(a) We are made in the image of Adam rather than in the image of God (*Gen.* 5: 3; cf. *I Cor.* 15: 48, 49).

(b) We are brought forth in iniquity and conceived in sin (*Ps.* 51: 5).

(c) We go astray from birth (*Ps.* 14: 3; 58: 3; *Isa.* 48: 8; *Rom.* 3: 11).

(d) There is not a righteous man on earth who does good and never sins (*Eccl.* 7: 20; *I Kings* 8: 46).

(e) Purity and righteousness are impossible to those who know only human birth (*Job* 15: 14; 25: 4).

(f) The Scriptures represent us as all under the bondage of sin (*Gal.* 3: 22).

(g) Our will is stubborn and evil (*Jer.* 16: 12).

(h) Our minds are impure: they are corrupted alike in reason and conscience (*Tit.* 1: 15; *Eph.* 4: 18).

(i) Spiritual things are folly to us, by nature (*I Cor.* 2: 14).

(j) Our heart is evil from our youth (*Gen.* 8: 21; 6: 5; *Jer.* 17: 9, 10; *Matt.* 15: 19).

(k) We are corrupt (*Gen.* 6: 12), not always able to understand our own actions (*Rom.* 7: 15).

(l) Knowing only the life of the flesh—that is to say, life lived without the knowledge of God—we set our minds on the things of the flesh (*Rom.* 8: 5; *John* 3: 6; *Rom.* 7: 18; 8: 7; *Eph.* 2: 3).

(m) If a man does not do right habitually, he is identifiable as a child of the devil (*I John* 3: 8, 10; *John* 8: 44). (The Bible does not teach the universal fatherhood of God, except in the general physical sense that God is the Creator of all.)

(n) We are, by nature, the children of wrath, deserving God's dreadful judgment (*Eph.* 2: 3; *John* 3: 36).

(o) By reason of our situation described above, it is impossible for us to please God whilst we remain in this position (*Rom.* 8: 8).

15. HUMAN EXISTENCE

Question: Why do I exist?

Answer: The original purpose of man's creation ceased to be fulfilled when man rebelled against God. Unreconciled, men cannot adequately answer this question. Reconciled, men discover themselves to exist in order to know God, to do His will, to glorify Him, and to enjoy Him for ever.

1. Why do I exist?

(a) This is one of those fundamental questions to which we see the answer but dimly; the full answer will be revealed and appreciated in the life to come (*I Cor.* 13: 12).

(b) The question can be answered adequately by God alone: we are assured that everything He made, including man, was made for a particular end (*Prov.* 16: 4).

(c) The question is extremely relevant in view of the futility of human life from so many points of view (*Ps.* 103: 15–16; *Jas.* 4: 14).

2. God's purposes for man in his creation give the first clues to the correct answer to the question, "Why do I exist?"

(a) We are here because God created the world, and He created man to inhabit it (*Gen.* 1: 26–28; 2: 7).

(b) Man was created to possess the earth (*Gen.* 1: 28):

(i) He was to make the earth serve him (*Gen.* 1: 28);

(ii) He was to rule all other creatures (*Gen.* 1: 28);

(iii) He was to cultivate God's creation (*Gen.* 2: 15; *Ps.* 104: 14);

(iv) He was intended to enjoy God's creation (*Ps.* 104: 14, 15).

(c) Man was created to know God:

(i) He was made in God's image, and in this was unique amongst all of God's creatures (*Gen.* 1: 27; *Ps.* 8: 5 f);

(ii) He was made to have fellowship with God (*Gen.* 3: 9; *Amos* 4: 13);

(iii) It was intended that he should find his highest satisfaction in having God Himself as his friend (*Ps.* 27: 1, 4);

(iv) He was created to live in devoted dependence upon God (*Luke* 10: 27; *Matt.* 4: 4).

(d) Man was created to do God's will:

(i) He was to obey God (*Gen.* 2: 16, 17; 3: 13; *Eccl.* 12: 13);

(ii) He was to live by faith and obedience (*Gen.* 2: 15–17);

(iii) He was made for God's pleasure, as was all of God's creation (*Heb.* 2: 10; *Rev.* 4: 11; *Gen.* 1: 31).

(e) Man was created with a capacity to enjoy God for ever:

(i) Man is not merely a physical creature (*Matt.* 4: 4);

(ii) Man has an eternal soul (*Mark* 8: 36).

(f) In view of God's creation of man the answer to the question "Why do I exist?" is "I am here to enjoy the earth, to know God, to do His will, and to enjoy Him for ever."

(g) But when man rebelled against God he lost his way and ceased to know the wonder of God's purposes for human life.

(i) Man is like a sheep gone astray (*Ps.* 119: 176; *Isa.* 53: 6).

(ii) Instead of worshipping the Creator, he worships more readily the created thing (*Rom.* 1: 25).

(iii) Yet there remains within man that which makes him feel after God; but he cannot find God without God's help (*Job* 11: 7).

(iv) Man's greatest need is to be reconciled to God (*II Cor.* 5: 20).

(v) On account of the saving work of Christ in dying for sinners, men may be reconciled to God and discover the full wonder of God's purpose for life, which was lost in the beginning (*II Cor.* 5: 17–19).

3. The question, "Why do I exist?" is very relevant to men and women who are not reconciled to God through Christ.

(a) The Lord is forbearing toward men, not wishing that any should perish: we are here to be given an opportunity of reaching repentance (*II Pet.* 3: 9) before His final judgment descends upon a world which ignores God and is unconcerned to know the answer to this question (*II Pet.* 3: 10).

(b) We are here to sow, by means of our lives, in order that we may reap an everlasting harvest—for good or ill (*Gal.* 6: 7).

4. The question has very positive answers when we are reconciled to God—for then we are in a position to enter into God's full purpose for life.

(a) We are here to know God (*John* 17: 3).

(b) We are here to know and fulfil God's perfect plan for our life (*Rom.* 12: 2).

(c) We are here to be agents for extending Christ's Kingdom (*Mark* 16: 15; *II Cor.* 5: 20).

(d) We are here to be made like Christ in character (*II Cor.* 3: 18).

(e) We are here to please God (*II Cor.* 5: 9).

(f) We are here to reflect God's glory (*Matt.* 5: 48; *I Pet.* 1: 16).

(g) Our chief purpose in life is to glorify God (*I Cor.* 10: 31).

(i) To glorify God is to appreciate Him (*Ps.* 92: 8); to adore Him (*Ps.* 29: 2); to love Him (*Deut.* 6: 5); to subject ourselves to Him (*Matt.* 2: 11; *Jas.* 4: 7).

(ii) Our desire is that God should be glorified in everything (*I Pet.* 4: 11).

(iii) We are here to glorify God in our bodies (*I Cor.* 6: 20): whatever we do—eating or drinking or anything else—should be done to bring glory to God (*I Cor.* 10: 31).

(h) Our glorious anticipation is of enjoying God for ever (*Ps.* 73: 25; *I Thess.* 4: 17): in the life to come we shall be satisfied with beholding God's likeness (*Ps.* 17: 15; *I Pet.* 1: 8).

16. THE LAW OF GOD

Question: Why has God given us His law—as, for example, in the ten commandments—if it is impossible for us to keep it?

Answer: While it is indeed impossible for us to keep the law of God perfectly, God has given it to mankind as a revelation of His righteousness, of His demands upon His creatures, and as a restraint upon the rebellion of mankind. By revealing to us our inability to please God, and the condemnation we deserve, God's Law enables us to see our need of Christ, and of the justification made possible by His cross.

1. The Law and the Ten Commandments.

(a) The word "law" is used in many senses. It may refer to the Old Testament as a whole (*Rom.* 3: 19), or just part of the Old Testament (*Matt.* 5: 17; 7: 12), or even the first five books of the Bible—the Pentateuch (*Luke* 24: 44). Sometimes it is used of those commandments given by God through Moses (*Rom.* 5: 13, 20; *Gal.* 3: 17, 19, 21). Often the term is used to describe the law of God as the expression of God's will (*Rom.* 3: 20; *Gal.* 3: 13).

(b) The fact recognised from the beginning was that it is God's right to command (*Gen.* 2: 16).

(c) Men have a law in themselves insofar as their own consciences endorse the existence of God's law, even though they may be ignorant of the law of God as it is set forth in the Bible (*Rom.* 2: 14, 15).

(d) The law of God was given to Adam and to Noah (*Gen.* 2: 16, 17; 9: 6; *Rom.* 5: 12–14), and the law of God, as we know it, came four hundred and thirty years after the promises of God to Abraham (*Gal.* 3: 17).

(e) The law was given to the Israelites (*Ex.* 20: 1–17; *Ps.* 78: 5) through the ministry of angels (*Acts* 7: 38; *Gal.* 3: 19; *Heb.* 2: 2) and a human intermediary, Moses (*Ex.* 31: 18; *John* 7: 19; *Josh.* 1: 7).

(f) The ten commandments are a comprehensive summary of the law of God: the first table of the law expresses man's duty toward God (*Ex.* 20: 3–11), and the second his duty toward his fellow men (*Ex.* 20: 12–17).

(g) The law is found for us, therefore, in the Scriptures (*Jas.* 2: 8).

(h) The law is a unity, expressing the undivided will of the supreme Lawgiver (*Jas.* 2: 11).

(i) The law makes demands upon men—it calls for works, for action (*Gal.* 2: 15, 16).

(j) The law is holy, just, good (*Rom.* 7: 12), spiritual (*Rom.* 7: 14), and royal—royal because it belongs to God's kingdom, and is given by the King of kings and the Lord of lords (*Jas.* 2: 8).

(k) Love is the fulfilling of the law (*Rom.* 13: 8, 10): the commandments of God relating to our fellow human beings are summed up in the commandment, "You shall love your neighbour as yourself" (*Rom.* 13: 9; *Gal.* 5: 14; *Jas.* 2: 8), and love for God Himself is seen in love for our fellow-men (*I John* 4: 20–21).

2. The law is meant to be kept.

(a) God requires that we should keep the whole of His law (*Gal.* 3: 21; *Jas.* 2: 10, 11).

(b) Thus the prophets conscientiously set the law of God before the people of God (*Dan.* 9: 10), and Jesus made it plain that He had not come to abolish the law but to complete it (*Matt.* 5: 17–19).

(c) The law of God is to be regarded as the voice of God speaking to us, and to transgress that law is to disobey God's voice (*Dan.* 9: 9, 11).

(d) It is man's duty to keep God's law (*Eccl.* 12: 13), and the right attitude to it is one of submission (*Rom.* 8: 7).

3. We cannot of ourselves keep God's law.

(a) The law requires perfect obedience (*Deut.* 27: 26; *Gal.* 3: 10; *Jas.* 2: 10).

(b) It requires the obedience of the heart (*Ps.* 51: 6; *Matt.* 5: 28; 22: 37).

(c) While God's image in man was unmarred by sin, men and women were able to keep God's law (*Gen.* 1: 26), and were sensitive to it, but now they have become callous (*Eph.* 4: 19).

(d) Fallen man finds it impossible to submit himself rightly to God's law (*Rom.* 8: 7); his nature finds it uncongenial (*Rom.* 7: 14).

(e) Man cannot render perfect obedience to the law of God (*I Kings* 8: 46; *Eccl.* 7: 20; *Rom.* 3: 10).

(f) Because the law is a unity, whoever otherwise keeps the whole law but fails in one point is none the less a law-breaker (*Jas.* 2: 10).

(g) We sin against the law (*Gal.* 2: 17, 18)—and all have transgressed it (*Rom.* 3: 9, 19).

(h) The law hushes every mouth, and holds the whole world accountable to God (*Rom.* 3: 19).

4. The law is not—and never has been—the basis upon which men have been justified.

(a) The law is not to be relied upon for justification because it brings a curse if full obedience is not rendered (*Gal.* 3: 10).

(b) Men cannot, therefore, be justified by the law (*Acts* 13: 39; *Rom.* 3: 20, 28; *Gal.* 2: 16; 3: 11). (It needs to be said, however, that when we are justified by God, it is in complete harmony with the law—*Rom.* 3: 31.)

(c) The law can produce no promise, only a threat of wrath to come (*Rom.* 4: 15): it has no power to bestow life (*Gal.* 3: 21).

(d) The law possessed only a dim outline of the benefits Christ would provide and did not actually bring any of those benefits to individuals (*Heb.* 10: 1): for example, by the works of the law no man receives the Spirit of God (*Gal.* 3: 2, 5).

(e) Thus the law has never been the basis upon which men have been justified or reckoned righteous —as, for example, in the case of Abraham (*Gal.* 3: 6, 7).

(f) The splendour of the law is completely outshone by the splendour of the gospel (*II Cor.* 3: 10).

5. The penalty for disobedience to God's law is death.

(a) It is a dreadful thing to reject the law of the Lord of hosts (*Isa.* 5: 24).

(b) If we do not fulfil the law of God, we sin, and that same law convicts us as transgressors (*Jas.* 2: 10).

(c) To reject God's law and not to keep God's statutes is to merit God's judgment (*Amos* 2: 4) and wrath (*Rom.* 4: 15).

(d) God's law which was meant to be a direction to life, we find to be a sentence to death (*II Cor.* 3: 6; *Rom.* 7: 10).

6. God's law is a schoolmaster to bring us to Christ.

(a) The law provided a preparatory discipline until Christ appeared to make possible the fulfilment of God's promise of the gospel.

(b) An obvious purpose of the law is the restraint of the lawless and the disobedient (*Gal.* 3: 23; *I Tim.* 1: 9).

(c) The real function of the law is to make men recognise and be conscious of sin (*Rom.* 3: 20): it is the straight-edge of the law which shows us how crooked we are (*Rom.* 7: 7).

(d) For example, we should never have felt guilty of the sin of coveting if we had not heard the law saying, "Thou shalt not covet" (*Rom.* 7: 7).

(e) The law was like a strict schoolmaster in charge of men until they could go to the school of Christ and learn to be justified by faith in Him (*Gal.* 3: 24, 25).

(f) Once they have such faith in Christ, they are free from the law's custodianship (*Gal.* 3: 25).

7. Christ redeems men and women from the necessity of keeping the law as the condition of justification and acceptance with God.

(a) Man's complete failure to obey God's law in its entirety makes it necessary for his salvation to depend, not on his own righteousness, but upon the righteousness of another—Jesus Christ (*Phil.* 3: 9; *Isa.* 64: 6).

(b) Christ became man for the purpose of removing sin—that is to say, the consequences of the breaking of God's law (*Heb.* 9: 28; *I John* 3: 5).

(c) Christ has redeemed us from the curse of the Law's condemnation by Himself becoming a curse in our place when He was crucified (*Gal.* 3: 13).

(d) Christ means the end of the struggle for righteousness by the law for everyone who believes in Him (*Rom.* 10: 4).

8. The law of God and the Christian life.

(a) The Christian is to recognise that the law is good in itself and has a legitimate function, particularly too as it is directed against any and every action which contradicts the wholesome teaching of the gospel (*I Tim.* 1: 8–11).

(b) The law is of continuing significance for the Christian: it is written on his heart, and set in his understanding—even as the Old Testament anticipated (*Heb.* 8: 10; *Jer.* 31: 31–34).

(c) The commandments of God are not burdensome (*I John* 5: 3).

(d) The Christian recognises that his first obligation is to love the Lord his God with all his heart and soul and strength and mind, and his neighbour as himself (*Matt.* 22: 37–40; *Rom.* 13: 10), and such love involves obedience to God's commandments (*I John* 5: 2, 3).

17. THE FIRST COMING OF CHRIST

Question: Why did Christ come?

Answer: As promised in the Old Testament Scriptures, Christ came into the world to save sinners by His death upon the Cross, according to the deliberate will and plan of God, that the way should be open for sinners to obtain a right relationship with God and the gift of eternal life.

1. Christ Himself declared certain purposes for which He did not come.

(a) He did not come to call the righteous (*Mark* 2: 17; *Matt.* 9: 13; *Luke* 5: 32).

(b) He did not come to judge the world (*John* 3: 17; 12: 47).

(c) He did not come to abolish the law and the prophets (*Matt.* 5: 17).

(d) He did not come to be served and waited upon (*Mark* 10: 45).

2. Christ came because it was the Father's will.

(a) He came from heaven (*John* 6: 38).

(b) He did not come of His own accord (*John* 7: 28).

(c) He was sent into the world (*John* 4: 34; cf. 3: 16).

(d) He came not to do His own will (*John* 6: 38).

(e) He came from the Father (*John* 8: 42; 16: 28; 17: 8).

(f) He came to do the Father's will (*John* 4: 34; 6: 38; 8: 29; *Luke* 2: 49).

(g) His aim throughout His earthly ministry was to do the will of the Father (*John* 5: 30).

3. Christ came to fulfil the Scriptures.

(a) He came as the One promised in the Old Testament as the Messiah and Saviour (*Luke* 7: 20; *John* 6: 14; 11: 27).

(b) He came to fulfil all the promises God had made about the coming One (*Matt.* 11: 3, 4, 5, 6): to announce good news to the poor, to proclaim release for prisoners and recovery of sight for the blind, to set at liberty the oppressed, to proclaim the year of the Lord's favour (*Luke* 4: 18, 19).

(c) Thus He came first to His own people—the Jewish people—to whom He had been promised (*John* 1: 11).

(d) Most of all He came to fulfil the Scriptures which show that the Messiah had to suffer and rise from the dead (*Mark* 14: 49; *Isa.* 53; *Acts* 8: 30–35; 17: 3).

4. Christ came to reveal the Father to men.

(a) He came to make the Father known—His grace and truth—for no one has ever seen God (*John* 1: 17, 18).

(b) He came to bear witness to the truth about God (*John* 18: 37).

(c) He came to complete the law, or, expressing the fact in another way, to reveal more completely what God requires of men (*Matt.* 5: 17).

(d) He came to give to men the

words of the Father (*John* 3: 34; 7: 16; 8: 26; 14: 24).

(e) He came to speak what the Father had commanded Him to say—and His words were the words of eternal life (*John* 12: 49, 50).

(f) One of the reasons why Christ is called "the Light" is that He revealed the Father (*John* 3: 19).

5. Christ came to save sinners— this is the stress of the Bible.

(a) He came into the world to save sinners (*I Tim.* 1: 15; *Mark* 2: 17).

(b) Acting on the principle that it is the sick who need a doctor and not the well, He came to call sinners to repentance (*Luke* 5: 32; *Matt.* 9: 12, 13).

(c) On account of His intent to save sinners, He spent His time with them, much to the disgust of the self-righteous (*Matt.* 11: 19).

(d) He came to seek and to save the lost (*Matt.* 18: 11; *Luke* 15: 1–32; 19: 10; *John* 10: 16).

(e) He came to be the Saviour of the world (*John* 12: 47; *I John* 4: 14)—to make it possible for God to save those in danger of perishing (*John* 3: 16).

(f) He came that men might believe on Him and be saved (*John* 6: 29; 3: 16, 17).

6. Christ came, therefore, to die.

(a) He made it clear to His disciples that He had to go to Jerusalem, there to suffer much from the elders, chief priests and scribes, to be put to death, and to be raised again on the third day (*Mark* 8: 31; *Matt.* 16: 21; *Luke* 9: 22)—all in accord with what was written of Him in the law of Moses, and in the prophets and Psalms (*Luke* 24: 44–47; 22: 37; *Isa.* 53: 12).

(b) He came into the world with the deliberate intention of dying upon the Cross (*John* 12: 27; *Acts* 2: 23).

(c) He came to give His life a ransom for many (*Mark* 10: 45).

(d) He came to be lifted up on the Cross as the serpent was lifted up by Moses in the wilderness (*John* 3: 14; 12: 34).

(e) He came to give His own flesh for the life of the world (*John* 6: 51).

(f) He was continually aware of the terrible suffering which awaited Him at the Cross (*Luke* 12: 50).

(g) The whole programme of His earthly life moved towards the Cross as its climax (*John* 7: 6, 8, 30; 8: 20; 12: 23, 27; 13: 1; 17: 1; *Luke* 24: 7).

(h) He came to be the propitiation for our sins (*I John* 4: 10).

7. Christ came that through His death for sinners, men might have a right relationship with God, and eternal life.

(a) He came that those who accept Him may receive a right relationship with the Father (*Matt.* 10: 40; *Luke* 10: 16; *John* 13: 20).

(b) He came that, by means of the Cross, He might be the way to God for us (*John* 14: 6).

(c) He came to proclaim the good news of peace through the reconciliation by the Cross (*Eph.* 2: 17).

(d) He came to bring spiritual life to men (*John* 5: 40; 6: 51, 58; 10: 10; 20: 31; *I John* 4: 9).

(e) He came so that everyone who has faith in Him as the crucified and risen Messiah should possess eternal life (*John* 3: 14, 15; 6: 40, 51, 58; 17: 3).

41

18. THE DEITY OF CHRIST

Question: How do we know that Christ is God?

Answer: The deity of Christ, confirmed by His perfect life and unique ministry and triumphantly attested by His Resurrection, is vigorously affirmed by the prophets, the apostles and the accumulative testimony of the Bible and by other direct and indirect means.

1. We have Christ's own claims to deity.

(a) There were occasions when He openly claimed to be the Messiah (*Mark* 14: 61–64; *Luke* 22: 66–71; *John* 4: 25, 26).

(b) To claim Messiahship was to claim deity (*Ps.* 2: 6–12; *Isa.* 9: 6; *Zech.* 13: 7).

(c) The Jews recognised this implication of Jesus' claim to Messiahship (*John* 10: 33).

(d) He made unique claims for Himself (*John* 6: 35; 8: 12; 10: 7, 9; 10: 11; 11: 25; 14: 6; 15: 1).

(e) He declared Himself to be one with the Father (*John* 10: 30; 5: 18).

(f) He accepted the declaration of Thomas, "My Lord and my God" (*John* 20: 28, 29).

2. Everything about His life serves to substantiate His claims to deity.

(a) There is the evidence of His supernatural conception and birth (*Luke* 1: 26–56; 2: 1–51; *Matt.* 1: 18–24).

(b) There is the evidence of His sinless life:

(i) He committed no sin and no guile was found on His lips (*I Pet.* 2: 22).

(ii) He could ask a question which only a perfect man would rightly dare to ask, "Which of you convicts Me of sin?" (*John* 8: 46).

(iii) Pilate's wife called Him "That just man" (*Matt.* 27: 19).

(iv) Judas said, "I have betrayed innocent blood" (*Matt.* 27: 4).

(v) The dying thief declared, "This man hath done nothing amiss" (*Luke* 23: 41).

(vi) The Roman soldier in charge of the crucifixion declared, "Certainly this man was innocent" (*Luke* 23: 47).

(vii) No amount of provocation caused Him to act wrongly (*I Pet.* 2: 23).

(c) There is the evidence of His remarkable insight and knowledge:

(i) He needed no evidence from others about a man, for He Himself could tell what was in a man (*John* 2: 24, 25);

(ii) He knew His betrayer from the beginning (*John* 6: 70, 71; 13: 10, 11);

(iii) He anticipated Peter's denial and restoration (*Luke* 22: 31–34).

(d) There is the evidence of His unique teaching: the authority of His teaching astonished all who heard Him (*Matt.* 7: 28, 29; *John* 7: 32, 45, 46). The prophets, for example, said, "Thus says the Lord", whereas Jesus said, "Verily I say to you . . ."

(e) There is the evidence of His miracles:

(i) These were never selfish or merely spectacular (*Matt.* 4: 5–7).

(ii) Those who witnessed the miracles sensed themselves to be in the presence of God (*Mark* 1: 27; *Luke* 5: 26; 7: 16; 9: 43).

(iii) The miracles were "signs" of Christ's deity (*John* 20: 30–31). The Jewish exorcists invoked the name of the Lord, but Jesus commanded, and evil spirits, the wind and the sea obeyed Him (*Mark* 1: 27; 4: 41).

(f) There is the overwhelming evidence of Christ's resurrection:

(i) All the gospel writers record it in detail (*Matt.* 28: 1–20; *Mark* 16: 1–20; *Luke* 24: 1–53; *John* 20; 21).

(ii) Both Peter and Paul make mention of it in their letters (*I Pet.* 1: 3, 21; *I Cor.* 15).

(iii) The apostolic preaching emphasised the Resurrection as the chief witness to Christ's deity (*Acts* 2: 32; 3: 15, 26; 4: 33).

(iv) God the Father declared Christ to be His Son by the resurrection, thus endorsing every claim Christ had made (*Rom.* 1: 4).

3. To the evidence of Christ's claims and unique life to His deity, there must be added the witness of the prophets, including John the Baptist.

(a) Some of the prophetic psalms spoke of a divine Messiah (*Ps.* 2: 6–12; cf. *Heb.* 1: 5; *Ps.* 45: 6, 7; cf. *Heb.* 1: 8, 9; *Ps.* 110: 1; cf. *Heb.* 1: 13).

(b) Isaiah spoke of the Messiah whose name should be called Wonderful, Counsellor, Mighty God, Everlasting Father, and Prince of Peace (*Isa.* 9: 6).

(c) Jeremiah declared that the Messiah would be called "The Lord is our righteousness" (*Jer.* 23: 5, 6; cf. *I Cor.* 1: 30).

(d) Micah speaks of the Messiah as One whose origins have been of old, from everlasting (*Micah* 5: 2).

(e) Zechariah records God speak-ing of the Messiah as His fellow (*Zech.* 13: 7).

(f) John the Baptist not only described his ministry as making straight the way of the Lord (*John* 1: 23; cf. *Isa.* 40: 3) but bore witness that Jesus was the Son of God (*John* 1: 34).

4. We have also the witness of the apostles to the deity of Christ.

(a) Peter's confession, "Thou art the Christ, the Son of the living God" (*Matt.* 16: 16), marked a vital stage in the training of the apostles.

(b) The apostles saw Christ's glory as He lived among them, such glory as befits the Father's only Son (*John* 1: 14; *I John* 1: 1).

(c) John bears witness:

(i) "The Word was made flesh and dwelt among us" (*John* 1: 14; cf. 1: 1–4);

(ii) John identifies the glory of the Lord which Isaiah witnessed (*Isa.* 6) as the glory of Christ (*John* 12: 41);

(iii) The truth of Christ's deity was the great fundamental for John (*John* 20: 31; *I John* 5: 20).

(d) Peter bears witness:

(i) He heard the testimony of God the Father concerning Jesus Christ His Son (*II Pet.* 1: 16–18);

(ii) He speaks in trinitarian terms of the Father, the Son and the Holy Spirit (*I Pet.* 1: 2).

(e) Paul bears witness:

(i) The first truth he proclaimed after his conversion was Jesus "is the Son of God" (*Acts* 9: 20).

(ii) The Church, he declares, was purchased by God "with His own blood" (*Acts* 20: 28).

(iii) In Christ dwells the whole fulness of deity bodily (*Col.* 2: 9).

5. Finally, we have the witness of the Bible itself.

(a) References to God in the Old Testament are in the New Testament applied to Christ.

Examples:

(i) Christ is the Lord (*Isa.* 40: 3; cf. *Matt.* 3: 3);
(ii) Christ is the First and the Last (*Isa.* 44: 6; *Rev.* 1: 17);
(iii) Christ is the Judge (*Eccl.* 12: 14; cf. *I Cor.* 4: 5).

(b) The works of God are ascribed to Him:

(i) The work of creation was His (*John* 1: 3; *I Cor.* 8: 6; *Col.* 1: 16; *Heb.* 1: 2);
(ii) The work of preservation in providence is His also (*Heb.* 1: 3).

(c) The characteristics which belong only to God are ascribed to Christ:

(i) He is everywhere present (*Matt.* 28: 20);
(ii) He is all-powerful (*Phil.* 3: 21; *Rev.* 1: 8);
(iii) He knows all things (*John* 16: 30; 21: 17; *Rev.* 2: 23);
(iv) He is unchanging (*Heb.* 13: 8);
(v) He forgives sins (*Col.* 3: 13; *Mark* 2: 7, 10).

Conclusions.

1. The deity of Christ throws amazing light upon the love of God: God Himself came to redeem men (*II Cor.* 5: 19).

2. Christ is worthy of our worship: all of God's angels worship Him (*Heb.* 1: 6), as does the whole of heaven (*Rev.* 5: 12).

3. His deity gives unique value to His death: by His death we may be redeemed for God and set free from all wickedness (*Rev.* 5: 9; *Tit.* 2: 14).

4. Christ is the object of the Christian's faith: men are urged to believe on the Lord Jesus Christ and be saved (*Acts* 16: 31).

5. The Church is built upon the fact of Christ's deity (*Matt.* 16: 18).

6. The Christian's relationship to Christ is the most important reality in his life (*Phil.* 3: 7–10).

19. THE INCARNATION

Question: How do we know that Christ is both God and man?

Answer: In both the Old and the New Testaments Christ is declared to be both God and man, united in one person; many infallible proofs of the truth of this mystery are provided.

1. The Old Testament prophecies spoke of the coming Messiah, or Christ, as both God and man.

(a) The Psalms provide many examples of such prophecies (*Ps.* 2; 22; 45; 72; 110).

(b) Christ's human and divine nature was portrayed by Isaiah (*Isa.* 9: 6, 7).

(c) The prophecies concerning the Messiah, which took for granted His deity, spoke also of His body, or His humanity (*Isa.* 50: 6).

(d) Micah prophesied that the Christ to be born was One whose "goings forth have been from of old, from everlasting" (*Micah* 5: 2).

2. The New Testament speaks of Christ as both God and man.

(a) Christ, who is God, was made

44

man, without ceasing to be God (*John* 1: 1–3, 14)—He bore the human likeness, He was revealed in human form (*Phil.* 2: 8).

(b) As the apostle John expresses it, the Word became flesh and dwelt among men, full of grace and truth; and men beheld His glory, glory as of the only Son from the Father (*John* 1: 14).

(c) The testimony of the apostles was that the man Christ Jesus was the Word, the Son of God (*I John* 1: 1–3).

(d) That Christ became flesh did not mean that His deity was any the less: in Him the whole fulness of deity dwells bodily (*Col.* 2: 9).

3. Christ's virgin conception points to the fact of His perfect deity and perfect humanity.

(a) He was born of a human mother, without any human father (*Luke* 2: 6, 7; *Gal.* 4: 4).

(b) He became flesh through being conceived by the power of the Holy Spirit in the womb of Mary (*Matt.* 1: 20); the Holy Spirit came upon her, and the power of the Most High overshadowed her; these facts explain the holiness of the child, and His identity as the Son of God (*Luke* 1: 35).

(c) The virgin conception had been promised by God through the prophet Isaiah (*Isa.* 7: 14; 8: 8; *Matt.* 1: 23); thus through this event God began to fulfil His promises made throughout the centuries that He would Himself visit and redeem His people (*Matt.* 1: 21 ff; Luke 1: 31 ff, 68–75; 2: 10 f, 29–32).

4. We are given ample proof of Christ's deity.

(a) Passages of Scripture in the Old Testament speaking of the Lord Jehovah are applied to Christ in the New Testament (*Num.* 21: 5, 6, cf. *I Cor.* 10: 9; *Ps.* 102: 25–27, cf. *Heb.* 1: 10; *Isa.* 6: 1–10, cf. *John* 12: 40, 41; *Isa.* 8: 13, 14, cf. *Luke* 2: 34; *Rom.* 9: 33; *Isa.* 40: 3, 4, cf. *John* 1: 23; *Isa.* 45: 22, 23, cf. *Rom.* 14: 11, *Phil.* 2: 10, 11; *Mal.* 3: 1, cf. *Matt.* 11: 10).

(b) Works and activity which particularly belong to God are said to belong to Christ: for example, creation (*John* 1: 3; *I Cor.* 8: 6; *Heb.* 1: 2); the sustaining of the universe (*Heb.* 1: 3; *John* 5: 17); and miracles (*John* 20: 30; cf. *John* 2: 11).

(c) Characteristics which belong to God alone are said to belong to Christ: for example, He is everywhere (*Matt.* 28: 20; *John* 14: 23; *Eph.* 3: 17); He is eternal (*John* 1: 1; *Rev.* 1: 11; *Micah* 5: 2); He is unchanging (*Heb.* 1: 11, 12; 13: 8); He knows all things (*John* 21: 17; *Rev.* 2: 23); He has majesty and glory equal to His Father (*John* 5: 23; *Rev.* 5: 13; *Phil.* 1: 2; 2: 6, 9, 10).

(d) The names given to Him bear witness to His deity: for example, He is definitely called God (*John* 1: 1; 20: 28; *Acts* 20: 28; *Rom.* 9: 5; *Phil.* 2: 6; *Heb.* 1: 8; *I Tim.* 3: 16); He is called the Son of God (*John* 1: 18; *Rom.* 8: 3); He is called Lord (*I Cor.* 8: 5, 6)—"Lord" being the word used in the Greek translation of the Old Testament to render the name of God, "Jehovah".

5. We are given ample proof of His humanity.

(a) God sent His own Son in the likeness of sinful flesh—the word "likeness" implies that Jesus was similar to sinful men in His earthly life, yet not absolutely like them (*Rom.* 8: 3; *Phil.* 2: 7), because He Himself was without sin (*Heb.* 4: 15).

(b) He shared our flesh and blood (*Heb.* 2: 14).

(c) He had all that is essential in a man: a body (*Luke* 24: 39; *Heb.* 2: 17; 10: 5; *I John* 1: 1); a soul (*Matt.* 26: 38; *Mark* 14: 34); and as a consequence a will (*Matt.* 26: 39), affections (*Mark* 3: 5; *Luke* 10: 21; *John* 11: 5), and particular abilities (*Luke* 2: 52).

(d) He knew tiredness (*John* 4: 6), thirst (*John* 4: 7; 19: 28), tears (*John* 11: 33 ff; *Heb.* 5: 7), and all the weaknesses of the flesh, with one exception (*Heb.* 4: 15).

(e) He shared fully in all our experiences, especially in the realm of temptation, except that He never sinned (*Heb.* 4: 15; *II Cor.* 5: 21; *I Pet.* 2: 22).

(f) Possessing a human body Christ endured bodily suffering (*I Pet.* 4: 1); He was put to death in the flesh (*I Pet.* 3: 18).

6. It was only by Christ being both God and man that salvation could be obtained for sinful men and women.

(a) Christ's body was a fundamental part of God's plan of salvation (*Heb.* 10: 5).

(b) God the Father caused Christ to be made flesh of a pure virgin, to live amongst men, that He might be obedient unto death, the death of the Cross (*Isa.* 50: 6; *John* 1: 14; *Luke* 1: 35; *Phil.* 2: 8; *I Tim.* 3: 16).

(c) The reconciliation which God purposed was accomplished by Christ's death in His body of flesh and blood (*Col.* 1: 22; *Eph.* 2: 15, 16).

(d) The new and living way for sinners into the presence of God by the blood of Christ was possible solely by means of Christ's taking flesh upon Himself (*Heb.* 10: 19, 20).

(e) It was by becoming a human being, that, going through death as a man, He destroyed him who had the power of death, that is, the devil, and set free those who lived their whole lives a prey to the fear of death (*Heb.* 2: 14, 15).

(f) Through taking human nature upon Him, He has made it possible for sinners to escape from the corruption that is in the world, and become partakers of the divine nature (*II Pet.* 1: 4).

(g) It was necessary that Christ should be man that the nature which had offended should suffer, and make satisfaction, so that Christ might be in every way a fit and sufficient Saviour for men (*Heb.* 2: 10–17); by becoming man He could mediate between God and men (*I Tim.* 2: 5).

(h) It was necessary that Christ should be God that He might be able to save absolutely those who come to God through Him (*Heb.* 7: 25).

7. Christ's perfect deity and perfect humanity are essentials of the Christian faith.

(a) Fundamental to the Christian faith is the fact that Christ, the Son of God, truly came "in the flesh" (*I John* 4: 2; *II John* 7).

(b) Any denial of the reality of Christ's "flesh", that is to say, that He was not truly a man, is heresy

(*I John* 2: 22–25; 4: 1–6; 5: 5–12; *II John* 7, 9 ff).

8. **The fact of Christ being the Word made flesh—what we call "The Incarnation"—is beyond the understanding of the human mind.**

That Christ is truly God and perfect man is a mystery, revealed to us in the Scriptures, yet beyond our complete understanding, being something which causes even the angels to admire the wisdom and goodness of God (*I Tim.* 3: 16; *I Pet.* 1: 12).

20. THE CROSS

Question: What happened when Christ died upon the Cross?

Answer: He offered up Himself as a sacrifice, bearing the punishment due to sinners, fulfilling the plan of God whereby men may be reconciled to Himself through Christ.

1. **The Cross cannot be understood unless the plight of man in his sin is realised.**

(a) Men are in danger of perishing (*John* 3: 16).

(b) Men have sinned against God (*Rom.* 3: 23).

(c) Sin has separated men from God (*Isa.* 59: 2).

(d) Sin has brought death upon men (*Rom.* 5: 12; 6: 23).

(e) Men are under the wrath of God (*John* 3: 36; *Eph.* 2: 3).

2. **The Cross was no accident but the deliberate will and plan of God** (*Acts* 2: 23).

(a) Before the world was founded God the Father determined that His Son should fulfil the function

of a Saviour for sinners (*I Pet.* 1: 20).

(b) The Father and the Son entered into a compact and a covenant: the Son was to accomplish the work assigned to Him (*John* 12: 27; 17: 2, 4), and the Father promised that as a result a great number of men and women from all nations should be given to Him as His inheritance (*Ps.* 2: 7–8) and He should be supreme Head to the Church (*Eph.* 1: 22; *Phil.* 2: 7, 9; *Heb.* 12: 2).

(c) The world was prepared for the great event of the Cross by many symbols and illustrations.

(i) The Old Testament sacrifices all looked forward to the coming of Jesus and His death upon the Cross for sinners (*Heb.* 9: 24; 10: 4, 10, 11, 12; *John* 1: 29, 36).

(ii) The Passover Lamb was a picture of Jesus also (*Ex.* 12: 21–23; *I Cor.* 5: 7) and Jesus used the feast of the Passover to establish the Lord's Supper as a reminder of the meaning of His death (*Luke* 22: 7–23).

3. **The initiative in the Cross was God's.**

(a) Loving the world so much God gave His Son (*John* 3: 16).

(b) It was the will of God to bruise Him (*Isa.* 53: 10).

(c) The bitter experience of the Cross was received by the Son from the Father (*Matt.* 26: 39, 42).

(d) The design of the whole plan of expiating sin by Christ's sacrificial death was the Father's (*Rom.* 3: 25).

4. **Christ willingly died upon the Cross.**

(a) From before the time the world was founded Christ had committed

47

Himself willingly to the Cross (*Isa.* 50: 4–6; *Heb.* 10: 5–10).

(b) He laid down His life (*John* 10: 11, 18).

(c) He poured out His soul to death (*Isa.* 53: 12).

(d) He gave Himself up as an offering and a sacrifice (*Eph.* 5: 2).

5. Christ bore the punishment due to sinners.

(a) He bore the sin of many (*Isa.* 53: 12; *I Pet.* 2: 24).

(b) He bore the wrath of God against sin which sinners deserve (*John* 3: 36; *Rom.* 1: 18; *I John* 2: 2; 4: 10—"propitiation" means the putting away of wrath).

(c) He bore the curse of the law which sinners through their disobedience deserve to experience—death and separation from God (*Gal.* 3: 10, 13; *Isa.* 59: 2; *Rom.* 5: 12; *Mark* 15: 34).

(d) He bore the pains of hell which the sinner deserves (*Ps.* 18: 5; *Mark* 15: 33, 34).

6. We cannot overemphasise either the worth or the eternal character of Christ's sacrifice.

(a) The punishment He suffered was sufficient to satisfy for the transgressions of all because He who suffered was not only a man, but God also. He was of infinitely more value than all those who had offended (*Rom.* 5: 9; *Heb.* 9: 13, 14).

(b) His sacrifice was final—once and for all—and utterly sufficient for all time (*I Pet.* 3: 18; *Heb.* 9: 26; 10: 11, 14).

7. The benefits achieved by Christ's death.

(a) The justice of God was satisfied (*Isa.* 53: 11).

(i) The punishment sin deserves has been allotted and carried out (*Isa.* 53: 4–6; *II Cor.* 5: 21).

(ii) God has shown Himself just and may justify any man who puts his faith in Jesus (*Rom.* 3: 26; *II Cor.* 5: 21).

(b) Redemption from the power of sin, death and hell was made possible for sinners:

(i) The price of redemption has been paid in full by Christ (*Matt.* 20: 28; *Mark* 10: 45; *I Tim.* 2: 6)—the price being His own precious blood (*Acts* 20: 28; *I John* 1: 7).

(ii) Christ has utterly overcome and defeated Satan, death and the powers of hell, that hold men captive. The devil's power is broken (*Heb.* 2: 14). As a consequence the power of death is broken too (*John* 5: 24; *Heb.* 2: 14; *I Cor.* 15: 55–57). Furthermore, hell need not be men's destination (*I Thess.* 1: 10).

(c) The new covenant which God had promised was confirmed.

(i) It was promised when Adam sinned (*Gen.* 3: 15).

(ii) Both Christ and the covenant were promised to Abraham (*Gen.* 12: 3; *Gal.* 3: 8, 16).

(iii) Yet more details were promised through the prophets (*Jer.* 31: 31–34; 32: 40).

(iv) This new covenant could come into operation only by the mediation of Jesus (*Heb.* 8: 6, 10–12).

(v) A testament or a covenant demands a death—a testament is operative only after a death—and Christ made valid the new covenant by the shedding of His blood (*Heb.* 9: 14–26; 13: 20).

(d) Grace and glory are assured

for all who enter into this new covenant:

(i) Having given His Son to die such a death, there is nothing which God will fail to lavish upon those who are saved by it (*Rom.* 8: 32; *Heb.* 4: 16).

(ii) Every spiritual benefit in this life and in that to come is assured (*Eph.* 1: 3 ff).

(iii) Eternal life is the gift of Christ to those who are saved by His death (*John* 17: 2; 14: 1–6).

(e) These benefits may be summed up in the word "reconciliation". Through God's work in Christ of reconciling the world to Himself, men's sins and misdeeds need no longer be held against them (*II Cor.* 5: 18, 19); united to Christ a man may receive a new life altogether (*II Cor.* 5: 17) and be declared righteous by God (*II Cor.* 5: 21).

8. Only by Christ's death may we be reconciled to God.

The message of the gospel is plain: be reconciled to God through Christ (*II Cor.* 5: 18, 20).

21. THE RESURRECTION

Question: What is the significance of the Resurrection of Christ?

Answer: God the Father raised Christ from the dead, in fulfilment of the Scriptures and of Christ's promises, declaring Christ to be His Son, and His acceptance of Christ's redemptive work, guaranteeing the justification, spiritual life and final resurrection of all believers.

1. The fact of the Resurrection is at the core of the gospel.

(a) The Resurrection was the work of the Father (*Acts* 2: 24; 3: 15; 10: 40; *Eph.* 1: 20; Col. 2: 12) by the power of the Spirit (*Rom.* 8: 11; *I Pet.* 3: 18).

(b) The centrality of the Resurrection is seen in the trouble to which the New Testament goes, and the Gospels especially, to give the facts concerning our Lord's appearances. Jesus appeared to Mary Magdalene (*Mark* 16: 9; *John* 20: 18), the women (*Matt.* 28: 9), Simon Peter (*Luke* 24: 34), two disciples (*Luke* 24: 13–31), all the apostles, except Thomas (*John* 20: 19, 24), Thomas himself (*John* 20: 26), the apostles at the Sea of Tiberias (*John* 21: 1), the apostles in Galilee (*Matt.* 28: 16, 17), about 500 brethren (*I Cor.* 15: 6), James (*I Cor.* 15: 7), all the apostles (*Luke* 24: 51; *Acts* 1: 9; *I Cor.* 15: 7), Paul (*I Cor.* 15: 8).

2. The fact of the Resurrection was central in the witness of the apostles.

(a) "We are witnesses" was their theme (*Acts* 2: 24; *Acts* 3: 15; *I Cor.* 15: 14, 15).

(b) To be an apostle a man had to be a witness to Christ's Resurrection (*Acts* 1: 22).

(c) The distinctive characteristic of their preaching was the power with which they bore witness to the Resurrection of Christ (*Acts* 4: 30, 33).

(d) They knew and preached a living Christ (*Acts* 25: 19; *II Tim.* 2: 8).

3. The Old Testament Scriptures demanded that the Resurrection should take place.

(a) The Messiah was not to be allowed to experience corruption (*Ps.* 16: 10; *Acts* 13: 34, 35).

(b) Everything written about Christ in the Law of Moses, the prophets and the Psalms demanded fulfilment (*Luke* 24: 44; *John* 20: 9; *Acts* 26: 22, 23).

4. Christ had foretold His Resurrection.

(a) At the beginning of His ministry He had hinted at it (*John* 2: 19–22).

(b) When Peter confessed Jesus as the Messiah, the first clear revelation about the Resurrection was given to the disciples (*Matt.* 16: 21).

(c) The experience of the Transfiguration was not to be reported until after the Resurrection (*Mark* 9: 9).

(d) Jesus clearly foretold His Resurrection to the disciples (*Matt.* 20: 19; *Mark* 14: 28).

5. The Resurrection was necessary to demonstrate irrefutably the truth of all Christ's claims.

(a) By His life, words and miracles Jesus had made many claims (*Luke* 11: 20; *John* 14: 6; 11: 25; 10: 18).

(b) From the lips of a mere man such claims would have been blasphemous (*Matt.* 26: 63–66). If such a one died and remained dead as other men then the charge of imposter would be true but if He rose again from the dead the truth of His claim—that He was from God and was the Son of God— would be vindicated. (*Matt.* 27: 63–66; cf. *Acts* 5: 38, 39, applying the latter words for the moment to the Resurrection.)

6. The Resurrection was necessary to give final proof of Christ's deity.

(a) The Resurrection was a declaration of the Father, as promised in the Old Testament, that Jesus is His Son (*Ps.* 2: 7; *Acts* 13: 33).

(b) By raising Christ to life again by the power of the Holy Spirit, God the Father patently marked Christ out as His Son— the Son of God, the Second Person of the Trinity (*Rom.* 1: 4).

(c) It was impossible for death to keep Christ in its grip (*Acts* 2: 24) —of God alone could such a claim be justly made.

7. Without the Resurrection we would not know that Christ's death achieved its objects so far as sin is concerned.

(a) Without it the gospel would be null and void (*I Cor.* 15: 14).

(b) Without it there would be no hope of forgiveness (*I Cor.* 15: 17).

(c) Without it men would be utterly lost with no possibility of salvation (*I Cor.* 15: 19).

(d) By the Resurrection the acquittal from every charge of all who believe is declared (*Rom.* 4: 25; 8: 34).

8. The Resurrection was necessary to provide a solid basis for faith.

(a) Christ showed Himself alive by many infallible proofs (*Acts* 1: 3).

(b) God's acceptance of Christ's work is demonstrated by the Resurrection (see 7, above): through Christ men may approach God with confidence (*I Pet.* 1: 21).

(c) The Resurrection gives our faith substance (*Rom.* 10: 9, 10; *I Cor.* 15: 17).

9. The Resurrection was necessary to give a living hope.

(a) The Christian's hope or assurance arises from Christ's Resurrection: through His Resurrection we receive new life (*I Pet.* 1: 3; *Rom.* 6: 4; *Col.* 2: 12).

(b) Believers have a living hope regarding the resurrection of the dead, for God who raised up Christ shall raise up them also (*I Cor.* 15: 20, 23; *Acts* 26: 23; *I Cor.* 6: 14; *II Cor.* 4: 14).

(c) Believers have a living hope regarding the resurrection of the body, for Christ's Resurrection is the pattern of theirs (*Luke* 24: 35, 39, 43; *John* 20: 20, 27; *Phil.* 3: 21; *Rom.* 6: 5; *I Cor.* 15: 49).

10. The Resurrection was necessary in order to demonstrate that Christ may be known today.

(a) Paul proved the truth of this experience in his day, at first to his great amazement (*Acts* 9: 1–9).

(b) Paul then made the knowing of Christ and the experiencing of the power of His Resurrection the objective of his life (*Phil.* 3: 10).

11. The Resurrection was necessary to give assurance of the just judgment of the world.

(a) Men wrongly condemned Christ; God the Father vindicated Him by the Resurrection, thereby judging those who dealt with Christ so falsely (*Acts* 2: 22–24).

(b) God will have the world judged and justly judged by Christ—He has given assurance of this by the Resurrection (*Acts* 17: 31).

12. The Resurrection was necessary to illustrate that the last word is always with God.

Men called Christ a "deceiver"; God the Father—by the Resurrection—declared Him "My Son" (*Matt.* 27: 63–66; *Ps.* 2: 7; *Rom.* 1: 4).

22. THE ASCENSION

Question: What happened when Christ ascended to heaven?

Answer: Christ returned to the Father and was glorified—the final proof of His completed sacrificial work. He entered then upon His work as priest and king upon the throne—no longer needing to offer atoning sacrifice to God—giving gifts to His Church, and guaranteeing her security and final presence with Him in heaven. He waits now for the time of His final victory.

1. The Ascension.

(a) The Ascension was a vital link in a chain of fulfilled prophecy, promised both in the Old Testament (*Ps.* 110: 1; *Acts* 2: 32–36) and by Christ Himself (*Matt.* 26: 64; *John* 6: 62; 7: 33; 14: 28; 16: 5; 20: 17).

(b) It took place forty days after the Resurrection (*Acts* 1: 3).

(c) It took place at the Mount of Olives (*Luke* 24: 50; cf. *Mark* 11: 1; *Acts* 1: 12).

(d) It was witnessed by the apostles, after He had talked with them (*Mark* 16: 19) and lifted up His hands to bless them (*Luke* 24: 50, 51).

(e) He was lifted up, and a cloud took Him out of their sight (*Acts* 1: 9).

(f) The return of Christ will be after the pattern of the Ascension (*Acts* 1: 11).

2. What the Ascension was.

(a) It was an act of God's power (*Eph.* 1: 19–22).

(b) It was the necessary completion of Christ's death and resurrection: it proved the full acceptance by God of His single sacrifice for sins for all time (*Heb.* 10: 12); it marked Christ out as Lord, even as the Resurrection marked Him out as the Son of God (*Phil.* 2: 9–11; *Acts* 2: 34–36; cf. *Rom.* 1: 4).

(c) It was the visible ascent of Christ, according to His human nature, from earth to heaven (*Mark* 16: 19; *I Pet.* 3: 22): He was exalted to the place in the universe He had laid aside when He humbled Himself to assume our humanity (*Eph.* 4: 9, 10).

(d) It marked Christ's return to the Father: He went to Him who had sent Him into the world (*John* 6: 62; 7: 33; 14: 28; 16: 5; 20: 17).

(e) It included a further glorification of the human nature of Christ: He carried His humanity with Him back to heaven (*Heb.* 2: 14–18; 4: 14–16), and He was highly exalted and glorified in doing so (*Acts* 2: 33; *John* 7: 39; *I Tim.* 3: 16), the Father honouring Him with the highest possible honour (*Eph.* 1: 20–22).

3. The significance of the Ascension.

(a) God the Father's acceptance of His Son into glory declared decisively and finally His acceptance of Christ's sacrifice for our sins (*Heb.* 1: 3; 9: 12; 10: 11–14).

(b) Christ entered upon His work as a royal priest upon the throne, no longer needing to offer atoning sacrifice to God (*Heb.* 7: 26; 8: 1; 10: 21); He entered into heaven to appear now before God on our behalf, representing our cause before the Father (*Heb.* 9: 24).

(c) Christ, demonstrated by the Ascension to be Lord (*Matt.* 28: 18; *Acts* 2: 36), entered upon His work as king; He is seated at the right hand of God (*Matt.* 26: 64; *Acts* 2: 33; *Rom.* 8: 34; *Col.* 3: 1; *Heb.* 1: 3; 10: 12; 12: 2; *I Pet.* 3: 22), a picture of the unique position the Father has given Him of kingly power and authority over angels, authorities and powers in heaven and on earth (*Heb.* 1: 13; *Dan.* 7: 13, 14; *Matt.* 26: 64; *Eph.* 1: 21, 22; 4: 10; *Col.* 1: 16–18; *I Pet.* 3: 22).

(d) Christ ascended to receive, as conqueror, the gifts promised Him for His Church (*Eph.* 4: 8; *Ps.* 68: 18): He ascended to send forth the Holy Spirit (*John* 7: 39; 16: 7; *Acts* 2: 33).

(e) The Ascension of Christ and the consequent outpouring of the Spirit made possible the numerous gifts of the Spirit which the Church enjoys (*Eph.* 4: 8, 11–13).

(f) Christ ascended to prepare a place for Christians (*John* 14: 2): He is their forerunner, preparing the way for them (*Heb.* 6: 20; cf. *Acts* 7: 56).

(g) Christians are already set with Christ in heavenly places, for they are made to share by grace, through faith, the Resurrection and Ascension of Christ (*Eph.* 2: 6): their citizenship is now in heaven and their thoughts and affections should be set there (*Phil.* 3: 20; *Col.* 3: 1, 2).

(h) In Christ's Ascension Christians have the assurance of a place in heaven (*II Cor.* 4: 14; *John* 14: 19) and of their own glorification (*Phil.* 3: 21): God's purpose in giving Christians a share in the Resurrection and Ascension of Christ is that in the coming ages He might show the immeasurable riches of His grace in kindness toward them in Christ Jesus (*John* 17: 24; *Eph.* 2: 7).

4. What Christ does at God's right hand.

(a) He lives for ever, holding a permanent priesthood (*Rev.* 1: 18; *Heb.* 7: 24).

(b) He rules and protects His Church as its Head (*Eph.* 1: 22, 23), helping the members in need (*Heb.* 2: 18; 4: 15), and giving the power to do great works (*John* 14: 12).

(c) He governs the universe, and to the end that God's purposes for the Church may be fulfilled (*Heb.* 1: 3; *Eph.* 1: 5-14).

(d) He intercedes for His people on the basis of His completed sacrifice (*Rom.* 8: 34): He is our Advocate with the Father (*I John* 2: 1).

(e) He waits for the time of His final victory: all His enemies shall be subdued (*Ps.* 110: 1; *Acts* 2: 35; *I Cor.* 15: 24-26; *Heb.* 10: 13).

(f) His Ascension in power is the prelude to His coming in power as the divine Judge (*Dan.* 7: 13, 14; *Matt.* 26: 64; *John* 14: 28; *Acts* 10: 42; *II Thess.* 1: 6-10).

23. THE HOLY SPIRIT

Question: Who is the Holy Spirit?

Answer: He is the Lord and Giver of Life, the third Person of the Trinity to be worshipped and glorified with the Father and the Son. He is most commonly presented to us as the Executor of God's purposes, whether in creation, revelation or redemption.

1. He is unique.

There is but one Spirit (*I Cor.* 12: 13; *Eph.* 4: 4).

2. He is a Person—not simply an influence or a power.

(a) He is spoken of as "He" and not as "It" (*John* 16: 13).

(b) He is spoken of as a Person—the Comforter or Advocate (*John* 14: 16, 26; 15: 26; 16: 7).

(c) He may be grieved (*Isa.* 63: 10; *Eph.* 4: 30).

(d) He is affronted by the apostate (*Heb.* 10: 29).

3. He is God.

(a) He is the Spirit of the living God (*II Cor.* 3: 3; *I Pet.* 4: 14).

(b) Sovereignty is ascribed to Him (*I Cor.* 12: 11).

(c) Old Testament references to God are revealed in the New Testament to have been references to the Holy Spirit (*Ex.* 17: 7; cf. *Heb.* 3: 7-9; *Isa.* 6: 3, 8-10; cf. *Acts* 28: 25-27; *Ps.* 78: 17, 21; cf. *Acts* 7: 51).

(d) The qualities ascribed to the Holy Spirit are the qualities ascribed everywhere to God alone: He is everywhere present (*Ps.* 139: 7-13; *I Cor.* 12: 13); He knows all things (*I Cor.* 2: 10); He has all power (*Luke* 1: 35; *Rom.* 8: 11; 15: 19).

(e) To lie to the Spirit is to lie to God (*Acts* 5: 3, 4, 5).

(f) He is to be obeyed (*Gal.* 5: 16-24).

(g) Blasphemy against Him is the worst of all sins (*Matt.* 12: 31 ff; *Mark* 3: 28 f; *Luke* 12: 10).

(h) His intercession is according to the will of God (*Rom.* 8: 27).

(i) To affront the Spirit is to deserve the severest judgment (*Heb.* 10: 29).

4. He is the Third Person of the Trinity.

(a) He is one with the Father and the Son (*Matt.* 28: 19; *II Cor.* 13: 14; *I Cor.* 12: 4-6; *Eph.* 4: 4-6).

(b) He is sent by both the Father and the Son and He acts for them both (*John* 15: 26).

5. He was the Agent of God's first creation.

(a) He was active in creation, bringing order out of chaos (*Gen.* 1: 2).

(b) By God's Spirit the heavens were made beautiful (*Job* 26: 13).

(c) Man was made by the Spirit of God (*Job* 33: 4; cf. *Gen.* 2: 7; *Ps.* 104: 29, 30).

6. He is the Author of the Scriptures.

(a) He inspired the Scriptures (*II Tim.* 3: 16): men impelled by the Holy Spirit spoke and wrote from God (*II Pet.* 1: 21; *Acts* 1: 16).

(b) The Scriptures are His testimony (*Heb.* 10: 15).

(c) He compelled the prophets to speak (*Ezek.* 11: 5; *Zech.* 7: 12; *Micah* 3: 8).

(d) He inspired men to prophesy (*Luke* 1: 67; 2: 26, 27, 29-32).

(e) He revealed to the apostles and prophets the truth concerning Christ and the gospel at the time determined by God (*Eph.* 3: 5, 6).

(f) He speaks today through the Scriptures (*Heb.* 3: 7).

7. He was active with regard to the Incarnation.

(a) By His power the virgin conception was accomplished (*Luke* 1: 35).

(b) Mary was found with child by the Holy Spirit (*Matt.* 1: 18, 20).

(c) The Spirit descended upon Jesus in a special manner at His baptism (*Mark* 1: 10 f).

(d) The Spirit led and directed Christ during His ministry (*Matt.* 4: 1; *Mark* 1: 12).

(e) The Spirit equipped Christ for His ministry (*Luke* 4: 1, 18; *Acts* 10: 38).

(f) Christ possessed the Spirit in a measureless manner (*John* 3: 34).

(g) Christ's works of power were by the power of the Spirit of God which was His (*Luke* 11: 20; cf. *Matt.* 12: 28; *Acts* 10: 38).

(h) The Spirit gave Christ joy during His earthly life and ministry (*Luke* 10: 21).

(i) The Spirit raised Christ from the dead (*Acts* 2: 24; cf. *I Pet.* 3: 18; *Heb.* 13: 20; cf. *Rom.* 1: 4).

8. He is the Agent of God's new creation in Christ—the Church.

(a) The Holy Spirit's activity in God's new creation is all-important:

(i) He puts the redeemed in possession of the results of the Father's love and the mediation of Christ (*II Cor.* 3: 8; *John* 7: 39);

(ii) Justification takes place through the name of the Lord Jesus and the Spirit of God (*I Cor.* 6: 11; *I Pet.* 1: 2);

(iii) Through the Spirit the redeemed are brought into the one body, the Church, this act being described as a baptism (*I Cor.* 12: 13);

(iv) The Spirit is the Author of the new birth (*John* 3: 5, 6; *II Cor.* 5: 17). Whereas the written law condemns to death, the Spirit gives life (*II Cor.* 3: 6; *Gal.* 5: 25). Where the Spirit is there is life (*Ezek.* 37: 1-14; *Rom.* 8: 2, 11; *John* 6: 63).

(b) The Holy Spirit is directly associated with the extension of God's new creation—the Church (*Matt.* 28: 19; cf. *Acts* 1: 4, 8):

(i) He ensures that messengers are raised up and men sent forth to proclaim the gospel (*Matt.* 9: 38; cf. *Acts* 13: 2, 4; 16: 6, 7, 10; 20: 28);

(ii) He accompanies the preaching of the gospel with His power (*I Pet.* 1: 12);

(iii) He shows men their need of salvation by convicting them of sin (*John* 16: 8–11);

(iv) He bears witness to Christ (*John* 15: 26), and by His influence men are enabled to say "Jesus is Lord" (*I Cor.* 12: 3);

(v) Given to every believer as a result of Christ's work (*John* 7: 39), He binds believers together in one body in spiritual unity (*Eph.* 4: 3, 4);

(vi) For the care of the Church the Spirit raises up guardians or pastors (*Acts* 20: 28);

(vii) He allots varying gifts to Christians (*Rom.* 12: 6–8);

(viii) In each Christian the Spirit desires to manifest Himself in some particular way, for some useful purpose (*I Cor.* 12: 4–11);

(ix) The Spirit's purpose in all this is to equip God's people for work in Christ's service, to the building up of the body of Christ (*Eph.* 4: 11–13).

24. THE HOLY SPIRIT AND THE CHRISTIAN

Question: What is the relationship of the Holy Spirit to the Christian?
Answer: The Holy Spirit is the gift of the Father and the Son to the believer to live within him: giving him spiritual life; assuring him of his sonship; and communicating to him the benefits of the gospel.

1. The Holy Spirit is Christ's promised gift to the believer.

(a) Christ asked the Father that the Spirit might be the believer's possession (*John* 14: 16).

(b) The Spirit is sent by Christ from the Father (*John* 15: 26; 16: 7).

(c) He is called sometimes "the Spirit of Christ" (*Acts* 16: 7; *Rom.* 8: 9; *I Pet.* 1: 11).

(d) He is received not by keeping the law but by believing the good news made known through Jesus Christ (*Gal.* 3: 2, 3, 14).

2. The Holy Spirit works in the believer the miracle of the new birth.

(a) Unless a man is born anew by the Holy Spirit he cannot see the kingdom of God (*John* 3: 3, 5).

(b) The life of the Christian is begun in the Spirit (*Gal.* 3: 3).

(c) If a man does not have the Spirit of Christ he does not belong to Christ (*Rom.* 8: 9).

3. The Holy Spirit is, therefore, the source of the believer's spiritual life (*Gal.* 5: 25).

(a) By nature men are spiritually dead (*Eph.* 2: 1).

(b) The Spirit brings spiritual life to dead men (*Eph.* 2: 1 f; cf. *Ezek.* 37: 14; *Rom.* 8: 2, 11; *John* 6: 63).

4. The Holy Spirit testifies with the Christian's spirit that he is a child of God (*Rom.* 8: 16).

(a) He makes the believer sure of his union with Christ (*I John* 3: 24; 4: 13).

(b) The Spirit cries in our hearts as the Spirit of God's Son, "Abba! Father!" (*Gal.* 4: 6).

5. The Holy Spirit dwells within the Christian believer.

(a) The possession of the Spirit is the Christian's distinguishing mark (*Rom.* 8: 9).

(b) The Christian's body is the shrine of the indwelling Holy Spirit (*I Cor.* 3: 16 f; 6: 19; cf. *Isa.* 57: 15; *II Tim.* 1: 14).

(c) By reason of the Spirit abiding with him, and in him, the Christian knows Him (*John* 14: 17).

(d) The Spirit dwells within the Christian for ever (*John* 14: 16 f).

6. The Holy Spirit sanctifies the Christian.

(a) The Holy Spirit makes the Christian holy—He sets him apart for God (*II Thess.* 2: 13; *I Pet.* 1: 2).

(b) The Holy Spirit is completely contrary in His desires to the desires of the Christian's lower nature (*Gal.* 5: 16), and He proceeds to fight against this lower nature (*Gal.* 5: 17).

(c) The Holy Spirit enables the Christian to put to death the deeds of the body—those activities of his lower nature—which displease God (*Rom.* 8: 13).

(d) By the power of the Spirit the Christian's character is transformed (*Gal.* 5: 22 f).

7. The Holy Spirit produces the character of Christ in the Christian.

(a) The Holy Spirit purposes to transfigure the Christian into the Lord's likeness, from splendour to splendour (*II Cor.* 3: 18).

(b) Love, joy, peace, patience, kindness, goodness, fidelity, gentleness, and self-control are His fruit (*Gal.* 5: 22, 23).

(c) We would expect the Holy Spirit to produce these characteristics for He is the Spirit of Christ (*Acts* 16: 7; *Rom.* 8: 9; *Gal.* 4: 6; *Phil.* 1: 19; *I Pet.* 1: 11).

8. The Holy Spirit strengthens the Christian.

(a) His resources are available to him (*Phil.* 1: 19).

(b) He upholds him (*Acts* 9: 31).

(c) He gives continuous help in times of difficulty and opposition (*I Pet.* 4: 14).

9. The Holy Spirit helps the Christian to pray.

(a) He helps him to pray at all times (*Eph.* 6: 18).

(b) He inspires prayer by the love He places in the Christian's heart for his fellow-believers (*Rom.* 15: 30).

(c) He prompts the Christian's "groanings"—those inner feelings which cannot find expression in words—for He is in them, and He conveys their meaning to the Father (*Rom.* 8: 26).

10. The Holy Spirit instructs the Christian, interpreting to him the Scriptures.

(a) The Holy Spirit explores everything: even the depths of God's own nature (*I Cor.* 2: 11).

(b) The Spirit alone knows what God is (*I Cor.* 2: 11).

(c) The Spirit reveals to the Christian things which would otherwise be hidden to him (*I Cor.* 2: 10).

(d) The Spirit makes known to the Christian all that God of His own grace gives him (*I Cor.* 2: 12).

(e) The Spirit bears witness pre-eminently to Christ (*John* 15: 26).

(f) The Spirit gives the Christian discernment (*I Cor.* 2: 14).

(g) The Spirit guides the Christian into all the truth (*John* 16: 13).

(h) The Spirit speaks to him today in the Scriptures (*Heb.* 3: 7).

11. The Holy Spirit gives power to the Christian's endeavours in witness.

(a) He gives power to witness and to fulfil the Lord's command to evangelise (*Matt.* 28: 19; cf. *Acts* 1: 4, 8).

(b) He makes preaching to carry conviction by spiritual power (*I Cor.* 2: 4 f).

12. The Holy Spirit guides the Christian.

(a) He guides the Christian into the way of victory over sin (*Gal.* 5: 16).

(b) He leads and directs the Christian in his service for God (*Acts* 16: 6, 7; *Rom.* 8: 14).

(c) He prompts right action at particular times (*Luke* 2: 27).

(d) He guides as to the right solution of difficult problems (*Acts* 15: 28).

13. The Holy Spirit imparts gifts to the Christian for the service of God (*Rom.* 12: 6–8).

(a) He equips the Christian to help in the task of building up Christ's Church (*Eph.* 4: 11–13).

(b) He gives the right gift or gifts for all varieties of service and the many forms of work there are (*I Cor.* 12: 4, 5, 6).

(c) He enables the Christian to fulfil a useful purpose within the Church (*I Cor.* 12: 7).

14. The Holy Spirit communicates the spiritual benefits of the gospel to the Christian.

(a) He makes God's love to flood his heart (*Rom.* 5: 5).

(b) He communicates joy (*Rom.* 14: 17; *I Thess.* 1: 6).

(c) He makes the Christian to overflow with the joy of the Christian hope (*Rom.* 15: 13; *Gal.* 5: 5).

15. The Holy Spirit is God's pledge to the Christian of what is to come to him in the future (*II Cor.* 1: 22).

(a) God has shaped the Christian for a wonderful future in glory (*II Cor.* 4: 16–5: 5).

(b) The Christian is reborn by the Spirit to a great and wonderful inheritance which nothing can destroy or spoil or wither (*I Pet.* 1: 4; *Eph.* 1: 14).

(c) The Spirit is the pledge that the Christian shall enter upon this inheritance (*Eph.* 1: 14).

16. The Christian's appropriation of the help of the Holy Spirit.

(a) The Holy Spirit's illumination is given in answer to prayer (*Eph.* 1: 16, 17).

(b) The Holy Spirit is given in His fullness to the Christian as the Christian seeks such from God (*Luke* 11: 13).

(c) As the Christian lives in obedience to God, so he knows more and more of the Spirit (*Acts* 5: 32).

(d) The Christian is to let the Spirit direct the course of his life (*Gal.* 5: 25).

25. DEFINING A CHRISTIAN

Question: What is a Christian?

Answer: A Christian is one who, having understood the ABC of the gospel of Christ, has received

Christ, has taken his stand upon Him, and experiences salvation through Him.

1. The gospel which has to be understood.

(a) The appointed time, concerning which the prophets in the Old Testament had spoken and to which the people of God had looked forward, has come. Through Christ, God has visited and redeemed His people (*Acts* 2: 16–21).

(b) This act of God, intervening in human history, is to be seen in the life of Jesus Christ, the Messiah, sent by God, rejected, and put to death by men, and raised up by God on the third day (*Acts* 2: 32, 36).

(c) By His death and resurrection Jesus Christ has conquered sin and death and opened the kingdom of heaven to all believers. In no one else is there to be found salvation (*Acts* 4: 12).

(d) The proofs of God's present power in the world are to be found in the fact of the resurrection and the evidences of the Holy Spirit's working in the Church (*Rom.* 1: 4; *Eph.* 1: 19, 20; *Acts* 4: 33).

(e) This is but the beginning of God's kingdom. Christ will come again as Judge, and God's kingdom will be finally established (*Acts* 3: 20, 21; 17: 30, 31; *II Thess.* 1: 7–10).

(f) Therefore all men everywhere should repent and be baptised in the name of Jesus the Messiah for the forgiveness of their sins, and thus receive the gift of the Holy Spirit (*Acts* 2: 38).

2. Fundamental to a person's understanding of the gospel is his appreciation, therefore, of at least the following truths:

(a) Jesus is the Christ, the Son of God (*John* 20: 31; *Acts* 8: 37).

(b) Christ's purpose in coming into the world and in dying upon the cross was to save sinners (*I Tim.* 1: 15).

(c) Christ's resurrection was God the Father's declaration of Christ as His Son and His satisfaction with His work (*Rom.* 1: 4).

(d) To enter into the benefits of Christ's work—to know forgiveness, the gift of God's Spirit and a place in His kingdom—repentance and open confession of Christ are required (*Acts* 2: 38).

(e) A Christian recognises his personal sinfulness (*Rom.* 7: 24).

(f) A Christian knows his personal indebtedness to Christ in that He gave His life a ransom for him (*Mark* 10: 45; *Gal.* 2: 20; *I Pet.* 2: 24).

3. The benefits the gospel promises.

(a) Deliverance from condemnation (*John* 3: 18; *Rom.* 8: 1).

(b) Justification (*I Cor.* 6: 11).

(c) The gift of the Holy Spirit (*I Cor.* 2: 12).

(d) Eternal life (*John* 3: 16, 36).

(e) Reconciliation with God (*II Cor.* 5: 18–21).

(f) Membership of the people of God (*I Pet.* 2: 9, 10).

(g) Membership of the kingdom of God (*Col.* 1: 13).

(h) The resurrection of the body (*I Cor.* 6: 14).

(i) Endless fellowship with Christ (*John* 14: 4; *I Thess.* 4: 17).

4. A Christian is one who, having

understood the ABC of the gospel, has received Christ.

(a) The words "believe" and "receive" are more or less identical (*John* 1: 12; *I Cor.* 15: 1, 2).

(b) The call to believe on the Lord Jesus Christ for salvation comes home to the individual with the conviction and power of the Holy Spirit (*I Cor.* 2: 1–5; *I Thess.* 1: 5).

(c) The call of God to believe on the Lord Jesus Christ is responded to (*Acts* 16: 31, 34; *I Cor.* 1: 9, 23, 24; *Rom.* 10: 9).

(d) Christ is received into the life, and spiritual birth takes place by the Holy Spirit (*John* 1: 12, 13; 3: 3, 7).

5. A Christian is one who, having understood the ABC of the gospel, has received Christ, and takes his stand upon Christ.

(a) He recognises that being bought with a price, he does not belong to himself any more (*I Cor.* 6: 20; 7: 23).

(b) The word "stand" speaks of assurance: he knows that he has eternal life (*I John* 5: 13; cf. *I John* 2: 3, 5; 3: 14; 4: 13).

(c) The expression "taking a stand" implies action: his stand is seen first by baptism (*Acts* 2: 38, 41; *I Cor.* 1: 13), and the confession of his lips that Jesus is Lord (*Rom.* 10: 9).

(d) He takes his stand by identifying himself with all who have similarly received the gospel (*Acts* 2: 41–47; *I Cor.* 1: 2; 6: 1, 2).

(e) He recognises himself to be a member of the body of Christ, the Church (*I Cor.* 12: 13, 27).

(f) He recognises himself to be God's—dedicated to God in Christ (*I Cor.* 1: 2; 6: 11).

(g) He loves the Lord Jesus Christ and shows that love by obedience (*I Cor.* 16: 22; *John* 14: 21).

(h) He waits expectantly for Christ (*I Cor.* 1: 7; 11: 26; 16: 22; *I Thess.* 1: 10).

6. A Christian is one who, having understood the ABC of the gospel, has received Christ, and having taken his stand upon Christ, experiences salvation through Christ.

(a) When the Christian first believed, he experienced salvation, e.g. he was washed, sanctified and justified (*I Cor.* 6: 11), he was enriched by Christ (*I Cor.* 1: 5); he found the cross the power of God (*I Cor.* 1: 18), and Christ became to him all he needed (*I Cor.* 1: 30).

(b) But salvation is also the Christian's present experience: he continues to call on the name of the Lord Jesus (*I Cor.* 1: 2); he continues to receive God's grace (*I Cor.* 1: 5; 15: 10; 16: 23); he continues to be enriched by Christ (*I Cor.* 1: 5).

(c) He is delivered from his old state of sin (*I Cor.* 15: 17); he is freed from the power of sin (*Rom.* 8: 2; *I Cor.* 6: 12; 8: 9).

(d) He knows the power of the Spirit in his life (*I Cor.* 6: 19, 20; 12: 7).

(e) He is kept by Christ (*I Cor.* 1: 8; *I Pet.* 1: 5).

7. Being a Christian.

(a) Belief in God alone does not make a man a Christian (*Jas.* 2: 19).

(b) Being a Christian is not a matter of being born in the right country or belonging to the right race (*John* 1: 13).

(c) Being a Christian is not just being zealously religious, for one can be such without being a Christian (*Rom.* 10: 2, 3).

(d) Being a Christian is not simply trying one's best to please God by good works (*Eph.* 2: 9).

(e) A Christian knows that what matters is not self-achieved righteousness gained by obedience to the law, but rather that genuine righteousness which God gives as we put our faith in Christ (*Phil.* 3: 9).

(f) The word "Christian" began as a description of the disciples of Christ (*Acts* 11: 26; 9: 1).

(g) A Christian is not self-made, but Christ-made (*II Cor.* 5: 17; *John* 3: 3, 7).

(h) All Bible definitions or descriptions of a Christian have one thing in common: they all imply a personal relationship to Christ (*I Cor.* 1: 9; *I John* 1: 3; *Col.* 3: 1).

(i) The name "Christian" is something which the Christian is to live up to (*I Pet.* 4: 16).

(j) When a man is a Christian, he would that all might become Christians too (*Acts* 26: 29; *Rom.* 10: 1).

26. REGENERATION

Question: What is regeneration?

Answer: It is the supernatural work of the Holy Spirit by which those who were dead in trespasses and sins are made spiritually alive.

1. Regeneration deals with men's dead spiritual state.

(a) Men are by nature dead in trespasses and sins (*Eph.* 2: 1).

(b) Human nature is sinful (*Rom.* 8: 3).

(c) Human life is governed very much by man's lower nature and its desires (*Rom.* 8: 4, 5).

(d) Whilst men's lives are governed by their lower nature, besides being in a state of hostility to God, they cannot please God (*Rom.* 8: 7, 8).

(e) Spiritual things are folly and beyond the grasp of unregenerate man (*I Cor.* 2: 14).

(f) Regeneration deals with this dead condition of men (*Eph.* 2: 1) —they are made alive.

2. Men's dead spiritual state is beyond the power of men to deal with.

(a) With lives governed by their lower nature men cannot please God (*John* 3: 6; *Rom.* 8: 7, 8).

(b) Deeds done by men in righteousness are not sufficient to accomplish the task of giving spiritual life (*Tit.* 3: 5).

(c) Men can do no more about it than they can change the colour of their skin or animals their fur (*Jer.* 13: 23).

3. Regeneration is the supernatural work of the Holy Spirit.

(a) It is supernatural because it is due to the immediate power of Almighty God—witnessed, for example, in Paul's regeneration (*Acts* 9: 1–9; *I Cor.* 15: 8; *Gal.* 1: 15, 16).

(b) The Holy Spirit makes men spiritually alive (*Eph.* 2: 1).

(c) He acts according to the will of God the Father (*John* 1: 13; *II Cor.* 5: 18; *Gal.* 4: 6; *Tit.* 3: 5; *Jas.* 1: 18).

(d) He acts on the grounds of Christ's saving work by His death and resurrection (*Tit.* 3: 6; *I Pet.* 1: 2, 3).

(e) The Spirit's work of regeneration is a work of tremendous power—of creative power (*II Cor.* 4: 6; 5: 17).

(f) His work is as sovereign, mysterious and irresistible as that of the wind (*John* 3: 8).

(g) It is as dramatic as birth (*John* 3: 3) and resurrection (*Eph.* 2: 5; *Col.* 2: 13).

(h) The unenlightened human mind finds the new birth impossible to understand because of its supernatural character (*John* 3: 4).

4. Various descriptions are given of this work of the Spirit.

(a) It is spoken of as a birth (*John* 3: 3, 6, 7, 8; *Jas.* 1: 18; *I Pet.* 1: 23).

(b) It is spoken of in terms of adoption: by it men become the children of God (*John* 1: 12, 13; *Rom.* 8: 15, 16).

(c) It is spoken of as a new creation (*II Cor.* 5: 17).

(d) It is spoken of as renewal (*Tit.* 3: 5).

(e) It is spoken of as passing out of death into life (*I John* 3: 14; 4: 7).

5. Regeneration is a necessity if men are to enter heaven.

(a) Unless a man is born anew, he cannot see the kingdom of God (*John* 3: 3).

(b) Only through being born anew can a man have "a living hope" (*I Pet.* 1: 3).

6. The Holy Spirit uses various means to bring to fulfilment His work of regeneration in men's lives.

(a) **The word of truth—i.e. the inspired Scriptures—is His main instrument.**

(b) The living and abiding Word of God is imperishable seed which brings forth spiritual life under the power of the Spirit (*I Pet.* 1: 23).

(c) The preaching of the gospel is the most frequent means, therefore, He uses to bring His work to light (*I Pet.* 1: 25).

(d) The Holy Spirit accompanies true gospel preaching with life-giving power (*I Cor.* 2: 2–5; *I Thess.* 1: 5, 6).

(e) He uses men, therefore, who preach the gospel (*I Cor.* 4: 15; *II Cor.* 5: 20).

7. There may be visible evidences sometimes that the Holy Spirit's work of regeneration is taking place but these evidences are for the most part beyond observation (*John* 3: 8).

(a) Conviction of sin is frequently seen to be present (*John* 16: 8–11; *Acts* 2: 37).

(b) It is as the regenerate man looks back after his regeneration that he realises that God was at work in his life before ever he realised it (*Gal.* 1: 11–16).

8. The work of regeneration may be said to have taken place when a man has saving faith in Christ (*John* 1: 12, 13; *II Thess.* 2: 13).

(a) Faith is more the effect of regeneration than the cause of it, insofar as it is the Holy Spirit who brings men to faith in Christ: He opens men's hearts to give heed to the message of the gospel (*Acts* 16: 14).

(b) Faith and regeneration, however, may take place at more or less the same time (*Acts* 2: 37–41; 8: 26–38).

9. The effects of the work of regeneration in a man's life.

(a) The most important truth is that he has a new life implanted in him by the Holy Spirit: the Holy Spirit enters the soul and abides there as a principle of a new life (*Rom.* 7: 6; 8: 9).

(b) He is made clean, or sanctified by the Spirit (*Tit.* 3: 5).

(c) He is renewed spiritually (*Tit.* 3: 5); he has newness of life (*Rom.* 6: 4).

(d) He has a new heart—a heart which wants to obey God (*Ezek.* 11: 19, 20).

(e) He is a new creation—the old has passed away, the new has come (*II Cor.* 5: 17; *Gal.* 6: 15).

(f) This new creation is seen in good works produced in the life, which are pleasing to God (*Eph.* 2: 10).

(g) God is at work in the man (*Phil.* 2: 13; *Heb.* 13: 21).

(h) The man is no longer enslaved by sin (*Rom.* 6: 6).

(i) He receives a new nature—the divine nature (*II Pet.* 1: 4)—created after the likeness of God in true righteousness and holiness (*Eph.* 4: 24; *Col.* 3: 10; *Rom.* 8: 29).

(j) This inner nature is renewed every day (*II Cor.* 4: 16).

(k) As a result of this new life and nature, he can appreciate spiritual things because he has spiritual discernment (*I Cor.* 2: 14; *II Cor.* 4: 6).

(l) He possesses a new appetite for spiritual things (*I Pet.* 2: 1, 2).

(m) He delights in the law of God in his inmost self (*Rom.* 7: 22).

(n) He may be said to know God (*Jer.* 24: 7; *Col.* 3: 10).

(o) He hates sin because his new nature cannot sin and is opposed to sin (*I John* 3: 9; 5: 18—notice here that the verb "to sin" is in the present tense, and speaks of continual and habitual action. John is not saying that the regenerate man cannot sin but rather that he cannot consistently and deliberately do so).

(p) He is preserved from the evil one (*I John* 5: 18) and will be presented faultless before God (*Phil.* 1: 6; *Jude* 24).

(q) He becomes, together with all the regenerate, the first-fruits of a new creation (*Jas.* 1: 18)—the kingdom of God (*John* 3: 3).

(r) He possesses this as a living hope through the resurrection of Jesus Christ from the dead—life after death, eternal life and an inheritance in heaven (*I Pet.* 1: 3–5).

(s) Three outstanding proofs of regeneration are given by John in his first epistle: the regenerate man believes that Jesus is the Christ (*I John* 5: 1), practises righteousness, i.e. does right things as a practice (*I John* 2: 29; 3: 9; 5: 18), and loves his Christian brethren (*I John* 4: 7).

27. CONVERSION

Question: What is conversion?

Answer: Conversion is turning from sin, to be the servant of the living and true God, through repentance and personal faith in Jesus Christ. It is a work in which God takes the initiative, and in which He requires

62

man's response as the gospel is understood.

1. Conversion is turning with sincerity to God.

(a) It is the turning of the life to the living God, our Creator (*Acts* 14: 15).

(b) It is the acknowledgment of God in a manner not practised previously (*Gal.* 4: 8, 9).

(c) Conversion conveys literally the idea of a turning *from* and a turning *to*: repentance and faith correspond to these two ideas (*I Thess.* 1: 9).

(d) Conversion must be of the heart to receive the benefits which God promises (*Deut.* 4: 29; *Acts* 15: 8).

2. Conversion is a possibility for men and women on the grounds of Christ's work on behalf of sinners.

(a) Conversion is for sinners (*Ps.* 51: 13).

(b) God sent His Son into the world so that it might be possible for sinners to be converted from their wickedness (*Luke* 24: 46, 47; *Acts* 3: 26; 5: 31).

3. Conversion's negative aspect is repentance.

(a) Conversion comes about as transgressors are taught God's ways (*Ps.* 51: 13).

(b) It is accompanied by an understanding of who God is and what He demands (*Jer.* 24: 7).

(c) It comes about when a man realises the ways of God and the contrast of his own ways (*Ps.* 119: 59).

(d) It means turning from wickedness (*Acts* 3: 26).

(e) It means turning from idols (*I Thess.* 1: 9), from vain worship and confused conceptions of God (*Acts* 14: 15).

(f) It means turning from darkness and the power of Satan (*Acts* 26: 18).

(g) It means ceasing to stray from God (*I Pet.* 2: 25).

(h) Repentance is an essential part of conversion (*Acts* 3: 19; 26: 20).

4. Conversion's positive aspect is faith in Christ.

(a) Conversion takes place when Christ is revealed to a person (*Gal.* 1: 16).

(b) It is the result of being confronted with the Person and claims of Christ (*Acts* 9: 5, 6).

(c) It is the expression of faith in Christ (*Acts* 11: 21).

(d) It means recognising Christ as the Shepherd and Guardian of one's soul and returning to Him (*I Pet.* 2: 25).

5. Conversion is a necessity for entry into the kingdom of heaven.

(a) Unless we are converted and become as little children, we cannot enter the kingdom of heaven (*Matt.* 18: 3).

(b) Essential blessings necessary for entry into the kingdom of heaven come by conversion alone:

(i) Forgiveness (*Mark* 4: 12; *Acts* 3: 19);

(ii) The cleansing of the heart (*Acts* 15: 9);

(iii) Deliverance from the wrath to come (*I Thess.* 1: 10);

(iv) A place amongst those who are sanctified by faith in Christ (*Acts* 26: 18).

6. Conversion marks the beginning of the Christian life in a person's experience.

(a) The converted person is a new creature (*II Cor.* 5: 17).

(b) At conversion an individual receives the gospel, takes his stand upon it, is saved by it, and holds it fast (*I Cor.* 15: 1, 2).

(c) He receives the forgiveness of sins (*Acts* 26: 18).

(d) He receives the gift of the Holy Spirit (*Acts* 15: 8).

(e) He begins to serve the living and true God (*I Thess.* 1: 9).

(f) He is committed to obedience to God (*Deut.* 30: 2).

(g) He discovers that God has a purpose for his life (*Gal.* 1: 16).

(h) He witnesses by means of baptism to what has happened in his life (*Acts* 2: 38; 8: 36–38; 9: 18; 16: 15; 16: 33).

7. The initiative in conversion is God's.

(a) Conversion is God's work (*John* 6: 44; *Acts* 11: 18; 21: 19; *II Tim.* 2: 25).

(b) It is God's work in us (*Jer.* 24: 7; *Acts* 8: 29; 16: 14; *Phil.* 1: 6).

(c) God sometimes uses unpleasant circumstances to bring conversion about in the lives of men and women (*Ps.* 78: 34).

(d) It is the result of God's grace to us (*Acts* 11: 21, 23; *Gal.* 1: 15).

(e) It takes place at God's will and choice (*Acts* 9: 3 ff; 15: 7; *Gal.* 1: 15).

(f) It is the consequence of the work of God the Holy Spirit (*Acts* 10: 44 ff).

(g) It is a blessing from God (*Acts* 3: 26).

(h) The praise is God's (*Gal.* 1: 24).

8. Conversion reveals the response God requires from man as he hears the gospel.

(a) Conversion is the step God requires of us if He is to restore us to Himself (*John* 12: 40).

(b) Man responds to God's command in conversion (*Acts* 17: 30).

(c) Conversion means becoming like children before God—completely submissive to what He commands we must do if we would enter His kingdom (*Matt.* 18: 3).

9. Conversion is the great work which God uses His servants to help bring about in the world amongst men.

(a) Conversion follows upon hearing the word of the gospel and believing (*Acts* 15: 7).

(b) God uses His messengers to bring conversion about in the lives of men (*Acts* 26: 18).

(c) Preaching has a vital place in conversion: God uses it to turn men to Himself (*Luke* 1: 16; *Acts* 26: 18).

(d) Conversion takes place as the messengers of the gospel are welcomed and their message obeyed (*I Thess.* 1: 9).

(e) Conversion may come about through the testimony of converted men to God's mercy and salvation (*Ps.* 51: 13).

(f) Conversion is the work of Christ which He is pleased to accomplish through His servants in the lives of those to whom they proclaim the message of repentance and faith (*Acts* 11: 21; *Rom.* 15: 18; *I Thess.* 1: 9).

10. Conversion is commanded by God.

(a) Men are exhorted to repent,

and to turn to God, so that their sins may be wiped out (*Acts* 3: 19).

(b) The delay in God's judgment of the world springs from His desire that men may heed His warnings and obey His command to be converted (*II Pet.* 3: 8, 9).

28. REPENTANCE

Question: What is repentance?

Answer: Repentance is turning from sin to God, as a result of a change of mind and heart about sin.

1. The necessity of repentance.

(a) God commands it on the part of all men (*Acts* 17: 30).

(b) Unless men repent, they will perish (*Luke* 13: 3, 5).

(c) Repentance is the first response demanded of men if they are to respond to the gospel of Jesus Christ (*Acts* 2: 38).

(d) Repentance is the first condition God imposes if men are to find Him (*Zech.* 1: 3, 4; *Acts* 20: 21).

(e) Repentance is a condition of cleansing (*Isa.* 6: 5).

(f) Repentance is a condition of forgiveness (*Luke* 24: 47; *Acts* 3: 19; 26: 18).

(g) Repentance is a condition of salvation (*Acts* 26: 18).

(h) Repentance is a condition of entry into the kingdom of heaven (*Matt.* 4: 17).

(i) Repentance is a condition of eternal life (*Acts* 11: 18).

(j) Repentance is a condition for escaping the judgment of God upon sin (*Acts* 17: 30, 31).

2. Repentance is turning from sin to God.

(a) Repentance is the result of the eyes of the mind being opened to understand the sinner's need before God (*Acts* 26: 18).

(b) Repentance is associated with the idea of turning (*Acts* 3: 19; 26: 20).

(c) Repentance is turning away from dead works (*Heb.* 6: 1); it is turning from wicked ways (*II Chron.* 7: 14); it is turning from iniquities to give heed to God's truth (*Dan.* 9: 13); it is turning away from sin to God (*Ezek.* 33: 11).

(d) Repentance involves the recognition of sin as failure to keep God's statutes (*Mal.* 3: 7).

(e) Repentance means seeing how awful sin is in God's sight (*Ps.* 51: 4), and recognising the affliction of the human heart which is sin (*I Kings* 8: 38).

(f) Conviction of sin is necessary for repentance to take place (*Acts* 2: 37, 38).

(g) Repentance involves a real sorrow and grief on account of sin (*Luke* 22: 62; *II Cor.* 7: 9, 10).

(h) Repentance brings such a sense of shame (*Ezra* 9: 6–15; *Jer.* 31: 19) that a man despises himself for his sin (*Job* 42: 6).

(i) Repentance is the wicked forsaking his way, and the unrighteous man his thoughts and returning to the Lord, that He may have mercy on him (*Isa.* 55: 7).

(j) Repentance means inevitably a fundamental break with the past (*Luke* 9: 23 f; 14: 26, 33).

3. Characteristics of true repentance.

(a) Unfortunately false repentance is a possibility: Saul (*I Sam.* 15: 24–30) and Ahab (*I Kings* 21: 27–29) provide examples of false repentance.

(b) True repentance springs from a recognition of God as the Lord (*Jer.* 3: 22).

(c) It is seen in grief for sin (*Joel* 2: 12; *II Cor.* 7: 9).

(d) It is rational and openly declared (*Hos.* 14: 2).

(e) It is accompanied by confession, renunciation and dedication (*Hos.* 14: 1–3, 8).

(f) It is wholehearted (*Joel* 2: 12, 13; *Hos.* 7: 14).

(g) It is humble (*Jonah* 3: 6; *II Chron.* 7: 14; *Jas.* 4: 9, 10).

(h) It is obviously a work and a gift of God (*Acts* 11: 18).

4. Motives for repentance.

(a) The character of God is a tremendous encouragement to repentance. He is gracious and merciful, slow to anger, and abounding in steadfast love (*Joel* 2: 13).

(b) God's patience should encourage repentance (*II Pet.* 3: 9).

(c) God's kindness is meant to lead men to a change of heart about sin (*Rom.* 2: 4).

(d) God pleads with men to repent (*Isa.* 30: 15).

(e) Repentance is never despised by God (*Jonah* 3: 9; *Luke* 15: 7, 10).

(f) Christ came to call sinners to repentance (*Matt.* 9: 13).

(g) Repentance is called for in the light of what God has accomplished for sinners through Christ's saving work (*Acts* 3: 18, 19; 5: 31).

(h) Repentance is the first part of conversion, and faith in the Lord Jesus Christ is the second (*Acts* 20: 21; *Mark* 1: 15).

5. Evidences of repentance.

(a) True repentance brings no regret but leads to salvation (*II Cor.* 7: 10).

(b) Practical reformation is assumed (*Judg.* 6: 25–27; *Luke* 19: 8).

(c) Actions follow which give proof of a change of mind about sin (*Joel* 2: 12; *Acts* 26: 20), especially restitution where necessary (*Ezek.* 33: 14, 15).

(d) Repentance yields appropriate fruit (*Matt.* 3: 8; *Luke* 13: 6–9).

29. FAITH

Question: What is faith?

Answer: Faith is both a decisive act and a sustained attitude. It begins as an act, by which a person abandons reliance on himself to merit salvation, has a firm conviction as to the truth of God's promises of mercy in Jesus Christ, and depends sincerely upon them. After this, faith becomes a habit of that person's life.

1. Faith rests on certain facts which the apostles were careful to preach (*I Cor.* 11: 23; 15: 1–3; *I Thess.* 2: 13; 4: 1, 2).

2. These facts are easy to determine.

(a) Jesus is the Christ, the Son of God (*John* 20: 31; *Acts* 9: 20).

(b) He died for our sins (*I Pet.* 2: 24).

(c) He was buried and was raised

to life again on the third day (*I Pet.* 1: 3; *Rom.* 4: 25).

(d) His death and resurrection took place according to the manner in which God had promised beforehand in the Old Testament Scriptures (*I Cor.* 15: 3, 4).

(e) On the grounds of what Christ accomplished men may receive forgiveness and the gift of the Holy Spirit (*Acts* 2: 38, 39).

3. These facts have to be received (*I Cor.* 15: 1).

(a) The facts themselves have to be understood (*Acts* 17: 2, 3; 18: 4, 19).

(b) Intellectual assent has to be given to them (*Acts* 28: 27; *Luke* 24: 45).

4. A stand has to be taken then upon these facts (*I Cor.* 15: 1).

(a) This stand involves a personal confession of Christ as the Son of God (*Matt.* 16: 16; *Acts* 8: 37; *Rom.* 10: 10).

(b) A personal belief that Christ died for our sins (*Gal.* 2: 20; *I Tim.* 1: 15).

(c) A personal belief that God raised Christ from the dead (*Rom.* 10: 9).

(d) Thus faith moves beyond the facts to trusting a Person—the Lord Jesus Christ (*Acts* 16: 31; *John* 1: 12; *John* 3: 16).

5. The stand which is taken upon these facts—significantly known as "the faith" (*Jude* 3)**—involves the abandonment of all confidence in human merit and works for the obtaining of salvation.**

(a) No confidence in externals, whether of race, social status, religious zeal, or legal rectitude is allowed (*Phil.* 3: 3–8).

(b) No confidence in one's good deeds is permissible (*Tit.* 3: 5).

6. When a person comes to true faith in Christ, faith becomes then a sustained attitude of that person's life.

(a) Faith gives substance to his hopes (*Heb.* 11: 1).

(b) Faith makes him certain of realities he cannot see (*Heb.* 11: 1).

(c) Faith is his guide (*II Cor.* 5: 7).

(d) He is defended in the battles of the Christian life by the shield of faith (*Eph.* 6: 16).

(e) He fights the good fight of faith (*I Tim.* 6: 12).

7. Such a habit of faith in a person's life makes a tremendous difference to his life. The men and women of faith, described in Hebrews 11, who did not fully know "the faith" of the gospel, provide helpful illustrations.

(a) Faith makes a man offer only his best to God—Abel (*Heb.* 11: 4).

(b) Faith makes a man reckon walking with God the most important thing in life—Enoch (*Heb.* 11: 5).

(c) Faith makes a man concerned for the saving of his household—Noah (*Heb.* 11: 7).

(d) Faith makes a man obey God, even blindly sometimes—Abraham leaving Haran (*Heb.* 11: 8).

(e) Faith makes a man live after the manner of a refugee in the world, holding lightly to its possessions—Abraham and his immediate descendants (*Heb.* 11: 9, 10, 13–16).

(f) Faith makes a man change his

mind about things thought impossible—Sarah (*Heb.* 11: 11, 12).

(g) Faith makes a man render implicit obedience to God no matter what He demands—Abraham and Isaac (*Heb.* 11: 17–19).

(h) Faith makes a man concerned for the spiritual well-being of the generations to follow—Isaac blessing Jacob and Esau (*Heb.* 11: 20).

(i) Faith gives a man confidence in the face of death—Jacob and Joseph (*Heb.* 11: 21, 22).

(j) Faith makes a man co-operative actively with the purposes of God as he knows them—Moses' parents (*Heb.* 11: 23).

(k) Faith makes a man live a life which is different and separate from the standard set by the world—Moses (*Heb.* 11: 24, 25).

(l) Faith takes away fear of man—Moses as to Pharaoh (*Heb.* 11: 27).

(m) Faith leads to the activity which comes from obedience—the Passover and the crossing of the Red Sea (*Heb.* 11: 28, 29).

(n) Faith brings victory and success—Jericho (*Heb.* 11: 30).

30. THE AWAKENING OF FAITH

Question: How do we come to saving Christian faith?

Answer: By the effective working of the Holy Spirit in our hearts, as the gospel is made known to us, calling us, without reference to our merits, from the dominion of darkness and transferring us to the kingdom of God's dear Son.

1. As the facts of the faith (see Question: What is faith?) are presented to us, the Holy Spirit convinces us of their truth.

(a) He is the Spirit of truth (*John* 16: 13).

(b) God's message is received, not as the word of men, but as what it truly is, the very Word of God (*I Thess.* 2: 13).

2. As we recognise the truth of the facts of the faith, the Holy Spirit enables us to apply them to ourselves.

(a) He uses the Law of God to reveal to us our sin (*Gal.* 3: 21–24; *Rom.* 7: 7).

(b) And thus He brings us to conviction of sin and repentance (*John* 16: 8–11; *Acts* 2: 37, 38).

3. Having convinced us of our sin, the Holy Spirit makes plain the remedy for our sin.

(a) The good news of Jesus and the benefits of His death and resurrection come home to the heart with strong conviction (*I Thess.* 1: 5).

(b) He glorifies Jesus in the eyes of the sinner, for He draws upon what is Christ's and discloses it to him (*John* 16: 14).

4. The result is faith built not upon human wisdom but upon the power of God (*I Cor.* 2: 5).

(a) Faith has come about not through the force of subtle arguments of men, but through the power of the Holy Spirit (*I Cor.* 2: 4).

(b) The Lord has added to the number of those whom He is saving (*Acts* 2: 40, 41; cf. 2: 47).

(c) No longer does the individual belong to the dominion of darkness but to the kingdom of God's dear Son (*Col.* 1: 13).

5. **This effective working of the Holy Spirit in our hearts to bring us faith in Christ is without reference at all to our merits** (*Tit.* 3: 5; *Rom.* 4: 5; *Tit.* 1: 1; *II Thess.* 1: 11).

31. JUSTIFICATION

Question: What is justification?

Answer: Justification is the free and undeserved act of God, by which He reckons to a sinner, through faith, the righteousness of Christ, declaring the sinner just and right before Him.

1. **Justification has to do with the justice and righteousness of God.**

(a) He is the just God and everything He does shows His justice (*Rom.* 3: 25, 26).

(b) He is the Lord and Judge of all the earth (*Gen.* 18: 25), who always does right.

(c) His righteousness is seen in His judgment and condemnation of those who disobey His laws (*Ps.* 7: 11; *Isa.* 5: 16; *Acts* 17: 31; *Rom.* 2: 5).

2. **Men and women are unrighteous before God.**

(a) No living person is righteous before the Lord (*Ps.* 143: 2).

(b) All have sinned and come short of the glory of God (*Rom.* 3: 23).

3. **Theoretically, the Law of God is a means of justification.**

(a) By perfect obedience to the Law of God an individual could be justified before God (*Rom.* 2: 13; 10: 5; *Lev.* 18: 5; *Jas.* 2: 10).

(b) But, in fact, all men everywhere have broken God's Law (*Rom.* 10: 5; cf. 9: 31)—it has served to bring an awareness of sin (*Rom.* 3: 20).

(c) The endeavour to keep the Law of God, therefore, can bring about neither righteousness before God nor justification (*Rom.* 3: 21; *Gal.* 2: 16, 21; 3: 11).

(d) Works or acts of obedience can neither satisfy God's justice, fulfil His Law nor stand up to His standard (*Ps.* 130: 3, 4; 143: 2; *Isa.* 64: 6; *Luke* 17: 10).

(e) The thought of God entering into judgment with man is, therefore, terrifying (*Ps.* 143: 2).

4. **God alone could deliver man from the condemnation which rightly awaits him; and the situation required an amazing solution.**

(a) Clearly, the wrong that was in men's and women's lives could not be righted by their obedience to the Law of God (*Rom.* 3: 21; 9: 31, 32; *Job* 9: 2, 3, 20; 25: 4).

(b) Whatever way God determined for righting the wrong that was in man, had to be adequate for all, without distinction; and it had to be consistent with His own justice (*Rom.* 3: 21, 22, 26).

(c) The answer was the gospel: it is the revelation of God's plan for imparting righteousness to sinful men (*Rom.* 1: 16, 17).

(d) The wonder of God's new covenant is that a man may be reconciled to God (*II Cor.* 5: 20), all the demands of God's law having been satisfied (*II Cor.* 3: 9).

(e) The Law and the prophets gave witness in advance of this way of justification which God purposed (*Rom.* 3: 21).

(f) Abraham is an example of God's justifying grace: he believed God, and it was reckoned to him as righteousness (*Gen.* 15: 6; *Rom.* 4: 3).

5. Justification, therefore, is necessarily an act of God, being beyond the power of man to accomplish.

(a) It is a legal term, meaning to acquit (*Rom.* 8: 33; cf. *Deut.* 25: 1; *Prov.* 17: 15).

(b) While God is the Judge, He is also the justifier (*Rom.* 3: 26, 30; 4: 5; 8: 33; *Gal.* 3: 8).

(c) The amazing thing is that He justifies the ungodly (*Rom.* 4: 5): for His own sake, He blots out their transgressions and will not remember their sins (*Isa.* 43: 25).

6. Justification depends upon what Christ has done for sinners.

(a) The grounds of it are what Christ accomplished for sinners (*Acts* 13: 39).

(b) God could justify the ungodly only through Christ's dying, at the right time, for the ungodly (*Rom.* 5: 6).

(c) He sets Christ before us as the One whose sacrificial death has atoned for our guilt and removed the judgment soon to happen which our rebellion against God has brought upon us (*Rom.* 3: 24, 25).

(d) Christ redeemed us from the curse of the Law, having become a curse for us (*Gal.* 3: 13).

(e) God caused Christ, who Himself knew nothing of sin, actually to *be* sin for our sakes, so that in Christ we might be made righteous with the righteousness of God (*II Cor.* 5: 21; *Isa.* 53: 5).

(f) Thus Jesus Christ, acting on behalf of sinners, has satisfied the claims of God's law and justice (*Gal.* 4: 4, 5), and has put away their sins by His blood (*Rom.* 3: 25; 5: 9).

(g) By justifying men on the basis of Christ's sacrificial death God demonstrates both His justice and His love (*Rom.* 3: 25, 26).

7. On the basis of Christ's sacrificial death, God reckons to believers the righteousness of Christ.

(a) Of Christ's righteousness there was no doubt (*Matt.* 3: 17; *I Pet.* 3: 18): justification is by the imputing of His righteousness to the sinner (*Rom.* 3: 22; 5: 18; *I Cor.* 1: 30; *II Cor.* 5: 21).

(b) To be justified is to receive the righteousness of Christ, for which alone the Lord accepts us as holy and righteous (*Isa.* 43: 25; *Rom.* 3: 23–26; 4: 5; *Phil.* 3: 9).

(c) God pronounces us to be free from all guilt and declares us to be righteous as He sees us in the righteousness of Christ (*Rom.* 3: 26).

(d) Christians are described as the righteous as a consequence (*I Pet.* 4: 18).

8. Justification is a free gift from God.

(a) Men and women are justified by God's free grace alone (*Rom.* 3: 24).

(b) The righteousness God bestows through Christ is a gift (*Rom.* 5: 17; *Phil.* 3: 9).

(c) Consequently, all room for human pride is removed (*Rom.* 3: 27).

9. The means of our entering into justification is by faith.

(a) The righteousness God offers is to be apprehended by faith

(*Rom.* 1: 17; 3: 22, 26; 4: 3 ff, 13; 9: 30; 10: 4, 6, 10).

(b) Justification depends upon faith to be effective (*Acts* 13: 39; *Rom.* 3: 25, 28; 4: 5).

(c) It is with the heart that men have faith which leads God to accept them as righteous (*Rom.* 10: 10).

(d) Faith, therefore, is reckoned as righteousness (*Gen.* 15: 6; *Ps.* 106: 31; *Rom.* 4: 3, 5 f, 9, 11, 22; *Gal.* 3: 6).

10. The benefits justification brings.

(a) The first benefit of justification is peace with God (*Rom.* 5: 1).

(b) It is to be acquitted of everything for which there was not acquittal under the law of Moses; it means the forgiveness of sins (*Acts* 13: 38, 39).

(c) It frees us from condemnation (*Isa.* 50: 8, 9; 54: 17; *Rom.* 8: 33, 34).

(d) No one can bring a charge against those whom God justifies (*Rom.* 8: 33).

(e) Being justified, the believer can rejoice in deliverance from the wrath of God to come (*Rom.* 5: 9).

(f) God has so justified the believer that he has nothing to fear at God's judgment seat (*Rom.* 8: 1).

(g) The peace justification brings carries with it access to God (*Rom.* 5: 2).

(h) Justification brings us into union with God and makes us sons and heirs of God (*Gal.* 3: 26; 4: 4 ff; *Rom.* 8: 14 ff).

(i) It is on the basis of his justification that the believer is in Christ, and knows Christ, together with all the benefits Christ has gained for him (*Phil.* 3: 9, 10; *Rom.* 8: 32).

(j) Justification brings tremendous joy: the joy of the hope of sharing the glory of God (*Rom.* 5: 2); joy in sufferings because we know God's good purposes are fulfilled in them for His children (*Rom.* 5: 3); and, supremely, joy in God Himself (*Rom.* 5: 11).

(k) Justification assures the believer that he will have eternal life (*Rom.* 8: 10; *Tit.* 3: 7).

(l) Justification means that absolutely nothing can separate us from the love of God in Christ Jesus our Lord (*Rom.* 8: 31–39).

(m) It is the basis of true happiness (*Rom.* 4: 6, 7; *Ps.* 32: 1, 2).

(n) No wonder it is the believer's most precious possession—nothing else can compare with its value (*Phil.* 3: 7–9).

32. BEING A CHRISTIAN

Question: What are the benefits and privileges of being a Christian?

Answer: The benefits and privileges of being a Christian are, principally, union with Christ, adoption by God into His family, Christian liberty, a spiritual right to the sacraments of the new covenant, the fellowship of all Christians, and the resurrection of the body.

1. Union with Christ.

(a) The purpose of all that Christ did was that Christians might be united with Him (*I Thess.* 5: 10):

(i) They were crucified with Him (*Rom.* 6: 6);

(ii) They were buried with Him (*Rom.* 6: 4; *Col.* 2: 12);

(iii) They died with Him (*Rom.* 6: 8; *II Tim.* 2: 11);

(iv) They were made alive with Him (*Col.* 2: 13);

(v) They were raised with Him (*Col.* 2: 12; 3: 1);

(vi) They are made joint-heirs with Him (*Rom.* 8: 17);

(vii) They are to suffer with Christ (*Rom.* 8: 17);

(viii) They shall be glorified with Him (*Rom.* 8: 17);

(ix) They shall be enthroned with Him (*Col.* 3: 1; *Rev.* 20: 4);

(x) They shall reign with Him (*II Tim.* 2: 12; *Rev.* 20: 4).

(b) The union is like that of a Head and a Body:

(i) Christ is the Head of the Body, the Church (*Col.* 1: 18), and Christians, like so many limbs and organs in a single body, constitute the one body of Christ (*I Cor.* 12: 12);

(ii) Christians are meant to grow up in every way into Christ, the Head (*Eph.* 4: 15).

(c) The union is like that of a Husband and Wife:

(i) Christ is the Head of the Church, even as the man is the head of the woman (*Eph.* 5: 23);

(ii) Christians are betrothed to Christ, to be as a pure bride to her husband (*II Cor.* 11: 2; *Eph.* 5: 25–27; *Rev.* 21: 9).

(d) The union is like that of a foundation to a building:

(i) Christ is the rock upon which we are built (*Matt.* 16: 18);

(ii) We become part of God's spiritual building or house, as we are joined to Christ, the chief corner stone, through faith (*Eph.* 2: 20–22; *I Pet.* 2: 4–7).

(e) The Holy Spirit brings the Christian into his living relationship and union with Christ, and there can be no such experience without the Holy Spirit (*Rom.* 8: 9, 11).

(f) It is through being in Christ that God gives us every possible spiritual benefit (*Eph.* 1: 3).

2. Adoption by God into His family.

(a) Before the foundation of the world God chose Christians to become, in Christ, His holy and blameless children, living within His constant care (*Eph.* 1: 4, 5).

(b) God's love has caused Him to bestow upon those who receive His Son the right to become His children (*John* 1: 12, 13; *I John* 3: 1).

(c) Christians receive the spirit of sonship, so that they are rightly able to cry, "Abba! Father!" (*Rom.* 8: 15–17).

(d) As God's children, Christians share His treasures, and all that Christ claims as His will belong to all of them as well (*Rom.* 8: 17).

(e) Christians wait for that redemption of their bodies which will mean that at last they will have realised their full sonship in Christ (*Rom.* 8: 23).

(f) The whole creation may be described as being on tiptoe to see the wonderful sight of the sons of God coming into their own (*Rom.* 8: 19).

3. Christian Liberty.

(a) Christ came to proclaim liberty to the captives, and the opening of the prison to those who are bound (*Isa.* 61: 1, 2; *Luke* 4: 18, 19): when Christ sets us free, we are free indeed (*John* 8: 32, 34, 36; *Gal.* 5: 1).

(b) Christ sets us free from the fear of death (*I Cor.* 15: 55–57; *Heb.* 2: 14, 15).

72

(c) Christ delivers from that slavish attitude of fear which so easily can characterise life without God (*Rom.* 8: 15).

(d) Christ has redeemed believers from the curse of the Law's condemnation, by Himself becoming a curse for them when He was crucified (*Gal.* 3: 13): no condemnation now hangs over the head of those who are in Christ Jesus (*Rom.* 8: 1).

(e) The burden of all the Jewish ceremonial is removed through Christ (*Acts* 15: 10, 11; *Gal.* 3, 4, 5).

(f) Christ makes us free from slavery to sin (*John* 8: 32, 34, 36): once the servants of sin, having honestly responded to the message of the gospel, Christians are released from the service of sin, and enter the service of righteousness (*Rom.* 6: 17, 18).

(g) The Christian's freedom, however, is not a freedom to do wrong, but a freedom to serve God (*I Pet.* 2: 16).

(h) The Christian is freed from the bondage of the law, but it remains for him a rule of life and holiness: God puts His law within the Christian and writes it upon his heart (*Jer.* 31: 31–33).

(i) The Christian no longer lives under the law, but under grace (*Rom.* 6: 14).

(j) The law is not undermined by the insistence on faith; rather the law is given its proper place (*Rom.* 3: 31).

4. A Spiritual Right to the Sacraments of the New Covenant.

(a) The first sacrament of the New Covenant is baptism:

(i) It was appointed by Christ Himself for all disciples (*Matt.* 28: 19, 20; *Mark* 16: 15, 16);

(ii) It is administered in the name of the Trinity (*Matt.* 28: 19);

(iii) It is a symbol of the individual's reception of the gospel (*Acts* 2: 37, 38, 41; 8: 12; 16: 14, 15);

(iv) It symbolises repentance and faith in the Lord Jesus (*Acts* 2: 38);

(v) It symbolises confession of Christ's Lordship (*Acts* 19: 5);

(vi) It symbolises admittance into the family of God (*Acts* 2: 38, 41, 47; 8: 12; 9: 18; *I Cor.* 12: 13);

(vii) It symbolises entry into all the benefits of Christ's death and resurrection (*Rom.* 6: 3, 4).

(b) The second sacrament of the New Covenant is the Lord's Supper:

(i) The Lord's Supper is a proclamation of the Lord's death by words and symbols (*I Cor.* 11: 26);

(ii) It was established and commanded by Christ (*Matt.* 26: 26–28; *I Cor.* 11: 23);

(iii) It continually reminds Christians of Christ's sacrifice for them (*Luke* 22: 19; *I Cor.* 11: 26);

(iv) By means of it Christians acknowledge their sharing in the benefits of Christ's death (*I Cor.* 10: 16, 17; 11: 25);

(v) In it Christians have fellowship with Christ and with one another (*I Cor.* 10: 16, 17, 21);

(vi) In it Christians make their thanksgiving to God (*I Cor.* 10: 16; *Rom.* 12: 1);

(vii) The Lord's Supper is to be continued until Christ returns (*I Cor.* 11: 26).

5. The Fellowship of all Christians.

(a) God has given His people one heart and one way (*Jer.* 32: 39).

(b) The people of God are one even as the Father and the Son are one (*John* 17: 22)—and Jesus' prayer to His Father had this unity as a main petition (*John* 17: 11, 21).

(c) Jesus, the Great and Chief Shepherd, has one flock to which all Christians belong (*John* 10: 16).

(d) The fellowship of believers— sometimes called "the communion of saints"—arises from Christians belonging to one Body, of which there is one Spirit (*Eph.* 4: 4).

(e) All Christians are baptised by the Spirit into one Body, whether Jews, Gentiles, slaves or free men, and they all have had experience of the same Spirit (*I Cor.* 12: 13).

(f) Though many, Christians are one body in Christ, and individually members one of another (*Rom.* 12: 5; *I Cor.* 12: 12).

(g) The fellowship or communion of believers, therefore, is the sense of identity and belonging we have with all believers through our common allegiance to the Lord Jesus, the truth (*Eph.* 4: 13; *II John* 1).

(h) The fellowship Christians have together arises from their fellowship with the Father and the Son (*I John* 1: 3).

(i) Christians should seek to express their fellowship and union outwardly by avoiding all dissensions among themselves, being united in the same mind and the same judgment (*I Cor.* 1: 10, 11; *Phil.* 2: 1, 2; *I Pet.* 3: 8).

(j) This fellowship of all Christians is given practical expression in the fellowship of the local church according to the pattern revealed in the New Testament (*Acts* 11: 26; 20: 17, 28; 14: 23; *I Cor.* 4: 17; *Heb.* 13: 17; 10: 25).

6. The Resurrection of the Body.

(a) God does not give the believer up to hell, but shows him the path of life, which leads to fullness of joy in God's presence, and pleasures for evermore at God's right hand (*Ps.* 16: 9–11).

(b) The believer has the assurance of the resurrection of the body through his living Redeemer (*Job* 19: 25–27; *I Thess.* 4: 14).

(c) The resurrection of the dead will be the first event of Christ's second coming (*I Thess.* 4: 16).

(d) Believers will be made alive through Christ (*I Cor.* 15: 22).

(e) Harvest provides us with a good illustration of the kind of thing that will happen: what you sow is not the body which is to be (*I Cor.* 15: 37); just as to every kind of creature and thing God has given a particular body, so He has determined the particular nature of the resurrection body (*I Cor.* 15: 38–42).

(f) The body characterised by decay, dishonour, weakness, and suited only for this present life, shall be raised an imperishable, glorious body, full of power, and perfectly fitted for life in the world to come (*I Cor.* 15: 42–44).

(g) The transformation will take place in a moment (*I Cor.* 15: 51, 52).

(h) The assurance of the resurrection of the body is a tremendous comfort and encouragement to the Christian (*I Thess.* 4: 18; *I Cor.* 15: 58).

(i) And after the glorious event, Christians shall be with Christ for ever (*I Thess.* 4: 17).

33. ASSURANCE

Question: How can we be sure that we are Christians?

Answer: By the conviction we have from the Holy Spirit, through our obedience to the gospel, that we are children of God and heirs of eternal life. The genuineness of this conviction is demonstrated by right belief in Christ, righteous conduct and love for other Christians.

1. First, we need to be clear as to what being sure includes.

(a) The spiritual benefits concerning which Christians are encouraged to be sure are many and include:

(i) Election (*Ps.* 4: 3; *I Thess.* 1: 4; *II Pet.* 1: 10);

(ii) Salvation and redemption (*Isa.* 12: 2; *Job* 19: 25; *Rom.* 5: 9; *I Cor.* 1: 30; *I Thess.* 5: 9);

(iii) Peace with God by Christ (*Rom.* 5: 1);

(iv) Adoption into the family of God (*Rom.* 8: 16; *I John* 3: 1, 2, 9, 10; 4: 4; 5, 2, 18, 19);

(v) Knowing God (*I John* 2: 3; 5: 20);

(vi) Union with God and Christ (*I Cor.* 6: 15; *II Cor.* 13: 5; *Eph.* 5: 30; *I John* 2: 5; 3: 24; 4: 13);

(vii) Membership of God's kingdom (*Col.* 1: 13; *Heb.* 12: 28);

(viii) Inseparability from the love of God (*Rom.* 8: 38, 39);

(ix) Deliverance from all evil (*Ps.* 3: 6, 8; 27: 3–5; 46: 1–3; *II Tim.* 4: 18);

(x) God's continuing and perfecting work in the life (*Phil.* 1: 6);

(xi) The right to pray and the assurance of God's answer (*I John* 3: 22; 5: 14, 15);

(xii) God's help in affliction (*Ps.* 73: 26; *II Cor.* 4: 8–10, 16–18);

(xiii) God's sure help in death (*Ps.* 23: 4; *Acts* 7: 59; *Phil.* 1: 23);

(xiv) A glorious resurrection (*Job* 19: 26; *Ps.* 17: 15; *Phil.* 3: 21; *I John* 3: 2);

(xv) Eternal life (*I John* 5: 13).

2. The grounds of our being sure that we are Christians, and all that this includes, as seen above.

(a) Firstly, God wants us to be sure (*II Cor.* 13: 5): His will is that those who believe in the name of the Son of God may know that they have eternal life (*I John* 5: 13).

(b) Secondly, the basis of any assurance we have concerning being Christians is that God has spoken to us through His Son Jesus Christ (*Heb.* 1: 1, 2), and all that He wants us to know is contained in the Scriptures, the Word of God (*II Tim.* 3: 15, 16; *I John* 1: 1–3).

(c) The Scriptures give to us the promises of God in Christ through which assurance comes (*II Cor.* 1: 20, 21).

(d) Understanding of God's truth brings a wealth of assurance through the knowledge of God Himself which comes to us as a result (*Col.* 2: 2).

(e) Thirdly, assurance springs from an understanding of God's character: for example, His holiness (*I John* 1: 5), His faithfulness (*I John* 1: 9), and His love (*I John* 4: 8, 9, 10, 16, 19).

(f) The Christian's assurance is not in himself, and not in the truth of God's Word alone, but in God Himself—"I know Whom I have believed . . ." (*II Tim.* 1: 12).

(g) Fourthly, assurance is particularly related to a full understanding of the gospel as being not the word of man, but the Word of God (*I Thess.* 2: 13; *I John* 2: 20, 21).

(h) In particular, our understanding concerns the Lord Jesus Christ and His finished work upon the Cross (*I John* 1: 1–3; 2: 22, 23; 4: 2, 3, 15; 5: 5, 10, 13, 20): Christ fully satisfied the Law's demands for us; Christ is freely offered to all who hear the gospel; all who receive Him and depend upon Him shall be saved (*I John* 2: 1, 2, 12; 3: 5, 8, 16; 4: 10; compare *John* 1: 12; 3: 16).

(i) Fifthly, a further ground of assurance is the awareness that we do believe in the manner God commands (*I John* 3: 23; 5: 13).

(j) Assurance is the result of faith in Christ (*Eph.* 3: 12; *Heb.* 11: 1).

(k) It is most important to realise that the work of assurance is the Holy Spirit's: He witnesses to us, in the first place, that the gospel message is true (*I John* 2: 20, 27; 3: 24; 4: 13); He gives an inward assurance to us that our response to the gospel is real (*I Thess.* 1: 5).

(l) His presence in our life is the proof that our response to the gospel has been genuine (*Acts* 2: 38, 39; 5: 32; 15: 8; *Rom.* 8: 15 f; *Gal.* 3: 2; 4: 6; *Eph.* 1: 13, 14; 4: 30).

(m) Assurance springs from the witness of the Holy Spirit within us (*I John* 3: 24; 5: 6, 8, 9, 10): we may know that we dwell in God and He in us because of the presence of His own Spirit in our life (*I John* 4: 13).

3. **The tests to be applied to our conviction that we are Christians to prove its genuineness.**

(a) It is necessary to apply these tests because a false assurance is possible; therefore, tests, such as an examination of the quality of our daily life (*Tit.* 1: 16), are to be applied.

(b) The first test is whether we possess right belief concerning the Lord Jesus Christ (*I John* 3: 23; 5: 13).

(c) Those who have right belief confess that Jesus is the Christ (*I John* 2: 22; 5: 1); that He is the Son of God (*I John* 3: 23; 5: 5, 10), and that He came in the flesh (*I John* 4: 2; *II John* 7).

(d) The second test is whether we are marked by righteous conduct: those who are born of God act righteously (*I John* 2: 29; 3: 10).

(e) Righteous conduct is described in many different ways:

(i) Walking in the light (*I John* 1: 7);

(ii) Obedience to God's commandments (*I John* 2: 3, 4, 5, 6; 3: 24);

(iii) The desire to live as Christ lived (*I John* 2: 6);

(iv) Deliverance from the spirit of this world (*I John* 2: 15–17; 3: 14–18; 5: 5, 19);

(v) Self-purification (*I John* 3: 3);

(vi) Ceasing to sin habitually (*I John* 3: 5, 6, 9; 5: 18).

(f) The third test is whether we love other Christians (*I John* 3: 10, 11, 12, 14, 15, 16, 17; 4: 7, 8, 11, 12, 20, 21): we know that we have passed from death to life because we love the brethren (*I John* 3: 14).

(g) By loving one another we show that we know God and are abiding in Him (*I John* 3: 23, 24; 4: 7).

(h) When our life stands up to

these tests we may assure our hearts before God that we are indeed Christians and children of God, even when we are conscious of our natural sinfulness (*I John* 3: 19).

(i) When, however, the application of these tests does not produce a satisfactory proof of genuineness any assurance people may seem to have is unjustified (*I John* 1: 6; 2: 4, 9–11, 23; 3: 6–10; 4: 8, 20; *II John* 9; *III John* 11).

4. The results of being sure that we are Christians.

(a) Joy (*I Pet.* 1: 8; *I John* 1: 4).

(b) The banishment of any unworthy fear of God (*I John* 4: 17–19).

(c) The avoidance of sin (*I John* 2: 1).

(d) Confidence in God and boldness before Him (*I John* 3: 19–22; 5: 14, 15; compare *Heb.* 10: 19–22).

34. PERSEVERANCE

Question: Can a true Christian go so far from God as to become lost?

Answer: A true Christian cannot go so far from God that he becomes lost, although he may backslide. He holds fast to the end because he is held fast by the Lord. Apostasy proves a person was never a true Christian.

1. The Christian must hold fast to the end—this is commanded.

(a) The Christian must hold fast to the end (*Matt.* 24: 13; 10: 22; *Mark* 13: 13).

(b) It is by standing firm that the Christian wins the well-being of his soul (*Luke* 21: 19, R.V.; cf. *Heb.* 10: 39).

(c) Continuance in the word of Christ is the proof of discipleship (*John* 8: 31).

(d) To him who by perseverance in well-doing seeks for glory and honour and immortality, the Lord will give eternal life (*Rom.* 2: 7).

(e) To him who is victorious Christ gives the right to eat of the tree of life (*Rev.* 2: 7).

(f) The Christian shares in all that Christ promises so long as he steadily maintains until the end the trust with which he began (*Heb.* 6: 11, cf. 3: 6, 14).

(g) The perseverance of the Christian is a condition of his reigning with Christ (*II Tim.* 2: 12).

(h) We are not left in any doubt as to the nature of this perseverance; it is perseverance in:

(i) Holiness (*Rom.* 8: 29; *II Thess.* 2: 13; *I Pet.* 1: 2);

(ii) The knowledge of God (*Col.* 1: 10);

(iii) The faith—i.e. being firm on the Christian foundations, never to be dislodged from the hope offered in the gospel (*Col.* 1: 23);

(iv) Christian conduct (*Col.* 1: 10);

(v) Loyalty to Christ (*Rev.* 14: 12);

(vi) Obedience (*Rev.* 14: 12; *Col.* 1: 9);

(vii) Running the race of the Christian life in faith and obedience (*Heb.* 12: 1, 2);

(viii) Good works (*Gal.* 6: 9; *Eph.* 2: 10; *I Thess.* 1: 3);

(ix) Fruitfulness (*Col.* 1: 10);

(x) The Lord (*Phil.* 4: 1).

2. The true Christian will hold fast to the end.

(a) Having begun a good work in the Christian's life, God brings it to completion, right up to the day of Jesus Christ (*Phil.* 1: 6; cf. *I Cor.* 1: 8).

(b) Stirred by the exhortations of the Bible, the true Christian will make every effort to enter into the promises of God, thus confirming his calling and election, adding to his assurance that there will be an abundant entrance for him into the eternal kingdom of our Lord Jesus Christ (*II Pet.* 1: 11).

(c) The warnings God has given against apostasy are used by the Holy Spirit to keep the true Christian from it (*Heb.* 2: 1; 6: 9; 10: 39).

(d) The testing of true faith brings perseverance (*Jas.* 1: 3—A.V. translates it "patience")—the reaction of the true Christian to testing gives proof of his spiritual sonship (*Rom.* 5: 3–5; *II Thess.* 1: 4; *Heb.* 10: 36; *Rev.* 13: 10).

(e) A fight there will be, but perseverance also (*Eph.* 6: 13).

(f) It is the Father's will that the Son should lose none of those whom He has given to Him (*John* 6: 39; 10: 27–29).

(g) The gifts and calling of God are irrevocable (*Rom.* 11: 29).

(h) Nothing is able to separate God's elect in Christ from His love (*Rom.* 8: 30–39).

3. The true Christian is not immune from backsliding although he cannot commit apostasy.

(a) Perseverance does not rule out backsliding, but it does rule out apostasy (*Rev.* 2: 2, with 4–7; 2: 9, with 20–29).

(b) The Christian may backslide (as some of the Hebrew Christians did) but he can never apostatise (*Heb.* 5: 11–6: 12, especially 6: 9).

(c) Though the Christian falls, he is restored through the help of the Lord (*Ps.* 37: 24).

4. The true Christian holds fast to the end because he is held fast by the Lord.

(a) The Christian does not keep himself; he is kept by the power of God, through faith unto salvation (*I Pet.* 1: 5; *Rom.* 14: 4).

(b) God will never forsake His people: His justice and His faithfulness forbid that He should (*Ps.* 37: 28; *II Thess.* 3: 3).

(c) He will fulfil His purposes for His people, and nothing can hinder them (*Ps.* 138: 8; *Rev.* 7: 1–8; cf. *John* 10: 27–29; *Ezek.* 9: 3–6).

(d) Even in the times of His people's ignorance and stupidity the Lord keeps His hand upon them (*Ps.* 73: 21–24).

(e) He sustains them to the end, according to His faithfulness and calling (*I Cor.* 1: 8, 9).

(f) Perseverance is the result of being strengthened by the Lord with all power, according to His glorious might (*Col.* 1: 11; *Eph.* 6: 13, 18).

(g) Satan's desires to have the Christian are not permitted by the Lord—Peter's case, for example (*Luke* 22: 31, 32).

(h) The glory or praise for the Christian's perseverance is entirely God's (*II Tim.* 4: 18).

(i) The Christian, therefore, may be sure of his security (*II Tim.* 4: 18; *Ps.* 37: 28; 73: 24).

(j) This fact should not lead to slackness but to diligence in the Christian life (*II Pet.* 1: 10; *Phil.* 2: 13).

5. Apostasy means a person was never a true Christian.

(a) Straightforward apostasy is the proof that a man was never, in fact, a Christian, although he appeared to be such (*I John* 2: 19).

(b) The parable of the sower indicates that perseverance is the test of reality (*Mark* 4: 3–8).

(c) Cases of falling away, or apostasy, are recorded (*I Tim.* 1: 19; *II Tim.* 2: 17, 18), but in no case is there proof that the persons concerned were true believers (*I John* 2: 19).

(d) We are reminded, therefore, that not everyone who calls himself a child of God is necessarily such (*Matt.* 7: 21–23; *Rom.* 9: 6–8).

6. Fundamental doctrines of the Christian faith underline the truth of what we call final perseverance.

(a) It follows on from election (*Jer.* 31: 3; *Matt.* 24: 22–24; *I Thess.* 1: 2–4).

(b) It follows from the covenant by which God the Father gave His people to His Son as the reward of His obedience and suffering (*Jer.* 32: 40; *John* 17: 2–6).

(c) It springs from the once-for-all nature of Christ's atoning death (*Heb.* 10: 14).

(d) It follows from the union of Christians with Christ (*Rom.* 8: 1; *Gal.* 2: 20; *John* 17: 19).

(e) It follows from the presence of the Holy Spirit in the Christian for ever (*John* 14: 16; *II Cor.* 1: 21, 22; *II Cor.* 5: 5; *Eph.* 1: 13, 14).

(f) It follows from the effective-ness of Christ's intercession for His people (*John* 17: 11, 15, 20; *Rom.* 8: 34; *Heb.* 7: 25; cf. *Luke* 22: 31, 32).

35. SANCTIFICATION

Question: What does God require of us most of all when we have become Christians?

Answer: The comprehensive words which sum up what God requires of us are sanctification and holiness. Sanctification is the process of which holiness is the completed state. In sanctification, God's will is that sinful attitudes and actions should be put to death in the Christian's life, his nature and character renewed after the image of God in Christ, his obedience to God increased, so that he lives to please God. All these things take place through the power and help of the Holy Spirit.

1. Sanctification and holiness.

(a) God's will for us is our sanctification (*I Thess.* 4: 3; *I Pet.* 1: 16).

(b) God's call to the Christian is to holiness (*I Thess.* 4: 7).

(c) The necessity for holiness springs from the fact that the Lord our God is holy (*Lev.* 11: 44; *I Pet.* 1: 16).

(d) That we might serve the Lord, without fear, in holiness and righteousness, all the days of our life is the purpose of God's redemption and of the gift of His Spirit (*Luke* 1: 75; *Ezek.* 36: 27).

(e) The supreme aim of the Christian is to be the achieving of holiness (*Heb.* 12: 14).

2. Sanctification—of which holiness is the completed state—is a continuous process.

(a) It is the continual endeavour to bring holiness to completeness (*II Cor.* 7: 1).

(b) It is a progressive work (*I Thess.* 5: 23), and involves the complete personality: the spirit, the soul and the body (*I Thess.* 5: 23).

(c) Entire sanctification will not be realised until our bodies are changed to be like Christ's body (*Phil.* 3: 21; *I John* 3: 2).

3. Sinful attitudes and actions are to be put to death in the Christian's life (*Rom.* 8: 13; *Col.* 3: 5).

(a) Belonging to the Lord brings the immediate obligation to depart from iniquity (*II Tim.* 2: 19).

(b) God's judgment and condemnation no longer rest upon the Christian because of his sin (*Rom.* 8: 1), but this does not mean that he may ever regard sin lightly (*Rom.* 6: 1, 2; *I John* 2: 1).

(c) The Christian is to throw off the sinful ways of his old life (*Eph.* 4: 22).

(d) While there is necessarily a battle with indwelling sin (*Rom.* 7: 14–25; *I John* 1: 8; 2: 1), sin is not to have the mastery over the Christian (*Rom.* 6: 12, 13).

(e) Sexual immorality and uncleanness are not to be given any place in the Christian's life (*I Thess.* 4: 3, 7).

(f) The more the Christian's sanctification proceeds the more he hates his sin (*Job* 42: 5, 6; *Isa.* 6: 5; *Rom.* 7: 24).

4. The Christian's nature and character are to be renewed after the image of God in Christ.

(a) Sanctification is a call to share God's moral perfection (*I Pet.* 1: 16).

(b) The goal of sanctification is always presented as likeness to Christ: God has chosen Christians to bear the family likeness of His Son (*Rom.* 8: 29; *Phil.* 1: 9–11; *II Pet.* 1: 5–8).

(c) God's purpose is that we should copy Christ and be like Him (*I Cor.* 11: 1; *Phil.* 2: 5).

(d) As our way of looking at things is made different and renewed by the Holy Spirit, so we are able to put on the new nature of God's creating, which shows itself in a just and devout life (*Eph.* 4: 23, 24).

5. Obedience to God is to grow and increase.

(a) Nothing we do outwardly has value to God without the willing obedience of the heart (*I Sam.* 15: 22).

(b) He requires that His commandments shall be upon our heart (*Deut.* 6: 5).

(c) Practical righteousness is walking (another word for "obeying") in all the commandments and ordinances of the Lord blameless (*Luke* 1: 6).

(d) We please God as we keep His commandments (*I John* 3: 22).

(e) We are to actively obey the Holy Spirit as He reveals to us what God requires (*Gal.* 5: 25).

(f) While our obedience is always imperfect (*Ps.* 130: 3), God will always receive the offering of our obedience and of ourselves to Him as holy and acceptable, when we are His children in Christ (*Rom.* 12: 1; *Phil.* 4: 18; *Heb.* 13: 16).

6. All these things take place by the power and help of the Holy Spirit.

(a) Our confidence as we seek to work out the salvation God has given us is that He Himself is at work in us, giving us the will and power to achieve His purpose (*Phil.* 2: 13).

(b) The Holy Spirit is the agent of our sanctification, even as of our regeneration (*I Cor.* 6: 11; *I Thess.* 4: 7, 8).

(c) Strength for the Christian life comes by the personal indwelling of the Holy Spirit (*Eph.* 3: 16; *II Cor.* 4: 16).

(d) The Holy Spirit assists the Christian in putting sin to death (*Rom.* 8: 13).

(e) The Holy Spirit assists in the gradual transformation of the Christian's character to that of Christ (*II Cor.* 3: 18; cf. *Rom.* 8: 29): He takes what is Christ's and declares it to the Christian (*John* 16: 14).

(f) The Holy Spirit assists believers in actual obedience: He implants a supernatural habit and principle in the believer enabling him to obey God's will (*Rom.* 8: 2).

(g) The Holy Spirit strengthens the believer's will to obey God's commandments (*I Pet.* 1: 2; *I John* 3: 24).

7. The instrument the Holy Spirit uses principally for our sanctification is the Word of God.

(a) It is declared to be God's chosen instrument (*John* 17: 17).

(b) Our way of life can be kept pure by guarding it according to God's Word (*Ps.* 119: 9).

(c) Holiness comes from instruc-tion in God's ways, and walking in His paths (*Isa.* 2: 2–5).

(d) It is for this reason that Christ gives, by His Spirit, gifts to enable the people of God to be instructed in the Word of God (*Eph.* 4: 11–16; *I Tim.* 5: 17).

(e) Our sharing in God's holiness involves chastisement on occasions and some of the experiences which lead to greater sanctification are not always pleasant at the time (*Heb.* 12: 10, 11).

8. Many incentives and motives for holiness and sanctification are set before the Christian.

(a) Reverence and respect for God (*II Cor.* 7: 1; *I Pet.* 1: 17).

(b) The mercies of God to us in Christ (*Rom.* 12: 1, 2).

(c) The promises of God (*II Cor.* 7: 1).

(d) The freedom to which we have been called in Christ, enabling us to please God (*Gal.* 5: 13–15).

(e) The prospect of Christ's return (*Tit.* 2: 12, 13; *I John* 3: 3).

(f) God's gift of the Holy Spirit to us and the implications of that gift (*Gal.* 5: 16–26; *I Thess.* 4: 8).

36. BAPTISM

Question: What is baptism?

Answer: It is an act of obedient discipleship, appointed by Christ, administered in the name of the Trinity, which symbolises repent-ance, faith in the Lord Jesus Christ, the confession of His Lordship, admittance into the family of God, entry into all the benefits of His death and resurrection, and the desire to live a new life through the power of the Holy Spirit.

1. Baptism was appointed by Christ Himself for all disciples.

(a) Christ Himself was baptised, thereby setting an example to all who would follow Him (*Mark* 1: 9–11; *Matt.* 3: 13–17; *Luke* 3: 21–22).

(b) Speaking of His own baptism, He declared it a rightful act of submission in order to conform to all that God requires (*Matt.* 3: 15).

(c) Baptism was a practice of Christ with regard to those who became His disciples during His ministry (*John* 3: 22, 26; 4: 1)—although Christ did not Himself baptise, leaving it to His disciples (*John* 4: 2).

(d) Baptism was part of the great commission, given to the apostles, after the Resurrection, to be the first thing in which believers were to be instructed of all that Christ commanded (*Matt.* 28: 19, 20; *Mark* 16: 15, 16).

2. It is administered in the name of the Trinity.

(a) It is to be administered always in the name of the Father, the Son and the Holy Spirit (*Matt.* 28: 19).

(b) The identity of the baptiser is unimportant (*John* 4: 2; *I Cor.* 1: 14–17)—this fact may explain why our Lord refrained from baptising disciples (*John* 4: 2), and why Paul appears to have done the same (*I Cor.* 1: 14–16; *Acts* 10: 48).

3. It is a symbol of the individual's reception of the gospel.

(a) It is the consequence of the Lord having opened the individual's heart to give heed to the gospel (*Acts* 16: 14, 15).

(b) It is a mark of a person's reception of the gospel—of the Word of the Lord (*Acts* 2: 37, 38, 41; 8: 12).

(c) It should follow immediately upon confession of faith in Christ (*Acts* 2: 38).

(d) It is the first act of obedient discipleship (*Acts* 9: 18; 16: 14, 15, 33; 22: 16).

(e) It is a badge of discipleship (*Matt.* 28: 19; *John* 3: 22).

(f) It is an experience which every Christian is to share (*Eph.* 4: 5).

(g) It is taken for granted in the New Testament that all believers will be baptised (e.g. *I Cor.* 1: 13; 6: 11; 10: 1 ff).

4. It symbolises repentance and faith in the Lord Jesus Christ.

(a) Baptism is an outward sign of repentance—of turning with contrition from sin to God (*Acts* 2: 38).

(b) It is the personal expression of faith in the Lord Jesus Christ and His gospel (*Mark* 16: 15, 16; *Acts* 8: 12, 13, 37; 16: 31–33).

5. Participation in baptism is the confession of Christ's Lordship.

(a) Baptism is always associated with Christ's name, in that the individual makes a confession concerning Him (*Acts* 2: 37, 38; 8: 16; 22: 16).

(b) It is the acknowledgment of Jesus as Lord (*Acts* 2: 38; 8: 37).

(c) It implies entrance into committed fellowship and allegiance to Christ (*Acts* 2: 38; 10: 48; *Gal.* 3: 27).

(d) It is the public testimony of the individual that he has become Christ's property (*Acts* 16: 15; 19: 5)—the expression "in the name" of someone being used commercially for the transfer of property.

(e) As Lord, Christ's command is to be obeyed (*Mark* 16: 16); to Him the believer must be faithful (*Acts* 16: 14, 15).

6. It symbolises admittance into the family of God.

(a) It marks the believer's admittance into the family of God, or the Church of Christ (*Acts* 2: 38, 41, 47; 8: 12 f, 36, 38; 9: 18, 19; 16: 33; 22: 16; *I Cor.* 1: 14–17).

(b) It is the outward sign of the believer's new birth into God's family (*John* 3: 5).

(c) It is a mark of his entry into the membership of Christ's body (*I Cor.* 12: 13).

7. It symbolises entry into all the benefits of Christ's death and resurrection.

(a) Baptism is a visual aid of the gospel, in that it portrays Christ's death and resurrection and the salvation which comes to men and women as they turn in repentance and faith to Christ (*Rom.* 6: 3, 4).

(b) It is a picture of an individual entering into the benefits of the new covenant, sealed with Christ's blood, even as Noah, believing the promises of God to him, entered the ark (*I Pet.* 3: 18–22).

(c) It is, therefore, a picture of the Christian's cleansing from sin through Christ's death (*Acts* 2: 38) —it is the outward and visible sign of inward and spiritual cleansing (*Acts* 22: 16; *Heb.* 10: 22).

(d) It speaks symbolically of the gift and blessing of new life by the gift and indwelling of the Holy Spirit (*Acts* 2: 38). In order to experience the reality of what baptism signifies, the individual must be born again of God's Spirit (*John* 3: 5; *I Cor.* 12: 13).

8. Participation in baptism expresses the desire the individual has to live a new life through the power of the Holy Spirit.

(a) It signifies his deliverance from the bondage of sin (*Rom.* 6: 3).

(b) It is a symbolical burial of the believer's old life (*Rom.* 6: 3, 4; *Col.* 2: 12), and renunciation of his old relationship to sin, because Christ's death has become his death by faith (*Rom.* 6: 12).

(c) It is a symbol of the beginning of the new life in Christ, of participation in the resurrection life of the Lord Jesus Christ, which is possible by the help and power of the Holy Spirit (*Rom.* 6: 4, 5; *Col.* 2: 12).

(d) It is a symbol of the believer's willingness to present his body to God as an instrument for the doing of God's will (*Rom.* 6: 13).

(e) It symbolises the end of a person's service of sin, and the beginning of his committed service to God (*Rom.* 6: 16, 17).

37. THE LORD'S SUPPER

Question: What is the Lord's Supper?

Answer: The Lord's Supper is the symbolic meal which Christ established and commanded; in which Christians remember Christ's sacrifice continually; in which they acknowledge their sharing in the benefits of His death; at which they

have fellowship with Christ and with other Christians; and make their thanksgiving to God.

1. The Lord's Supper is a symbolic meal.

(a) The Lord's Supper is a proclamation of the Lord's death by words and symbols (*I Cor.* 11: 26).

(b) Christ's body is represented by the bread (*I Cor.* 11: 24).

(c) Christ's blood is represented by the wine (*I Cor.* 11: 25).

(d) The bread is broken and the wine is poured out as symbols of Christ's death upon the Cross (*Matt.* 26: 26; *Mark* 14: 22; *Luke* 22: 19, 20; *I Cor.* 11: 24, 25).

(e) Both the bread and the wine are to be distributed to Christians as they sit at the Lord's Table (*Matt.* 26: 26, 27; *Mark* 14: 22–28; *Luke* 22: 19, 20; *I Cor.* 11: 23, 24, 26).

(f) The Lord's Supper was prepared for, in symbol, by the Jewish Passover (*I Cor.* 5: 7, 8; *Ex.* 12: 21–28): even as the Passover proclaimed the mercy of God in redeeming His people under the old covenant, so the Lord's Supper proclaims God's redeeming mercy under the new covenant (*I Cor.* 11: 26).

(g) The Lord's Supper took place at the Passover feast and was established on the pattern of the Passover (*Matt.* 26: 17–19; *Mark* 14: 1, 2, 12–16; *Luke* 22: 14–20; *John* 13: 21–30; compare *Ex.* 12).

(h) The bread that was eaten with the lamb in the Passover feast was put to a new use (*Matt.* 26: 26).

(i) The third cup of the Passover, "the cup of blessing" (compare *I Cor.* 10: 16) was also put to a new use (*Matt.* 26, 27, 28).

(j) By reason of its significance, the Lord's Supper must be regarded as quite distinct from all other meals (*I Cor.* 11: 29).

2. The Lord's Supper was established and commanded by Christ.

(a) The Lord Jesus Christ established this regular act at the Last Supper on the night of His betrayal (*Matt.* 26: 26–28; *I Cor.* 11: 23).

(b) Christ gave certain actions to be imitated every time the symbolic meal was repeated (*I Cor.* 11: 23 ff).

(c) The Lord's Supper, in its institution, was a meal which Christ earnestly desired to share with His disciples (*Luke* 22: 15).

(d) In establishing the symbolic meal Christ commanded that it should be continually repeated (*Luke* 22: 19b; *I Cor.* 11: 25).

(e) Because Christ established the meal it is called the Lord's Supper (*I Cor.* 11: 20), and also the table of the Lord (*I Cor.* 10: 21). It is also described as the breaking of bread (*Acts* 2: 42; 20: 7) because Christ broke the bread (*Luke* 22: 19; 24: 30, 35). It is also called the "eucharist" or "thanksgiving" (*I Cor.* 10: 16) because Christ gave thanks when He took the cup (*Matt.* 26: 27).

(f) The apostle Paul received a direct revelation from Christ regarding the institution of the Lord's Supper and the importance of its continuation (*I Cor.* 11: 23; cf. *Gal.* 1: 12; 2: 2).

(g) We are not surprised, therefore, that the Lord's Supper was a regular act of the early church (*Acts* 2: 42); they used to assemble on the first day of the week for the breaking of bread (*Acts* 20: 7).

3. By means of the Lord's Supper Christians remember Christ's sacrifice continually.

(a) The Lord's Supper sets forth Christ's death for us (*I Cor.* 11: 26).

(b) The purpose is that we should recall to mind Christ's sufferings on our behalf (*Luke* 22: 19; *I Cor.* 11: 24, 25).

(c) It is a remembrance, or a memorial, meal (*I Cor.* 11: 23–25).

4. By means of the Lord's Supper Christians acknowledge their sharing in the benefits of Christ's death.

(a) The Lord's Supper declares that the new covenant that God promised has been established through the saving work of His Son (*I Cor.* 11: 25).

(b) It reminds us of our sharing by faith in the benefits of His death (*John* 6: 53, 63; *I Cor.* 10: 16).

(c) The Lord's Supper is a symbol of our sharing or partaking of Christ (*I Cor.* 10: 17).

5. In the Lord's Supper Christians have fellowship with Christ and with other Christians.

(a) The Lord's Supper is an act of communion with Christ (*I Cor.* 10: 16).

(b) Christians, therefore, who take part in the Lord's Supper should be in uncompromised fellowship with the Lord Jesus Christ (*I Cor.* 10: 21).

(c) The Lord's Supper is an act of fellowship with other Christians: it is the time when Christians "come together" (*I Cor.* 11: 17, 18, 20, 33, 34; *I Cor.* 10: 17; *Acts* 20: 7).

(d) The Lord's Supper expresses the union of Christians with one another (*I Cor.* 10: 17; 12: 13).

(e) The fellowship which believers have with the Lord Jesus Christ in the Lord's Supper is a pledge of the fulfilled fellowship they will have in the kingdom of God (*Mark* 14: 25; *Luke* 22: 16).

6. In the Lord's Supper Christians make their thanksgiving to God.

(a) The Lord's Supper is a reminder of the death of Christ to bring forth our thanksgiving (*I Cor.* 11: 24, 25).

(b) We are to give thanks for the bread and wine as Christ did, remembering that they are symbols of His broken body and of His outpoured blood (*I Cor.* 11: 23, 24).

(c) Thus the Lord's Supper is the particular time when we offer our thanksgiving to God for Christ and His redeeming work (*I Cor.* 10: 16).

(d) Being more aware of God's mercies towards us at the Lord's Supper than at any other time the sacrifice of thanksgiving should include the offering of ourselves to God (*Rom.* 12: 1).

(e) Christians who take part in the Lord's Supper should be willing to dedicate themselves completely to Christ (*I Cor.* 10: 21).

(f) To take part properly in the Lord's Supper we need to have done with our old kind of life and to be living to the full our new life in Christ (*I Cor.* 5: 7, 8): renewed dedication of ourselves to this end is part of our thanksgiving.

7. The Lord's Supper is a tremendous help to the spiritual life of Christians.

(a) The Lord's Supper strengthens our faith and refreshes our souls—this fact is true every time we consider the love of God to us (*I John* 3: 1-3; *Rom.* 8: 35-39).

(b) At the Lord's Supper we may feed spiritually upon Christ (*John* 6: 32, 33, 35, 50, 51): those who rightly receive the bread and the wine, by living faith, receive Christ and the benefits of His passion (*I Cor.* 10: 16).

8. Unfortunately, it is possible for Christians to take part in the Lord's Supper unworthily.

(a) The Lord's Supper needs to be entered upon with care (*I Cor.* 11: 27).

(b) Christians should examine their lives before they eat their share of the bread and drink from the cup (*I Cor.* 11: 28).

9. The Lord's Supper is to be continued until Christ returns.

(a) The Lord's Supper looks forward to the Lord's return (*I Cor.* 11: 26).

(b) The Lord's Supper will no longer be necessary when Christ returns (*I Cor.* 11: 26).

38. THE CHURCH

Question: What is the Church of Christ?

Answer: The Church consists of those of every race, every land and every age who have been chosen by God the Father, purchased by Christ's blood and sanctified by the Holy Spirit.

1. The Descriptions given of the Church in the Bible.

(a) God's very own people (*Ex.* 6: 7; *II Cor.* 6: 14-18; *Rev.* 21: 2, 3).

(b) The new and true Israel, established in Christ (*Gal.* 3: 29; 6: 16; *I Pet.* 2: 9).

(c) The company of those whom the Lord has called to Himself (*Acts* 2: 39).

(d) Those who are in Christ (*Phil.* 1: 1).

(e) The company of those who in every place call upon the name of Jesus Christ the Lord (*I Cor.* 1: 2).

(f) The company of those who believe (*Acts* 4: 31, 32).

(g) The household of God (*Heb.* 10: 21), and the household of faith (*Gal.* 6: 10).

(h) God's building (*I Cor.* 3: 10).

(i) God's temple (*I Cor.* 3: 16, 17), i.e. the temple of the Spirit (*Eph.* 2: 22).

(j) Christ's flock (*Heb.* 13: 20; *Acts* 20: 28).

(k) The Body of Christ (*I Cor.* 12: 14-27; *Eph.* 1: 23; 5: 30; *Col.* 1: 24).

(l) The bride of Christ (*Eph.* 5: 21-33; *Rev.* 21: 2, 9; 22: 17).

2. The members of the Church are chosen by God the Father.

(a) They were chosen in Christ before the foundation of the world (*Eph.* 1: 4).

(b) They were destined in God's love to be His sons in Jesus Christ (*Eph.* 1: 5).

(c) Being chosen, they are called by God to be members of Christ's Church (*Rom.* 8: 28-30; 9: 11, 24; 11: 5; *Gal.* 1: 15; *I Thess.* 1: 4).

(d) The Church is made up of those who have been called of God, out of darkness into His marvellous light (*Rom.* 1: 5, 6; *II Tim.* 1: 9; *I Pet.* 2: 9).

3. The members of the Church are cleansed from sin through Christ's blood.

(a) The Church was purchased by the blood of Christ (*Acts* 20: 28; *Eph.* 5: 25; *Heb.* 9: 12).

(b) Christ loved the Church and gave Himself up for her, that she might be cleansed and sanctified (*I Cor.* 6: 11; *Eph.* 5: 25–27).

(c) Christ gave Himself to redeem her members from all iniquity (*Tit.* 2: 14).

(d) Thus the Church is made up of those who were once alienated from God by sin but have been brought nigh to Him through the blood of Christ (*Eph.* 2: 11–13).

(e) They are members of the Church through the blood of the new and eternal covenant (*Heb.* 13: 20).

4. The members of the Church are sanctified by the Holy Spirit who lives within them to this end.

(a) Members of Christ's Church were chosen that they should be holy and blameless before God (*Eph.* 1: 4), conformed to the image of God's Son (*Rom.* 8: 29), and purified (*Tit.* 2: 14).

(b) This work of sanctification is the Holy Spirit's, which He never ceases to perform throughout the Christian's life (*I Pet.* 1: 2; *I Thess.* 4: 7, 8; *Phil.* 1: 6).

(c) Thus the Church is the company of those who have received the Holy Spirit through faith in the Lord Jesus Christ (*Rom.* 8: 9; *Acts* 11: 17), who have been born again of God's Spirit (*John* 3: 5–8).

5. Some of the conclusions the Bible draws for us.

(a) The Church belongs to God (*Gal.* 1: 13; *I Tim.* 3: 15).

(b) God alone knows exactly who are the true members of the Church (*II Tim.* 2: 19).

(c) The sole right of adding new members to the Church is the Lord's (*Acts* 2: 47).

(d) The Church is made up of those of every race who have been brought together in Christ, and are indwelt by the Holy Spirit (*Eph.* 2: 11–22; *Rev.* 5: 9, 10).

(e) Thus the Church of Christ ignores all divisions of race or social distinctions, making all its members one (*I Cor.* 12: 13).

39. BECOMING A MEMBER OF THE CHURCH

Question: How do we become members of the Church?

Answer: Through the new birth by living faith in Jesus Christ.

1. Christ is the foundation of the Church.

(a) There is no other foundation save Jesus Christ (*I Cor.* 3: 11).

(b) The Church is built upon Him (*Matt.* 16: 18).

2. Living faith in Christ, therefore, is essential.

(a) It is by coming to Him, the living foundation stone of the Church, that we become part of God's spiritual building — the Church (*I Pet.* 2: 4, 5).

(b) As we believe that Jesus is the

Son of God and confess Him as Lord, through the help of the Holy Spirit, we become members of the Church of Christ (*Matt.* 16: 16, 17; *John* 20: 31; *I Cor.* 12: 3).

(c) Those who thus hear God's call to become members of Christ's Church do so by means of the Word of God and the work of the Holy Spirit (*John* 3: 8; *Acts* 16: 14; *I Cor.* 4: 15; *I Pet.* 1: 23).

3. **Such living faith means that the new birth has taken place.**

(a) We become members of the Church by new birth (*John* 3: 5–8).

(b) We belong to Christ and His Church through our possession of the Holy Spirit (*Rom.* 8: 9).

(c) All believers are brought into the one Body of Christ—the Church—by the one and the same Holy Spirit (*I Cor.* 12: 13).

4. **The Church of Christ is made up, therefore, of those who have a personal relationship to Christ.**

(a) They know Him (*Phil.* 3: 10; *II Pet.* 3: 18).

(b) He is their Shepherd (*John* 10: 14; *I Pet.* 2: 25; 5: 4).

(c) As members of His Body, they have a living relationship to Him, the Head (*Eph.* 4: 14–16).

40. BELONGING TO THE CHURCH

Question: What does belonging to the Church of Christ involve?

Answer: It involves, first and foremost, obedience to Christ's control, and the recognition in practice of the implications of the relationship we have towards all other members of the Church: fellowship; caring for one another; submitting to necessary discipline; maintaining spiritual unity; and offering together spiritual sacrifices acceptable to God.

1. **Membership of the Church of Christ involves, first and foremost, obedience to Christ's control.**

(a) The Church is His Body (*Eph.* 1: 23).

(b) The Church, therefore, is to be subject to Christ in everything (*Eph.* 4: 15, 16; 5: 24).

(c) Christ is to be reverenced in the heart as Lord (*I Pet.* 3: 15).

(d) The love of the members of the Church for Christ, the Head, is seen in their obedience to His commandments (*John* 14: 15); for example, in their zeal for good works (*Matt.* 5: 16, compared with *Tit.* 2: 14).

2. **Membership of the Church of Christ involves recognising the relationship we have to all other Christians.**

(a) We are members of the same Body (*I Cor.* 12: 4–27; *Eph.* 1: 23; 5: 30; *Col.* 1: 24); and, therefore, individually members one of another (*Rom.* 12: 5).

(b) We constitute together the people of God (*I Pet.* 2: 9, 10).

(c) We belong to the same family or household (*Gal.* 6: 10; *Heb.* 10: 21).

(d) We are sheep of the same flock (*Heb.* 13: 20; *Acts* 20: 28).

(e) We are citizens of the same kingdom (*Phil.* 3: 20; *Heb.* 11: 16; 12: 28; *Rev.* 21: 2, 3).

(f) We are together a chosen race, a royal priesthood and a holy nation (*I Pet.* 2: 9, 10).

3. Membership of the Church of Christ involves fulfilling the implications of this relationship which we have with all other Christians.

(a) By living in fellowship (*Acts* 2: 42–47; *Heb.* 10: 24; *I John* 1: 3, 7; 2: 19).

(b) By caring for one another (*I Cor.* 12: 7; *Gal.* 6: 10; *I Pet.* 5: 2; *I John* 3: 16, 17).

(c) By accepting the family discipline (*I Cor.* 5: 12, 13; *Heb.* 13: 17; *Rev.* 2: 12–29).

(d) By maintaining spiritual unity (*Eph.* 4: 2, 3; *Phil.* 2: 1, 2).

(e) By offering together the spiritual sacrifices of our spiritual priesthood which are acceptable to God by Jesus Christ (*I Pet.* 2: 5): for example, praise (*Heb.* 13: 15), thanksgiving (*Ps.* 50: 14; 107: 22), prayer (*Ps.* 141: 2), the dedication of our bodies to Him (*Rom.* 12: 1), doing good and sharing what we have with others (*Heb.* 13: 16).

41. THE WORK AND DESTINY OF THE CHURCH

Question: What is the work of the Church? And what is going to happen to the Church?

Answer: The work of the Church—in brief—is to proclaim the gospel of Christ, making disciples of all who believe, until, as the bride of Christ, she is presented to Christ at His return.

1. The work of the Church is to proclaim the gospel of Christ.

(a) Christians are to declare the wonderful deeds of Him who has called them out of darkness into His marvellous light—principally by the change which the gospel has brought into their lives (*I Pet.* 2: 9).

(b) The main function of the Church is testimony to Jesus Christ (*Rev.* 11: 7; 12: 11, 17).

(c) The purpose the Lord Jesus Christ had for the Church from the beginning was the preaching of repentance and forgiveness of sins in His name to all nations (*Luke* 24: 47; *Mark* 16: 15; *Acts* 1: 8).

2. The work of the Church is to make disciples of all who believe the gospel.

(a) Believers are to be baptised in the name of the Father, and of the Son, and of the Holy Spirit (*Matt.* 28: 19).

(b) They are to be taught to observe all that Christ has commanded (*Matt.* 28: 20).

(c) They are to be warned and instructed, according to all that God would have them know, so that they are brought to their full maturity as members of Christ's Body, the Church (*Col.* 1: 28).

3. The end always in view is the return of Christ and the presentation of the Church to Him as His bride.

(a) No matter how dark the days may be, and how apparently hopeless the Church's situation may appear, she shall triumph and the powers of hell will not prevail against her (*Matt.* 16: 18).

(b) Christ loves the Church, and He will demonstrate that love before the enemies of the Church (*Rev.* 3: 9; compare *II Thess.* 1: 5–10).

(c) The Church will be gathered from every part of the earth, with no member missed, at Christ's return (*Matt.* 24: 31; *Mark* 13: 27; *Luke* 21: 28).

(d) Her destiny is to be presented glorious before Him at the last (*Eph.* 5: 27), His bride (*II Cor.* 11: 2; *Rev.* 21: 2).

42. MEMBERSHIP OF A LOCAL CHURCH

Question: Why belong to a church?

Answer: The teaching of the New Testament takes it for granted that every Christian will join together with other Christians in the membership of a local congregation for only then can the implications of common membership of the Church of Christ find expression—that is to say, in fellowship, mutual care, submission to necessary discipline, the maintenance of spiritual unity, and the offering together of spiritual sacrifices acceptable to God—and the work of the Church be effectively carried out—that is to say, in the proclamation of the gospel and the making of disciples in a particular area.

1. **The New Testament gives an essential place to the local church in the life of the Christian.**

(a) The local church is not to be despised by the Christian (*I Cor.* 11: 22).

(b) The New Testament refers to patterns of behaviour in the church, meaning the local church (*I Cor.* 14: 19, 28, 35); and the directions given by the apostles were given in the first place to churches (*I Cor.* 16: 1).

(c) As the work of evangelism progressed in the first century, Christians were gathered together as soon as possible into churches (*Acts* 13: 1; 14: 23; 15: 41; 20: 17; *Rev.* 1: 11).

(d) Usually, wherever Christians were to be found there were ordained elders (*Acts* 14: 22, 23), and a local situation was defective where elders had not been appointed (*Tit.* 1: 5).

(e) Christians were assumed to be in such a close relationship together that they acknowledged certain men as leaders (*Heb.* 13: 7), and the latter knew themselves to be guardians of the local company of Christians (*Acts* 20: 28).

(f) The New Testament takes it for granted that Christians living in the same locality will have regular fellowship, assembling together as a company of believers (*I Cor.* 1: 2; 14: 23; *II Cor.* 1: 1; *I Tim.* 3: 15).

(g) Christians are instructed not to neglect meeting together (*Heb.* 10: 25).

(h) The early Christians were in such an established relationship with one another that they could speak of some who "went out from us" who "were not of us" (*I John* 2: 19).

(i) Christians are to strive to excel in building up the local church (*I Cor.* 14: 12).

(j) The instinctive act of Paul after his conversion was to identify himself with the Christians in Damascus, and with those at Jerusalem on his arrival there (*Acts* 9: 19, 26).

2. **The Descriptions the Bible gives of the Church as a whole demand that Christians meet together as ordered congregations in their localities.**

(a) The flock of God gathers together under the leadership of the under-shepherds whom the Chief Shepherd, Christ, has appointed (*Heb.* 13: 20; *I Pet.* 2: 25; 5: 2, 4).

(b) The members of the Body of Christ are members of one another and are intended, therefore, to be in the closest possible association together (*I Cor.* 12: 26, 27).

(c) The picture of the church as the household of faith implies a close relationship together (*Gal.* 6: 10).

(d) A brick is only a building as it is together with other bricks, properly joined to them: so too with the Christian (*I Pet.* 2: 4, 5).

3. **To belong to a church is a practical demonstration of the recognition of our relationship in Christ to our fellow-believers.**

4. **It enables us to live in fellowship.**

(a) The logical consequence of receiving the Holy Spirit is to want to live in fellowship with other Christians (*Rom.* 8: 9; *Phil.* 2: 1).

(b) Constant fellowship is possible through the local church as in no other way (*Acts* 2: 42).

(c) The fellowship is to be so close that mutual encouragement can be given both to love and to do good works (*Heb.* 3: 13; 10: 24).

5. **It enables us to fulfil Christ's command to remember His death and its meaning by means of the Lord's Supper.**

(a) To do this together is a vital part of Christian fellowship (*Acts* 2: 42; *I Cor.* 10: 16, 17).

(b) The early Christians gathered together on the Lord's Day to break bread in remembrance of Christ's death (*Acts* 20: 7).

(c) Christians need to come together regularly in the local church for the Lord's Supper (*I Cor.* 11: 23–34).

6. **It enables us to get to know our fellow-believers and thus to care for one another.**

(a) We may do good effectively to those who are of the household of faith only as we know who they are by coming together in the fellowship of the local church (*Gal.* 6: 10).

(b) By close association with one another Christian love is able to find the positive and practical expression it needs (*John* 13: 35).

(c) Through church-membership we are able to strengthen one another (*Luke* 22: 32), restore one another when fallen (*Gal.* 6: 1), and bear one another's burdens (*Gal.* 6: 2).

(d) By means of the local church the exercise of spiritual gifts to the benefit of one another is made possible (*I Cor.* 12: 24–28).

7. **It shows our acceptance of the family discipline of the Church, expressed, as it can only be, through the local church.**

(a) The Lord Jesus Christ taught that the local church was essential for maintaining the right kind of discipline amongst God's people (*Matt.* 18: 15–20).

(b) It is taken for granted in the New Testament that all Christians will be so committed to a local church that they will be within the discipline of that church (*I Thess.* 5: 12; *I Tim.* 5: 17; *Heb.* 13: 17; *I Pet.* 5: 1–5).

(c) Christians are to be in such an association of membership together that they can discipline members who bring dishonour to Christ (*I Cor.* 5: 2, 4, 12, 13).

8. It is a practical expression of spiritual unity.

(a) Christians feel within themselves the desire to express the oneness there is in Jesus Christ (*Gal.* 3: 28).

(b) No effort is to be spared to make fast with the bonds of love the unity which the Spirit gives (*Eph.* 4: 2, 3).

(c) The common life Christians have in Christ brings a common care for unity (*Phil.* 2: 1, 2).

9. It enables us to offer regularly the corporate spiritual sacrifices which honour God.

(a) By means of the local church, Christians make their praise and prayers corporate (*Heb.* 13: 15; *Acts* 2: 42, 47; 12: 5, 12).

(b) Through the knowledge Christians have of one another's needs, associated as they are in the local church, they are able to do good and share what they have with others (*Heb.* 13: 16).

(c) They are able to fulfil their financial obligations too to the work of Christ's Church (*I Cor.* 16: 2; *Phil.* 4: 14–19).

10. It is the instrument God uses to proclaim the gospel of Christ in an area.

(a) The testimony of the corporate life of a local church should be such a powerful influence for evangelism, that the Lord adds to the number of His people (*Acts* 2: 42–47).

(b) The local church is the means of sounding forth the word of the Lord in an area (*I Thess.* 1: 1, 8).

11. It is the provision God has made for the instruction of believers that they should be mature disciples.

(a) Christians are to be instructed in all that the Lord Jesus Christ commanded that they should do and observe (*Matt.* 28: 19): to this end God gives to local churches pastors and teachers, so that Christians may be fed and built up by the Word of God (*Acts* 20: 28; *Eph.* 4: 12, 15, 16; *I Pet.* 2: 2; 5: 2).

(b) The most important part of the elders' work is the ministry of the Word of God (*I Tim.* 5: 17; *I Pet.* 5: 2).

(c) Christians are expected to be in a situation where they will be contributing to the financial support of those who give themselves to preaching and teaching (*Gal.* 6: 6; *I Tim.* 5: 17, 18).

(d) The local church, faithfully taught, is one means God uses to preserve the pure teaching and preaching of the gospel (*II Tim.* 2: 2).

43. THE DEVIL

Question: What do we know about the devil?

Answer: The devil is the great enemy of God and man, the opposer of all that is good and the promoter of all that is evil. He has been defeated already by Christ's death and resurrection, and this defeat will be complete and clear to all at the end of this present age.

1. The devil's history.

(a) He is one of the fallen angels exalted in rank and power above all the rest (*Jude* 6; *II Pet.* 2: 4).

(b) He fell from the truth in which he once stood (*John* 8: 44).

(c) He is represented as a star fallen from heaven to earth (*Rev.* 9: 1).

(d) He sinned probably by reason of pride (*I Tim.* 3: 6).

(e) From the time of his first rebellion against God, the devil has sinned continuously (*II Pet.* 2: 4; *I John* 3: 8).

2. He is called by many names.

(a) He is called Satan (*Matt.* 16: 23; *Luke* 22: 31; *Rev.* 12: 9; 20: 2).

(b) He is the wicked one (*I John* 2: 13, 14; 3: 12; 5: 18).

(c) He is the prince of the power of the air (*Eph.* 2: 2).

(d) He is the prince of the devils (*Matt.* 9: 34; 12: 24).

(e) He is the god of this world (*II Cor.* 4: 4).

(f) He is called Beelzebub (*Matt.* 12: 24, 27; *Luke* 11: 15, 18, 19).

(g) He is the tempter (*Matt.* 4: 3; *I Thess.* 3: 5).

(h) He is called the old serpent (*Rev.* 12: 9).

(i) He is called the dragon (*Rev.* 12: 3, 4, 7, 9, 13, 16, 17; 20: 2).

3. The devil's power.

(a) He has great power: he showed Christ all the kingdoms of the world in a moment of time (*Matt.* 4: 8; *Luke* 4: 5).

(b) All who are without Christ and the new birth are under the authority and power of the devil and his agents (*Eph.* 6: 12; *I John* 5: 19)—to be outside of the Church of Christ is to belong to Satan (*I Cor.* 5: 5; *I Tim.* 1: 20).

(c) The whole world is in his power (*I John* 5: 19), for he is its ruler (*John* 12: 31; 14: 30; 16: 11; *II Cor.* 4: 4; *Eph.* 2: 2; 6: 12).

(d) Men and women have the devil as their father, and they are his children (*John* 8: 44; *I John* 3: 10).

(e) To be in his power is to be imprisoned, to be spiritually blind, and in spiritual darkness, under God's condemnation (*Acts* 26: 18).

(f) He is likened to a strong man, whose house contains men and women as chattels or goods. He must be bound before his house can be broken into (*Matt.* 12: 29; *Mark* 3: 27; *Luke* 11: 21, 22).

(g) His power is such that Christ prayed against him on behalf of His disciples (*John* 17: 15).

4. Some of the devil's characteristics.

(a) He is the enemy of all righteousness, full of deceit and villainy, whose activity is to make crooked the straight paths of the Lord (*Acts* 13: 10).

(b) He is wicked (*Matt.* 6: 13; *John* 17: 15; *I John* 2: 13, 14; 3: 12; 5: 18, 19).

(c) He is a liar and the father of lies (*John* 8: 44): he has nothing to do with the truth, because there is no truth in him.

(d) He is subtle and deceitful (*Gen.* 3: 1; *II Cor.* 11: 3, 4; *Eph.* 6: 11).

(e) He is proud and presumptuous (*I Tim.* 3: 6; *Job* 1: 6; *Matt.* 4: 5, 6).

(f) He is malignant: he makes malicious accusations and pleads false charges (*Job* 1: 6–12; 2: 4; *Zech.* 3: 1; *Rev.* 12: 9–11).

(g) He is fierce and cruel (*Luke* 8: 29; 9: 39, 42): he prowls around like a roaring lion (*I Pet.* 5: 8).

(h) He is a murderer (*John* 8: 44; *I John* 3: 12).

(i) His activity is ceaseless (*Rev.* 12: 10).

5. His activity in general.

(a) Sin is his characteristic activity (*I John* 3: 8): he was the originator of the Fall (*Gen.* 3: 1, 6, 14, 24).

(b) He is active in doing evil (*Job* 1: 7; 2: 2).

(c) He masquerades as an angel of light (*II Cor.* 11: 14), and so too do his agents (*II Cor.* 11: 15).

(d) He causes false beliefs to arise (*I Tim.* 5: 15): every anti-Christian movement and spirit is a result of his activity (*II Thess.* 2: 9).

(e) He encourages men in lies and deceit (*II Thess.* 2: 10; *Rev.* 3: 9).

(f) He engineers pretended signs and wonders and wicked deception (*II Thess.* 2: 9, 10; *Rev.* 16: 14).

(g) He misapplies the Scriptures to gain his own wicked ends (*Matt.* 4: 6).

(h) Through depending upon human wisdom rather than divine, men can become his agents without being aware of the fact (*Matt.* 16: 23; *Mark* 8: 33): the devil put it into the heart of Judas Iscariot to betray Jesus (*John* 13: 2).

(i) He opposes God's work (*Zech.* 3: 1; *Matt.* 13: 39; *I Thess.* 2: 18): especially the preaching of the gospel (*Matt.* 13: 19; *II Cor.* 4: 4; *Mark* 4: 15; *Luke* 8: 12).

6. His attacks upon Christians.

(a) He does battle against every individual who would keep God's commandments and bear testimony to Jesus (*Luke* 22: 31; *I Pet.* 5: 8, 9; *Rev.* 12: 17).

(b) He is always looking for an opportunity of causing trouble to the Christian (*Eph.* 6: 11; *I Tim.* 3: 7; *Jas.* 4: 7; *Rev.* 12: 10).

(c) He seeks to gain the advantage over believers (*II Cor.* 2: 11): he tells of the pleasures of sin but not of its consequences (*Gen.* 3: 4 f); he tells half-truths for the truth (*Gen.* 3: 5).

(d) He seeks to tempt believers by any means possible, trying one temptation after another (*Matt.* 4: 1–10; *Mark* 1: 13; *Luke* 4: 2, 13).

(e) He tempts along the line of the appetites frequently (*Gen.* 3: 1 ff; *Matt.* 4: 2, 3; *Luke* 4: 2, 3; *I Cor.* 7: 5).

(f) He tempts Christians to use spiritual powers selfishly (*Matt.* 4: 3; *Luke* 4: 3), and to presume upon God's care (*Matt.* 4: 5, 6; *Luke* 4: 9–11).

(g) He encourages doubts and questionings, together with compromise (*Gen.* 3: 1, 4; *Matt.* 4: 8, 9; *Luke* 4: 5, 6, 7).

(h) He gets at the Christians through their lack of balance (*I Cor.* 7: 5).

(i) He seeks to bewitch them so that they take their eyes off Christ crucified (*II Cor.* 11: 14; *Gal.* 3: 1).

(j) He would encourage them in evil—even to lie to the Holy Spirit (*Acts* 5: 3).

(k) He inspires the persecution of Christians (*Rev.* 2: 10, 13).

7. Christ's conquest of the devil at the Cross.

(a) The devil had no power over Christ (*John* 14: 30); his power and authority are inferior to those of Christ (*Mark* 3: 7; *Luke* 11: 19, 20, 21, 22).

(b) Christ partook of flesh and blood that through death He might destroy him who had the power of death, that is, the devil (*Heb.* 2: 14; *I John* 3: 8).

(c) Christ's conflict with the devil came to a head at the Cross: He disarmed the devil and all his powers, and made a public example of them at His resurrection, triumphing over them (*John* 12: 31; 16: 11; *Heb.* 2: 14; *Col.* 2: 15; *I John* 3: 8).

(d) So far as Christ is concerned, the devil is a conquered enemy (*Luke* 10: 18).

(e) Christ's people enter into His victory over the devil (*Rom.* 16: 20).

8. The devil's limits.

(a) The devil's power has been given to him, and can, therefore, be taken away from him by God (*Luke* 4: 6): he knows his time is short (*Rev.* 12: 12).

(b) He is allowed liberty, within bounds, to test and tempt Christians (*Job* 1: 1–12; 2: 1–6; *Luke* 22: 31; *II Cor.* 10: 13; *Rev.* 20: 2, 7).

(c) The Father is able to keep from the evil one those whom He has given to His Son out of the world (*John* 17: 15).

(d) His activity can even be used by God to accomplish some good purpose (*I Cor.* 5: 5; *II Cor.* 12: 7).

9. The devil's end.

(a) His final defeat will take place at the last day, and his ultimate condemnation and punishment are sure at the judgment of that day (*Jude* 6; *Rev.* 20: 10).

(b) He is to be crushed by God (*Rom.* 16: 20).

(c) Eternal fire is prepared for the devil and his angels at the final judgment (*Matt.* 25: 41).

10. Meanwhile, the devil is to be overcome by Christians.

(a) Christians are not to be ignorant of his devices (*II Cor.* 2: 11).

(b) They are dependent upon Christ's protection and activity on their behalf for deliverance from the devil (*Luke* 22: 31).

(c) The devil is overcome by the blood of the Lamb and by the word of Christians' testimony (*Rev.* 12: 11).

(d) As Christians resist the devil, he will flee from them (*Jas.* 4: 7).

(e) The spiritual equipment God provides for the Christian is alone sufficient to enable him to stand against the devil's wiles (*Eph.* 6: 11): using this equipment, the Christian cannot be defeated (*Eph.* 6: 13).

44. THE RETURN OF CHRIST

Question: Will Christ come again?

Answer: Christ will come again, as promised, at a time not told us, in the same way as He was seen to return to heaven.

1. Christ's second coming is clearly promised in the Bible.

(a) The Lord Jesus Christ Himself promised, "I will come again" (*John* 14: 3; *Matt.* 25: 31).

(b) His second coming is promised by the Old Testament prophets (*Dan.* 7: 13; *Zech.* 14: 5).

(c) The apostles bore witness to Christ's second coming (*Acts* 3: 20).

(d) Peter declares that Christ will be revealed (*I Pet.* 1: 13).

(e) John declares that Christ will appear and Christians will see Him (*I John* 3: 2).

(f) Paul preached with urgency in view of the appearing of our Lord Jesus Christ yet to come (*I Tim.* 6: 14).

(g) The Lord's Supper is intended to be a perpetual reminder of the Lord's second coming for it is an "interim" measure—it is "until He comes" (*I Cor.* 11: 26).

(h) A common greeting amongst the early Christians seems to have been "Maranatha"—"the Lord is coming" (*I Cor.* 16: 22).

2. Signs of Christ's coming again are indicated in the Bible.

(a) The second coming of Christ will be preceded by disturbances in nature, and distress among the nations (*Luke* 21: 25).

(b) There will be signs in sun and moon and stars (*Luke* 21: 25; *Matt.* 24: 29).

(c) The second coming will be preceded by concern and fear over coming events: men will faint with fear and with foreboding of what is coming to the world (*Luke* 21: 26).

(d) The second coming will be preceded by the appearance of many antichrists (*I John* 2: 18).

(e) Many shall depart from the faith and false teaching shall be on the increase (*I Tim.* 4: 1–3).

3. The precise time of Christ's second coming is not stated.

(a) It is natural for us to want to know the timing of everything (*Mark* 13: 4).

(b) But no one knows the day or the hour of Christ's second coming, except the Father (*Mark* 13: 32; *Matt.* 24: 36).

(c) We are not intended to know the exact time (*Acts* 1: 6, 7).

(d) Christ shall be sent by the Father at the appointed time (*Acts* 3: 20, 21).

(e) Christ's coming will be at the unexpected moment (*Matt.* 24: 44; *Luke* 12: 40)—in the twinkling of an eye (*I Cor.* 15: 51–52).

(f) His coming will be sudden (*Mark* 13: 36)—like lightning (*Matt.* 24: 27) or a thief in the night (*I Thess.* 5: 2; *II Pet.* 3: 10; *Rev.* 16: 15).

(g) The world will be totally unprepared for the second coming of Christ even as it was unprepared for the coming of the flood (*Matt.* 24: 38).

(h) There is no delay about the Lord's coming (*Heb.* 10: 37): the only reason for any appearance of delay in the Lord's return is His forbearance, in that He does not wish that any should perish, but that all should reach repentance (*II Pet.* 3: 9).

(i) The coming of the Lord Jesus draws near with the passing of each day (*Heb.* 10: 25).

(j) His coming will be soon (*Rev.* 22: 7, 12, 20).

(k) His coming is always to be considered as being at hand (*Rom.* 13: 12; *Phil.* 4: 5; *I Pet.* 4: 7).

4. We are told something of the manner in which Christ will come.

(a) He will come in the same way

as He was seen to go into heaven (*Acts* 1: 9, 11).

(b) He will come from heaven (*Acts* 3: 21; *Phil.* 3: 20; *I Thess.* 1: 10; 4: 16).

(c) He will come visibly (*Matt.* 24: 30; *Mark* 13: 26; 14: 62; *I John* 3: 2; *Rev.* 1: 7).

(d) He will come openly (*Matt.* 24: 27), and personally (*Acts* 1: 11) —His coming will mean His presence after His absence (*John* 14: 2, 3).

(e) He will come in clouds with power and great glory (*Matt.* 24: 30; 26: 64; *Rev.* 1: 7)—the glory of His Father (*Matt.* 16: 27).

(f) He will come with His angels (*Matt.* 16: 27; 25: 31; *Mark* 8: 38; *II Thess.* 1: 7), and with all His saints, in flaming fire (*I Thess.* 3: 13; *II Thess.* 1: 8).

5. Christ's second coming should influence Christians in their character and conduct continually.

(a) We are to rest the full weight of our hopes on the grace that will be ours when the Lord Jesus Christ returns (*I Pet.* 1: 13).

(b) We are to anticipate the sight of the Lord Jesus Christ (*I Pet.* 1: 8).

(c) We are to love His appearing (*II Tim.* 4: 8), looking (*Phil.* 3: 20; *Tit.* 2: 13), waiting (*I Cor.* 1: 7; *I Thess.* 1: 10) and praying for it (*Rev.* 22: 20).

(d) Having this hope before us, we shall find ourselves stimulated to pursue holiness (*I Thess.* 3: 13; *II Pet.* 3: 11, 12; *I John* 3: 3).

(e) Our conduct will be influenced and regulated by this truth as it is ever before us (*I Pet.* 4: 7–11).

(f) We shall use the apparent "delay" to bring about men's salvation by the preaching of the gospel (*II Pet.* 3: 15), at the same time hastening the coming of the Lord by this activity (*II Pet.* 3: 12).

(g) We shall aim at being ready for the Lord Jesus when He comes (*Matt.* 24: 42; 25: 6; *Mark* 13: 33, 35–37; *Luke* 12: 40; 21: 36).

(h) We shall always act and live remembering that time is short (*I Cor.* 7: 29).

(i) We need constantly reminding of Christ's coming (*Rev.* 22: 7, 12, 20).

6. Unbelievers find the Second Coming a cause for scoffing.

(a) Unbelievers often scoff at Christ's coming (*II Pet.* 3: 3, 4).

(b) Men, who prefer to follow their own passions, scoff at the promise of Christ's coming, deliberately ignoring the Word of God (*II Pet.* 3: 3–7).

(c) Unbelievers shall, nevertheless, be overtaken and surprised by the reality of the Lord's second coming (*Matt.* 24: 37–39; *I Thess.* 5: 2; *II Pet.* 3: 10).

45. THE CONSEQUENCES OF CHRIST'S RETURN

Question: What will happen when Christ returns?

Answer: Christ's glory will be seen, and the resurrection of the dead and the transformation of all believers will take place. The judgment will follow, with the final division of all men and women, either to being with Christ for ever or to suffering the punishment of eternal destruction

and exclusion from the presence of the Lord. The end of all things as we know them will come, and the Father will be glorified in it all.

1. Christ's glory will be seen.

(a) The second coming will be an occasion of glory for Christ (*Matt.* 25: 31).

(b) Everyone will see Him (*Mark* 13: 26; *Rev.* 1: 7).

(c) He will be seen sitting at the right hand of Power, and coming with the clouds of heaven (*Mark* 14: 62).

(d) His glory will be revealed to the world (*I Pet.* 4: 13).

(e) He will be glorified amongst His own and adored among all believers (*II Thess.* 1: 10).

2. The resurrection of the dead will take place, and the transformation of all believers.

(a) Christ's grace will be revealed to believers in a manner unknown before (*I Pet.* 1: 13).

(b) The completeness of the Christian's salvation will be revealed (*Heb.* 9: 28; *I Pet.* 1: 5).

(c) A most important aspect of this completeness will be the resurrection of the dead (*I Cor.* 15: 23, 51–54).

(d) Christians shall be made like Christ (*I John* 3: 2): at His coming the Lord Jesus Christ will change our lowly bodies to be like His glorious body, by the power which enables Him to make all things subject to Himself (*Phil.* 3: 21).

3. Following the resurrection of the dead, believers will be gathered together.

(a) At His coming Christ will gather together all believers (*Matt.*

24: 31; *I Thess.* 2: 19; 3: 13; 4: 15–17; 5: 23; *I John* 2: 28).

(b) Christ will send out the angels and gather His elect from the farthest bounds of earth to the farthest bounds of heaven (*Mark* 13: 27).

(c) Christ will gather His people to Himself (*II Thess.* 2: 1)—both those who had died before His coming and those alive on earth at the time (*I Thess.* 4: 16, 17; *John* 14: 2, 3).

(d) The gathering together of all His people is likened to the gathering in of the harvest (*Rev.* 14: 14–16).

4. Then the judgment will be held.

(a) Every man and woman will acknowledge Christ as the Lord (*Phil.* 2: 9–11) and therefore as the supreme judge (*Acts* 17: 31).

(b) The second coming will be a time of reckoning (*Luke* 12: 40–48).

(c) Christ will be ashamed of those who have been ashamed of Him, and of His words in this adulterous and sinful world (*Mark* 8: 38).

(d) He will bring to light, at His coming, the things now hidden in darkness and will disclose the purposes of the heart (*I Cor.* 4: 5).

(e) His coming will bring distress to some, because of the judgment He will bring (*Rev.* 1: 7).

(f) The Lord's coming will mean the giving of account to Christ by Christians (*I Thess.* 2: 19): this giving account will not be with regard to the condemnation they deserve because of sin (*Rom.* 5: 1; 8: 1) but as to the rewards they shall receive on account of faithfulness to Christ (*I Cor.* 3: 8, 14).

5. The final division of men and women will come after the judgment.

(a) Men and women without the knowledge of God and who have refused to obey the gospel of our Lord Jesus Christ shall suffer the punishment of eternal destruction and exclusion from the presence of the Lord and from the glory of His might (*II Thess.* 1: 8, 9).

(b) The judgment of God will be executed by God's angels on unbelievers (*Rev.* 14: 17–20).

(c) Believers will enter into the full wonder of everlasting life and the enjoyment of God's presence for ever (*II Thess.* 1: 10; *I Thess.* 4: 17).

(d) Christ will take believers to Himself that where He is they may be also (*John* 14: 2, 3).

6. The end of all things as we now know them will take place.

(a) The coming of the Lord will herald the end of things as we know them on this earth (*II Pet.* 3: 7, 10, 11, 12, 13).

(b) The heavens will pass away with a loud noise, and the elements will be dissolved with fire, and the earth and the works that are upon it will be burned up (*II Pet* 3: 10).

(c) After the dissolution of this world, there will be revealed new heavens and a new earth in which righteousness dwells (*II Pet.* 3: 13).

7. The Father will be glorified in all that happens.

(a) All that He ever spoke by the mouth of His holy prophets shall be established (*Acts* 3: 21).

(b) As all men and women will be compelled to confess Christ as Lord, that act will have one great end—the glory of God the Father (*Phil.* 2: 11).

(c) After destroying every rule and every authority and power, there will come the end of all the events connected with Christ's coming, when Christ will deliver the kingdom to God the Father (*I Cor.* 15: 24).

(d) When all things are subjected to Christ, then He Himself will be subjected to the Father who put all things under Christ (*I Cor.* 15: 28).

46. THE JUDGMENT

Question: What will happen at the judgment?

Answer: Christ will be the Judge and all will appear before Him. The perfect justice of God and the undeniable guilt of all men and women will be plain and beyond dispute. Those justified through faith in Christ will be acquitted from the guilt of sin and will receive rewards according to their faithfulness; the unbelieving will receive their final condemnation.

1. The timing of the judgment.

(a) Our Lord Jesus Christ spoke of a judgment which was still future (*Matt.* 12: 41).

(b) Judgment is the certainty which follows men after death (*Heb.* 9: 27).

(c) God has fixed a day on which He will judge the world by righteousness by a man whom He has appointed, and of this He has given assurance to everyone by raising Him from the dead (*Acts* 17: 31; *Rom.* 2: 16).

(d) The judgment will take place at the coming of the Lord Jesus Christ (*Matt.* 25: 31 ff; *II Tim.* 4: 1; *II Pet.* 3: 7).

(e) The judgment will be preceded by the resurrection of the dead (*John* 5: 28, 29).

(f) The day of judgment will be followed by the dissolution, by means of fire, of the heavens and earth that now exist, according to God's promise (*II Pet.* 3: 7).

2. Christ will be the Judge.

(a) God the Father judges no one (*John* 5: 22), but has committed to the Son the task of judging all men and women (*John* 5: 22, 27).

(b) The Lord Jesus Christ is the One ordained of God to be the Judge of the living and the dead (*Acts* 10: 42; *II Tim.* 4: 1).

(c) The separation of the wheat from the chaff (*Matt.* 3: 12; *Luke* 3: 17), and the sheep from the goats (*Matt.* 25: 32, 33) will be His responsibility.

(d) Christ will come the second time, therefore, as Judge (*Matt.* 25: 31–46).

3. All will appear before the judgment seat.

(a) The Old Testament declares that God will judge the righteous and the wicked, for He has appointed a time for every matter and for every work (*Eccl.* 3: 17).

(b) Judgment will be held on all nations (*Matt.* 25: 32; *Joel* 3: 12).

(c) The judgment will include all men and women (*Heb.* 9: 27)— the small and the great (*Rev.* 20: 12), the living and the dead (*II Tim.* 4: 1; *I Pet.* 4: 5).

(d) We must all appear before the judgment-seat of God, so that we may each one receive good or evil, according to our faith and works (*Rom.* 14: 10, 12; *II Cor.* 5: 10).

(e) The fallen angels will also be finally judged at the judgment (*II Pet.* 2: 4; *Jude* 6).

4. The perfect justice of God will be seen.

(a) The judgment is pictured as a harvest—there will be no doubt which is wheat and which is chaff (*Joel* 3: 13; *Matt.* 3: 12; *Luke* 3: 17).

(b) God's just judgment will be revealed (*Rom.* 2: 5; 3: 4–6)—the judgment shall be in righteousness (*Ps.* 98: 9; *Acts* 17: 31).

(c) God's judgment will be a precise and just retribution (*Obad.* 15), perfectly related to people's ways and deeds (*Hos.* 12: 2), and according to God's perfect records (*Dan.* 7: 10; *Rev.* 20: 12).

(d) The judgment will be in proportion to the opportunities and privileges of men and women: every one to whom much has been given will find much is required (*Luke* 12: 48).

(e) The judgment will be individual and personal (*Matt.* 25: 42–45).

(f) God will render to every man according to his works (*Rom.* 2: 6).

(g) Those who have had no opportunity of knowing the law given to Moses, or the gospel, will be judged according to the law of conscience (*Rom.* 2: 12, 14, 15).

(h) All who have had the law of Moses will be judged by it (*Rom.* 2: 12).

(i) Neglected opportunities of repentance and faith increase the condemnation men and women shall experience at the judgment (*Matt.* 11: 20–24; *Luke* 11: 31, 32).

(j) If men and women have sinned deliberately after receiving the knowledge of the truth, their condemnation will be all the worse (*Heb.* 10: 26).

(k) Although all our questions about the judgment cannot be answered now, we know that the Judge of all the earth will do right (*Gen.* 18: 25).

5. The guilt of all will be plain.

(a) Account will be rendered for words spoken (*Matt.* 12: 36).

(b) Every secret thing, including the purposes of the heart, will be brought under judgment (*Eccl.* 12: 14; *I Cor.* 4: 5).

(c) Actions will be judged (*Eccl.* 11: 9; 12: 14; *Rev.* 20: 13) and the ill deeds of men and women shall return upon their heads (*Obad.* 15, 16).

(d) None can stand before such a judgment and deserve to live (*Ps.* 130: 3), for no living man is righteous before God (*Ps.* 143: 2) on the grounds of what he is in himself.

(e) All will be found guilty: those without the law have perverted the light which comes from nature (*Rom.* 1: 21 ff), and those with the law have failed to keep it (*Gal.* 3: 10–12).

(f) No one will have anything to say in self-defence—all excuses will die upon men's lips (*Rom.* 3: 19).

(g) The word of Christ will be a witness against those who have rejected Christ and refused His sayings (*John* 12: 48).

(h) The judgment is clearly a fearful prospect (*Heb.* 10: 27).

(i) The first part of the judgment will be the separation of those who have accepted God's way of salvation from those who have gone about to gain salvation by dependence on their own efforts (*Matt.* 25: 31–33).

(j) Those whose names are in the book of life shall escape the judgment of condemnation on account of sin (*Luke* 10: 20; *Phil.* 4: 3; *Rev.* 20: 12; 21: 27) because, having seen the folly of trusting in their own righteousness (*Isa.* 64: 6), through faith in Christ they have become the righteousness of God in Him (*II Cor.* 5: 21).

6. Acquittal from the guilt of sin will be granted to those who have been justified by faith.

(a) The final judgment will be determined by works and faith in Christ (*Rev.* 20: 13–15).

(b) There is no condemnation for those who are justified by faith in the Lord Jesus Christ (*Rom.* 5: 1; 8: 1).

(c) Christians have complete confidence for the day when Christ shall judge all men and women (*I John* 4: 7; *John* 5: 25); they will not be ashamed at His coming (*I John* 2: 28).

(d) Christ will acknowledge Christians openly in the presence of the Father (*Matt.* 25: 34–40; *Rev.* 3: 5), presenting them guiltless (*I Cor.* 1: 8; *I Thess.* 3: 13), having declared them free from sin (*Rom.* 8: 1, 33, 34).

(e) The key to deliverance from this judgment, therefore, is a personal relationship to the Lord Jesus Christ (*Matt.* 10: 32, 33; *Mark* 8: 38; *Heb.* 10: 29).

(f) Salvation from the judgment

which sin deserves is possible through the Lord Jesus Christ alone (*I Thess.* 5: 9, 10).

(g) Having been acquitted from all guilt, Christians will join with Christ in the judgment of the world (*I Cor.* 6: 2; compare *Matt.* 19: 28; *Luke* 22: 28 ff; *Dan.* 7: 22; *Rev.* 20: 4).

7. Those who have refused to acknowledge God and to obey the gospel of our Lord Jesus Christ will be condemned.

(a) Eternal judgment is a first principle, an elementary doctrine, of the gospel (*Heb.* 6: 2; *Acts* 24: 25).

(b) The children of the wicked one will be revealed and their destiny made known (*Matt.* 13: 24–30, 36–43, 47–50).

(c) The judgment will be a time of misery for those who have rejected the Lord Jesus Christ (*Rev.* 1: 7; *II Thess.* 1: 8, 9).

(d) Those who have disobeyed the truth and obeyed wickedness will experience the wrath of God and eternal punishment (*Rom.* 2: 8; *Jude* 15; *Rev.* 20: 15).

(e) The punishment of evildoers will be final and complete (*Matt.* 13: 40–42; 25: 46).

(f) No one will be able to resist the judgment (*Matt.* 3: 12; *Luke* 3: 17; *Amos* 9: 1–4).

8. Christians will be rewarded by Christ.

(a) To those who by patience in well-doing seek for glory and honour and immortality, Christ will give eternal life (*Rom.* 2: 7; *Jude* 24; *Rev.* 20: 12, 15).

(b) He will come as the righteous Judge, judging His people by the gospel—the law of liberty (*Jas.* 2: 12)—that He may reward them for their faithfulness (*II Tim.* 4: 8; *Jas.* 1: 12; *Luke* 19: 17, 19).

(c) Every Christian's service will be subject to scrutiny and examination (*I Cor.* 3: 9–14): there will be rewards for faithful service (*I Cor.* 3: 9–13; *II Tim.* 4: 8; *Rev.* 11: 18).

(d) Christians will discover the value of the work they have done for Christ (*II Cor.* 1: 14; *Phil.* 2: 16).

9. The effect the knowledge of the coming judgment should have upon Christians.

(a) The certainty of judgment is a great incentive to urgent preaching (*II Cor.* 5: 11; *II Tim.* 4: 1, 2).

(b) Unbelievers are to be warned of the future judgment (*Acts* 24: 25): this warning provides an incentive to repentance (*Acts* 17: 30, 31) and to faith in Christ (*Isa.* 28: 16, 17; *John* 3: 17, 18).

(c) The certainty of the judgment is an incentive to holiness (*II Pet.* 3: 11, 14): the fact that Christians must stand too before the judgment seat of Christ is not to promote fear but the desire to please Him now, so that they may be pleasing to Him then (*II Cor.* 5: 9, 10).

47. THE RESURRECTION OF THE BODY

Question: Will our bodies be raised to life again?

Answer: All will rise from the dead, believers to the resurrection of life, and unbelievers to the resurrection of judgment. Christ's resurrection will be the pattern of the believer's.

1. **There will be a resurrection both of the righteous and the wicked.**

(a) The resurrection of the dead will take place at the second coming of the Lord Jesus Christ (*I Cor*. 15: 23; *I Thess*. 4: 14).

(b) The resurrection of the dead is a fundamental part of the Christian gospel (*I Cor*. 15: 12, 13; *Heb*. 6: 2).

(c) Many of the details of the resurrection of the dead are not revealed to us (*I Cor*. 15: 51) but it will take place by the power of God (*Matt*. 22: 29), who gives life to the dead and calls into existence the things that do not exist (*Rom*. 4: 17).

(d) The resurrection of the dead will take place in a moment, in the twinkling of an eye (*I Cor*. 15: 52).

(e) The actual fact of resurrection will be true of everyone: all in the tombs and graves will hear Christ's voice, and come forth, those who have done good, to the resurrection of life, and those who have done evil, to the resurrection of judgment (*John* 5: 28, 29).

(f) For some the resurrection of the dead will mean awaking to everlasting life and for some to shame and everlasting contempt (*Dan*. 12: 2).

(g) There will be a resurrection of both the just and the unjust (*Acts* 24: 15), of those whose names are in the book of life and those whose names are not (*Rev*. 20: 11–15).

(h) The Scriptures assure us of the resurrection of the dead (*Matt*. 22: 29).

(i) The resurrection of the dead was anticipated and promised in the Old Testament:

(i) It was hinted at in God's words to Moses, "I am the God of Abraham, the God of Isaac, and the God of Jacob" (*Ex*. 3: 6; *Matt*. 22: 32).

(ii) It was promised that the dead should live, their bodies should rise (*Isa*. 26: 19).

(iii) It was promised that many of those who sleep in the dust of the earth should awake, some to everlasting life, and some to shame and everlasting contempt (*Dan*. 12: 2).

(j) The Lord Jesus Christ spoke of raising up believers at the last day (*John* 6: 39, 40, 44).

(k) By His own resurrection Christ abolished death and brought life and immortality to light through the gospel (*II Tim*. 1: 10)—the Christian confidence concerning the resurrection of the dead springs from Christ's resurrection (*I Cor*. 15: 12, 13, 15, 16).

(l) The apostles preached the resurrection of the dead through Jesus (*Acts* 4: 2).

2. **Addressed as it is to Christian believers, the New Testament concentrates on the resurrection of believers.**

(a) Christ will raise up at the last day all who have believed in Him and inherited eternal life, according to the will of the Father (*John* 6: 40).

(b) By God's great mercy Christians have been born anew to a living hope through the resurrection of Jesus Christ from the dead (*I Pet*. 1: 3)—Christians are children of the resurrection (*Luke* 20: 36).

(c) Christ's resurrection is the pledge of the believer's resurrection (*II Cor*. 4: 14).

(d) That there should be no

resurrection of the dead is inconceivable in the light of Christ's resurrection (*I Cor.* 15: 12).

(e) Even as Christ was raised from the dead, so shall believers be raised (*I Cor.* 15: 20): by Christ, the man, has come the resurrection of the dead, even as by man came death (*I Cor.* 15: 21).

(f) The precise details of the resurrection of the dead will cause some to question, almost inevitably (*I Cor.* 15: 35)—"How will it happen? With what kind of body do they come?"

(g) The resurrection body will be something quite beyond our present experience (*I Cor.* 15: 35–37): there will, for example, be no marriage after the resurrection, and thus sexual relations will end (*Mark* 12: 25).

(h) Harvest provides us with an illustration of the kind of thing that will happen at the resurrection: the body that is sown is not the body which shall be, but the two are directly related (*I Cor.* 15: 36, 37).

(i) The resurrection body will be a real body: even as to every kind of creature and thing God has given a particular body, so He has determined the particular nature of the resurrection body (*I Cor.* 15: 38–42).

(j) The perishable body sown in death will be raised imperishable (*I Cor.* 15: 42); the body sown in dishonour at death will be raised in glory (*I Cor.* 15: 43); the body sown in weakness will be raised in power (*I Cor.* 15: 43): the physical body sown in death will be raised a spiritual body (*I Cor.* 15: 44).

(k) Even as the physical body bore the image of the man of dust—of Adam—so the spiritual body will bear the image of the man of heaven—Christ (*I Cor.* 15: 49).

(l) Believers will all be changed at the resurrection of the dead (*I Cor.* 15: 51): the imperishable will replace the perishable; the immortal will replace the mortal (*I Cor.* 15: 53).

(m) The dead in Christ shall rise first, being given their resurrection bodies (*I Thess.* 4: 16); and then shall all living believers be caught up together to meet the Lord in the air; and so we shall always be with the Lord (*I Thess.* 4: 17).

(n) Those still alive at Christ's coming will experience the change of body necessary to their entry into heaven (*Phil.* 3: 21)—that is to say, they will be given a body identical with those raised from the dead.

(o) The resurrection of the dead will be followed by entry into God's presence (*II Cor.* 4: 14): from the resurrection of the dead onwards we shall be forever with the Lord (*I Thess.* 4: 17).

3. **The resurrection of Christ tells us something of the nature of the resurrection body of the believer.**

(a) Christians shall be like Christ (*I John* 3: 2): Christ will change their lowly body to be made like His glorious body by the power which enables Him even to subject all things to Himself (*Phil.* 3: 21).

(b) From what we are told (*I John* 3: 2; *Phil.* 3: 21), we know that the resurrection body will be like Christ's resurrection body.

(c) Our Lord's resurrection body seems to have been similar to His body as it was before:

104

(i) The disciples were able to hold the Lord Jesus by the feet as they worshipped Him (*Matt.* 28: 9).

(ii) He could be handled (*Luke* 24: 40; *John* 20: 27).

(d) But Christ's body was clearly different in some ways:

(i) His body appears to have passed through the grave clothes (*John* 20: 6, 7).

(ii) When He walked on the road to Emmaus with the two disciples they did not immediately recognise Him (*Luke* 24: 13–35).

(iii) He was able to eat food, if He desired (*Luke* 24: 41–43).

(iv) He was able to pass through shut doors (*John* 20: 19, 26).

(e) Uncertain of so many aspects not yet revealed to us about the resurrection of the body, of the fact of it we are certain, for Christ was the first-fruits, by His own resurrection, of the resurrection of the dead to come (*I Cor.* 15: 20, 23).

4. The encouragement which the assurance of the resurrection brings to the believer.

(a) The resurrection of the dead is a tremendous comfort to the Christian (*I Thess.* 4: 18)—those who have fallen asleep in Christ have not perished (*I Cor.* 15: 18).

(b) The resurrection of the dead is a great encouragement to our continuance in service (*I Cor.* 15: 58).

(c) The assurance of life after death means that life here and now is not thought precious if it is endangered for the sake of the gospel—the reward of this life can be reaped in the life to come (*I Cor.* 15: 32).

(d) The assurance of the resurrection of the dead makes a difference to conduct (*I Cor.* 15: 33).

(e) The assurance of the resurrection of the dead takes away fear of death—it gives men a confidence in the face of death and the terrors which can be associated with it (*I Cor.* 15: 31; *Heb.* 11: 35).

(f) Christians are to be envied indeed for the glorious assurance they have of resurrection on the grounds of Christ's (*I Cor.* 15: 19).

48. LIFE AFTER DEATH

Question: What happens when we die?

Answer: The body returns, as dust, to the earth as it was, and the spirit returns to God. The body may be described as asleep, and for the Christian the return of the spirit to God means to be consciously with Christ.

1. The body sleeps.

(a) The picture of sleep is frequently used of the dead (*Matt.* 9: 24; 27: 52; *John* 11: 11; *I Cor.* 11: 30; *I Thess.* 4: 13).

(b) The description of the dead as asleep would seem to have particular reference to the body rather than the spirit: at death the body returns to dust, and the spirit to God (*Eccl.* 12: 7); whilst the body may sleep (*Acts* 7: 60), the spirit may be with God (*Acts* 7: 59).

(c) To die before the coming again of the Lord Jesus is to leave the flesh (*Phil.* 1: 24).

(d) The human body is but a temporary shelter for the human

spirit, to be replaced by something better (*II Cor.* 5: 1–5).

2. The spirit lives.

(a) It is important to remember that, for the Christian, eternal life has begun already: he who has heard Christ's word and believed God who sent Him, has eternal life; he does not come into judgment, but has passed from death to life (*John* 5: 24).

(b) The soul—"soul" and "spirit" are often used as meaning the same—is not affected by the death of the body (*Matt.* 10: 28).

(c) That the dead lived in spirit was implied in the Old Testament (*Ex.* 3: 6; *Matt.* 22: 32).

(d) Death is gain for the Christian (*Phil.* 1: 21).

(e) When the Christian dies, he lives; in fact, he cannot really die (*John* 11: 25, 26).

3. The Christian's spirit is immediately with Christ from the moment of death.

(a) Jesus told the penitent thief, "Today you will be with Me in Paradise" (*Luke* 23: 43).

(b) Statements made by the apostle Paul have no meaning unless they speak of conscious existence immediately following death:

(i) To be away from the body is to be at home with the Lord (*II Cor.* 5: 8);

(ii) To die and to be with Christ is far better than to continue ordinary human existence (*Phil.* 1: 23);

(iii) The spirit is with Christ, and is made perfect (*Heb.* 12: 23).

(c) In the light of what we have seen from the Scriptures we may say that the Christian who has died before the coming of the Lord Jesus is without his body, but has conscious enjoyment of the Lord's presence. Even as the Lord Jesus Christ was quickened in His human spirit before His body was raised from the tomb (*I Pet.* 3: 19), so the Christian's quickened spirit awaits the day of resurrection when it will be united with the resurrection body.

4. Death holds no fear for the Christian.

(a) Our Lord Jesus Christ has abolished death for the Christian (*II Tim.* 1: 10; *Heb.* 2: 14).

(b) The Christian shall never taste real death (*John* 8: 51; 11: 26).

(c) Death cannot separate the Christian from God (*Rom.* 8: 38, 39).

(d) Death has lost both its victory and its sting (*I Cor.* 15: 55).

(e) Victory over death is so complete that it can be described as belonging to the Christian (*I Cor.* 3: 22).

(f) The Christian's attitude to death is the very opposite of despair (*Phil.* 1: 21–23).

(g) The Christian, seeing things aright, would rather be away from the body, and at home with the Lord (*II Cor.* 5: 8).

49. HEAVEN

Question: What do we know about heaven?

Answer: Heaven is the eternal dwelling place of God and of His angels, the place from which Christ came at His Incarnation and to which He returned at His Ascension.

All the language the Bible uses to describe heaven expresses the perfection of the eternal life which Christians will experience there. With such assurance may Christians regard it as their eternal home that they are described as citizens of heaven whilst here on earth.

1. Heaven is the eternal dwelling place of God (*Matt.* 5: 16; 12: 50; *Rev.* 3: 12; 11: 13; 20: 9) and of His angels (*Matt.* 18: 10; 22: 30; *Rev.* 3: 5).

(a) The Father is said to be "in heaven" (*Matt.* 5: 45; 6: 1, 9; 7: 11, 21b; 10: 33; 12: 50; 16: 17; 18: 10b, 14, 19; *Mark* 11: 25 f).

(b) He is the architect and maker of heaven (*Heb.* 11: 10)—He is the Lord of heaven (*Dan.* 5: 23; *Matt.* 11: 25).

(c) He reigns in heaven (*Ps.* 11: 4): He does according to His will in the host of heaven and among the inhabitants of the earth (*Dan.* 4: 35; *Ps.* 135: 6).

(d) He fills heaven (*I Kings* 8: 27; *Jer.* 23: 24); His glory (*Acts* 7: 55) and His majesty (*Heb.* 8: 1) are manifested there.

(e) Heaven is the place from which God speaks to men today (*Heb.* 12: 25); He answers His people from heaven (*I Chron.* 21: 26; *II Chron.* 7: 14; *Neh.* 9: 27; *Ps.* 20: 6).

(f) God sends His judgments from heaven (*Gen.* 19: 24; *I Sam.* 2: 10; *Dan.* 4: 13, 14; *Rom.* 1: 18).

2. Christ came from heaven and returned to heaven.

(a) From heaven Christ came to become Incarnate (*John* 3: 13, 31, 32; 6: 38, 42, 50; *I Cor.* 15: 47).

(b) At His Ascension He returned to heaven (*Mark* 16: 19; *I Pet.* 3: 22).

(c) Heaven, since the Ascension, is the scene of His present life and activity (*Acts* 7: 55; *Eph.* 6: 9; *Heb.* 8: 1).

(d) At God's right hand, He pleads the cause of His people (*Rom.* 8: 34; *Heb.* 9: 24).

(e) He prepares a place in the Father's house for His people (*John* 14: 2, 3).

(f) He is all-powerful in heaven (*Matt.* 28: 18): angels, authorities, and powers have been made subject to Him (*I Pet.* 3: 22).

(g) He is the King of heaven (*Matt.* 25: 40).

(h) From heaven He will descend at His second coming (*I Thess.* 4: 16; *Phil.* 3: 20; *Matt.* 24: 30; *II Thess.* 1: 7).

3. Heaven is not part of this creation and is quite different from it (*Heb.* 9: 11). We must distinguish "heaven" from "the heavens" where birds, clouds, sun and stars, etc., are to be found.

(a) Heaven is the place of the "real" (*Heb.* 8: 5).

(b) Heaven is a place of peace (*Luke* 19: 38).

(c) Heaven is holy (*Deut.* 26: 15; *Ps.* 20: 6; *Isa.* 57: 15).

(d) Heaven is everlasting (*Ps.* 89: 29).

(e) Heaven is indescribable in its happiness and satisfaction (*Rev.* 7: 17).

4. Descriptions given of heaven to aid our understanding.

(a) It is described as paradise (*II Cor.* 12: 2, 4).

(b) It is likened to a granary—

Christians being the wheat (*Matt.* 3: 12).

(c) It is called the Father's house (*John* 14: 2).

(d) It is described as a city, prepared by God for His people (*Heb.* 11: 16)—Mount Zion, the city of the living God, heavenly Jerusalem (*Heb.* 12: 22).

(e) It is described as a heavenly country—better than anything known on earth (*Heb.* 11: 16).

(f) It is described as a rest (*Heb.* 4: 9).

(g) It is described as the Christian's inheritance (*I Pet.* 1: 4; *Matt.* 25: 34).

5. The grounds of entry into heaven.

(a) The inheritance of heaven is not by legal right but by promise (*Gal.* 3: 18).

(b) Those who inherit it will recognise that they do not deserve to do so by reason of their own merits (*Matt.* 25: 37–39).

(c) All who gain entry into heaven do so on the grounds of the mediation of Jesus Christ and the efficacy of His sacrifice (*Heb.* 12: 24).

(d) Heaven will be made up of those of every nation and tongue who have been redeemed by Christ (*Matt.* 25: 32; *Rev.* 5: 9, 10).

6. Entry into heaven is impossible for some.

(a) Entry is impossible for those who are not "born again" (*John* 3: 3).

(b) Those whose lives are characterised by the works of the flesh have no place there (*Gal.* 5: 19–21; *Eph.* 5: 5).

(c) The devil and his angels can have no place in heaven (*Matt.* 25: 41).

7. What heaven will mean to the Christian.

(a) To enter heaven will be to be blessed of the Father (*Matt.* 25: 34).

(b) There he shall have the things he has hoped for (*Col.* 1: 5).

(c) In heaven he will be perfect and holy, and thus able to see the Lord (*Heb.* 12: 14).

(d) In heaven he will have his glorified body (*II Cor.* 5: 1).

(e) He will be able to look upon Christ's glory (*John* 17: 24).

(f) He will receive his reward (*Matt.* 5: 12; 25: 34–40; *Heb.* 10: 34, 35).

(g) He will enjoy never-failing treasure which he has laid up for himself (*Matt.* 6: 20; *Luke* 12: 33).

(h) The partial will have vanished and wholeness will have come (*I Cor.* 13: 10).

(i) His knowledge will be whole, like God's knowledge of him now (*I Cor.* 13: 9, 10).

(j) All the puzzles of this human life will be resolved (*I Cor.* 13: 12).

8. The relationship of the Christian to heaven now.

(a) He is an heir of heaven: since the foundation of the world God has been preparing it for him and all like him redeemed by Christ (*Matt.* 25: 34).

(b) His name is enrolled in heaven (*Luke* 10: 20; *Heb.* 12: 23)—a ground for true rejoicing.

(c) He is a citizen of heaven (*Phil.* 3: 20).

(d) He knows heaven to be his true home (*Heb.* 13: 14).

9. The effect the fact of heaven should have upon the Christian.

(a) There should be a great longing for heaven in his heart (*Heb.* 11: 16; cf. 11: 10).

(b) He should set his standards by those of heaven—as he knows them from the Scriptures—rather than by those of this world for he knows his citizenship is in heaven (*Phil.* 3: 20).

(c) He should hold loosely to his earthly possessions, never allowing them to be all-important (*Heb.* 10: 34).

(d) He should let his thoughts dwell on that high realm, where Christ is, rather than on this earthly life (*Col.* 3: 2).

50. HELL

Question: What do we know about hell?

Answer: Hell is the place of everlasting punishment and banishment from God's presence, the future dwelling place of all who have neglected God and disobeyed the gospel of Christ.

1. Hell is the place of banishment and punishment.

(a) Hell is the place of banishment from God's presence (*Matt.* 7: 23; 25: 41).

(b) It is the sphere of the manifestation of the wrath to come, from which Christ delivers the believer (*I Thess.* 1: 10); there there will be the revelation from heaven of the wrath of God against all ungodliness and unrighteousness (*Rom.* 1: 18).

(c) To be cast into hell is to be separated from Christ, to be cursed, to be cast into the eternal fire prepared for the devil and his angels, and to be eternally punished (*Matt.* 25: 41, 46).

(d) Hell means eternal exclusion from the radiance of the face of the Lord and the glorious majesty of His power (*II Thess.* 1: 9).

(e) A person's presence in hell is the direct result of his choices made during his earthly life (*Luke* 16: 19–31).

(f) It is the dwelling place of all who have lived their human life neglecting God (*Ps.* 9: 17).

(g) The cowardly, the faithless, and the vile, murderers, fornicators, idolators and liars of every kind will be cast into hell (*Rev.* 21: 8), that is to say, those who do not know God and do not obey the gospel of our Lord Jesus Christ (*II Thess.* 1: 8, 9).

(h) The body suffers in hell (*Matt.* 5: 29).

(i) The soul suffers also in hell (*Matt.* 10: 28).

(j) The punishment of hell is eternal (*Isa.* 33: 14; *Rev.* 20: 10).

(k) There is no transfer from hell to heaven (*Luke* 16: 26).

(l) We are born on the road to hell, and the majority remain upon it (*Matt.* 7: 13, 14).

2. The descriptions given of hell in the Bible.

(a) Hell is described as a dark imprisonment (*II Pet.* 2: 4) and outer darkness (*Matt.* 22: 13).

(b) It is like a bottomless pit (*Rev.* 9: 1).

(c) It is a place of bondage, darkness and weeping (*Matt.* 22: 13).

(d) It is like fire—everlasting burnings (*Isa.* 33: 14), unquenchable *Matt.* 3: 12; *Mark* 9: 44), a furnace (*Matt.* 13: 42), devouring (*Isa.* 33: 14), everlasting (*Matt.* 18: 8; 25: 41), a lake of fire (*Rev.* 20: 14).

(e) It is a place of torment (*Luke* 16: 23)—there is no rest, day or night (*Rev.* 14: 10, 11).

3. The right attitude to hell.

(a) God has no desire that men should remain on the road to hell but that they should reach repentance (*II Pet.* 3: 9); our desire for them should be the same.

(b) Christ came to deliver men from hell (*John* 3: 16).

(c) He who is wise avoids hell (*Prov.* 15: 24).

(d) Christians should seek to save men and women from the road to hell (*Jude* 23).

BIBLE DEFINITIONS

ADOPTION is an act of God by which He bestows on those who are justified in Christ, the status or standing of His sons and daughters (*John* 1: 12). They are made members of His family, and possess all the privileges of that family. The Holy Spirit is the Spirit of adoption because He makes believers the sons and daughters of God and enables them to call God their Father and to have the feelings towards God which go with the relationship (*Rom.* 8: 15).

ADVOCATE is a title given to both our Lord Jesus Christ and the Holy Spirit. The word carries the idea of calling someone alongside to help, and was used in legal matters for the counsel for the defence. In the references to the Holy Spirit in John's Gospel, where the word is translated "Comforter", "Helper" would be the most apt word (*John* 14: 16, 26; 15: 26; 16: 7). In *I John* 2: 1, where it is used of the Lord Jesus Christ, it is translated "Advocate", indicating its more legal use.

An advocate does two things: first, he stands and pleads on behalf of his client; secondly, he advises his client how to speak when he has to. Christ acts for believers in the first sense: He appears in God's presence on our behalf, interceding there by His presence and on the basis of His finished work on the Cross (*Heb.* 7: 25).

The Spirit acts for believers in the second sense: He comes alongside believers in prayer, for example, and puts pleas and words into their mouths (*Rom.* 8: 26–27).

ALIENATED describes the condition of men in relation to God before reconciliation. They are cut off from the life of God through sin and ignorance (*Eph.* 4: 18). The evil in their lives makes them God's spiritual enemies (*Col.* 1: 21).

ANGEL OF THE LORD. This angel appears in the Old Testament as a messenger of God, but constantly acts and speaks in a way which implies that He is Himself God. All divine titles are given to Him, and worship is offered also (*Gen.* 16: 10–13; 18: 13, 14, 19, 25, 33; 22: 11 ff; 48: 15, 16; *Ex.* 3: 2, 6, 14; 13: 21; 14: 19; 23: 20; *Josh.* 5: 13–15; *Judg.*

6: 11; 13: 3 ff). As the Old Testament revelation unfolds, this angel or messenger of the Lord is called the Son of God, the Messiah (*Isa.* 42: 1 ff; *Mal.* 3: 1).

The angel of the Lord is spoken of quite differently in the New Testament (*Luke* 1: 19). Many hold, with reason, that the angel of the Lord in the Old Testament was none other than the Son of God, who later became flesh as Jesus.

ANGELS are created beings, who act as God's messengers (*Acts* 7: 53; *Gal.* 3: 19; *Heb.* 2: 7), and as God's heavenly servants (*Heb.* 1: 14). Their presence with God always represents the glorious nature of God (*Rev.* 5: 11). There are evidences of a fall amongst the angels, with Satan as their leader (*Job* 4: 18; *Matt.* 25: 41; *II Pet.* 2: 4; *Rev.* 12: 9).

ANTICHRISTS are opponents or adversaries of the Messiah who appear in the last days. They are men who put forth teaching which fundamentally opposes and denies Christ (*I John* 2: 18, 22; 4: 3; *II John* 7). Such teaching may be deceitful in that it pretends to be true Christian teaching (*II John* 7: 8).

APOSTATE, APOSTASY, APOSTATISE. Apostasy is falling away from allegiance to Christ, departing from the faith (*I Tim.* 4: 1). The apostate is a person who having shown all the outward signs of faith in Christ and obedience to Him, then loses all interest and even becomes hostile to Christ and His claims (*Heb.* 6: 6).

It is persistence in sin, sinning wilfully after knowing the truth as it is in Christ (*Heb.* 10: 26). It is the result often of a superficial profession of Christ (*Matt.* 13: 5, 6, 20, 21).

To "apostatise" is to become an apostate. See *Question* 34.

APOSTLES. The word "apostle" means a person sent by another. The title belongs strictly in the New Testament to the twelve apostles and Paul who joined their number later. They were chosen, called and sent forth by Christ Himself (*John* 6: 70; 13: 18; 15: 16, 19; *Gal.* 1: 6); they were His witnesses, especially of His resurrection (*Acts* 1: 8, 22; *I Cor.* 9: 1; 15: 8; *Gal.* 1: 12; *Eph.* 3: 2–8; *I John* 1: 1–3). In a particularly marked sense they knew the help of the Holy Spirit, who led them into all truth (*Matt.* 10: 20; *John* 14: 26; 15: 26; 16: 7–14; 20: 22; *I Cor.* 2: 10–13; 7: 40; *I Thess.* 4: 8). God confirmed the value of their work by signs and miracles (*Matt.* 10: 1, 8; *Acts* 2: 43; 3: 2; 5: 12–16; *Rom.* 15: 18, 19; *I Cor.* 9: 2; *II Cor.* 12: 12; *Gal.* 2: 8).

ASCENSION. See *Question* 22.

ASSURANCE is the conviction Christians have from the Holy Spirit (*Rom.* 8: 15, 16; *I John* 3: 24), through their obedience to the gospel, that they are children of God and heirs of eternal life (*I John* 5: 13). The genuineness of this conviction is demonstrated by right belief in Christ (*I John* 2: 22; 5: 1), righteous conduct (*I John* 2: 3–6; 3: 3) and love for other Christians (*I John* 3: 10–17; 4: 7–12, 20, 21). See *Question* 33.

BACKSLIDE, BACKSLIDING. Backsliding describes the state of the believer when his spiritual life declines and he loses his spiritual vitality through deliberate disobedience to the Lord. It consists of faithlessly turning or drawing back from what the Lord demands (*Jer.* 3: 6–14; *Hos.* 11: 7).

BAPTISED, BAPTISM. See *Question* 36.

BELIEVE is the verb from which we obtain the noun "faith" expressing confidence in God. It describes awareness of God's existence (*Heb.* 11: 6), assurance concerning His trustworthiness, active confidence in His help and self-committal to His care (*John* 3: 16; *Acts* 16: 31, 34; 27: 25; *Rom.* 10: 9, 10; *II Tim.* 1: 12).

BELIEVER is the name given to those who believe and trust in Christ as the only Saviour and the Lord (*Acts* 2: 36), and who find themselves added to the Lord and to His Church (*Acts* 5: 14; 2: 41, 44, 47). See BELIEVE.

BLASPHEMY is some open insult to the majesty of God. At first specific words of reviling and defamation were thought of, as offending in this way (*Lev.* 24: 16; *Mark* 2: 7), but it came to be realised that words which encroach upon God's sole rights in some way are blasphemy. This explains the false charge which the religious authorities made con-

cerning the Lord Jesus Christ (*Mark* 14: 64). It is never a mark of the Holy Spirit's influence (*I Cor.* 12: 3) but rather it is characteristic of the devil and his agencies (*Rev.* 13: 1, 5, 6).

BLOOD OF CHRIST is an expression often used in the New Testament to express the fact of Christ's death as a sacrifice for sins. It is a particularly apt way of describing His death in view of the ceremonial offerings of the Old Testament which had prepared the way for it by their symbolism (*Heb.* 10: 1–17). His blood purges the conscience of moral guilt, and provides the forgiveness which gives the sinner peace (*Heb.* 9: 13, 14). Its power to cleanse is continuous, enabling the believer to maintain fellowship with God (*I John* 1: 7).

BODY. The body represents many aspects of human life, besides describing man's purely physical being: the main characteristic of life is that it is "in the body" (*II Cor.* 5: 8). The body is the organ of man's activity (*I Cor.* 6: 20; *Rom.* 12: 1), the instrument of human experience and suffering (*II Cor.* 4: 10; *Gal.* 6: 17), and the seat of the sexual function during man's present earthly life (*Rom.* 4: 19; *I Cor.* 7: 4).

The Christian's present lowly body is destined to be changed into a glorious body—even as Christ's glorified body—at the resurrection from the dead on Christ's return (*Phil.* 3: 21; *I Cor.* 15: 44).

The word "body" is also used to describe the community of Christians, the Church as a unified body, especially as the body of Christ (*Rom.* 12: 5; *I Cor.* 10: 17; 12: 13, 27; *Eph.* 1: 23; 2: 16; 4: 12, 16; 5: 23, 30; *Col.* 1: 18, 24; 2: 19; 3: 15).

BOOK OF LIFE a pictorial expression of the fact, often expressed, that the Lord knows those who belong to Him (*II Tim.* 2: 19), and that their entry into the full enjoyment of eternal life is absolutely certain (*Phil.* 4: 3; *Rev.* 3: 5).

BORN AGAIN or "regeneration", as it is called, is the supernatural work of the Holy Spirit by which those who were dead in trespasses and sins are made spiritually alive (*John* 3: 3, 6, 7, 8; *Eph.* 2: 1; *Jas.* 1: 18; *I Pet.* 1: 23). See *Question* 26.

CALLED, CALLING, CALLS. Calling is an act of God alone by which the elect are brought into fellowship and union with Christ (*I Cor.* 1: 9) so that they benefit from all the fruits of His redeeming and saving work on their behalf. It is the first step in the application of God's salvation to the individual (*Rom.* 8: 28–30; cf. *Acts* 16: 14). The call carries with it the grace of God sufficient to enable the individual to answer the call and to believe on the Lord Jesus Christ and be saved (*Acts* 16: 31). This grace is, in fact, what we call regeneration.

There is also the "call" to service. It is the individual's duty to recognise that call, and for the local church, when involved at all, to recognise it also and to act accordingly (*Acts* 13: 2; 16: 10).

CHASTISEMENT is the careful and gracious disciplining and correcting of our characters by means of unpleasant circumstances and trials. God's object in chastisement is always the spiritual development and maturity of the believer (*Heb.* 12: 5–7). A company of people, or a local church, or a single individual may all be the subjects of it.

CHOSEN. In the Old Testament the expression was used of the Israelites (*I Chron.* 16: 13; *Ps.* 89: 3) whom God chose from the peoples of the world, not for any merit, to fulfil His eternal purposes in the world (*Deut.* 7: 6, 8; *Isa.* 42: 1; 43: 20, 21).

In the New Testament it is a designation of those whom God has chosen from all mankind, apart from race and nation, and drawn to Himself through living faith in His Son, Jesus. The word reminds Christians that their faith rests on the work of God in them, and not on their own merits, and that they are chosen for God's own purposes (*Eph.* 1: 4; 5: 27; *Col.* 1: 22).

CHRIST is a Greek word meaning "The Anointed One"—the meaning of the word "Messiah". Anointing was a symbol of being set apart for a special task by God. The Jews looked for the coming of a Great One, called the Messiah, who would accomplish God's purposes for His people. Jesus accepted the title but only infrequently, for it would appear the Jews thought mainly of the Messiah

as a political deliverer and Jesus had not come as such (*Matt.* 16: 16, 17; *Mark* 14: 61, 62; *John* 4: 26; cf. *Matt.* 1: 18; 2: 4; *Luke* 2: 11, 26).

CHRISTIAN. Christians are those who are connected with Christ— Christ's men and women. Believers were first called Christians in Antioch (*Acts* 11: 26). To believe the apostolic message of the gospel was to become a Christian (*Acts* 26: 28). To be known as a Christian, in some circumstances, became the basis for persecution (*I Pet.* 4: 16).

CHURCH. The word "church" is used mainly in two ways: first, of the whole company of those redeemed through Christ (*Matt.* 16: 18; *Acts* 9: 31; *I Cor.* 6: 4; 12: 28; *Eph.* 1: 22; 3: 10, 21; 5: 23 ff, 27, 29, 32), and secondly, of a company of professing believers in a particular area or district (*Matt.* 18: 17; *I Cor.* 1: 2; 10: 32; 11: 16, 22; 15: 9; *II Cor.* 1: 1; *Gal.* 1: 13; *I Thess.* 2: 14; *II Thess.* 1: 4; *I Tim.* 3: 5, 15; *Acts* 20: 28).

CLEANSED, CLEANSING is what we need from our sin (*Ps.* 51: 2). It normally describes physical cleansing, but it has another meaning in the Bible. Sin pollutes the soul, and makes it an object of dislike to God. The removal of sin, both in its condemning and corrupting influences, through the blood of Christ, is very appropriately described as cleansing (*Heb.* 1: 3). This cleansing is continuously available to the Christian as he endeavours to live in obedience to God, confessing all known sins as they arise (*I John* 1: 7–9).

COMFORTER. By its Latin derivation, and in older English, the word meant "encourager". The same Greek word is translated elsewhere in the New Testament as "Advocate" (*John* 14: 16, 26; 15: 26; 16: 7). See ADVOCATE.

COMMUNION is sharing and participating, and translates the same word in the New Testament which we more often translate as "fellowship". Communion is a particularly apt word for describing the Lord's Supper because by participating in it, not only does the Christian express his own personal fellowship with Christ and sharing in the benefits of His completed atoning work, but he does so in fellowship with other

113

Christians because of the essential spiritual unity and identity of all who share the benefits of Christ's redeeming work (*I Cor.* 10: 16, 17).

COMMUNION OF SAINTS is another way of expressing the fellowship of Christian believers. This fellowship, or communion, of believers is the identity, sympathy and belonging we have with all believers through our common allegiance to the Lord Jesus Christ (*Eph.* 4: 6, 13). The more fellowship with God the Father and the Son is enjoyed, the more is communion with God's people experienced (*I John* 1: 3).

CONDEMNATION, CONDEMNED. Condemnation describes the result of man's sinful condition before God. Deserving the wrath of God, sinners are sentenced to just punishment—death (*Ezek.* 18: 4; *John* 3: 16-19). Through Christ, the believer's sin is adequately and finally dealt with, and all condemnation is removed (*Rom.* 8: 1; *I John* 4: 10).

CONFESS, CONFESSION. The same word is used with regard to a few different matters. First, confession is the acknowledgment before God of our individual sins; and upon such confession depends our experience of His forgiveness and cleansing (*I John* 1: 9). Secondly, confession is our consistent declaration before men that Jesus is the Son of God and has become our Saviour and Lord, to whom we give total allegiance (*Rom.* 10: 9, 10; *Phil.* 2: 11; cf. *Matt.* 10: 32; *Luke* 12: 8). Thirdly, confession is the acknowledgment we make and the witness we give to the truths of the faith (*I Tim.* 6: 12; *Heb.* 10: 23).

CONSCIENCE is that part of us which registers disapproval when we go against what we know is right, and approval when we do the right thing. Like a witness, it declares facts (*Rom.* 2: 15; 9: 1; *II Cor.* 1: 12), like a trusted adviser, it prohibits evil (*Acts* 24: 16; *Rom.* 13: 5), and like a judge, it assesses what is deserved (*Rom.* 2: 15; cf. *I John* 3: 20 f). Conscience on its own is not the standard of right and wrong; it needs to be instructed and informed by the Word of God and the Holy Spirit. Before a person is a Christian, conscience tends to be either bad or asleep. When the work of conviction begins a man's conscience is made sensitive, and he knows he has a bad conscience before God. When he is reconciled to God, as a gift from God, his conscience is purged through the effectiveness of the blood of Christ on his behalf (*Heb.* 9: 14). A conscience "void of offence" (*Acts* 24: 16) is maintained as he seeks to do God's will and allows no sin to remain unconfessed (*I John* 1: 6-10).

CONTRITION is brokenness of spirit through a right appreciation of the sinful nature of sin. A man's pride is properly humbled by this appreciation and he is in a fit position then to receive the grace and forgiveness of God (*Ps.* 34: 18; 51: 17; *Isa.* 57: 15; 66: 2).

CONVERSION. See *Question* 27.

CONVICTION is the work of the Holy Spirit, who, through the Scriptures as they are preached, convicts the conscience of its sin before God, bringing a conviction of the justice and certainty of God's wrath upon sin, and a hatred of sin on the part of the individual (*John* 16: 8, 9; cf. *Acts* 2: 37; *I Thess.* 1: 5, 9, 10).

CORRUPTION is used first in a physical sense of the body decaying and dying (*Ps.* 16: 10; cf. *Acts* 2: 27), and secondly in a spiritual sense of man's state before God as a consequence of his sinful rebellion (*Ps.* 14: 1). Left to himself man gets worse and worse, and everything he does is infected by his sin.

COVENANT. A covenant is a compact or a contract. When the word is used in connection with God, it has the idea of a one-sided arrangement made by a superior party. In the covenant with Adam, for example, God placed him on probation, promising life, if he were obedient (*Gen.* 2: 17).

The word is used particularly, however, of those obligations which God imposes upon Himself, for the reconciliation of sinful men and women to Himself (*Gen.* 17: 7; *Deut.* 7: 6-8; *Ps.* 89: 3-4; *Heb.* 13: 20).

CREATION. The God and Father of our Lord Jesus Christ is the creator of all things (*Neh.* 9: 6; *Ps.* 90: 2; *Isa.* 42: 5; *Acts* 17: 24, 25;

114

I Cor. 8: 6). God the Son and God the Holy Spirit were active in the creation (*Gen.* 1: 2; *Job* 26: 13; *John* 1: 3; *Col.* 1: 16; *Heb.* 1: 2), and God the Father has ordained that all creation shall ultimately belong to the Son (*Heb.* 1: 2). In the final analysis, the absolute creation of all things by God is a matter for faith rather than scientific proof (*Heb.* 11: 3). See *Question 9.*

CROSS. The cross was an upright stake or beam used in punishing and executing criminals, particularly by the Romans. The word describes the painful form of death Jesus endured, but it is more often used as a one-word summary of the good news of salvation, that Jesus "died for our sins". "The word of the cross" is "the preaching of the gospel" (*I Cor.* 1: 17 ff).

CURSE is a sentence of destruction called down upon someone because of a misdemeanour. In the Bible it does not refer to blasphemous language as today. It is used of the Lord Jesus Christ who is said to have become a curse for sinners. The failure of sinners to keep God's law brings upon them the curse of God which, in fact, is death (*Gal.* 3: 10; *Rom.* 6: 23). Christ willingly stood in the place of sinners at the Cross, taking their death upon Himself. In this way He became a curse for them (*Gal.* 3: 13).

DAY OF JUDGMENT. See JUDGMENT.

DEPRAVED is used to describe man's corrupt state before God as a result of his sin. Man is said to be totally depraved, not in the sense that he is as bad as he can possibly be, but rather that sin has corrupted every part of his being, his mind, will and affections. Men's hearts are full of evil and madness (*Eccl.* 9: 3; *Matt.* 15: 11, 15–20; *Mark* 7: 15, 20–23), and correction sometimes only makes him sin the more (*Zeph.* 3: 7).

DESTRUCTION describes the eternal death, damnation and ruin which is the punishment of the wicked (*Matt.* 7: 13; *Rev.* 17: 8, 11).

DEVIL. See *Question 43.*

DISCIPLE was something of a technical term used of a person who attached himself to a particular teacher. A disciple is someone under instruction. Jesus chose the twelve, to bring them under His instruction so that they should be able to convey His teaching later to others (*Matt.* 28: 20; cf. *II Tim.* 2: 2). But many more besides the twelve were called "disciples" (*Luke* 10: 1 ff) and the term was given generally to all professing Christians (*Acts* 11: 26). Jesus requires faithfulness and obedience to what He says as the major condition of discipleship (*John* 8: 31).

DISOBEDIENCE can describe either the deliberate and obstinate rejection of the will of God (*Eph.* 2: 2; 5: 6) or the refusal to hear God's words (*Jer.* 11: 10; 35: 17). It can, of course, describe both aspects at once.

ELDERS were the spiritual leaders of the early Christian churches. They were appointed from the earliest times (*Acts* 11: 30). Their precise functions are not clear, although pastoral care and rule fell to them as their particular responsibilities and some had the further task of teaching and preaching the Word of God. The qualifications for elders and bishops are more or less identical (*Tit.* 1: 6–9; *I Tim.* 3: 1–7) and it is generally agreed that the two titles were interchangeable, referring to the same spiritual office.

ELECT, ELECTION. Election is God's eternal, unconditional choice of guilty sinners to be redeemed and born again of His Spirit so that they may be brought at the last to His everlasting glory (*Rom.* 8: 30; *Eph.* 1: 3–12; *I Pet.* 1: 2). The believer's experience of salvation, sanctification, and glory all flow from God's election (*II Thess.* 2: 13, 14) which had no regard at all to any works or merit on the believer's part (*Rom.* 11: 6; *II Tim.* 1: 9).

ETERNAL always conveys the idea of something which is without end (*Luke* 16: 9; *Acts* 13: 46), and, sometimes, when God is spoken of, of that without beginning (*Gen.* 21: 33; *Isa.* 26: 4; *Rom.* 16: 26; *Heb.* 9: 14).

ETERNAL LIFE, EVERLASTING LIFE is never-ending life, the very opposite of death and corruption (*Rom.* 6: 22; *Gal.* 6: 8). It is the gift of God, and the present possession of the Christian through believing in the Lord Jesus Christ (*Rom.* 6: 23; *John* 3: 16; 10: 28). Its essence is everlasting fellowship with God (*John* 17: 3).

EVIL describes that which is bad, and contrary to law, such as crime, sin and wrong-doing. It begins in the human heart (*Matt.* 9: 4), and unchecked leads to further evil (*Eccl.* 8: 11).

EVIL ONE is a name given to the devil because of his wicked, bad, base and vicious activities (*Matt.* 13: 19; *John* 17: 15; *Eph.* 6: 16; *I John* 2: 13 f; 5: 18, 19).

EXPIATE, EXPIATION. To expiate is to pay the penalty of sin, and to make amends for it. Christ is the expiation for our sin in that to Him were transferred our sins, and He died for our sins, so that we might be brought near to God (*I Pet.* 3: 18). By giving up Himself sacrificially, Christ annulled the power of sin to separate between God and the believer (*Heb.* 2: 17; *Rom.* 3: 25).

FAITH. See *Question* 29.

FALL, The. See *Question* 13.

FATHER (See **GOD**). The word is the distinguishing name of the first Person of the Trinity in relation to the second Person—the Son (*John* 14: 6; 20: 17; *Rom.* 15: 6; *II Cor.* 1: 3). The relationship has no like anywhere, and is beyond our understanding.

The word is used, secondly, of the relationship God the Father has with those who believe in His Son (*Rom.* 1: 7; *I Cor.* 1: 3; *II Thess.* 2: 16). Such are taught by the Holy Spirit to call Him "Father" (*John* 1: 12; *Rom.* 8: 15; *I John* 3: 1).

The relationship which God has to men in general is seldom spoken of as fatherhood, indeed the opposite is the case (*John* 8: 44).

FELLOWSHIP is a favourite Christian word and is the name for the common sharing of Christians in the grace of God, the salvation Christ brings, and the indwelling Holy Spirit which is the spiritual birthright of all Christians. The fellowship which Christians have with one another, therefore, springs from the fellowship they have with the Father,

Son and Holy Spirit (*I John* 1: 3). Fellowship with God is a relationship in which Christians receive from, and respond to, all three Persons of the Trinity in a relation of friendship (*John* 14: 23; *Rom.* 5: 5; 8: 16; *Eph.* 4: 30). Such fellowship is the life of heaven begun on earth (*I Pet.* 1: 8).

FLESH is used to describe an important part of our bodies, and as such no blame is attached to it (*I Cor.* 15: 50; *Luke* 24: 39).

But generally it is used to describe the sinful and corrupt nature of men. It represents the lower part of man's nature, where his natural desires have unhindered scope, leading to all kinds of sin (*Rom.* 7: 18; *Gal.* 5: 19–21; *Eph.* 2: 3). In the person who is born again, the deeds of the flesh are put to death as the Holy Spirit is obeyed. But in those who are not Christians, the flesh dominates (*Rom.* 8: 4–9, 12, 13).

FORGIVENESS is the cancelling by God (*Micah* 7: 19; *Eph.* 1: 7) of the sinner's debt and guilt on the basis of Christ's death for sinners (*Matt.* 26: 28; *Mark* 14: 24). The conditions are repentance and faith in Christ (*Acts* 2: 38; 5: 31; 10: 43; *I John* 1: 9).

GENTILES was, to begin with, a term for "nations". The Jews knew themselves to be distinct from all other peoples and they used this term to describe all such peoples. In the New Testament the term usually has the Greeks especially in mind, and now, of course, covers all who are not of Jewish race.

GLORY is used of God Himself to sum up the perfection of all that He is and all that He does, not least His grace, power and righteousness—the latter revealing especially how far short men fall of God's standards (*Rom.* 1: 23; *Eph.* 1: 17; *Jude* 24).

The word is also used to describe the eternal happiness which Christians are to enjoy in the life to come (*Rom.* 8: 18, 21; *I Pet.* 5: 1, 10).

GOD is Spirit (*John* 4: 24): invisible (*I Tim.* 6: 15, 16; *John* 1: 18), personal (*Ex.* 3: 14), great beyond human estimation (*Isa.* 40: 18; 45: 6; *Rom.* 11: 33–34), life-giving (*Gen.* 1; *John* 5: 26; *Acts* 17: 25) and supre-

116

mely powerful (*Ps.* 115: 3; *Isa.* 40: 15, 17).

There is but one God (*Deut.* 6: 4), but one in three Persons, Father, Son and Holy Spirit (*Matt.* 28: 19; *II Cor.* 13: 14).

Although no one has ever seen God the Father (*John* 1: 18), God has given clues to His existence both in creation (*Gen.* 1: 1; *Ps.* 19: 1; *Acts* 17: 24; *Rom.* 1: 18–20) and in the nature of man (*Ps.* 139: 14; *Rom.* 2: 14, 15), and in the glorious revelation of Himself in the Person of His Son, Jesus Christ (*II Cor.* 4: 6; *John* 1: 14, 18; 14: 9; *Col.* 1: 15–17; *I John* 1: 1–3).

Added to these evidences, there is the witness of the Bible (*II Tim.* 3: 16), and of those who have found God (*Acts* 4: 20; *I John* 5: 20).

GOD (god) is a word used of divine beings generally, and of the one true God, the God and Father of our Lord Jesus Christ. It is also used of idols who are so-called "gods", and of Satan who is the god of this world (*II Cor.* 4: 4). In using this term to describe idols and evil spirits the Bible does not acknowledge their deity—indeed the opposite is the case —but it recognises the false worship which men may foolishly give to them.

GODHEAD is an expression standing for the very being of God, or His essential nature; an alternative word is deity (*Acts* 17: 29; *II Pet.* 1: 3, 4).

GOOD WORKS are the good actions which are to be produced in the Christian's life following upon his experience of being justified (*Eph.* 2: 10). Even as the health of a tree is shown by its fruit, so too is the health of a Christian shown by his good works (*Matt.* 5: 16; 7: 15–20). They necessarily contain imperfections but they are pleasing to God because they arise from living faith in Christ.

Good works are worthless, however, as a means of justification and for gaining merit before God (*Eph.* 2: 9; *Tit.* 3: 5).

GOSPEL means "good news"— the good news concerning God's Son Jesus Christ. The good news is that Christ died for sinners, and that through repentance and faith in Christ sinners can possess His righteousness before God, and receive the gift of the Holy Spirit and everlasting life.

GOSPELS. The four gospels— Matthew, Mark, Luke and John— are the books in which the story of Christ's life and teaching is found. They are not so much biographies of Jesus as written copies of the apostles' preaching and teaching, putting the emphasis on the events through which God's salvation was made available to men and women—the "good news" after which the gospels are named. According to the four gospel writers, there is but one gospel —the gospel of Jesus Christ, the Son of God—delivered to, and preached by the apostles (*Acts* 2: 42; *I Cor.* 15: 1–4).

GRACE is the undeserved love of God to men revealed in Christ, giving them through Him help and countless gifts and benefits which they could never merit (*Rom.* 3: 24; 5: 15; 6: 1; *Eph.* 1: 6; 2: 5, 7, 8).

GUILT is the deserving of punishment because of law-breaking or failure to do something required. All men, since the first rebellion of man (*Rom.* 5: 12), are guilty before God since all have sinned and fallen short of His glory (*Rom.* 3: 23) and are accountable to Him (*Rom.* 3: 19). Salvation rescues from guilt (*Eph.* 1: 7), the sacrifice of Christ completely removing the guilt of sin (*Heb.* 10: 4, 18).

HEART covers the whole inward life of a man: his thinking, feeling and will (*Matt.* 13: 15). Sin has its roots in the heart (*Matt.* 15: 19, 20) and it is in the hearts of men, therefore, that God's work of salvation begins (*Matt.* 13: 19; *Rom.* 2: 15; *II Cor.* 3: 3; *Heb.* 8: 10) so that men believe in their own heart (*Acts* 15: 9; *Rom.* 10: 9, 10).

HEATHEN. Used in the Bible, the word means "nation". Being the sole people in the Old Testament to whom God had revealed Himself in a covenant relationship, the Jews regarded other nations as completely separate and different. All other peoples, not having the covenant relationship with God, were the heathen. The term "heathen" describes men and women everywhere who are without the true knowledge of God.

HEAVEN. See *Question 49.*

117

HELL. See *Question* 50.

HOLINESS, HOLINESS OF GOD.
Holiness is a term which above all others expresses the perfection of God's character. He is entirely free from moral evil, and possesses infinite purity. He is absolutely distinct from all His creatures, and is exalted above them in infinite majesty. The idea behind the word "holy" and "holiness" is that of being cut off, separated, or set apart. God sets apart His people from other peoples, and He calls them to separate themselves from all that displeases Him and is contrary to His will. He calls them to be like Himself (*I Pet.* 1: 15, 16).

HOLY GHOST is another way of describing the Holy Spirit. Both "Spirit" and "Ghost" are translations of the same word in the New Testament. "Spirit" is a better word than "Ghost" for other uses are inclined to mislead us when we think of the Holy Spirit by the title of "Ghost".

HOLY SPIRIT. The Holy Spirit is the Lord (i.e. Himself God) and the Giver of life, the third Person of the Trinity, to be worshipped and glorified with the Father and the Son (*Matt.* 28: 19; *I Cor.* 12: 4–6; *II Cor.* 13: 14; *Eph.* 4: 4–6). He is most commonly presented to us as the Executor of God's purposes, whether in creation (*Gen.* 1: 2; *Job* 26: 13), revelation (*II Tim.* 3: 16; *II Pet.* 1: 21) or redemption (*Luke* 1: 35; *John* 3: 5, 6; *Acts* 2: 24; *I Cor.* 12: 3). He is the gift of the Father and the Son to the believer to live within him (*John* 14: 16; 15: 26; 16: 7): giving him spiritual life (*Gal.* 5: 25; *Eph.* 2: 1); assuring him of his sonship (*Rom.* 8: 16); and communicating to him the benefits of the gospel (*Rom.* 5: 5; 15: 13). See *Questions* 23, 24.

HOPE as used in the New Testament, has behind it no idea of clinging to a mere possibility, but rather the happy and confident expectation of enjoying some unseen and future promise of God. The living hope of the resurrection from the dead and the inheritance to follow are examples (*I Pet.* 1: 3–4).

IMMORTALITY is deathlessness, and belongs to God alone. Christians receive it as a gift, but God Himself is the source (*I Tim.* 6: 16). Immortality is not merely the survival of the soul after the death of the body, but the self-conscious existence of the whole person, body and soul together, in a state of eternal happiness (*I Cor.* 15: 53 f).

IN CHRIST is a characteristic description of Christians, signifying the spiritual union which every Christian has with Christ, from which springs his experience of all the benefits of Christ's finished work and the knowledge of Christ living within him by the Holy Spirit (*John* 15: 4, 5; *Rom.* 8: 9–11; *I Cor.* 1: 30; *II Cor.* 5: 17; *Gal.* 2: 20; *Phil.* 1: 1).

INCARNATION. The word itself comes from Latin, meaning "becoming-in-flesh", and describes the amazing fact of Christ, the Son of God, becoming flesh (*John* 1: 14). In both the Old and New Testaments Christ is declared to be both God and man (*Ps.* 2; 22; 45; 72; 110; *John* 1: 1–3, 14; *Col.* 2: 9). His perfect deity and perfect humanity are essentials of the Christian faith (*I John* 2: 22–25; 4: 1–6; 5: 5–12; *II John* 7), although these glorious facts are beyond the understanding of the human mind (*I Tim.* 3: 16). See *Question* 19.

INFINITE describes that which is boundless, endless and very great. It is used commonly of God because no limitation can be set to His being. He is far greater in His being and perfection than we can know or think.

INHERITANCE. In the Old Testament the land of Canaan, promised to Abraham and his descendants, was called the "inheritance" (*I Kings* 8: 36).
In the spiritual sense, the Lord Himself is said to be His people's inheritance (*Jer.* 10: 16) and the Lord speaks of His true people as His inheritance (*Deut.* 4: 20; 32: 9; *Ps.* 2: 8).
In the New Testament the "inheritance" is the kingdom of God with all its benefits (*Matt.* 25: 34; *I Cor.* 6: 9; *Gal.* 5: 21; *I Pet.* 1: 3, 4). As the children of God through faith in Christ, believers are to share God's treasures and Christ's glory (*Rom.* 8: 17).

INIQUITY is persistent wickedness and disobedience to God's laws (*Isa.* 53: 6; *Rom.* 6: 19; *Tit.* 2: 14).

INSPIRED, INSPIRATION. The word used in the New Testament for "inspired" means "God-breathed" (*II Tim.* 3: 16). The Scriptures came about not by the impulse of man, but through men being moved by the Holy Spirit to speak from God (*II Pet.* 1: 21). The responsibility of such men was to transmit what they received (*I Pet.* 1: 10–12). The authority of the Bible springs from its divine inspiration (*II Tim.* 3: 16, 17). The conviction that the Scriptures are the Word of God is brought about in the heart of the Christian by the Holy Spirit (*I Cor.* 2: 4, 5; *I Thess.* 1: 5; 2: 13).

INTERCESSION is the continuing work of Christ in heaven for Christians. On the grounds of His sacrifice on their behalf, He unfailingly claims every spiritual benefit for them, secures forgiveness for all their sins and makes their worship and service acceptable to God (*Rom.* 8: 34; *Heb.* 7: 27; 9: 24; 13: 15; *I John* 2: 1).

A different kind of intercession is the Holy Spirit's work in the Christian by which He disposes, teaches and helps the Christian to pray according to God's will. The Spirit gives both the inclination and the ability to pray (*Rom.* 8: 26, 27).

ISRAEL was the name given by God to the patriarch Jacob (*Gen.* 32: 28; 35: 10) and to all the descendants of Jacob. The name was given then to the whole nation of Israel. In the New Testament it is used also of Christians, whether Jews or Gentiles, as the true nation of Israel (*Gal.* 6: 16) for whom circumcision is a matter of the heart, not of the body (*Rom.* 2: 29).

JESUS is the Greek form of the Hebrew name Joshua, meaning "God is salvation" or "God is the Saviour". In obedience to God's command, it was given to the Son of God when He became man, as a symbol of God's promise that Christ would rescue God's people from the guilt and power of their sins (*Matt.* 1: 21; *Luke* 1: 31; 2: 21).

JEWS. The title "Jew" was used first for members of the tribe of Judah or of the two tribes of the Southern Kingdom (*II Kings* 16: 6; 25: 25). Later it was used of any Hebrew who returned from the Captivity. Now it covers all of the Hebrew race anywhere in the world (*Esth.* 2: 5; *Matt.* 2: 2).

JUDGE, The. Sometimes God the Father is spoken of as the Judge (*Heb.* 12: 23), and sometimes the Lord Jesus Christ (*Acts* 10: 42; *II Tim.* 4: 1, 8). God the Father has fixed a day on which He will judge the whole world in justice by Christ the Judge whom He has appointed (*Acts* 17: 31).

JUDGMENT, JUDGMENT DAY. Judgment is the condemnation of God which rightly falls upon sinners (*Rom.* 2: 2) and which will be executed at the judgment when Christ will be the Judge and all will appear before Him (*Matt.* 25: 31–46; *John* 5: 22, 27). The perfect justice of God and the undeniable guilt of all will be plain and beyond dispute (*Gen.* 18: 25; *Acts* 17: 31; *Rom.* 2: 5, 6). Those justified through faith in Christ will be acquitted from the guilt of sin and will receive rewards according to their faithfulness (*Rom.* 5: 1; *I Cor.* 3: 9–13; *II Tim.* 4: 8); the unbelieving will receive their final condemnation (*Rom.* 2: 8; *II Thess.* 1: 8, 9; *Jude* 15; *Rev.* 20: 15).

The day of judgment is the day when Christ returns (*I Thess.* 5: 4; *Heb.* 10: 25; *I Cor.* 3: 13), when all these things will take place. See *Question 46*.

JUDGMENT SEAT. Both Greek and Roman judges sat on either a raised platform or seat in a public place and justice was seen to be done. Because of the absolutely fair and public nature of the last judgment, the picture is taken up to illustrate the judgment day when Christ shall publicly and justly judge all men (*Rom.* 14: 10; *II Cor.* 5: 10).

JUST describes men who are upright or righteous in that they conform to the laws of God and man; this is only possible to us through the new birth (*I John* 2: 29). It is used of God Himself to describe the perfect fairness of His judgment of men and nations (*Ps.* 7: 11; *II Tim.* 4: 8). It is used of Jesus, who is the perfect standard of obedience and uprightness (*Matt.* 27: 19; *Acts* 7: 52; *I Pet.* 3: 18).

JUSTIFICATION, JUSTIFY. See *Question* 31.

KINGDOM, KINGDOM OF GOD, KINGDOM OF HEAVEN. The kingdom of God or the kingdom of heaven, is spoken of in two ways: first, as that of which Christians are members because Christ, through the new birth (*John* 3: 3, 5), actively rules as King in their hearts; and secondly, as that which they possess as an inheritance in the future (*Matt.* 25: 34; *Luke* 22: 16; *II Tim.* 4: 18; *Heb.* 12: 28).

LAMB is a picture used of Christ to set Him forth as the One promised in the Old Testament to obtain for others deliverance from God's judgment by the sacrifice of Himself for sin (*John* 1: 29; *I Pet.* 1: 19). In the Old Testament the lamb was the principal sacrificial animal, and all such sacrifices looked forward to the one sacrifice which would deal with sin once and for all—the sacrifice of Jesus as the Lamb of God (*Heb.* 10: 1–14). While meekness characterised Jesus as the Lamb of God in His earthly ministry (*Isa.* 53: 7; *I Pet.* 2: 22, 23), the symbol is used in the Book of Revelation to express His position as the Conqueror and the Mighty One (*Rev.* 5: 6; 7: 14 ff; 12: 11).

LAST DAY, LAST DAYS. The Last Day is usually a reference to Christ's second coming (*John* 6: 39, 40, 44, 54) and the events which will then occur, principally the judgment and the resurrection of the dead.

The last days are sometimes thought of as beginning with the birth of Christ (*Heb.* 1: 2) in that God's new and final order of things through the redeeming work of His Son, and the consequent birth of the Church, then comes into operation.

The last days also describes the period of history immediately preceding the second coming of Christ (*II Tim.* 3: 1), the great event which will mark the completion of the present age.

LAW is used to describe the whole of the Scriptures (*Josh.* 1: 8; *Ps.* 119: 97) and more particularly the Law of God, as summed up in the Ten Commandments (*Ex.* 20: 1–17). It is the Law of God which makes us aware of our sin against God (*Rom.* 3: 20) and thus drives us to realise our need of the salvation achieved by Christ for sinners (*Gal.* 2: 15, 16, 21). See *Question* 16.

LORD describes God, and is the word used in the Greek translation of the Old Testament to render the name of God, "Jehovah". It is used regularly of Christ, meaning that He is divine Lord, having the highest place of all, worthy of our worship, service and obedience (*Acts* 2: 36; *I Cor.* 16: 22; *Phil.* 2: 9–11; *Col.* 3: 24). It is also used of the Spirit (*II Cor.* 3: 18).

Significantly, references to the LORD God in the Old Testament are applied to Christ in the New Testament (*Isa.* 40: 3; cf. *Matt.* 3: 3; *Isa.* 44: 6; *Rev.* 1: 17).

LOST is used to describe the condition of men and women who live without Christ and therefore without the hope of eternal life. Like lost sheep, they are separated from the Shepherd they need (*Matt.* 10: 6; *Luke* 15: 4; 19: 10). The lost need to be found and saved through Christ, or else they will perish (*Matt.* 18: 12–14; *John* 3: 16).

LOVE is the foremost characteristic of God, together with His holiness (*I John* 1: 5; 4: 8). It is a love which is utterly independent of the merits of those loved, a fact so perfectly illustrated in the Cross, when Christ died for us, while we were yet sinners (*John* 3: 16; *Rom.* 5: 8). Christ perfectly expressed the love of God for men (*II Cor.* 5: 14; *Eph.* 2: 4; 3: 19; 5: 2).

Christian love is the fruit of the Holy Spirit's presence in the Christian (*Gal.* 5: 22). Love for God is seen in obedience to His commandments (*John* 14: 15, 21, 23; 15: 10; *I John* 2: 5; 5: 3; *II John* 6). Love for others is seen in seeking their best interests, irrespective of the attitude or response received (*Rom.* 15: 2; *I Cor.* 13; *Gal.* 6: 10).

MEDIATOR, MEDIATION. A Mediator, literally, is a go-between. He mediates between two parties to

120

produce peace by removing disagreement.

Christ is the one Mediator between God and men (*I Tim*. 2: 5). He was uniquely qualified to mediate being Himself both God and man. Christ voluntarily took His stand between the offended God and the offending sinner, so as to deliver the sinner by taking upon Himself the wrath of God which the sinner deserved.

By His unique sacrifice for sins on behalf of men peace between God and man was made possible. Christ Himself is our peace (*Eph*. 2: 14).

MERCY is warm affection demonstrated to the needy, helpless and distressed. In sending Christ to be the Saviour of sinners, the amazing mercy of God was shown (*Luke* 1: 78; *Tit*. 3: 5). His abundant mercy is seen in the manner in which He blots out the penitent sinner's transgressions (*Ps*. 51: 1).

MESSIAH means "Anointed" and was the name given to the coming deliverer promised in the Old Testament. The word indicated that the deliverer or saviour was to be specially consecrated for his tasks, in the same way as a king or a priest might be. Among the Greeks the title Messiah was translated "Christos", or "Christ" as we spell it.

Jesus accepted the title (*Matt*. 16: 16) but He used it cautiously to describe His mission, for many of the Jews looked upon the Messiah as merely a political deliverer rather than a spiritual Saviour. He always emphasised the sufferings which had to be His as the Messiah before He could enter upon His glory (*Matt*. 16: 16, 20, 21).

MIND represents man's ability to think, his understanding—and the word "understanding" often translates the Greek word for "mind" in the New Testament. The mind of the unregenerate man is described as blinded (*II Cor*. 3: 14; 4: 4), darkened (*Eph*. 4: 18), alienated (*Col*. 1: 21), puffed up (*Col*. 2: 18), corrupt (*I Tim*. 6: 5), and defiled (*Tit*. 1: 15). Regeneration brings a new awakening of the mind to love God, to understand His will and to do it (*Rom*. 12: 1, 2; *Eph*. 4: 23; *I Pet*. 1: 13).

MIRACLE. A miracle is an act or a work of supernatural origin or character, which would not be possible by ordinary or natural means. The deeds of power of Jesus were miracles in this sense (*Matt*. 13: 54, 58; *Luke* 19: 37).

NEW BIRTH. See *Question* 26.

NEW COVENANT, NEW TESTAMENT. The word "testament" means "covenant" rather than our modern "testament". The term "New Testament" came into general use in the later part of the second century to describe these twenty-seven writings which fall into four divisions: the four gospels; the Acts of the Apostles; twenty-one letters; the Book of Revelation.

The great message of the New Testament is that God's promises of redemption have been fulfilled in the life, death and resurrection of Jesus. His blood has secured the provision of a new covenant, according to God's will, so that all who believe and obey become God's people and Christ's Church.

OBEDIENCE, OBEY. Obedience is the obeying of God's voice in His commandments (*Josh*. 22: 2; *Ex*. 19: 5; *Jer*. 17: 23; *Deut*. 5: 10). The revelation God has given us in the Scriptures is to be the rule of the individual's whole life (*II Tim*. 3: 16, 17). Christ is the perfect example of obedience (*John* 15: 10; *Heb*. 10: 7).

Obedience is, in effect, our response to the Word of God (*Matt*. 13: 23). It is almost identical with a sensitive conscience, constantly educated and informed by the Holy Spirit through the Scriptures, and consistently obeyed (*Acts* 23: 1; 24: 16; *II Tim*. 1: 3).

Obedience is the work of God in the Christian, as a result of the new birth, for God inspires both the will and the deed, for His own good pleasure (*I Pet*. 1: 2, 14; *Phil*. 2: 13, 14).

By obedience we please God (*I John* 3: 22), dwell in Christ's love (*John* 15: 10), sustain our fellowship with God (*John* 14: 23-24; *I John* 1: 3, 7), grow in holiness (*Luke* 1: 6; *I Pet*. 1: 14-16), and perfect our love for God (*I John* 2: 5).

OFFERING. Sacrifices and offerings

are linked in the Old Testament (*Heb.* 10: 5; *Ps.* 40: 6). The "sacrifices" were animal offerings and the "offerings" vegetable offerings. The word "offering" carried with it the idea of drawing near. It was that with which a man drew near to God. The sin of man is such that he cannot enter into the presence of God without some preparation: to this fact the offerings bore witness.

Leviticus 1–7 describes them. They are of great interest because we know how the Lord Jesus fulfilled their deepest significance for us by the one offering of Himself, opening up the way for us into the presence of God by His blood (*Heb.* 10: 10, 19–22).

OLD TESTAMENT. The word "testament" means "covenant" rather than our modern "testament". The term "Old Testament" came into general use in the later part of the second century to describe the writings we know by that title.

The thirty-nine books were arranged by the Jews in three divisions: the Law, the Prophets and the Writings. They deal particularly with the promises, or covenant that God made with Israel. They are the record of the working out of God's redemption on behalf of His people, and they always look forward to the spiritual redemption to take place in the future with the coming of the Messiah.

OMNIPOTENCE means possessing all power, and is characteristic, therefore, of God alone who can do all things so that no purpose of His can be thwarted (*Job* 42: 2). There is no power higher than God's (*Ps.* 135: 6; *Rev.* 1: 8). His limitless power is expressed in the title "God of Sabaoth" or "Lord of hosts" (*Jas.* 5: 4; cf. *Judg.* 5: 20; *II Kings* 6: 17; *Isa.* 5: 9; *Rom.* 9: 29; *Isa.* 1: 9).

OMNIPRESENCE means being everywhere at the same time and is an ability and quality possessed by God alone (*Amos* 9: 2–4; *Ps.* 139: 7–12).

OMNISCIENCE means possessing all knowledge and wisdom and is a characteristic of God alone. Nothing can escape the knowledge of God (*Ps.* 139: 2, 3, 6; 145: 7). He is the only wise God (*Rom.* 16: 27).

PARADISE is an oriental word, first used by the Persians of an enclosed garden or park. It was taken over by the Greeks and it expressed the idea of a place of supreme happiness above the earth. Our Lord used it of the heavenly home to which the believer's spirit goes at death (*Luke* 23: 43).

PASSOVER was the name given to the feast appointed by God to keep in memory the deliverance of the Israelites from Egypt (*Ex.* 12). It was so called because the Lord "passed over" or "spared" the Israelites when He punished the Egyptians. The Israelites had to offer up a lamb or a kid in order that the destroying angel might pass over them. The passover lamb is a picture of Christ, and He is called "our Passover" (*I Cor.* 5: 7) because His death has saved us from the judgment of God's wrath which we deserve.

PEACE is harmony with God restored, made possible by the reconciliation God has already accomplished through the death of Christ (*II Cor.* 5: 20, 21), into which we enter by faith (*Rom.* 5: 1). This peace brings with it glorious access to God (*Rom.* 5: 2).

PENTATEUCH is the name given to the first five books of the Bible (Genesis, Exodus, Leviticus, Numbers, Deuteronomy), the actual word itself meaning a five-volumed book. In the Old Testament, the Pentateuch is described as the Law (*Josh.* 8: 34; *Neh.* 8: 2) or the book of the Law of God (*Josh.* 24: 26; *Neh.* 8: 18), and sometimes as the book of Moses (*Ezra* 6: 18; *Neh.* 13: 1), in view of his responsibility in writing down God's revelation and dealings with God's people.

In the New Testament also, these first five books are associated particularly with God's law (*Gal.* 3: 10; *Matt.* 12: 5; *Luke* 16: 16; *John* 7: 19; *Luke* 2: 23, 24) and with Moses (*Luke* 2: 22; *Mark* 12: 26; *John* 7: 23; *Luke* 20: 28).

The period covered by the Pentateuch is from the creation to the beginning of Joshua's leadership, after the death of Moses.

PERISH means to die, with all the consequences of death, and eternal separation from God—the opposite, in fact, of everlasting life (*John* 3: 16)

PERSEVERANCE describes the New Testament teaching that once a man is truly saved, he remains saved for ever (*John* 6: 39; 10: 27–29; *II Tim.* 4: 18). God does not keep a man living the Christian life, however, without exertion, diligence and watchfulness on the man's part (*John* 8: 31; *I Tim.* 2: 15; *II Pet.* 1: 11). The strength to persevere in the faith is from God alone (*Phil.* 1: 6). The believer holds fast to the end because he is held fast by the Lord (*I Pet.* 1: 5). Apostasy proves a person was never a true Christian.

PRAYER is not simply making requests of God, but rather conversation with God. In prayer God makes Himself known to the soul, revealing His glory and His love. Christians must endeavour always to pray in the way God has laid down: through Christ and the Holy Spirit. Through Christ Christians have confidence to come before God (*Heb.* 10: 19) and by the Holy Spirit they are enabled to offer true prayer (*Rom.* 8: 9, 26, 27).

PRESERVATION is a term used to describe, first, God's preserving and maintaining the creation which He made so that it continues to exist and function (*Neh.* 9: 6). The Son and the Holy Spirit are also spoken of as having their functions to fulfil in the upholding and continuing of God's creation (*Ps.* 104: 30; *Heb.* 1: 3).

The term is used, secondly, for describing God's preserving or keeping of believers in faith and grace, even using trials and difficulties to the strengthening of their faith (*Phil.* 1: 6; 2: 13; *II Tim.* 4: 18; *I Pet.* 1: 6, 7; *Jude* 24).

PROPHECIES, PROPHECY. Prophecy in the Bible represents the speaking forth of the mind and counsel of God. Although prophecies sometimes referred to future events, prophecy was not necessarily foretelling the future. Rather it was the setting forth of truth which could not be known by natural means. Prophecy apparently passed away when all the Bible books were available to the Christian church. Teaching from the whole Scriptures has taken the place of the prophecy which was necessary before the complete Scriptures were available (cf. *II Pet.* 2: 1).

PROPHETS were God's spokesmen:

individuals supernaturally instructed in God's will, and inspired and commissioned to make known that will to men, both as to present and future events (*Jer.* 1: 9; *Isa.* 51: 16; *II Pet.* 1: 20, 21). The Holy Spirit who inspired them caused some to write down their messages for the benefit of future generations.

PROPITIATION. To propitiate is to "placate" or "appease". The reaction to sin of God's holiness is wrath, displeasure and vengeance. The purpose of propitiation is the removal of God's displeasure. By His death upon the Cross for our sins, Christ propitiated the wrath of God and rendered God well disposed to His people—and this He did as the provision of God the Father's great love for the sinner (*I John* 4: 8, 9, 10).

PROVIDENCE is God's good, kind, and unceasing activity and control of all things, working out everything in agreement with the counsel and design of His own will (*Ps.* 100: 5; *Eph.* 1: 11). Wars, suffering, and such like, are permitted by Him only in so far as they may serve to fulfil His purposes; His final and sure purpose being that they shall cease.

PSALMS means "praises" and gives its name to the longest book in the Bible. The 150 psalms came from different authors, although many—73—are said to have been written by David. They were like a hymnbook for Solomon's temple. Reflecting as they do so many different varieties of experience amongst God's people, strength and help is readily found in them by the Christian believer in his own particular experience.

RECONCILE, RECONCILED, RECONCILIATION. The idea behind the word "reconciliation" is that of making peace again after a quarrel, the bringing together of two parties who have been estranged. The harmony which man knew with God in the beginning has been completely spoiled by man's sin, so that God's attitude of wrath is the only right one man can deserve. Men constitute themselves God's enemies (*Rom.* 5: 10; *Col.* 1: 21), because God's demand for righteousness means that He is always opposed to evil.

Reconciliation, in this situation, is

effected by God's dealing with the root cause of the quarrel—human sin. By the death of His Son God dealt with sin finally and effectively (*Rom.* 5: 10, 11). God caused Christ, who Himself knew no sin, actually to be sin for sinners, so that in Christ they might be made righteous and acceptable to Him (*II Cor.* 5:21). Man may now be reconciled to God as he responds to God's gracious offer in Christ (*II Cor.* 5: 20).

REDEEM, REDEMPTION. Redemption is a term by which Christ's work for sinners may be viewed. Redemption is deliverance from captivity, bondage or death, by purchase. The Biblical picture behind it is that of slavery. By nature we are slaves to sin, deserving the punishment of death (*John* 8: 34). The price paid to purchase sinners from the slavery of sin was the death of the Lord Jesus Christ (*I Cor.* 6: 20; *Eph.* 1: 7). Through Christ, believers become free from the power of sin and death, but they have a privileged obligation, as a consequence, to glorify God in their bodies (*I Cor.* 6: 20).

REGENERATION. See *Question* 26.

REPENTANCE is turning from sin to God (*Ezek.* 33: 11; *Acts* 3: 19; 26: 20), as a result of a change of mind and heart about sin.

RESURRECTION. God the Father raised Christ from the dead (*Acts* 2: 24; 3: 15; *Eph.* 1: 20; *Col.* 2: 12), in fulfilment of the Scriptures (*Ps.* 16: 10; cf. *Acts* 13: 34, 35; *Luke* 24: 44) and Christ's promises (*John* 2: 19–22; *Matt.* 16: 21; 20: 19; *Mark* 9: 9; 14: 28), declaring Christ to be His Son (*Rom.* 1: 4), and His acceptance of Christ's redemptive work (*I Cor.* 15: 14, 17, 19), guaranteeing the justification of all believers (*Acts* 26: 23; *I Cor.* 15: 20, 23, 49).

RESURRECTION OF THE BODY. See *Question* 47.

RESURRECTION OF THE DEAD. This event will take place at Christ's return (*I Thess.* 4: 14–16). All will rise from the dead, believers to the resurrection of life, and unbelievers to the resurrection of judgment (*Dan.* 12: 2; *John* 5: 28, 29; *Acts* 24: 15; *Rev.* 20: 11–15). The resurrection of the dead is a fundamental of the Christian message (*I Cor.* 15: 12, 13; *Heb.* 6: 2; *II Tim.* 2: 18).

RETRIBUTION is generally recompense for evil, although sometimes for good. The wheels of God's vengeance may appear to move slowly (*Eccl.* 8: 11) but vengeance belongs to God, and He will righteously recompense evil (*Rom.* 12: 19; *Rev.* 18: 6). At His return, Christ will carry His recompense with Him, to repay everyone according to his deeds (*Rev.* 22: 12).

REVELATION is God's making known of Himself and His will to men in a way which otherwise they could not themselves discover. It is God speaking to us so that we both know what He is like, and come to know Him.

God has revealed facts about Himself in His creation (*Ps.* 19: 1–4; *Rom.* 1: 20 f), and His providence (*Ps.* 145: 9; *Matt.* 5: 45; *Acts* 14: 16 f), and in man's conscience (*Rom.* 1: 32; 2: 14 f). These things all men everywhere may discern, and they do not bring a knowledge of God's salvation. God speaks to men in a supernatural way through the Scriptures, called "the Word of God", and through His Son, who is also called "the Word"—the One through whom God perfectly reveals Himself to man (*John* 1: 1; *Heb.* 1: 1, 2).

REWARDS have nothing to do with the earning of salvation, for salvation is a free gift (*Rom.* 6: 23; *Eph.* 2: 8). When the gift of salvation has been received, however, God is graciously pleased to give rewards for faithful service (*Matt.* 19: 28; *Mark* 10: 29–30; *Luke* 18: 28, 29).

The parable of the talents teaches that where there is unequal ability but equal faithfulness, the reward will be the same in both cases (*Matt.* 25: 14–30).

The parable of the pounds teaches that where there is equal ability but unequal faithfulness, the reward will be graded (*Luke* 19: 11–27).

RIGHTEOUS, RIGHTEOUSNESS is a characteristic of God, expressing the rightness of all that He is and does (*Rom.* 3: 5). It is used to describe, too, whatever is pleasing to God (*Matt.* 3: 15; 5: 6, 10, 20). The most important use is when it describes the right relationship men are brought into with God when they believe in Christ (*Rom.* 10: 10). They are made righteous in Him, that is to say, they become in Christ all that God requires a man to be (*I Cor.* 1: 30; *II Cor.* 5: 21).

SACRAMENT. A sacrament is an outward sign by which God confirms to believers' consciences His promises of goodwill towards them. The sacraments provide believers with an opportunity of declaring their devotion and allegiance to God.

The two commonly accepted sacraments of the Christian Church are baptism and the Lord's Supper. Most Protestants maintain that these are the only two because our Lord Jesus specifically ordained them (*Matt.* 28: 19; *I Cor.* 11: 23–25). Some prefer the word "ordinances" in place of "sacraments", therefore, because baptism and the Lord's Supper were "ordained" by the Lord.

SACRIFICE, SACRIFICES. A sacrifice was an act of worship by which an offering was made to God of some object belonging to the worshipper, the purpose being to please God and to obtain His favour.

The animal sacrifices of the Old Testament were intended by God to teach the method of salvation. They always had the idea of cleansing behind them and the indispensable element was the shedding of blood (*Heb.* 9: 22, 23) but their repetition only served to point out their effectiveness (*Heb.* 10: 2). Thus the sacrifices reminded men of sin, revealed the need of atonement, and prepared the way for the coming of Christ.

The expression is used of the sacrificial death of Christ, for He offered for all time a single sacrifice for sin (*Heb.* 10: 12), doing what the Old Testament sacrifices could never do. His sacrifice is effective for all time, guaranteeing perfect forgiveness (*Heb.* 9: 26).

SACRIFICE, SACRIFICES (Spiritual). Christ's single sacrifice for sin for all time has completely done away with the need for animal and ceremonial sacrifices.

But God still requires sacrifices of another kind from those who are saved through Christ's one perfect sacrifice. As spiritual priests, Christians may offer to God acceptable spiritual sacrifices (*I Pet.* 2: 5, 9) by means of praise, thanksgiving, prayer, contrition, obedience, sharing and doing good to others (*Ps.* 50: 14; 51: 17; 107: 22; 141: 2; *Rom.* 12: 1; *Heb.* 13: 15, 16; *Jas.* 1: 27). By such means we worship God in the Spirit, for these are all part of the Holy Spirit's activity in the Christian (*Phil.* 3: 3).

SAINT serves as a name for all believers, and is not given in the Bible only to people of outstanding holiness and saintliness.

The word means "separated" or "dedicated". Christians are called upon to separate themselves from evil (*II Tim.* 2: 19), and to dedicate themselves to God's service (*Rom.* 12: 1, 2), because He has set them apart to be His own possession (*I Pet.* 2: 9, 10). For these reasons Christians are called "the saints".

SALVATION is deliverance from the guilt and penalties of sin to enjoy, instead, the unchanging favour of God for ever through repentance and faith in the Lord Jesus Christ (*Acts* 4: 12; *Rom.* 10: 10). It is known and felt in the present by the gift of the Holy Spirit (*Acts* 2: 38) and the forgiveness of sins (*I John* 1: 9), but it will be completely disclosed in the future in the full enjoyment of everlasting life and all its benefits (*Acts* 2: 38–40; 16: 30, 31; *I Thess.* 5: 8, 9, 10; *I Pet.* 1: 5, 13).

SANCTIFICATION. See *Question 35.*

SANCTIFIED when applied either to persons or to things indicates their consecration, dedication, or inclusion in the inner circle of what is holy, because of their association with God in some way. Thus Christians, because of their relationship to God through Christ which sets them apart as His, are described as "sanctified" or as "saints", as the word is sometimes translated.

SATAN is the name of the prince of evil, the adversary, commonly called the devil. He is the great enemy of God and man, the opposer of all that is good and the promoter of all that is evil. He has been defeated already by Christ's death and resurrection, and this defeat will be complete and clear to all at the end of this present age. See *Question 43.*

125

SAVIOUR. A Saviour is a deliverer or preserver, and as a title for Christ is especially appropriate because of His saving work on the Cross on behalf of sinners, promised by God throughout the centuries (*Luke* 2: 11; *Acts* 13: 23; *Phil.* 3: 20). As the Saviour He offers forgiveness of sins on true repentance (*Acts* 5: 31), and life and immortality (*II Tim.* 1: 10).

SCRIPTURES. The word means simply "writings", and in the New Testament is used to refer to the Old Testament (*Luke* 24: 44, 45; *I Cor.* 15: 3 f). The term is often used by Christians to describe both the Old and New Testaments.

SEPARATION FROM GOD. God's holiness demands that He shall be entirely separate from sin. Men's iniquities make a separation between them and God so that fellowship is impossible (*Isa.* 59: 2). The reality of that separation which sin brings is probably best illustrated in the cry of separation which Jesus uttered upon the cross (*Matt.* 27: 46; *Mark* 15: 34), when He who knew no sin was made to be sin, so that in Him we might become the righteousness of God (*II Cor.* 5: 21).

SIGN. A sign, like a miracle, is a work or an event which is contrary to the usual course of nature.

The miracles of Jesus in John's Gospel are all described as "signs" for besides being supernatural in nature, they provided direct evidence of His deity, sufficient to bring a man to living faith in Jesus (*John* 20: 30, 31).

SIN. See *Question* 12.

SON, SON OF GOD was an expression Jesus rarely used, although He spoke of Himself sometimes as "the Son" (*Matt.* 11: 27; *Mark* 13: 32). He is not the Son in the same sense as men may become sons of God through faith (*Matt.* 11: 27; *Luke* 2: 49; *John* 20: 17). He is uniquely God's one Son, His wellbeloved (*Mark.* 12: 6), in a way no one else can be. He and the Father are one, a fact which the disciples fully appreciated at the resurrection (*John* 20: 28; *Rom.* 1: 3, 4). All the works, glory and perfection of God may be attributed to Him (*John* 1: 3; *Col.* 1: 16, 17; *Heb.* 1: 2; *Mark* 2:

5, 7). He is one with His Father, He is equal with God.

SOUL is, firstly, the seat and centre of the inner life of a man in its varied aspects, and it can represent man's feelings and emotions. But, secondly, it is also the seat and centre of that life that goes beyond this life. As such, the soul can receive God's salvation (*Jas.* 1: 21; *I Pet.* 1: 9). Men cannot harm it, but God can give it over to destruction (*Matt.* 10: 28).

It is because it is capable of partaking of the nature of God (*I Pet.* 1: 22; cf. *II Pet.* 1: 4) that its worth is so tremendous—indeed nothing man possesses is more precious (*Matt.* 16: 26; *Mark* 8: 37).

SOVEREIGNTY is supreme authority and absolute dominion.

Such sovereignty by right is God's alone. He accomplishes all things according to the counsel of His own will (*Eph.* 1: 11). He is over all things and He does what He will (*Rom.* 9: 5, 18).

SPIRIT is sometimes used in place of the word "soul" (*Luke* 23: 46; *Acts* 7: 59; *I Cor.* 5: 3, 5; *Eccl.* 12: 7), and compared with the body is the more important, being that part of us which thinks, feels and wills and lives for ever (*Matt.* 16: 26; *II Cor.* 5: 8; *II Tim.* 4: 22).

It is also used to describe God's nature: He is spirit, that is to say, there is nothing material in His nature (*John* 4: 24), He has no body. Like the wind—the same word, in fact—spirit is invisible, immaterial, and powerful, and these characteristics perfectly belong to God.

SPIRIT OF CHRIST is a title given to the Holy Spirit, the Third Person of the Trinity, on several occasions in the New Testament (*Rom.* 8: 9; *Gal.* 4: 6; *Phil.* 1: 19; *I Pet.* 1: 11).

The title expresses the close link that exists in the Bible between the two Persons. The Spirit was promised by the Son as well as by the Father (*John* 14: 17, 26). It is by the Spirit that Christ lives in believers' hearts (*Eph.* 3: 16, 17). The ministry of the Spirit has been and is, to take of the things of Christ and to make them known to men (*I Pet.* 1: 11; *John* 16: 14).

TEMPTATION is used both in a good and a bad sense, and can have the meaning of test as much as tempt. In the good sense God tests men so that they may prove themselves true (*Heb.* 11: 17) and in this sense Christ was tested by God (*Heb.* 2: 18; 4: 15).

In the bad sense there is the enticement to sin, which is the devil's work (*I Cor.* 7: 5; *Matt.* 4: 1; *Gal.* 6: 1; *Jas.* 1: 13).

TESTAMENT. A testament, like a covenant, is an undertaking or engagement made between God and man, at God's initiative through His promises.

The Old Testament relates to the promises, relating principally to this life, which God made to the Jews. The Old Testament was built upon the keeping of God's law.

The New Testament relates to those everlasting promises which God makes in Christ throughout all the Scriptures. This testament is built on faith and not on works (*John* 3: 16).

TESTING describes the use God makes of varying and difficult circumstances to make known to men their real character, and often to prove to them the reality and strength of their faith and obedience (*Gen.* 22: 1, 12; *Heb.* 11: 17; *I Pet.* 1: 7; 4: 12).

TRANSFIGURATION is the term used in the gospels to record what three of the apostles witnessed of Christ's glory. For a few moments the heavenly glory of Christ, which was usually hidden by the conditions of Christ's human life, shone through His body and its clothing (*Matt.* 17: 2; *Mark* 9: 2). This revelation was accompanied by a statement of God's approval of His Son.

TRANSGRESSION is the violation of God's law, the picture behind the word being the stepping over the bounds laid down by the law. When we do what God's law forbids, we transgress—we step over the bounds God has set (*Dan.* 9: 11).

TRESPASS. To trespass is to make a false step, to turn aside from right and truth, to sin either against men (*Matt.* 6: 14, 15) or against God (*Rom.* 5: 15, 17; *Gal.* 6: 1).

TRINITY. See *Question* 8.

UNJUST is used to describe those who do contrary to what is right in the sight of God—all men, by nature, find themselves rightly so described (*Matt.* 5: 45; *Acts* 24: 15; *I Pet.* 3: 18).

UNRIGHTEOUSNESS is wrongdoing or the persistent doing of that which is wrong—the characteristic of man as a sinner (*I John* 1: 9; 5: 17). See **INIQUITY** which is almost identical.

WASHED is a description of the Christian when forgiveness of sins is thought of in terms of inward and spiritual cleansing (*Acts* 22: 16; *I Cor.* 6: 11; *I John* 1: 7-9).

WICKED describes a person or a thing that is evil, bad, base, worthless, vicious or degenerate. The wicked man's life is governed by transgression; he has no fear of God (*Ps.* 36: 1). The prosperity he appears to enjoy is a fleeting experience (*Ps.* 37: 13).

WICKED ONE. See EVIL ONE.

WICKEDNESS is baseness, maliciousness and sinfulness. It is the characteristic of this present age (*Gal.* 1: 4) and comes from within man, from the heart (*Mark* 7: 22). Wickedness multiplies and its intense multiplication will be a mark of the end (*Matt.* 24: 11).

WILL is the ability we possess as persons to decide or think ourselves as deciding upon action, without any other cause. It represents the act of willing or desiring. This exercise of will is necessary to our personality and to our responsibility as rational beings. The will is always free, and we have the power of choice. We also have to say, however, that the will is not always good, for, since the fall of man, it is diseased, impaired and always prone to evil.

WORD OF GOD, The. The expression is used in three particular senses. Firstly, our Lord Jesus Christ is called the Word of God (*John* 1: 1), in that God has spoken to us in Christ, giving us His final and complete revelation in Him (*Heb.* 1: 1, 2).

Secondly, the gospel is called the Word of God (*Mark* 4: 14; *Luke* 5: 1; 8: 11; 11: 28) because it is God's message to sinful men (*Rom.* 1: 16; 15: 16).

Thirdly, the Scriptures are the Word of God. Christ and the apostles spoke of the Old Testament and quoted it as God's Word (*Mark* 7: 13; *Acts* 3: 22–25; *Rom.* 1: 2; *II Tim.* 3: 16).

And then the Word of God taught by the Lord and the apostles is the content of the New Testament, thus constituting the whole Bible the Word of God. This fact makes the Bible the sole authority in everything which concerns faith and life. When the Bible speaks, God speaks. See *Questions* 3, 4.

WORKS (Human) i.e. deeds of men. A man cannot be made acceptable to God by what he does or achieves (*Rom.* 3: 20, 28; *Gal.* 2: 16; *Eph.* 2: 8, 9). His acceptance by God depends upon his relationship to Christ. But good works are the demanded and expected result of a right relationship with God through Jesus Christ (*Eph.* 2: 10; *Tit.* 2: 7, 14; 3: 1, 8).

WORLD is used sometimes simply to describe the world in a geographical sense (*John* 1: 10), or the men and women of the world (*John* 3: 16, 17). Most frequently, it refers to the life of men as dominated and organised by the god of this world, Satan (*II Cor.* 4: 4; *I John* 2: 15–17).

WORSHIP is the acknowledgment by the believer of the worth-ship of God with every part of his being (*Rom.* 12: 1, 2). Such worship is only acceptable to God as it is offered through Christ, the Mediator and our great High Priest (*Heb.* 13: 15, 16). This worship cannot be separated from practical conduct bearing out what has been professed by the lips (*Jas.* 1: 27).

WRATH is the inevitable reaction of the holiness of God against sin, which demands that He, the righteous Judge, shall finally reckon with it (*John* 3: 36; *Rom.* 1: 18; *I Thess.* 1: 10; 5: 9).

Bible Guidelines

I. LOYALTY TO GOD

Exodus 20: 3: "You shall have no other gods before me."

Question: What does the first commandment teach?

Answer: The first commandment teaches that our first loyalty is to be to the Lord Himself, and idolatry of any sort is forbidden. The loyalty that is acceptable to God is sincere, unreserved, and carefully maintained.

1. Loyalty to God is His proper due for two principal reasons: God's uniqueness, and the redemption He has provided.

God's uniqueness.

(a) There is only one God (*Deut.* 4: 39; *II Sam.* 22: 32; *I Cor.* 8: 4): He is God in heaven above and on the earth beneath (*Deut.* 4: 39).

(b) God made us (*Ps.* 100: 3): He is the almighty Creator who spreads the canopy of the sky over chaos and suspends the earth in the void (*Job* 26: 7); He alone has power over creation (*Jer.* 14: 22).

(c) None can be compared with God: He is altogether different and unique in His majesty and glory (*Ps.* 98: 6–8; *Isa.* 44: 6).

(d) While to some people, there are a great many gods, both in heaven and on earth (*I Cor.* 8: 5, 6), these have no existence in the real world (*I Cor.* 8: 4), and are impotent (*Jer.* 14: 22).

(e) When other so-called gods are confronted with the Lord, men and women are compelled to acknowledge that "the Lord is God" (*I Kings* 18: 39); He has every right to our exclusive loyalty and the false gods of men's creation are not worthy to be mentioned in the same breath (*Isa.* 45: 5, 21–23; *Jer.* 10: 1–10).

(f) We are to understand the Lord's uniqueness and take it to heart (*Deut.* 4: 39), the only proper conclusion being that we should obey His laws (*Deut.* 4: 40).

God's provision of redemption.

(g) The Lord liberated His people from their slavery in Egypt (*Ex.* 20:2), and Christians know a similar and even greater deliverance and redemption (*I Pet.* 1: 18, 19).

(h) The supreme loyalty of the Christian is to the Lord Jesus Christ (*Eph.* 5: 21), who loved him and gave Himself for him (*Gal.* 2: 20).

(i) Even as the passover feast served to keep fresh in the Israelites' memory the deliverance God had given them (*Ex.* 12: 14), so the Lord's Supper keeps fresh in Christians' memories the redemption God has achieved for them through the death of His Son, our Lord Jesus Christ (*I Cor.* 11:20–26).

2. Loyalty to God forbids idolatry in any form.

(a) The heathen worship idols of gold, silver, bronze, iron, wood and stone, made by their own hands (*Ps.* 135: 15–17; *Dan.* 5: 4, 23).

(b) By such idolatry men exchange the glory of the immortal God for images representing mortal man or birds or animals or reptiles (*Rom.* 1: 23), and then trust in them (*Hab.* 2: 18).

(c) The error of idolatry is that it worships the created thing rather than the Creator (*Judg.* 8: 24–28; *Rom.* 1: 25; *Eph.* 5: 5).

(d) But idolatry is not limited to the worship of material idols of man's manufacture, for anything or any person claiming our primary loyalty becomes "another god" (cf. *Col.* 3: 5).

(e) Idolatry begins in the heart (*Deut.* 11: 16), and that which has most of our heart and thoughts is our god (*Luke* 12: 34).

(f) Whatever men boast of tends to be a god to them: for example, wisdom (*Jer.* 9: 23, 24), human strength or resourcefulness (*Jer.* 17: 5), good works (*Isa.* 64: 6), respectability and reputation (*Luke* 18: 11).

(g) Wealth is a most common idol (*Mark* 10: 22; *Job* 31: 24; *Matt.* 13: 22), and covetousness is identified as idolatry (*Eph.* 5: 5; *Col.* 3: 5).

(h) Men make a god of pleasure (*II Tim.* 3: 4), especially of their appetites (*Phil.* 3: 19), insofar as they are proud of what they should be ashamed of and this world is the limit of their horizons.

(i) Having the heart set on the good things of this life is a form of idolatry (*II Tim.* 4: 10; *I John* 2: 15, 16).

(j) Even Christian leaders can become idols, having the place in people's affections and loyalty which belongs to God (*I Cor.* 1: 11, 12).

(k) Idolatry dishonours God (*Dan.* 5: 23): it represents man's rejection of God (*Rom.* 1: 18–23), his forsaking of God (*Jer.* 1: 16), his refusal to hear God's words (*Jer.* 13: 10, 11) and his breaking faith with God (*Judg.* 2: 17).

(l) Idolatry is spiritual harlotry (*Hos.* 12: 12–14) or adultery (*Judg.* 2: 17; cf. *Jas.* 4: 4).

(m) Idolatry brings forth God's judgment (*Hos.* 8: 4; *Amos* 5: 25–27; *Micah* 1: 7): those who fall into idolatry find many sorrows, in marked contrast to those who serve the Lord (*Ps.* 16: 4, 8–11).

(n) Idolatry must be rooted out (*Micah* 5: 14), utterly destroyed and the Lord's rightful place re-established (*Judg.* 6: 25–27), for He can be served only as other gods are put away (*Josh.* 24: 14).

3. Loyalty to God must be sincere, unreserved and carefully maintained.

Sincere loyalty.

(a) The Lord is to be served with sincerity (*Josh.* 24: 14).

(b) Professions of loyalty which are insincere serve only to increase sin (*Hos.* 8: 11); our motives must be right as well as our actions (*Amos* 5: 18–27).

(c) Loyalty to God is a spiritual matter, and includes, in the light of God's uniqueness and redemption, the presenting of our bodies as a living sacrifice, holy—the kind He can accept (*Rom.* 12: 1).

(d) God looks for loyalty which springs from a willing mind (*I Chron.* 28:9).

Unreserved loyalty.

(e) God demands our first loyalty (*Josh.* 24: 14); He will countenance no rival, for He is a jealous God (*Ex.* 20: 5; 14: 14), in that He will not share His praise—which includes our loyalty—with anyone else (*Isa.* 42: 8).

(f) We have to choose whom we will worship: the one true God, the Lord, or the so-called gods which abound around us (*Josh.* 24: 14, 15; *I Thess.* 1: 9).

(g) Love for God must be absolute: He is to be loved with all our heart, soul, and mind (*Matt.* 22: 37).

(h) "I belong to the Lord" should be our glad testimony (*Isa.* 44: 4).

Carefully maintained loyalty.

(k) We are to cleave to the Lord our God (*Josh.* 23: 8), which means being very careful to keep on loving the Lord our God (*Josh.* 23: 11).

(l) To avoid idolatry we have to watch our heart (*Deut.* 11: 16), deliberately shunning the worship of idols of any sort (*I Cor.* 10: 14), and keeping ourselves away from anything that might take God's place in our hearts (*I John* 5: 21).

(m) This carefully maintained watchfulness is necessary because behind idolatry of every kind there is the activity of Satan (*I Cor.* 8: 5; 10: 19; cf. *Acts* 5: 3), and he is unceasing in his wiles and deceits (*I Pet.* 5: 8).

(n) We are to be always thinking of the Lord (*Ps.* 16: 8), having our eyes ever looking to Him (*Ps.* 25: 15).

5. Loyalty to God is rewarded by God.

(a) There is no limit to the benefits which come when we are faithful in our loyalty to the Lord (*Deut.* 28: 1ff).

(b) Loyalty to the Lord—the supreme wisdom—brings a long, good life, riches, honour, pleasures and peace (*Prov.* 3: 17).

(c) Those committed to the Lord have the secret of joy (*Isa.* 56: 7).

(d) When the Lord is our God, we may be sure of His blessing (*Ps.* 67: 6), knowing that the whole of our life is under His control, with everything fitting into His good purposes (*Rom.* 8: 28).

(e) The rewards of loyalty extend beyond this life with the promise of the gift of the kingdom of God (*Luke* 12: 32), and a never-ending share in God's glory and honour (*I Pet.* 5: 4).

2. WORSHIP OF GOD

Exodus 20: 4–6: "You shall not make for yourself an idol in the form of anything in heaven above or on the earth beneath or in the waters below. You shall not bow down to them or worship them; for I, the Lord your God, am a jealous God, punishing the children for the sin of the fathers to the third and fourth generation of those who hate me, but showing love to thousands who love me and keep my commandments."

Question: What does the second commandment teach?

Answer: The second commandment teaches that God alone is to be worshipped, without any visual symbols of Himself, and in strict accordance with the manner in which He has revealed Himself to us.

1. God is to be worshipped.

(a) Worship is God's due as our Creator (*Ps.* 100; *Rom.* 1: 25): it is the natural expression of our obedience to the first commandment (*Ex.* 20: 3).

(b) Worship is the giving of glory, honour, and thanks to God (*Rev.* 4: 9); and in our worship of the Lord we acknowledge that He alone is worthy to receive such (*Rev.* 4: 11).

2. God alone is to be worshipped.

(a) The Lord Himself is the proper object of all worship (*Ex.* 20: 2, 3).

(b) He is jealous of His honour as the one Lord (*Ex.* 20: 5); He will not give His glory to anyone else (*Isa.* 42: 8).

(c) He will share neither our affection nor our obedience with any other (*Ex.* 20: 5, 6).

3. God is to be worshipped without any visual symbols of Himself.

(a) We are forbidden by this commandment both to worship images of other so-called gods and to use images of the one true God (*Ex.* 20: 4).

(b) God is against any representation of Himself (*Lev.* 26: 1): we are not to make for ourselves "an idol in the form of anything in heaven above or on the earth beneath or in the waters below" (*Ex.* 20: 4).

(c) Men act corruptly when they make an image of God, in the form of any figure whatsoever (*Deut.* 4: 15–19), so that we may conclude that idolatry is not only the worship of false gods, but even the worship of the one true God by images.

(d) This demand that the Lord should be worshipped without visual images is reinforced in the Old Testament by the reminder that the Israelites saw no form of God on the day that the Lord spoke to them at Horeb. Since the Lord did not give a visible form of Himself, but instead spoke to them, so now we are not to seek visual symbols of Him but simply to obey His Word (*Deut.* 4: 15–19).

Reasons for the prohibition of visual symbols of God.

(e) God's glory is jeopardised when images are used in worship (*Isa.* 40: 18–31): wherever we go in creation, all things were created by the Lord, and are subject to Him, thus making it ridiculous to seek a likeness of Him in the created order (*Ex.* 20: 4; *Deut.* 5: 8).

(f) When men picture their god in human form they soon reckon to him their own human weaknesses (*I Kings* 18: 26–29).

(g) Furthermore, it is impossible for man to make an image of God because God is spirit (*John* 4: 24): He cannot be made static or controlled as the manufactured images would suggest.

(h) The Lord requires us to guard against unworthy conceptions of Him, and of creating false images of Him in our hearts (*Ex.* 20: 4, 5).

4. God is to be worshipped in the manner He has laid down.

(a) The second commandment insists that worship must be in accord with divine revelation; we are warned against ways of worship that lead us to dishonour God and to put aside His truth (*Ex.* 20: 4, 5).

(b) We are to receive nothing, practise nothing, and own nothing in the worship of God but what is of His appointment (*Rev.* 22: 8, 9).

(c) We are summoned to recognise that God is so great that we may worship Him acceptably only when we do so in the manner He chooses to lay down (*Isa.* 55: 8, 9; *Rom.* 11: 33, 34).

(d) There is a wrong as well as a right way to worship God (*John* 4: 23, 24): God is spirit and those who worship Him must worship in spirit and in truth—i.e. spiritually and truly.

(e) The New Testament reveals that there is only one image of God that is wholly true and worthy, and that is the Lord Jesus Christ Himself who is the image of the invisible God (*Col.* 1: 15ff): thus all Christian worship centres around God's Son because in His face we see the glory of God as nowhere else (*II Cor.* 4: 6; *John* 1: 14, 18).

5. God desires worship springing from love, and expressed in obedience (Ex. 20: 6).

(a) Worship is in vain if the feelings of the heart do not correspond with the expression of the lips (*Isa.* 1: 11–17; *Amos* 4: 4; 5: 18–27; *Matt.* 15: 8, 9).

(b) Acceptable worship is a response

to the mercies of God (*Rom.* 12: 1ff): we love Him because He first loved us (*I John* 4: 19).

(c) Our worship is expressed in obedience to His Word rather than any respect for visual images of God (*Deut.* 4: 15–19).

(d) True worship presupposes the willingness to obey the Lord (*Josh.* 5: 14, 15; *Isa.* 6).

(e) At conversion we turn away from idols to worship and serve the true and living God with joy (*I Thess.* 1: 6–9).

3. REVERENCE

Exodus 20: 7: "You shall not misuse the name of the Lord your God, for the Lord will not hold anyone guiltless who misuses his name."

Question: What does the third commandment teach?

Answer: The third commandment teaches us to avoid all wrong use of God's Name, to treat His Name with the greatest respect, and to make it our deliberate purpose to honour and reverence Him.

1. **The Special Use of the word "Name" in the Bible.**

(a) Names have meanings, and this particularly applies to the Name of God (*Ex.* 3: 13–15).

(b) God's Name proclaims and reveals His character (*Ex.* 33: 19), all that He is and all that He does (*Ex.* 34: 5, 6).

(c) God's Name is linked, therefore, with His attributes and characteristics, and the Psalms provide many illustrations:

righteousness (*Ps.* 89: 15, 16);
faithfulness (*Ps.* 89: 24);
salvation (*Ps.* 96: 2);
holiness (*Ps.* 99: 3, 4);
goodness (*Ps.* 100: 4, 5);
mercy (*Ps.* 109: 21);
love (*Ps.* 138: 2);
truth (*Ps.* 138: 2);
glory (*Ps.* 148: 13).

(d) The adjective most commonly associated with God's Name is "holy" (*Ps.* 33: 21; 103: 1; 106: 47; 111: 9; 145: 21).

(e) So close is the identification of the Lord with His Name that He may be spoken of as The Name (*Prov.* 18: 10; *Isa.* 30: 27).

2. **Ways in which God's Name is used wrongly.**

(a) **Perjury.** Perjury is the sin of taking an oath in the Name of God and then uttering falsehood (*Lev.* 19: 12; *Num.* 30: 2; *Deut.* 6: 13; *Ps.* 15: 4; *Zech.* 5: 4).

(b) God's Name is defiled or polluted when men shrug aside promises and oaths made in His Name, holding them of little account (*Jer.* 34: 16), and when they make a vow they never intend to keep (*Deut.* 5: 11).

(c) Solemn and legal oaths are not prohibited; it is the abuse of them that is wrong (*Lev.* 19: 12; cf. *Rom.* 9: 1; *II Cor.* 1: 23).

(d) **Rash and unnecessary swearing.** When men introduce the Name of God into their conversation by an oath simply to strengthen what they are saying, they use His Name wrongly (*II Kings* 9: 20).

(e) Even swearing by heaven is swearing by God's throne, and swearing by the earth swearing by God's footstool (*Matt.* 5: 34, 35; cf. *Matt.* 23: 21, 22).

(f) Jephthah, for example, rashly swore an oath in God's Name which was entirely out of keeping with God's character (*Judg.* 11: 31).

(g) **Blasphemy.** Blasphemy is to treat

irreverently the Majesty of God, to utter His Name, and then to curse Him (cf. *Lev.* 24: 11).

(h) Blasphemy occurs when men deliberately defy God by mentioning His Name and casting doubt upon His character (*II Kings* 19: 4, 10, 22).

(i) **Unnecessary and irreverent use of God's Name in ordinary conversation** (*Matt.* 7: 21–23).

(j) Sarah, for example, wrongly put the whole weight of blame upon Abraham for their shared mistake concerning Hagar, and unnecessarily brought God's Name into her conversation for emphasis (*Gen.* 16: 5).

(k) **Offering religious worship while living a godless life** (*Mal.* 2: 13–16).

(l) To say we are the Lord's by the performance of religious worship but not to obey Him, so that our worship is mere words, reeled off by heart, is to use God's Name wrongly (*Isa.* 29: 13).

(m) God's Name is brought into disrepute by bad conduct on the part of those who profess loyalty to Him (*Prov.* 30: 9).

(n) Absalom, for example, expressed the desire to worship the Lord, and went through the forms of doing so, only to further a political conspiracy (*II Sam.* 15: 7, 8, 12); he used God's Name for a completely unworthy purpose.

3. **Ways by which we honour and reverence God's Name.**

(a) **Praise and Thanksgiving.** We honour God's Name by praising Him for the wonders of His grace towards us (*Joel* 2: 26), and for the glorious truth that everything about Him is good (*Ps. 54: 6).*

(b) **Meditation and study.** We reverence the Lord by thinking about His Name, and pondering all He has revealed to us of Himself (*Mal.* 3: 16).

(c) **Love.** We show our reverence for God by loving His Name (*Ps. 5: 11), and being jealous for His interest (*Ps. 69: 9; John 2: 17).

(d) **Carefulness.** We reverence God's Name by keeping before us His holiness, and speaking about Him with care, encouraging one another to serve and worship Him with holy fear and awe (*Ps. 89: 7; Heb. 12: 28, 29).

(e) **Obedience.** We show our respect for God's Name by living in conformity to the will and character that Name reveals (*Micah* 4: 5).

(f) **Prayer.** We honour God by calling upon Him in prayer for help because it is His Name, His unchanging character, which gives us the assurance that He hears and answers prayer (*Ps.* 99: 6).

(g) **Confidence.** We reverence God by showing publicly that our confidence is in the Lord, and that, having committed ourselves to Him, we can wait with assurance and without impatience for His answer (*Ps.* 52: 9).

(h) **Evangelism.** We reverence God's Name by taking seriously the fact that He alone is the supreme Lord, whose saving deeds need to be known in all the world around (*Isa.* 12: 4).

(i) **Truthfulness.** We honour and reverence God's Name by being committed to complete truthfulness in every sphere for one of the main purposes of the third commandment is to prevent us ever calling upon God to confirm a lie (*Ex.* 20: 7). God is truth (*John* 1: 14; 14: 6) and He calls us to commitment to truth (*Eph.* 4: 25; 5: 9; 6: 14).

136

4. REST

Exodus 20: 8-11: "Remember the sabbath day by keeping it holy. Six days you shall labour and do all your work, but the seventh day is a sabbath to the Lord your God. On it you shall not do any work, neither you, nor your son or daughter, nor your manservant or maidservant, nor your animals, nor the alien within your gates. For in six days the Lord made the heavens and the earth, the sea, and all that is in them, but he rested on the seventh day. Therefore the Lord blessed the sabbath day and made it holy."

Question: What does the fourth commandment teach?

Answer: The fourth commandment teaches that the keeping of one day in seven as a sabbath is a special means of honouring God our Creator and Redeemer and of renewing our minds, bodies, and souls in the manner their constitution and well-being require.

It encourages us, upon a weekly basis, to lay aside material considerations, so that the worth of God, the worth of our soul, and spiritual issues and concerns, may occupy our thoughts and more effectively influence our living.

1. **The change from Saturday, i.e. the original sabbath, to Sunday.**

(a) The vital element in the commandment is that there should be six days of work and a day of rest— the particular day set apart is not the essence of the commandment (*Ex.* 20: 9, 10).

(b) The first Christians soon recognised that the Old Testament regulations for the Sabbath are part of the ceremonial law which has been fulfilled in our Lord Jesus Christ, so that they are no longer binding on God's people (*Rom.* 14: 5-6; *Col.* 2: 16, 17).

(c) In principle, every day is the Lord's Day, and is equally suitable for worship (*Acts* 2: 46).

(d) Yet it was also appreciated that if the purposes of the day are to be fulfilled it should, as far as possible, be the same day for all (*Acts* 20: 7; notice in *I Cor.* 11: 17-20 the emphasis on "coming together as a church").

(e) It soon became the practice to meet on Sunday in honour of our Lord's resurrection from the dead "on the first day of the week" (*John* 20: 1ff).

(f) The Lord Jesus appeared to His disciples on the first Easter Sunday, and again on the following Sunday.

(g) There are references to Christians meeting on "the first day of the week" (*Acts* 20: 7; *I Cor.* 16: 2), and it would seem to have been the recognised day for Christians to assemble together.

(h) The change not only bore witness to the fact of the Resurrection, but it emphasised the difference between the Christian Sunday and the Jewish Sabbath; the Jewish Sabbath came at the end of six days and spoke of a rest to come, the Christian Sunday comes at the beginning of the week symbolising "the rest" which Jesus Christ has won for those who trust in Him.

2. **The reasons for the appointment of the sabbath.**

First, God's own glory.

(a) It is His sabbath (*Ezek.* 20: 16, 21, 24).

(b) God's glory is His own Person: when we observe the sabbath we display the likeness of God in a

137

pattern of work and rest for He made us in His own image (*Gen.* 1: 26, 27).

(c) The sabbath provides us with a special opportunity for remembering and meditating upon His work of creation and redemption. We cannot do this without wanting to praise Him, and thus to glorify Him (*Ps.* 50: 23).

(d) By our proper use of the sabbath we honour God by acknowledging His claim upon our time and service (*Ex.* 23: 25).

Secondly, man's own good.

(e) God blessed the sabbath, i.e. made it for man's blessing (*Gen.* 2: 3).

(f) The sabbath was made for man, not man for the sabbath (*Mark* 2: 27): that is to say, it was made for man's own true well-being in body, mind and soul. The need for one day's rest in seven is built into man's physical and mental constitution. It is not something that was peculiar to the Jews as part of their religious heritage, but something which is a necessity for all. As man needs daily rest, so he needs a weekly rest.

Thirdly, a covenant sign.

(g) It is a reminder of the covenant between God and His people for ever (*Ex.* 31: 13, 17; *Ezek.* 20: 12).

(h) It helps God's people to remember that they have a special and unique relationship to the Lord who sets them apart for Himself, for His own possession (*Ex.* 31: 13).

3. **Our duties regarding the sabbath or Sunday.**

(a) **To remember it.**

(i) The word "remember" (*Ex.* 20: 8) bears the meaning of **imprint** or **mark** so as to be recognised. We are to imprint its importance upon our minds, and by our speech and actions mark it out as recognisably different from other days.

(ii) To remember it is to hold it as a delight (*Isa.* 58: 13).

(iii) To remember it is to count the keeping of it as an honour and privilege (*Isa.* 58: 13).

(b) **To keep it holy** (*Ex.* 20: 8).

(i) The idea behind the word "holy" is that of being cut off, separated, or set apart.

(ii) God calls upon us to set one day in seven apart, and to view it, and use it differently from the rest.

(iii) We keep it holy by using it in such a way that we show that the Lord has our first loyalty.

(c) **To lay aside our daily work** (*Ex.* 20: 9, 10).

(i) Work is an essential element in God's plan for human life (*Gen.* 2: 15) but man needs rest from work (*Ex.* 23: 12).

(ii) We are, therefore, commanded to rest (*Ex.* 31: 15): "You shall not do any work" (*Ex.* 20: 10).

(iii) We are to put aside our ordinary callings on this one day (*Neh.* 13: 15–18).

(iv) The Hebrew word **shabbâth** translated "Sabbath" means **cessation, intermission** or **rest**.

(d) **To allow others the same opportunity of rest** (*Ex.* 20: 10).

(i) We are to do our utmost to ensure that in so far as our own conduct is concerned, others may enjoy rest too.

(ii) We have a measure of responsibility for others to see that they have the opportunity of rest: "You shall not do any work, neither you, nor your son, or daughter, nor your manservant or maid servant, nor your animals, nor the alien within your gates."

138

(e) **To remember God's mighty acts of creation and redemption.**

(i) We are to remember God's rest from His great work of creation (*Ex.* 20: 11): God Himself "worked" for the first six days and "rested" on the seventh day (*Gen.* 1: 31; 2: 1–3).

(ii) We are to remember God's redemption: the Jews were instructed to remember on the sabbath how they were servants in the land of Egypt, and the Lord their God brought them out of Egypt with a mighty hand and an outstretched arm (*Deut.* 5: 15).

(iii) Christians remember on the Lord's Day a far greater deliverance in which they were ransomed from the empty folly of their lives lived without God by the precious blood of Jesus Christ, in whom they have come to trust knowing that He was raised from the dead on the first day of the week for their justification (*I Pet.* 1: 18, 19; *Rom.* 4: 25).

(iv) The particular focus of Christian worship, therefore, will be the glory of the Risen Lord (*Rev.* 1: 10ff).

(v) We delight ourselves in the Lord, calling the sabbath a delight for it gives us the opportunity of occupying ourselves with the Lord (*Isa.* 58: 13, 14).

(f) **To engage in humanitarian action.**

(i) It is lawful to do good on the sabbath (*Matt.* 12: 12).

(ii) It is imperative to do good on the sabbath (*Luke* 13: 10–17 notice the word "ought" in verse 16).

(iii) We are to seize the special opportunities it affords of doing good to others (e.g. *Mark* 2: 1–5; *Luke* 13: 10–17; 14: 1–6; *John* 9), and that probably includes activities such as visiting a hospital, opening our homes to the lonely, and calling in to see the elderly.

(iv) The Lord's Day is never to be an excuse for avoiding rightful duties to our fellow men (*Mark* 3: 1–6).

(g) **To remember that it is God's institution.**

(i) The choice of one day in seven was not man's, but God's: God hallowed it (*Gen.* 2: 3).

(ii) "In six days the Lord made the heavens and the earth, the sea, and all that is in them, but he rested on the seventh day. Therefore the Lord blessed the sabbath day and made it holy" (*Ex.* 20: 11).

4. **Benefits of observing the sabbath principle.**

(The reason for using the term "the sabbath principle" is that contemporary life with its complex machinery and shift systems frequently involves some working on the recognised "sabbath," i.e. Sunday. Where this is the case, both employers and employees should be strongly encouraged to observe the **principle** still by giving another day that week in lieu, and insisting that it should be taken as a day of rest.)

(a) **Blessing from God.**

(i) We shall find joy in God (*Isa.* 58: 14).

(ii) We shall have God-given success in our endeavours (*Isa.* 58: 14).

(iii) We shall obtain our full share of the blessings promised us (*Isa.* 58: 14).

(b) **Rest and renewal.**

(i) By rest both we and all associated with us, including animals, are refreshed (*Ex.* 23: 12).

(ii) We shall renew our strength, according to His promise to those who wait upon Him (*Isa. 40: 31*).

(c) **A necessary corrective is imposed**

139

upon our proneness to self-seeking (*Amos* 8: 5).

(i) We deliberately turn aside from our own business, from seeking our own interests or attending to our own affairs and honour the Lord (*Isa.* 58: 13).

(ii) By putting aside "getting" for a day at least, we symbolically reject covetousness as a motive for living (*Col.* 3: 5–8).

(iii) We remember on the "sabbath" that this world is not everything and that there is another world and kingdom to be put first (*Matt.* 6: 33; *Col.* 3: 1, 2).

(iv) We deliberately turn aside for a brief while from the natural preoccupations of our daily work so that the well-being of our soul, and spiritual issues and concerns occupy our thoughts and more effectively influence our living (*Ps.* 73: 17; 77: 13; *II Cor.* 4: 18; *Heb.* 10: 10, 13–16).

(d) **The proper exercise of our soul in the worship of God.**

(i) We delight ourselves in the Lord (*Isa.* 58: 13, 14), making the sabbath a day of joy as we do so.

(ii) We esteem a day in His courts better than a thousand elsewhere (*Ps.* 84: 10).

(iii) We are provided with the opportunity to cultivate our spiritual life to which we are continually exhorted (*Ps.* 27: 4, 8; *II Pet.* 3: 18).

(e) **The strengthening of family life and unity.**

(i) All the members of a family are instructed and encouraged to rest together (*Ex.* 20: 10).

(ii) It is a day for being at home—being "in one's place" (*Ex.* 16: 29).

(f) **The encouragement and profit of Christian fellowship.**

(i) We are able to enter into the worship and fellowship of God's people (*Ps.* 55: 14; 122: 1; 132: 7).

(ii) We are able to benefit from the teaching of God's Word (*Luke* 4: 31; 6: 6; *Acts* 13: 13, 14, 15, 44; *Acts* 17: 2; 18: 4).

(iii) Assembling ourselves together, we may stir up one another to love and to good works (*Heb.* 10: 24).

(g) **A helpful anticipation and reminder of the everlasting rest God prepares for His believing people.**

(i) God's rest on the seventh day is a type of the messianic rest which God will yet give to His people (*Heb.* 4: 4, 9).

(ii) Our Lord Jesus Christ, having completed His work for us by His death and resurrection, has entered into His rest, and one day we are going to share in that eternal heavenly rest (*John* 14: 2, 3).

5. RESPECT FOR, AND SUBMISSION TO, PROPER AUTHORITY

Exodus 20: 12: "Honour your father and your mother, so that you may live long in the land the Lord your God is giving you."

Question: What does the fifth commandment teach?

Answer: The fifth commandment teaches us the general principle of paying respect to whom respect is due, and honour to whom honour is due by underlining the fundamental and specific responsibility children have to honour their parents, a responsibility which is at the very heart of a nation's well-being.

1. **The meaning of the word "honour."**
(a) The Hebrew word for "honour" is "kabed" with the basic meaning of "to be heavy" from which comes the sense of making weighty, and of

lading respect upon a person. Thus, to honour our parents is to regard them as eminently worthy of respect—to recognise that they deserve a "weight" of respect.

(b) The Greek equivalent of the Hebrew word, used in the New Testament, "timaō," conveys the thought of fixing a valuation, and, by implication, to revere.

(c) Thus, to honour our parents is to fix a right valuation upon their worth, causing us to revere them.

(d) The honour we give to parents is to be a reflection of the honour we know we ought to give to God our heavenly Father (*Mal.* 1: 6).

(e) The honouring of parents is part of practical holiness (*Lev.* 19: 2, 3).

2. The duties of children to their parents.

Reverence and respect.

(a) Children are to revere their parents (*Lev. 19: 3*).

(b) Negatively, this means never to despise or mock them (*Prov.* 30: 17), curse them (*Ex.* 21: 17; *Prov.* 20: 20), strike them (*Ex.* 21: 15) or speak evil of them (*Matt.* 15: 4).

(c) Positively, it means to deliberately honour them by speaking well of them, respecting their persons, and showing them courtesy (cf. *Gen.* 47: 7, 11, 12; *I Kings* 2: 19, 20).

Demonstrated and genuine love.

(d) The love of children for their parents is always assumed in the Bible: such love is a first, and entirely natural, love (*Matt.* 10: 37).

(e) Love, to be acceptable to God, must be genuine and without hypocrisy (*Rom.* 12: 9).

(f) Children should be unashamed of showing their affection for their parents (*Gen.* 46: 29).

Obedience to their commands.

(g) Both parents are to be obeyed (*Deut.* 21: 18), and they are to be obeyed in everything (*Eph.* 6: 1; *Col.* 3:20).

(h) To honour parents, therefore, is the opposite of stubbornness and rebelliousness towards them (*Deut.* 21: 18).

(i) We honour our parents by giving deference or regard to their requests (*I Kings* 2: 20), neither despising their instruction nor their direction (*Prov.* 1: 8; 15: 5).

Submission to their discipline.

(j) The rightful submission of children to parents is to respect them for the discipline they exercise (*Heb.* 12: 9).

(k) Proper discipline, rightly appreciated, is not a disadvantage to a son or daughter but a privilege (*Prov.* 3: 11–12; *Heb.* 12: 5–8).

Faithfulness to their interests.

(l) Children can fall into the peril of regarding lightly their parents' property: a man who, in effect, robs his father or mother and says, "It's not wrong" is no better than a murderer (*Prov.* 28: 24).

(m) To honour our parents is to give them joy by living wisely, and we do the right thing when we aim at giving them this joy (*Prov.* 23: 24, 25).

Repaying the love, care and trouble they have given.

(n) To honour our parents is to care for them, and to provide for them when they are in need, in other words, to make some return to them, not least financially, if that is the help required (*I Tim.* 5: 4).

(o) Children are not to conceive excuses—least of all religious excuses—for not fulfilling their obligations to their parents (see the

"Corban" argument in *Matt.* 15: 1–6; *Mark* 7: 1–13).

The limitations of the rightful submission of children to parents.

(a) The obedience and subjection God commands are neither absolute nor universal—they are "in the Lord" (*Eph.* 6: 1), i.e. in such things as parents require us to do with the Lord's authority.

(b) If anyone, including parents, commands that which is contrary to the law and will of God, then we ought to obey God rather than men (*Acts* 5: 29).

(c) Furthermore, the day must come when children recognise their independence of their parents, and, for the majority, this comes through marriage in particular (*Matt.* 19: 5, 6; *Mark* 10: 7, 8).

(d) Prior to marriage a man or woman has his or her closest bond with parents, and owes to them the greatest obligation; the new bond and obligation which marriage involves transcends the old (*Eph.* 5: 31).

(e) A man's duty to his wife, and a woman's duty to her husband, and their united duty to their children, clearly bring a change of priorities so far as their relationship and duties to their parents are concerned, although no lessening of their respect and sense of responsibility for them (*Eph.* 5: 21–33).

(f) If at any stage parents seek to make loyalty to themselves a priority over their children's loyalty to the Lord, they demand that which is unlawful: love for the Lord ought to be so great that the best of human loves is hatred by comparison (*Luke* 14: 26).

(g) Nevertheless, all commands about loyalty to Jesus Christ must be seen in the context of genuine filial piety as a Christian duty (*Mark* 7: 13).

(h) We may be quite sure that the priority of loyalty to God will never be detrimental to the wellbeing of those we love most, much as we may not see how it can be so at the time (see Abraham and Isaac in *Genesis* 22).

4. The responsibilities rightful submission of children to parents places upon the parents.

(a) Parents must realise their responsibilities for their children for they are the first and foremost educators of their children (*Prov.* 4: 1–4).

(b) Parents must manage their own households well, keeping their children submissive and respectful in every way (*I Tim.* 3: 4).

(c) Parents should be clear as to the kind of children to be proud of, so that they don't place false objectives before their children (*Prov.* 23: 22–25).

(d) Children are gifts from the Lord (*Gen.* 4: 1; 25: 21; *Ruth* 4: 12, 13; *I Sam.* 1: 5, 6, 11), given to parents for a while, and parents do well to give their children back to the Lord, as it were, lending them to Him for as long as they live (*I Sam.* 1: 11, 27, 28).

(e) Children are given to parents to rear and to train up in the way they should go (*Prov.* 22: 6): they are to be nurtured like tender plants with a view to their future fruitfulness in character (*Ps.* 128: 3).

(f) God desires godly offspring from the marriage union (*Mal.* 2: 15).

(g) Parents' **actions** and **words** in relation to their children are all to be with their spiritual good in view—what the New Testament calls "the discipline and instruction of the Lord" (*Eph.* 6: 4).

(h) Parents' **actions** must be right towards their children, particularly in regard to the discipline they exercise because, first, foolishness is bound up in the heart of a child and it takes more than words to dislodge it (*Prov.* 22: 15), and, secondly, character is a plant which grows more sturdily for some cutting back (*Prov.* 15: 32, 33; 5: 11, 12; *Heb.* 12: 11), and from early days (*Prov.* 13: 24b; 22: 6; 29: 15).

(i) The motive of love is to be behind all exercise of discipline (*Prov.* 13: 24), and love demands that a restraint should be placed upon children by their parents when they do wrong (*I Sam.* 3: 13).

(j) Parents' words must be right towards their children, for they are to be instructed from their earliest days in the law of God (*Eph.* 6: 4; *Josh.* 8: 35) with loving persistence (*Prov.* 1: 8; 3: 21; 4: 8, 9, 12).

(k) Parents need to be in that tender relationship to their children in which their children expect to receive instruction from them (*Prov.* 4: 1–4).

(l) Parents are not to make it difficult for their children to obey the commandment, "Honour your father and your mother" by making unreasonable demands (*Col.* 3: 21), needlessly provoking them to anger (*Eph.* 6: 4), perhaps by favouritism (*Gen.* 25: 29) or by neglect (*II Sam.* 14: 13, 28).

(m) The important factor in a child's upbringing is not the money parents have with which to supply their children's needs but rather the example they set (*Prov.* 20: 7): parents pass on a heritage for good or ill according to their fear of God (*Ps.* 25: 12, 13; *Hos.* 4: 6).

(n) Parents themselves are to be an example of loyalty to God, never allowing their children to take precedence over their own discipleship of our Lord Jesus Christ (*Mark* 10: 29; *Luke* 18: 29; *Matt.* 19: 29).

(o) Parents are to be an example themselves too of dutiful children in relation to their own parents (*Luke* 6: 31).

5. **Examples of obedience to this commandment.**

(a) Joseph is a conspicuous example of obedience to this commandment in his concern for his father (*Gen.* 45: 3), his provision for him (*Gen.* 45: 9–13), his demonstrated affection (*Gen.* 46: 28–34), his filial pride (*Gen.* 47: 7, 27–31), and his obedience (*Gen.* 50: 1–14).

(b) Our Lord Jesus Christ is the supreme example of obedience to this commandment, as to all others, in His earthly submission and obedience (*Luke* 2: 51), and His concern and provision for His widowed mother (*John* 19: 26, 27).

6. **Examples of disobedience to this commandment.**

(a) The two sons of Eli, Hophni and Phinehas, are sad examples of disobedience to this commandment in that they refused to listen to the voice of their father (*I Sam.* 2: 25), and had no regard for the Lord or His commandments, with disastrous consequences (*I Sam.* 2: 12; 4: 11, 17).

(b) A second example of disobedience is the manner in which the Jews evaded obedience to the implications of this commandment to maintain needy parents by instead vowing their property insincerely to

143

the Temple (*Mark* 7: 1–13; *Matt.* 15: 1–6).

7. **The fundamental importance of this principle of respect for, and submission to, parents.**

(a) This commandment is the application of a general Christian principle: we are to pay respect to whom respect is due, and honour to whom honour is due (*Rom.* 13: 7 cf. *Mark* 12: 17).

(b) Parents are the first authority we learn to respect and the pattern of submission we learn towards them influences our submission to all men, for we are taught to honour all men (*I Pet.* 2: 17), so that, for example, we rise up before the hoary head (*Lev.* 19: 32), and honour widows and such like by caring for them financially and in other ways open to us (*I Tim.* 5: 3).

(c) Inevitably the pattern of submission we learn from our earliest years influences our submission in other spheres, whether towards our teachers, our rulers or our employers: those who show proper respect and submission to parents are unlikely to find difficulty in honouring the civil authorities (*I Pet.* 2: 17) or treating earthly masters or employers with all respect (*I Pet.* 2: 18): in other words, the well-being of a people or a nation begins in the home.

6. RESPECT FOR LIFE

Exodus 20: 13: "You shall not murder."

Question: What does the sixth commandment teach?

Answer: The sixth commandment condemns murder, which is the deliberate, malicious and unlawful taking of life, and teaches us the sanctity of human life which, as a gift from God, is to be neither violated nor threatened, whether by actions, threats, motives or words.

1. **Life is a gift from God and is sacred.**

(a) Man's breath is God's prerogative (*Gen.* 2: 7; *Isa.* 42: 5; *Dan.* 5: 23).

(b) Man's life is sacred (*Gen.* 9: 6), so sacred that even the life of a murderer is not to be carelessly taken away (*Gen.* 4: 15).

(c) Man's life is sacred because man was made in the image of God (*Gen.* 1: 27; 9: 6).

(d) Man's life is his dearest possession (*Matt.* 16: 26; *Mark* 8: 37; *John* 15: 13; cf. *Acts* 27: 18, 19, 22).

(e) Man's redemption in and through our Lord Jesus Christ emphasises the sanctity of human life (*John* 10: 10, 28; *Rom.* 5: 21).

2. **Murder violates God's commandment.**

(a) It despises God's sixth commandment and is evil in God's sight (*II Sam.* 12: 9).

(b) It offends, more than any other sin, the commandment "Love your neighbour as yourself" (*Rom.* 13: 9).

(c) It offends the special value given to the life of man because of the awareness that all men are brethren (*Acts* 17: 26).

(d) God hates murder (*Prov.* 6: 16, 17).

(e) Murder cannot be concealed from God (*Isa.* 26: 21; *Jer.* 2: 34) and it cries out for God's vengeance (*Gen.* 4: 10).

3. **Human attitudes and emotions which can give rise to murder are forbidden by this commandment.**

(a) At first sight the sixth commandment appears to be concerned with nothing more than the murderous act (*Ex.* 20: 13), but the Lord Jesus gave the commandment a further and deeper meaning: all sins which lead to murder and are the occasions of it are forbidden (*Matt.* 5: 21–26). Anger and hatred are perhaps the two most obvious examples.

Anger

(b) Anger, like a fire can be kindled and do great damage (*Ps.* 124: 3).

(c) Anger is a work of the flesh (*Gal.* 5: 20).

(d) Anger can be foolishly harboured and kept alive (*Amos* 1: 11; *Eccl.* 7: 9).

(e) Anger and insult can constitute both the spirit of murder (*Matt.* 5: 22), and cause murder (*Gen.* 49: 6).

(f) A distinction is recognised between anger and malice, in that the former under control is sometimes allowable (*Eph.* 4: 26, 27), but malice—mental murder—is always evil (*I John* 3: 15).

Hatred

(g) Hatred is synonymous with darkness, and walking in darkness (*I John* 2: 9).

(h) Hatred distorts our perspective (*I John* 2: 11).

(i) Murder is the fruit of hatred (*I John* 3: 15).

(j) Murder is first committed in the heart and then completed by actions: e.g. Cain and Abel (*Gen.* 4: 5, 8), Saul (later known as Paul) who breathed out threats of murder against the disciples of the Lord (*Acts* 9: 1) and was a "man-slayer" before his conversion (*Acts* 9: 1, 4, 5; 22: 4, 7; 26: 10).

4. **There are important exceptions in the taking of human life which are not infringements of this commandment.**

The civil authority and capital punishment.

(a) The just punishment of crime by magistrates is not murder: the powers that be are ordained of God to bear the sword and execute wrath (*Rom.* 13: 1–7; *I Pet.* 2: 13–17).

(b) The assumption is always present that there are crimes worthy of death (*Gen.* 9: 6; *Acts* 25: 11).

(c) Under the Mosaic law the death penalty was prescribed for certain offences (*Ex.* 2: 12, 14, 23–25; *Lev.* 24: 17; *Num.* 35: 21; *Deut.* 19: 11–13), and the institution of capital punishment for murder would seem to be of permanent obligation (*Gen.* 9: 5, 6).

War

(d) The lawfulness of defensive war is distinctly recognised in the Bible, and the taking of life in time of war is not murder (*Judg.* 5: 23; *I Sam.* 15: 2, 3).

(e) When consulted through the Urim and Thummin, or by the prophets, as to the rightness of military enterprises, God answered (*Judg.* 20: 27; *I Sam.* 14: 37; 23: 2, 4; *I Kings* 22: 6).

(f) Since magistrates are given power of life and death over their citizens, they plainly have the right to declare war in self-defence (*Rom.* 13: 1–7; *I Pet.* 2: 13–17).

Manslaughter

(g) The life of a person taken away by accident is not murder (*Deut.* 19: 5).

(h) The cities of refuge were intended to provide refuge for those guilty of manslaughter so that their case could be properly judged (*Num.* 35: 9–28).

(i) The life of a person taken in self-defence is not murder (*Ex.* 22: 2).

5. The implications of this commandment are many.

(a) Love for our neighbour means the protection and preservation of his life (*Luke* 10: 25–37).

(b) The opposite of murder is self-sacrificing love (*I John* 3: 11–18), which should be the Christian norm (*Phil.* 2: 5–8; *I Pet.* 2: 21–25).

(c) We need to guard our hearts if we would avoid breaking this commandment (*Prov.* 4: 23; *Matt.* 5: 21–26).

(d) We should never let the sun go down on our anger (*Eph.* 4: 26), or any other harmful and wrongful attitude of heart.

(e) Human relationships matter to God (*I John* 4: 21; 5: 1).

(f) Attitudes and works recognised as incitements to murder are to be recognised by the Christian as belonging to his old life, and are to be put away, e.g. bitterness, anger, clamour, slander, and malice (*Eph.* 4: 31; *Col.* 3: 5; cf. *I Pet.* 2: 1).

7. THE SANCTITY OF MARRIAGE

Exodus 20: 14: "You shall not commit adultery."

Question: What does the seventh commandment teach?

Answer: The seventh commandment teaches the sanctity of marriage and, by implication, forbids all impurity of thought, speech and behaviour.

1. **God's institution of marriage.**

(a) Marriage is a divine institution (*Gen.* 2: 24).

(b) It was founded before the existence of civil society, and it is, therefore, not simply a civil institution but a creation ordinance (*Gen.* 2: 18–24).

(c) It was founded on the nature of man as constituted by God: He made male and female and ordained marriage as an indispensable condition for the continuance of the human race (*Gen.* 1: 27, 28; 2: 18–24).

(d) One of God's purposes in marriage, therefore, is procreation and fruitfulness (*Gen.* 1: 28; *Ps.* 127: 3, 5).

(e) Children are to be brought up within the marriage relationship (*Prov.* 5: 16, 17), and God desires godly offspring from the marriage union (*Mal.* 2: 15).

(f) The other equally important purpose of marriage is the support and help that marriage partners are able to give one another (*Gen.* 2: 20–22).

(g) For the welfare of the human race marriage is not to be within certain close family relationships (*Lev.* 18: 6ff; 20: 11–21; *Deut.* 22: 30; 27: 20–23).

(h) Beneficial as marriage is, the marriage relationship is not to be coveted (*I Cor.* 7: 1ff; *Ex.* 20: 7).

(i) Marriage brings its own cares and distractions, and can in some measure bring divided loyalties in that God is not served with the same freedom from entanglements as before marriage (*I Cor.* 7: 32–34).

(j) Considerations arising from the kingdom of God and its best interests may cause some men and women to forego the privileges and joys of the marriage state (*Matt.* 19: 11, 12; *I Cor.* 7: 7).

(k) Marriage is a relationship limited to this life, for at the resurrection men and women do not marry but are like the angels in heaven (*Matt.* 22: 30; *Mark* 12: 25; *Luke* 20: 35).

2. The proper pattern of behaviour in marriage.

(a) The natural aim of marriage partners is to please one another (*I Cor.* 7: 32–34).

(b) The passion of lust is not to characterise the sexual relationship within marriage but rather holiness and honour (*I Thess.* 4: 4, 5), with a proper recognition of the other partner's conjugal rights (*I Cor.* 7: 3).

(c) The marriage relationship is to be modelled upon that between the Lord Jesus Christ and His Church: the husband is to love, protect and cherish his wife as himself; and the wife is to love, honour and obey her husband (*Eph.* 5: 21–30).

(d) The secret of happy marriage is that neither party should demand his or her rights but each should give to the other appropriate love and service willingly and freely (*Eph.* 5: 22, 25).

(e) Marriage partners need to appreciate the real nature of their oneness, and its mystery, which means understanding that to hurt one's partner is to hurt oneself (*Eph.* 5: 28–33).

(f) The marriage couple are to find joy in one another, and to keep strictly to one another; they are each other's cistern from which alone they are to drink (*Prov.* 5: 15, 18, 19).

3. The sanctity of marriage.

(a) At marriage two people become one (*Matt.* 19: 5, 6; *Mark* 10: 7, 8).

(b) Marriage is for life, and this is the Lord's ruling (*Matt.* 19: 9; *Mark* 10: 11, 12; *Luke* 16: 18; *I Cor.* 7: 10, 11, 39).

(c) Marriage is a compact between a man and a woman to live together, as husband and wife, until separated by death (*Gen.* 2: 23, 24; *Rom.* 7: 2, 3), and God is witness to that covenant (*Mal.* 2: 14).

(d) It is the most intimate and sacred relationship which can exist between human beings, and all other human relationships must be reckoned as secondary to it if necessary (*Gen.* 2: 24; *Eph.* 5: 31).

(e) It is the point at which adult children rightly recognise their independence of their parents, and enter into a oneness with a marriage partner which is deeper than that known with their respective parents (*Matt.* 19: 5, 6; *Mark* 10: 7, 8).

(f) The marriage compact is permanent, and cannot be dissolved at the will of either of the parties (*Matt.* 5: 31, 32; 19: 3–9; *Mark* 10: 2–12; *Luke* 16: 18).

(g) The union is properly dissolved only by the death of one of the parties (*Matt.* 19: 6; *Mark* 10: 6).

(h) Marriage is to be held in honour among all, and the marriage bed is to be undefiled—that is to say, the sexual act is a sanctuary sacred to the husband and his wife (*Heb.* 13: 4).

(i) The sanctity of marriage is underlined by the fact that it is made the symbol of the relationship between God and His people (*Isa.* 62: 5; cf. *Hos.* 2: 14–23).

(j) It is used to illustrate the union between the Lord Jesus Christ and His Church (*Eph.* 5: 22–33; *Rev.* 19: 7, 9; 21: 9).

(k) The uncompromising nature of our Lord Jesus Christ's teaching on marriage surprised even His disciples (*Matt.* 19: 10).

4. Adultery.

(a) To commit adultery is to sin against God as well as against another human being (*Gen.* 20: 6), for it offends God's law (*Ex.* 20: 14).

(b) We cannot break the seventh commandment without in some way cheating our fellow men (*I Thess.* 4: 6).

(c) Adultery offends the commandment, "Love your neighbour as yourself" (*Rom.* 13: 9).

(d) Adultery is the final expression of thoughts given place to in the heart and expressed in the eyes (*Matt.* 5: 28, 29).

(e) Adultery is the putting asunder of those whom God has joined together (*Matt.* 19: 6; *Mark* 10: 9).

(f) If a man arbitrarily puts away his wife and marries another, he commits adultery (*Matt.* 19: 9; *Mark* 10: 11, 12); similarly, a wife is an adulteress if she lives with another man while her husband is alive (*Rom.* 7: 3).

(g) Marriage can be dissolved through the unchastity on the part of one partner, the implication being that the mysterious sense in which the Bible declares a husband and wife to be one has been dreadfully abused and marred (*Matt.* 19: 9).

(h) If a man repudiates his wife on the above grounds, however, and marries another, he commits no offence, and likewise with the wife if she is the offended party (*Matt.* 19: 9; *Mark* 10: 11, 12).

(i) Adultery displays an absence of the fear of God (*Mal.* 3: 5).

(j) To fail to recognise the sanctity of marriage is to bring God's judgment upon the individual (*Heb.* 13: 4), and His judgment is sure (*I Cor.* 6: 9, 10).

(k) Divorce is contrary to the whole purpose of God in marriage (*Mark* 10: 1–12; cf. *Gen.* 12: 17–20), and its sinfulness should remind men and women of the seriousness of marriage before they embark upon it (*Matt.* 19: 10).

5. **The implications of this commandment in regard to personal purity.**

(a) The commandment forbids all impurity of thought, speech and behaviour (*Matt.* 5: 27–30; *Eph.* 5: 4).

(b) In other words, it extends to the heart, mind and imagination as well as to the body and external actions (*Matt.* 5: 28).

(c) To fix our eyes upon a person of the other sex with lascivious desire is adultery of the heart (*Matt.* 5: 27–28).

(d) We need to keep a strict watch, therefore, over our heart for from it flow the springs of life (*Prov.* 4: 23; *Matt.* 15: 19; *Mark* 7: 21).

(e) The will of God is our sanctification which means abstaining from all forms of sexual immorality (*I Thess.* 4: 3).

(f) Every one of us is to learn to control his or her body, keeping it pure and treating it with respect, and never regarding it as an instrument for self-gratification (*I Thess.* 4: 4, 5).

(g) The calling of God is not to impurity but to the most thorough purity, and anyone who makes light of the matter is not making light of a man's ruling but of God's commandment (*I Thess.* 4: 8).

(h) Christian believers in particular must preserve their chastity because their bodies have become the temples of the Holy Spirit (*I Cor.* 6: 15, 19).

8. RESPECT FOR PROPERTY

Exodus 20: 15: "You shall not steal."

148

Question: What does the eighth commandment teach?

Answer: The eighth commandment teaches us to have a proper respect for other people's property, and forbids all forms of theft. By implication, it teaches the right of private property, and the honourableness of lawfully acquired wealth.

1. **The right of private property.**

(a) The earth is the Lord's (*Ps.* 24: 1; 50: 10–12), so that although man has been granted use of the property and wealth of the world his right remains a derived and temporary right (*Gen.* 1: 28–30).

(b) God has so constituted man that he desires and needs this right of exclusive possession, and the foundation of the right of property, therefore, is the will of God (*Ex.* 20: 15).

(c) In the Old Testament every man held his piece of land as an inheritance from the Lord, and the removal of the landmark indicating that inheritance was an offence against the Lord Himself (*Deut.* 19: 14).

(d) The prophets looked forward to the coming days of universal peace which included private property as one of the great blessings yet to be (*Micah* 4: 3, 4).

(e) Personal property is to be respected (*Deut.* 23: 25), and throughout the Scriptures the individual's right to his property is maintained (*I Kings* 21: 1–16).

(f) Even the community of goods which the early Church chose to practice for a period did not involve the denial of the rights of property (*Acts* 5: 4).

(g) The eighth commandment, therefore, forbids all violations of the rights of property (*Ex.* 20: 15).

2. **Examples of the many different forms of theft.**

(a) Borrowing, and then failing to return what has been borrowed (*Ps.* 37: 21).

(b) Failure to clear oneself of debt when able to do so (*II Kings* 4: 7).

(c) False weights and measures (*Amos* 8: 5; *Micah* 6: 10, 11).

(d) General dishonesty in buying and selling (*Lev.* 25: 14).

(e) Misuse of one's employer's property or time (*Tit.* 2: 10).

(f) Wasting someone else's possessions (*Luke* 16: 1).

(g) Failure to seek the owner of something we have found (*Lev.* 6: 4).

(h) Taking unfair advantage of either the ignorance or the needs of our fellow men (*Prov.* 11: 26).

(i) Paying bad wages, or withholding or delaying the payment of wages (*Lev.* 19: 13; *Mal.* 3: 5; *Jas.* 5: 4).

(j) Indifference of children in their use of their parents' property (*Prov.* 28: 24).

(k) Failing as adult sons or daughters to make some return to our parents when they need help (*Prov.* 28: 24; *Mark* 7: 11; *I Tim.* 5: 4, 8).

3. **The importance of honesty and trustworthiness in regard to other people's possessions.**

(a) We are to seek the good of our neighbour rather than just seeking our own good (*I Cor.* 10: 24).

(b) As employees we are to show complete faithfulness to our employer's interests (*Tit.* 2: 10).

(c) Honesty is to characterise the work we do (*Eph.* 4: 28).

(d) We are to strive after honesty in little things for that sets the pattern for larger things (*Luke* 16: 10).

149

(e) We are not to give any encouragement to others in defrauding those who have committed some trust to them (*Ps.* 50: 18; *Prov.* 29: 24).

(f) In regard to other people's property and possessions, justice and only justice is what we are to follow (*Deut.* 16: 20).

(g) Theft offends the commandment, "Love your neighbour as yourself" (*Rom.* 13: 9).

(h) At the root of all forms of stealing is selfishness (*Eph.* 4: 28).

(i) Theft is an abomination to God (*Jer.* 7: 9, 10), and brings God's judgment upon the thief (*Zech.* 5: 3, 4).

4. **Wealth is not in and of itself wrong, but it must be obtained lawfully and honourably.**

(a) The eighth commandment requires that whatever wealth we possess should be lawfully obtained (*Ex.* 20: 15).

(b) Property is not evil in itself but like all material possessions it can present dangers to our spiritual well-being (*Deut.* 6: 10–12; *Luke* 12: 15).

(c) The more easily we obtain our wealth, the sooner we shall probably lose it (*Prov.* 13: 11); whereas the harder it is to earn, the more we shall possess most likely in the long-term (*Prov.* 13: 11).

(d) The most lawful and honourable means of obtaining wealth is to work for it (*Eph.* 4: 28).

(e) In fulfilling our daily work we are to think not only of ourselves but also of those who are in any kind of material need whom we can help (*Isa.* 58: 10; *Eph.* 4: 28; *I John* 3: 17)—the implication being that possessions are a trust from God.

(f) The clear implication of the eighth commandment, therefore, is

that we are to restore anything that we have unjustly obtained or taken from others (*Lev.* 6: 4; *Luke* 19: 8; *Eph.* 4: 28).

9. TRUTHFULNESS

Exodus 20: 16: "You shall not give false testimony against your neighbour."

Question: What does the ninth commandment teach?

Answer: The ninth commandment forbids in principle all untruth and falsehood, and in particular perjury, and proclaims the necessity of truthfulness of speech.

1. **Implicit in the ninth commandment is the importance of the tongue.**

(a) Truthfulness has special reference to our speech (*Eph.* 4: 25; *Col.* 3: 9).

(b) The abuse of the gift of speech and the wrong use to which words are put are sins to which the Scriptures draw considerable attention (e.g. *Ps.* 120: 1–3; cf. *Ps.* 5: 9; 12: 2–4; 36: 1–4; 52: 1–4; 64: 1–4.)

(c) We sin most easily in our speech (*Eccl.* 5: 1, 2; *Isa.* 6: 5).

(d) If anyone makes no mistake in what he says, he is a perfect man, able to keep his whole body in check (*Jas.* 3: 2).

(e) The tongue can be deceitful in the mouth (*Micah* 6: 12), full of venom (*Rom.* 3: 13), and a dreadful scourge (*Job* 5: 21).

(f) The tongue can be used to deceive (*Rom.* 3: 13), to express malice (*Dan.* 3: 8), and to bring about mischief (*Ps.* 36: 3).

(g) The tongue has a terrifying power, comparable to that of poison and of fire (*Jas.* 3: 1–12).

150

(h) In the light of the tongue's potential for good or evil, we are instructed to be extremely careful in the manner in which we speak of others (*Lev.* 19: 16).

2. God's own character is necessarily reflected in this commandment as in all others.

(a) The Lord is revealed to us as the true God (*II Chron.* 15: 3; *Jer.* 10: 10; *John* 17: 3; *I Thess.* 1: 9f; cf. *I John* 5: 20).

(b) Our Lord Jesus Christ is the truth (*John* 14: 6): everyone who loves truth recognises His voice (*John* 18: 37).

(c) The Holy Spirit is the Spirit of truth (*I John* 5: 6; *John* 15: 26): He guides those whom He indwells into everything that is true (*John* 16: 13).

(d) God is the God of truth and all truth derives its sanctity from Him (*John* 17: 3; *I John* 5: 20).

(e) God cannot lie (*Tit.* 1: 2; *Heb.* 6: 18; cf. *Rom.* 3: 4); to lie would be to contradict Himself, and God cannot deny Himself (*II Tim.* 2: 13).

(f) It is God's perfection to be consistent with Himself, and all His ways are truth (*Ps.* 111: 7, 8; cf. *Deut.* 32: 4; *Isa.* 25: 1).

(g) God requires truth in our inward being (*Ps.* 51: 6).

(h) The Lord has a controversy with us when we choose to put aside truth (*Hos.* 4: 1, 2).

3. In particular, the ninth commandment forbids perjury.

(a) The ninth commandment exemplifies what is the worst form of lying: taking a solemn oath in court and then by failure to tell the truth, or by deliberately misrepresenting the truth, to put someone's reputation or very life in danger (*Ex.* 20: 16).

(b) The commandment forbids the uttering of a false report, or conspiring with others to misrepresent the truth (*Ex.* 23: 1).

(c) False witness takes place when an individual states what is untrue in order to safeguard the interests of someone else, perhaps for personal gain (*Isa.* 5: 23).

(d) The commandment, therefore, forbids us to have anything to do with a false charge, and to have no involvement in the harming of the innocent and the righteous (*Ex.* 23: 7).

(e) The commandment forbids the taking of a bribe, for a bribe blinds men's eyes to justice, and injures the cause of those who are in the right (*Ex.* 23: 6–8).

(f) A man who bears false witness against his neighbour always does him harm (*Prov.* 25: 18).

(g) By bearing false witness we may even put a man's life in jeopardy (*I Kings* 21: 13; *Ps.* 35: 11).

(h) The false witness is a betrayer (*Prov.* 14: 25).

(i) False witness, like other sins, arises from the evil corruption of men's hearts (*Matt.* 15: 19).

(j) The bearing of false witness shows an absence of the fear of God (*Mal.* 3: 5).

(k) God hates false oaths (*Zech.* 8: 17), and He sees to it that a false witness will not go unpunished (*Prov.* 19: 5).

4. In principle, the commandment forbids all untruth and falsehood.

(a) **Slander,** for example, consists of making false statements about a person in order to defame or injure him, and is, in effect, fighting and injuring people with the tongue (*Jer.* 18: 18).

(b) We are not to injure others by initiating or accepting lies or false reports which are harmful to people's good names (*Col.* 3: 9).

(c) Hatred is frequently at the back of slander (*Ps.* 41: 7; 109: 3).

(d) Slander comes from an evil heart (*Luke* 6: 45), and is an abomination to the Lord (*Prov.* 6: 16, 19).

(e) **Deceit** (*Ps.* 120: 2; *Rom.* 3: 13), **lying** (*Eph.* 4: 25), and **flattery** (*Ps.* 5: 9; 78: 36) are likewise forbidden.

(f) **False judgments** and wrong forms of **criticism** are also snares into which we may fall, which constitute sin in the light of this commandment. The command forbids all rash and unwarrantable judging of other men's hearts and destinies which is usually accompanied by ignorance of our own (*Matt.* 7: 1, 3); we are all in danger of rising too quickly to criticise others (*Mark* 9: 38–41; *Luke* 9: 49, 50).

(g) **Tale-bearing** and **backbiting** are both aspects of slander (*Lev.* 19: 16; *Prov.* 17: 9; *Rom.* 1: 30; *II Cor.* 12: 20; *I Tim.* 5: 13).

(h) All these and similar departures from truth bring strife (*Prov.* 26: 20), separate friends (*Prov.* 16: 28; 17: 9), and are utterly destructive (*Prov.* 11: 9).

(i) Everyone who loves and practises falsehood is excluded from the kingdom of God (*I Cor.* 6: 10; *Rev.* 22: 15).

(j) Untruth and falsehood are Satan's habitat (*John* 8: 44), and both lying (*Acts* 5: 3) and slander (*Rev.* 12: 10) are identified with him.

(k) We shall be judged for every careless word we utter (*Matt.* 12: 36, 37).

(l) The Christian, therefore, is to put away from him every form of untruth and falsehood (*Eph.* 4: 25, 31; *I Pet.* 2: 1; 3: 10; cf. *Ps.* 34: 13).

5. **The ninth commandment proclaims the necessity of truthfulness of speech.**

(a) The commandment aims at the preservation and promoting of truthfulness among men: men should speak the truth to one another (*Zech.* 8: 16; *Eph.* 4: 29).

(b) The Lord Jesus Christ, our example in everything, demonstrated this necessity: no deceit was in His mouth (*I Pet.* 2: 22).

(c) Truth is that to which we are to cling (*I Tim.* 1: 19).

(d) Truth is to be spoken from the heart (*Ps.* 15: 2).

(e) We should mean what we say, ensuring that our speech is both direct and clear (*Matt.* 5: 37; *Jas.* 5: 12).

(f) Truthful speech may be expected to be accompanied by the power of God (*II Cor.* 6: 7).

(g) The necessity of truthfulness in us rests upon God's truthfulness (*I Pet.* 1: 15, 16; cf. *John* 18: 37); upon our exercise of truthfulness depends our experience of fellowship with God (*I John* 1: 5–10).

10. CONTENTMENT

Exodus 20: 17: "You shall not covet your neighbour's house. You shall not covet your neighbour's wife, or his manservant or maidservant, his ox or donkey, or anything that belongs to your neighbour."

Question: What does the tenth commandment teach?

Answer: The tenth commandment forbids wrong attitudes to the possessions and position of others, especially the attitudes of uncontrolled

desire, envy and jealousy. It teaches rather that we should be content with what God has given to us, and covet those things He desires us to have and which will never harm anyone.

1. Defining covetousness.

(a) Covetousness, like all other sins, comes from within, out of our hearts (*Mark* 7: 21–23).

(b) It relates particularly to our desires, and our desires find their source in our hearts (*Ps.* 37: 4; *Rom.* 1: 24).

(c) Desires characterise both the body and mind, and prior to the experience of new birth they dominate our lives (*Rom.* 6: 12; *Eph.* 2: 3): we are tempted when we are lured and enticed by our desires (*Jas.* 1: 14, 15).

(d) Covetousness is essentially selfish desire (*Prov.* 21: 26; *Luke* 12: 1), indicating a basic discontent with what we already possess (*Heb.* 13: 5).

(e) The desires of our hearts and minds are prompted usually by what our eyes see and choose to focus upon (*Gen.* 3: 6; *Josh.* 7: 21; *Prov.* 27: 20).

(f) Covetousness, then, establishes a place in our thoughts (*Luke* 12: 17), usually in the form of secret thoughts about the possessions of others (*Micah* 2: 1, 2).

(g) Covetousness is an aspect of loving the world, and the things in the world, with the sad consequence that love for God is absent (*I John* 2: 15).

(h) It is God's law which brings home to us a real awareness of what covetousness is (*Rom.* 7: 7).

2. Some of the objects of covetousness.

(a) Objects of covetousness are mentioned in the commandment itself— for example, our neighbour's home, wife, employees and possessions (*Ex.* 20: 17)—and there are many forms of covetousness (*Luke* 12: 15; *Rom.* 7: 8).

(b) Covetousness finds its preoccupation with all that is in the world (*I John* 2: 16).

(c) Covetousness may have material possessions as its principal object, such as clothes (*Josh.* 7: 20, 21; *Acts* 20: 33) or property (*I Kings* 21: 2).

(d) Covetousness may have its focus upon money (*Acts* 20: 33; *I Tim.* 3: 3; 6: 9)—see, for example, Gehazi (*II Kings* 5: 20–24); Judas (*Matt.* 26: 14, 15; *John* 12: 6); and Ananias and Sapphira (*Acts* 5: 1–10).

(e) Covetousness may have as its wrongful object a physical or sexual relationship (*Eph.* 4: 19; 5: 3, 5, 6)— covetousness can lead a man into adultery (*Matt.* 5: 28).

(f) Covetousness may have as its object position and prestige (*I John* 2: 16—"the pride of life") or power (*Acts* 8: 18, 19).

3. Some of the snares of covetousness.

(a) It leads to deceit in that the lips will try to cover up often the desires that are in the heart (*Ezek.* 33: 31; *I Thess.* 2: 5).

(b) It makes us slaves to our inward passions and desires (*Tit.* 3: 3; *II Pet.* 2: 19).

(c) It makes us blind to the fact that life is more than food, and the body more than clothing (*Luke* 12: 23).

(d) It makes us essentially selfish in that we think principally of ourselves (*Luke* 12: 19, 21).

(e) It leads us to store and hoard rather than to use our possessions to profit others (*Matt.* 6: 19).

(f) It causes us to store up for a future that may never be (*Luke* 12: 20), as well as neglecting the final accounting with God we must all make (*Luke* 12: 30).

(g) It shuts our life to the helpful influence and transforming power of God's Word (*Mark* 4: 19).

(h) It encourages us to put aside and ultimately destroy all other moral values (*II Tim.* 3: 2ff).

(i) It brings problems to others who are connected with us (*Josh.* 7: 20, 21), especially to our own family (*Prov.* 15: 27).

(j) It always brings antagonisms and conflicts in human relationships (*Jas.* 4: 1, 2) because by it malice, envy and hatred enter into our lives (*Tit.* 3: 3).

(k) It brings no true satisfaction (*Eccl.* 5: 10; *Hab.* 2: 5), but misery (*I Tim.* 6: 10) and ultimate poverty (*Prov.* 28: 22).

4. The sinfulness of covetousness.

(a) It is disobedience to the tenth commandment (*Ex.* 20: 17).

(b) It is idolatry, in that the covetous worship a false god (*Eph.* 5: 5): the original desire may be after something lawful in itself but it grows to such a selfish intensity that it gains the place which God alone should have in our soul (*Col.* 3: 5).

(c) It lies behind many disagreements and disputes which spoil human relationships (*Luke* 12: 13, 14; *Jas.* 4: 1ff).

(d) It breaks one of the great summaries of the commandments, "Love your neighbour as yourself" (*Rom.* 13: 9).

(e) It is on account of covetousness that we break often the other commandments of God: e.g. covetousness leads to not providing for and honouring our parents (*Mark* 7: 11), murder (*Prov.* 1: 18, 19; *Jer.* 22: 17; *Ezek.* 22: 12, 27), adultery (*II Sam.* 11: 2ff), theft (*Josh.* 7: 21), lying (*II Kings* 5: 22–25), and false accusation (*Acts* 16: 19–21).

5. The commandment teaches us to be content with what God has given to us—the opposite of covetousness.

(a) The willingness to work honestly for our living is put in opposition to covetousness (*Acts* 20: 33, 34).

(b) The awareness that our heavenly Father knows our needs and supplies them as is best for us leads us to appreciate how inappropriate regrets or complaints are in regard to what we possess (*Matt.* 6: 31, 32; *Rom.* 8: 28).

(c) Contentment for Christian believers is based upon the certainty of our Lord Jesus Christ's promises, and His presence (*Heb.* 13: 5), and the glorious assurance that He gives us all we need (*Ps.* 16: 5).

(d) Our contentment needs to be not in what we expect others to give, or what we may strive after, but in what God unfailingly provides for us by one means or another (*Phil.* 4: 10–13).

(e) Contentment does not come easily to the majority of us, but it is a virtue that can be learned (*Phil.* 4: 11), as the Lord Jesus becomes the strength of our life (*Phil.* 4: 13).

(f) Those who follow the example of the Lord Jesus Christ remember and act upon His words, "It is more blessed to give than to receive" (*Acts* 20: 35).

6. There is a right kind of coveting.

(a) We usually associate the word "coveting" with unlawful desires but it can be used in a good sense as, for example, of the men and women of faith throughout the centuries who have coveted a better country, that is, a heavenly one, so that God is not ashamed to be called their God (*Heb.* 11: 16).

(b) There is a place for coveting spiritual leadership if God has given the necessary potential, and the honest desire is for the well-being of God's people and the glory of Jesus Christ (*I Tim.* 3: 1; *I Pet.* 5: 2–4).

(c) It is right to covet the best for others (*II Cor.* 11: 2; cf. *Rom.* 10: 1).

(d) Christians are to covet earnestly the best gifts, and most of all love (*I Cor.* 12: 31; 13: 1)—coveting like this does harm to no one but only good!

II. TEMPTATION

Question: What is temptation? and how is it to be viewed and overcome?

Answer: Temptation is seduction into disobedience to God. It is to be viewed as a constant peril, and is overcome only by daily watchfulness and dependence upon God.

1. **Defining and describing temptation.**

(a) To be tempted is to be faced with the seeming attractiveness of sin so as to be in danger of being drawn into it—an experience common to all (*I Cor.* 10: 12).

(b) Temptation forces us to decide for or against God, and Satan tries by means of it to separate us from God (*Gen.* 3: 1–19).

(c) God is never the author of temptation (*Jas.* 1: 13), so that He can never be charged with being responsible for our sins.

(d) Satan, the ruler of this world (*John* 12: 31; 14: 30; 16: 11), is the tempter, who endeavours to take advantage of our desires (*I Cor.* 7: 5; *I Thess.* 3: 5; *Jas.* 1: 14).

(e) Some distinction must be made between temptations and trials, especially as the New Testament usually employs the identical Greek word for both, the right translation into English being determined by the context—when God's involvement is clear, testing is in view rather than temptation (*Gen.* 22: 1–19; cf. *Heb.* 11:17–19; *Job* 1: 6–22; 2: 1–7).

(f) Temptation may come in various ways, but most obviously through our senses (*II Sam.* 11: 2; *Job.* 31: 1; *Matt.* 5: 27, 28), our desires (*I Cor.* 7: 5) and the weakness of our flesh (*Mark* 14: 38).

(g) Temptation may come through pride of position or status which inflates us and makes us forget our place before God (*Acts* 12: 21–23).

(h) Temptation may come through striving to help someone else, as we find ourselves tempted by the sins into which they have fallen (*Gal.* 6: 1).

(i) Temptation may come through the most unlikely instrumentality, like a best friend who misinterprets God's will for us, and wants us to choose an easy way rather than God's way (*Matt.* 16: 22, 23).

2. **The encouragement of our Lord's temptation to the Christian.**

(a) The temptations He experienced immediately after His baptism and again in the Garden of Gethsemane placed Him in a situation of open choice between surrender to God's will and revolt against it (*Matt.* 4: 1–11; 26: 36–46; *Mark* 1: 12, 13; 14: 32–42; *Luke* 4: 1–13; 22: 40–46).

(b) The three temptations were attempts to reduce the Lord Jesus to disobedience: first, to use His power for purposes out of keeping with His mission (*Matt.* 4: 3; *Luke* 4: 3); second, to invoke God's help on His own behalf (*Matt.* 4: 5; *Luke* 4: 9–11); third, to give up His obedience to God, and to follow Satan (*Matt.* 4: 8, 9; *Luke* 4: 5–7).

(c) It is because He Himself has been tempted by such suffering that He is able to help so adequately those who are now being tempted in the same way (*Heb.* 2: 18)—although He Himself did not sin (*Heb.* 4: 15).

(d) His perfect understanding encourages us to approach the throne of grace in His Name with perfect confidence, that we may receive mercy and find help in time of need (*Heb.* 4: 16).

(e) When we do fall before temptation, He acts as our High Priest, and we receive forgiveness in Him (*Col.* 1: 12, 13; *Heb.* 4: 14–16), as we honestly and contritely confess our sins (*I John* 1: 9).

3. **Overcoming temptation.**

(a) As a fruit of self-knowledge we must recognise our weakness (*Matt.* 26: 41; *Mark* 14: 38).

(b) We must recognise our essential dependence, therefore, upon our Lord Jesus Christ (*John* 15: 5; *Phil.* 4: 13).

(c) We must practice spiritual watchfulness (*Mark* 14: 38; *I Cor.* 10: 12; *Gal.* 6: 1; *I Pet.* 5: 8), sometimes taking preventative actions (*I Cor.* 7: 5).

(d) We must learn lessons from our past mistakes (*Job* 31: 1) and our previous experience of God's faithfulness (*I Cor.* 10: 13).

(e) We must deliberately put on the full armour of God (*Eph.* 6: 10–17), and then use our two principal weapons—the Scriptures (*Eph.* 6:

17; cf. *Matt.* 4: 4, 7, 10; *Luke* 4: 4, 8, 12) and prayer (*Mark* 14: 38; *Eph.* 6: 18).

(f) We must pray for discernment to know when to flee temptation (*II Tim.* 2: 22) and when it is God's will to withstand Satan and his temptations (*Jas.* 4: 7; *I Pet.* 5: 9), by the exercise of faith in the Lord Jesus (*Eph.* 6: 16).

(g) We must be in no doubt that God's purpose is that by the power of His Son, we may be able to stand our ground, and after we have done everything, to stand (*Eph.* 6: 10, 13).

12. WORLDLINESS

Question: What is worldliness? and why is it so serious?

Answer: Worldliness is essentially love of the world as it manifests itself in the lust of the flesh, the lust of the eyes, and the pride of life. It is so serious because it is in complete opposition to love of God.

1. **Worldliness needs to be seen against the background of the Christian's position in the world.**

(a) As God made the world, it was good (*Gen.* 1: 31; *I Tim.* 4: 4).

(b) The course of this world, however, has been tragically affected by man, through whose fall, on account of disobedience, death came into the world and rules over it (*Rom.* 5: 12ff).

(c) The whole world lies in the power of the prince of this world, the devil (*John* 12: 31; 16: 11; *Eph.* 2: 2; *I John* 5: 19).

(d) The whole world of mankind has become guilty before God (*Rom.* 3: 19); and even the created world has been subjected to frustration and longs for liberation (*Rom.* 8: 20–22).

(e) But it is into this world as it is, a world which has fallen into the power of sin and destruction, that God has sent His Son in order to reconcile it to Himself (*II Cor.* 5: 19ff).

(f) Christians are those who have been delivered from this present evil world (or age) through the giving of the Lord Jesus Christ of Himself for their sins (*Gal.* 1: 3), and they appreciate now that they live in a world which in its present form is passing away (*I Cor.* 7: 31).

(g) Because Christians live in the world, they must have dealings with the world (*I Cor.* 5: 10; *Phil.* 2: 15), but they must resist the world's pressures to squeeze them into its mould (*Rom.* 12: 2), and they must endeavour to live as those who are dead to it (*Gal.* 6: 14).

(h) Christians are assured that everything belongs to them—including the world—but they themselves do not belong to the world any more (*John* 15: 19; 17: 14, 16; *Col.* 2: 20) but to the Lord Jesus Christ (*I Cor.* 3: 21ff).

(i) Christians are to see the world as the sphere of their obedience to Christ (*Matt.* 28: 19, 20): it is God's harvest field (*Matt.* 9: 38; *Luke* 10: 2), in which they are harvesters, and also sowers by functioning as salt and light (*Matt.* 5: 13, 14), always holding out the word of life, the gospel (*Phil.* 2: 16).

(j) Because Christians are not taken out of the world at their new birth, the important thing is for them not to be conditioned any longer by the world (*Jas.* 1: 27).

2. Defining worldliness.

(a) Worldliness is the expression of the state of a man's heart (*Mark* 7:

21ff), by his love of the world as a matter of deliberate choice (*Jas.* 4: 4; cf. *II Tim.* 4: 10), by which he lives according to worldly wisdom rather than the wisdom God gives (*Jas.* 3: 13; cf. 1: 5).

(b) Worldliness revolves, first, around **the lust of the flesh,** our human desires (*I John* 2: 16).

(c) Without a right relationship to God, man's life is dominated by the lusts and desires of this world, for there is little else for which he can live (*Tit.* 2: 12; *I Pet.* 4: 2–4; *II Pet.* 1: 4), and before their new birth Christians lived their lives obeying the promptings of their instincts and notions (*Eph.* 2: 3).

(d) Selfish desires within are always fighting for their own satisfaction, wanting us to indulge them, often leading us into personal conflicts and quarrels (*Jas.* 4: 1, 3, 4).

(e) Our lower nature's desires would constantly set themselves against the guidance and direction of the Holy Spirit (*Gal.* 5: 16); and Satan would fill our lives with wrong desires (*John* 8: 44).

(f) This aspect of worldliness with its emphasis on natural desires constituted the first temptation to which our Lord was subjected in the challenge to command a stone to be made bread (*Luke* 4: 1).

(g) Worldliness revolves, secondly, around **the lust of the eyes** (*I John* 2: 16), one manifestation of which is covetousness.

(h) Eyes are the organs of desire (*Josh.* 7: 21): the eye is the lamp of the whole body—when our eyes are good, our whole body is full of light, but sadly the converse is also true (*Luke* 11: 34f).

(i) The desires of our eyes may often

act on the philosophy that stolen water is sweet and bread eaten in secret is pleasant (*Prov.* 9: 17).

(j) Sometimes the lust of the eyes has a sexual connotation (*Job* 31: 1; *Matt.* 5: 29).

(k) Covetousness can lead to other sins, such as dishonesty (*II Kings* 5: 19–27) and murder (*I Kings* 19: 1–19; *Jas.* 4: 3).

(l) This aspect of worldliness was the second temptation Satan placed before our Lord when in a flash he showed Him all the kingdoms of this world, and offered them to Him at a price (*Luke* 4: 5, 6).

(m) Worldliness revolves, thirdly, around **the pride of life,** the empty pride we so often have in possessions and position (*I John* 2: 16).

(n) It is lust for advantage (*Matt.* 20: 21ff).

(o) It is lust for status (*Acts* 12: 21–23).

(p) It is lust for self-importance, revealed often in boasting (*Luke* 18: 11, 12; *Jas.* 4: 16).

(q) It is lust for possessions (*Gen.* 13: 11; *Josh.* 7: 21; *Luke* 12: 13–21).

(r) The wrongful preoccupation with possessions is the cause of much of human anxiety (*Matt.* 6: 34).

(s) This aspect of worldliness was the third temptation Satan placed before the Lord Jesus as he encouraged Him to claim an open manifestation of God's protecting power, purely for personal prestige and pride of position (*Luke* 4: 9–11).

(t) Worldliness, in essence, therefore, is love of the world or the things in the world (*I John* 2: 15).

3. The seriousness of worldliness.

(a) It finds its roots in a man's heart rather than in the things he does or the places he frequents (*I John* 2: 15,

16), and God looks on the heart (*I Sam.* 16: 7).

(b) In direct opposition to God's will for man (*I John* 2: 17), it is in total opposition to love for the Father (*I John* 2: 15), and constitutes unfaithfulness to God or spiritual adultery (*Ps.* 73: 27; *Jas.* 4: 4), a direct opposite of godliness (*Tit.* 2: 14).

(c) It indicates a failure to appreciate the passing nature of this world (*Heb.* 12: 27; *I John* 2: 17), and the neglect of the all-important question: What shall it profit a man if he gain the whole world and lose his own soul? (*Mark* 8: 36; *Matt.* 16: 26; *Luke* 9: 25).

(d) It demonstrates where a man's heart is (*Luke* 12: 33f), and where his treasures are to be found (*Matt.* 6: 19ff), for it is impossible to serve God and mammon (*Matt.* 6: 24; *Luke* 16: 13).

(e) It boasts of itself rather than of God and treats life as if God does not exist (*Jas.* 4: 13–17).

(f) Worldliness is serious because it grows: it begins in the mind, shows itself in conduct, and becomes established in attitude (*Ps.* 1: 1).

(g) It chokes spiritual growth and fruitfulness (*Luke* 8: 14), and it may indicate that an individual is without the Spirit (*Jude* 13).

(h) When a Christian is worldly in spirit and attitude he grieves the Spirit (*Jas.* 4: 5).

(i) Worldliness will take away the Christian's appreciation of the means of grace (*Ps.* 84: 10; cf. *Heb.* 10: 25).

(j) Worldliness may make a man turn aside from that to which he has set his hand, a task which he has known to be God's will (*II Tim.* 4: 10).

(k) It may even reach a point at which his last state becomes worse than his first, in that his entanglement with the world's defilements is worse at the end than at the beginning (*II Pet.* 2: 20, 21).

4. The antidote to worldliness is the constant practice and pursuit of a number of objectives.

(a) An understanding that the purpose of our redemption by the death of Christ is that we, having been set free, purified from all wickedness, made God's chosen people, and inspired to do good (*Tit.* 2: 14; cf. *Gal.* 1:4; *I Pet.* 1: 18f; *II Pet.* 2: 20), should give up ungodliness and worldly desires, and, here and now, live lives that are disciplined, righteous and godly, while we await our Saviour's return (*Tit.* 2: 12, 13; cf. *II Pet.* 1: 3, 4).

(b) The realisation of our true character now in the world as strangers and passing travelers (*Heb.* 11: 13), and our essential foreignness (*I Pet.* 1: 17; 2: 11) because of our heavenly citizenship (*Eph.* 2: 19; *Phil.* 3: 20) and our commitment to seek first God's kingdom and His righteousness, leaving it to God to add to us what He knows we need of this world's possessions (*Matt.* 6: 33).

(c) The understanding that we are called upon to enter into the privilege of being friends of God (*Gen.* 2:23; *John* 15: 14; *Jas.* 4. 4, *Rev.* 3: 20), a privilege which demands wholehearted obedience to Him as a condition of our enjoyment of this unspeakable privilege (*John* 14: 21, 23).

(d) The daily renewed offering of ourselves to God without reserve, in the light of His mercies towards us, so that instead of being conformed to this world we are instead transformed by the renewal of our mind, so that we prove in daily experience what is good and acceptable and perfect (*Rom.* 12: 1, 2), resolving to discover and to do God's will in everything (*I Thess.* 4: 3; *I Cor.* 10: 31).

(e) Honesty with ourselves both to examine ourselves (*I Cor.* 10: 12; 11: 28; *II Cor.* 13: 5), and to exercise self-control over our desires where they war against the best interests of our soul (*I Pet.* 2: 11); and if ever we are uncertain as to the rightness of our desires to present them to God in prayer for His judgment and guidance (*Jas.* 4: 2, 3).

(f) The key antidote to worldliness is the frank recognition of its seriousness and the active pursuit of sanctification, guided by the Word of God (*John* 17: 17).

13. SPIRITUAL DECLINE

Question: What is spiritual decline or backsliding?

Answer: Spiritual decline, or what the Bible calls "backsliding," is turning back from following the Lord. It takes a variety of forms, but it always begins with the thoughts, and eventually it shows itself in a life which is no longer wholehearted in its devotion to the Lord Jesus Christ.

1. Spiritual decline describes what the Bible calls "backsliding."

(a) It is the Christian ceasing to make every effort to progress in holiness and obedience (*II Pet.* 1: 5ff).

(b) It is to turn back by degrees from following the Lord (*Zeph.* 1: 6).

(c) It is the turning of the heart away from God (*I Kings* 11: 9), so that the

159

heart is not wholly true to God (*I Kings* 11: 4).

(d) It is to gradually forget God and the indebtedness the individual should feel to God (*Hos.* 2: 13).

(e) It is to deal faithlessly with the Lord (*Hos.* 5: 7), for inevitably the attempt is made to serve two masters (*Matt.* 6: 24).

(f) It is the abandonment of the love for Christ which the Christian knew at first (*Rev.* 2: 4).

(g) It is the pushing of Christ outside of the life (*Rev.* 3: 20).

(h) It is spiritual adultery (*Hos.* 1: 2; *Jas.* 4: 3).

2. The form which spiritual decline or "backsliding" takes varies a great deal but certain stages, not always in the order outlined, may be discerned.

(a) It all begins with the thoughts: the thoughts are led astray from a sincere and pure devotion to Christ (*II Cor.* 11: 3).

(b) Little by little the private aspects of the Christian life—such as private prayer—are neglected (*Jas.* 4:2; *Luke* 18: 1).

(c) Slackness in service soon follows (*Heb.* 6: 10, 11).

(d) Appreciation of the opportunities for fellowship, public worship, and the ministry of God's Word lessens, and this lessening of appreciation leads to neglect of them (*Ps.* 84: 10; *Heb.* 5: 11, 12; 10: 25).

(e) In spite of this obvious decline, there may be complete complacency about the situation in the individual's mind, a spiritual short-sightedness (*Amos* 6: 1, 4–7; *II Pet.* 1: 9; *Rev.* 3: 17).

(f) It is more than likely that the individual will be inclined to criticise his more spiritual fellow-Christians (*Phil.* 1: 15, 16).

(g) He begins to forget and lose the wonder of the Cross—the manner in which he was first cleansed from his sins (*II Pet.* 1: 9).

(h) Whereas he ought to be able to teach others the Christian faith, he needs, in fact, someone to teach him again the ABC's of God's Word (*Heb.* 5: 12).

(i) He loses his appreciation of the deeper truths of the faith and of the Bible (*Heb.* 5: 12; *I Cor.* 3: 2).

(j) He becomes unskilled in using the Bible, whereas once he had facility in doing so (*Heb.* 5: 13).

(k) He loses his ability to discern good from evil in the everyday situations of life (*Heb.* 5: 14).

(l) The promises of God no longer seem very great and precious, and they cease to influence the course of his life (*II Pet.* 1: 4; *Heb.* 6: 12).

(m) Guidance in daily life is no longer sought (*Zeph.* 1: 6).

(n) Compromise, in situation after situation, makes the individual's spiritual life—and life in general—more and more unstable (*Jas.* 1: 6–8), and the process accelerates (*Gal.* 5: 9).

(o) In the end he becomes completely ineffective and unfruitful in the knowledge of our Lord Jesus Christ (*II Pet.* 1: 8).

3. The causes of spiritual decline or "backsliding" are many and it may be caused by just one such cause or the combination of several.

(a) The neglect of prayer; or, on the other hand, the offering of prayer but from the wrong motives, with conduct completely contrary to God's revealed will (*Jas.* 4: 2, 3).

(b) Giving in to sin, with the sin unrepented of and unconfessed (*Ps.* 51: 3, 4; *Gal.* 6: 1).

(c) Disobedience to the obvious and known will of God for the individual's life (*Jonah* 1: 2–3; *Jer.* 8: 5–7; *Neh.* 9: 26; *I Cor.* 10: 23).

(d) Love of the world (*Luke* 8: 14; *Rom.* 12: 2; *II Tim.* 4: 10; *I John* 2: 15–17; *Jas.* 4: 1–3; *Rev.* 3: 4).

(e) A human relationship—especially with someone of the other sex—taking the place which God alone should have (*I Kings* 11: 4; *II Cor.* 6: 14).

(f) Discouragement, through the power of unbelief—this was the case apparently with the Hebrew Christians addressed in the Epistle to the Hebrews (*Heb.* 6: 9–20).

(g) Never having been properly established in the Christian life, as was the case with some of the Corinthian believers (*I Cor.* 3: 1–3).

(h) Self-assurance—instead of self-distrust and trust in Christ—is a cause of spiritual decline (*Prov.* 16: 18; *Mark* 14: 29, 31; *I Cor.* 10: 12).

(i) The pursuit of false and unworthy ambitions (*Jas.* 4: 3).

(j) A lack of self-examination (*I Cor.* 11: 31).

4. **The consequences of spiritual decline or "backsliding."**

(a) It grieves the Holy Spirit (*Eph.* 4: 30).

(b) It makes the Christian good-for-nothing or useless in fulfilling God's purposes in the world (*Matt.* 5: 13).

(c) It removes the joy of God's salvation (*Ps.* 51: 12).

(d) The sense of God's presence is lost (*Num.* 14: 43; *Isa.* 59: 2, 9–11).

(e) The ability to teach others the way of God is lost (*Ps.* 51: 13).

(f) Some form of idolatry is soon practised (*Zeph.* 1: 4–6).

(g) All kinds of sins may follow (*Prov.* 14: 14; *Isa.* 1: 5–6; *Hos.* 4): not least those which arise from unlawful associations (*Hos.* 5: 7).

(h) The backslider may find himself so carried away that he discovers himself to be contending for the world against God (*Judg.* 6: 28–32).

(i) Backsliding leads to a complacency which is full of danger (*Rev.* 3: 17; *I Cor.* 10: 12).

(j) It makes the Christians concerned nauseating to Christ (*Rev.* 3: 16).

(k) Unchecked, it is liable to increase (*Jer.* 8: 5; 14: 7).

(l) It brings the believer under the displeasure of God (*Ps.* 78: 57, 59).

(m) It brings the discipline and judgment of God (*Hos.* 11: 5–7); it brings reproof and chastisement from Christ (*Rev.* 3: 19).

14. SPIRITUAL RESTORATION

Question: How may the Christian in spiritual decline, i.e. the backslider, be restored?

Answer: The Christian in spiritual decline, i.e. the backslider, may be restored when he comes to himself, realises the seriousness of his position and fulfils carefully the conditions given in the Scriptures. As the conditions are fulfilled, God's promises come into operation to accomplish full and glorious restoration.

1. **The restoration of the backslider or the Christian whose spiritual life is in decline is clearly taught in the Bible.**

(a) The backslider's state is not hopeless (*Ps.* 37: 24; *Prov.* 24: 16).

(b) Nothing, however, can be done for the backsliding Christian until he

161

feels restless and miserable (*Mark* 14: 72)—his conscience needs to be probed and stirred (*John* 21: 15–17).

(c) Restoration is achieved only by the help of God (*Hos.* 12: 6).

(d) Backsliders are exhorted to return to the Lord (*II Chron.* 30:6; *Isa.* 31:6; *Jer.* 3: 12, 14, 22; *Hos.* 14: 1–3).

(e) The Lord uses chastisement to bring the backslider back to Himself (*Hos.* 2: 6; 5: 15; 6: 1).

(f) A spiritual Christian may be used by the Lord to restore a backsliding Christian (*Gal.* 6: 1; *Jas.* 5: 19)—perhaps by a pointed question (*Gal.* 4: 15) or by direct accusation (*II Sam.* 12: 1–13).

(g) Restoration can take place only when the backslider has come to himself (*Luke* 15: 17), perhaps through seeing the chastising hand of God in his circumstances (*Jonah* 2: 2–4).

2. The Lord promises the pardon of the backslider and the reviving of the Christian whose spiritual life is in decline on certain conditions (II Chron. 7: 14).

(a) The recognition that deliverance belongs to the Lord—it is not in the power of the Christian on his own to effect (*Jonah* 2: 9).

(b) The remembrance of the rightful jealousy God has for His people (*Deut.* 32: 16, 21; *Ex.* 20: 5; 34: 14; *Zech.* 8: 2; *Jas.* 4 5).

(c) All arrogance must be removed—self-assurance must be put aside (*Jas.* 4: 6).

(d) Submission to God—the backslider's return must be accompanied by the humbling of his pride, or else his profession of seeking God is of no avail (*Jas.* 4: 6; cf. *Hos.* 5: 5–7).

(e) Resistance to the devil, for he will surely contest the move to return to the Lord (*Jas.* 4: 7; *I Pet.* 5: 8, 9; *Eph.* 6: 16).

(f) Drawing near to God (*II Chron.* 7: 14; *Jas.* 4: 8)—prayers for restoration are provided in the Bible for our help and guidance (*Ps.* 80: 3; 85: 4; *Lam.* 5: 21).

(g) The sin of backsliding is to be confessed (*Jer.* 3: 13, 14; 14: 7–9) and the merits of Christ's atoning death depended upon, even as when the Christian was first converted (*I John* 1: 7, 9).

(h) The things which have turned the individual aside are to be resolutely abandoned (*Isa.* 1: 16–20; *II Chron.* 7: 14; *Ps.* 24: 4; *Jas.* 4: 8)—backsliding is soon renewed if repentance is not real (*II Cor.* 7: 10); remorse, therefore, is not to be mistaken for repentance (*Judg.* 2: 4, 5, 11–23).

(i) Self-humbling before God (*Prov.* 3: 34; *Jas.* 4: 6; *I Pet.* 5: 5).

3. As the conditions God lays down are fulfilled, so His promises come into operation to accomplish restoration.

(a) Praying now out of the right motives, the individual will receive that for which he asks (*Jas.* 4: 2, 3).

(b) The Holy Spirit, who has been grieved, will immediately assist the Christian in his efforts to return to the Lord (*Jas.* 4: 5).

(c) As the Christian seeks to humble himself before God in submission, he will be given grace from God (*Jas.* 4: 6); this grace will include help in resisting the devil to the end that the devil may flee from him (*Jas.* 4: 7).

(d) As he draws near to God, so God will come closer to him (*Jas.* 4: 8).

(e) As he confesses his sin, God is just, and may be trusted to forgive him his sins and to cleanse him from every kind of sin (*I John* 1: 9).

(f) As he continues to humble himself before the Lord, so the Lord will lift him up anew into the joys of new life in Christ (*Jas.* 4: 10).

(g) His desire and ability to teach transgressors God's ways will be regained (*Ps.* 51: 13).

(h) There is no doubt whatsoever about the Lord's healing, love and reviving, if the conditions are fulfilled (*Hos.* 14: 4–7; *Jer.* 3: 22)—the love that first pardoned the Christian's sins heals backsliding (*Micah* 7: 18).

4. From what has been deduced from the Bible about spiritual decline or "backsliding," certain results obviously follow upon restoration after such an experience.

(a) The regaining of the joy of God's salvation (*Ps.* 51: 12).

(b) A greater appreciation of Jesus Christ—the Saviour and Restorer of the soul.

(c) An increased hatred of sin.

(d) A more sensitive awareness to the first approaches of sin and temptation.

(e) A new appreciation of the means of grace, and a more diligent use of them.

(f) A renewed and deepened dedication to the service of Christ (*Jonah* 3. 1, *John* 21: 15–17).

15. CHRISTIAN WORSHIP

Question: What does the Bible teach about worship?

Answer: Worship is our acknowledgement of God in a manner acceptable to Him which means a wholehearted dependence upon Jesus Christ and the way He has opened up for us into God's presence; a recognition of the inwardness and spiritual nature of true worship; and an obedient awareness that the worship of God cannot be separated from conduct which glorifies Him.

1. Worship is the acknowledging of God in a manner worthy and pleasing to Him.

(a) The English word "worship" means simply "worthship," and denotes the worthiness of the person receiving the special honour due to his worth. Worship and service are presented to us as being virtually the same—the identical Hebrew word can be used for either "worship" or "service" and the same holds true in the New Testament in the use of the Greek word for "worship."

(b) Worship is rejoicing in all that God is, and giving Him the glory, i.e. ascribing to Him the things which rightly belong to Him, such as glory, honour, power, salvation, and thanksgiving (*Rev.* 4: 9, 11; 19: 1, 7).

(c) Worship can be simply that of the individual (*Gen.* 24: 26), but the emphasis is more generally upon corporate worship (*Ps.* 42: 4).

2. God alone is to be worshipped.

(a) The primary reference of worship is Godward—it is "to God" (*Col.* 3: 16).

(b) Worship presupposes that God is, that He rewards those who seek Him (*Heb.* 11: 6).

(c) God does not live in temples made by man. He is in fact not far from each one of us: "In Him we live and move and have our being" (*Acts* 17: 24, 27, 28).

(d) God wants men to seek Him, in the hope that they might feel after Him and find Him (*Acts* 17: 27).

(e) God alone is to be worshipped, and the revelation God has given forbids us to worship anyone besides God (*Ex.* 20: 3; *Matt.* 4: 10; *Rev.* 19: 10).

(f) We must beware of worshipping either the gifts or the messengers of God (*Rom.* 1: 25; *Rev.* 19: 10; 22: 9).

(g) Worship is God's due as our Creator (*Ps.* 100: 1, 2; *Rom.* 1: 25; *Rev.* 4: 11)—He is the Maker of the world and everything in it, the Lord of heaven and earth (*Acts* 17: 24).

(h) Worship is God's due as our Redeemer (*John* 3: 16); God the Father is the source of all blessing, and is thus to be Himself blessed (*Eph.* 1: 3).

(i) God in Christ is the definite, special object of Christian worship (*Eph.* 5: 19): spiritual worship of God is synonymous with joy in Christ, and a renunciation of all confidence in the flesh (*Phil.* 3: 3).

(j) In worshipping Christ we worship the Father (*Eph.* 5: 19, 20; *Col.* 3: 16), for He is the Son of God (*Matt.* 14: 33), the visible image of the invisible God (*Heb.* 1: 3; *Col.* 1: 15).

(k) Our praise and thanksgiving go to the Father through the Lord Jesus Christ and in His Name (*Eph.* 5: 20).

(l) The Lord Jesus, as the Lamb who was slain, is rightly the centre of our worship (*Rev.* 5: 8–14), to the glory of God the Father (*Phil.* 2: 11).

(m) Christians are to meet together for worship (*I Cor.* 14: 26; *Heb.* 10: 24), and such worship is appropriate as often as God's people have the opportunity of meeting together (*Acts* 2: 46, 47).

(n) The particular day for worship, however, is the first day of the week, the Lord's Day (*Acts* 20: 7; *Rev.* 1: 10).

3. The basis of worship.

(a) Whenever men would worship God, they are confronted with the great and glorious, but awesome truth, that God is holy (*Ps.* 24: 3, 4; *Isa.* 6; *I John* 1: 5–7).

(b) Worship rests upon revelation from God as to how worship is possible for sinful men; and Christian worship rests upon the revelation of Jesus Christ and the way He has opened up for us into God's presence (*Eph.* 2: 13–18; *Rev.* 1: 12–17).

(c) Worship depends upon God's grace: He is graciously willing to be approached (*Ps.* 5: 7; 138: 2).

(d) We can approach God solely on the grounds of what the Lord Jesus Christ has done for us: by virtue of His blood shed for us, we may have confidence to come before God (*Heb.* 10: 19).

(e) The Lord Jesus Christ has opened up for us a new and living way into God's presence (*Heb.* 10: 20).

(f) We may draw near to God with a true heart and with fullest confidence, knowing that our guilty consciences have been purified by the sprinkling of Christ's blood, just as our bodies are cleansed by the washing of clean water (*Heb.* 10: 22).

(g) In view of such a provision, worship is indeed part of our gratitude to God (*Heb.* 12: 28): the soul, the heart, and the flesh of the believer long to express worship to God (*Ps.* 84: 2).

(h) Every new experience of God's grace in Christ increases our desire to worship the Lord (*Ps.* 27: 6; *Luke* 5: 8; *Rev.* 1: 12–17).

(i) Worship should be our instinctive reaction to the discovery of some token of God's working on our behalf (*Judg.* 7: 15).

4. Characteristics of true worship.

(a) The place of worship is not important, but the manner of worship is (*John* 4: 20–24).

(b) Worship of God must be on the basis of a knowledge of God that is true (*Acts* 17: 23)—a fact which underlines the importance of the understanding given to us in the Scriptures (*John* 4: 22); worship must be according to God's Word, and not according to the ideas and precepts of men (*Isa.* 29: 13; *Mark* 7: 6–8).

(c) Expressed another way, worship requires some glimpse of God's glory (*Josh.* 5: 13–15; *Isa.* 6; *II Cor.* 4: 6).

(d) Awe and reverence are to characterise our worship of God (*Ps.* 5: 7; *Heb.* 12: 28).

(e) We should never enter into worship carelessly, allowing our lips to be rash and slick in expression of worship (*Eccl.* 5: 1, 2).

(f) The worship we offer to God is to be spiritual, that is to say, inspired and aided by God's Holy Spirit (*John* 4: 23, 24; *Phil.* 3: 3), for God delights not in outward acts but in the spiritual worship of the heart (*Ps.* 40: 6; 50: 7–15).

(g) The worship we offer to God is to be sincere (*Isa.* 1: 11–15): it is acceptable to Him only as our motives are right (*Amos* 5: 18–27).

(h) Worship is in vain if the feelings of the heart do not correspond with the expression of the lips (*Mark* 7: 6, 7); God has regard to our worship when it is sincere and the best we can

offer; but He has no regard to that which is formal and less than our best (*Gen.* 4: 3, 5).

(i) Worship is to combine fervour with the use of the mind (*I Cor.* 14: 14, 15); the mind and understanding are to be active in our worship of God (*I Cor.* 14: 14).

(j) Worship should always include the spirit of submission to God (*Josh.* 5: 14), for it cannot be separated from obedience (*Josh.* 5: 14, 15; *I Sam.* 15: 22; cf. *Gen.* 22: 5).

(k) Worship should cost us something (*II Sam.* 24: 22–24; *Mal.* 1: 6–11; cf. *Gen.* 4: 1–7): it is better not to worship God at all than to offer that which is knowingly and deliberately inferior.

(l) Worship is to be conducted decently and in order (*I Cor.* 14: 40), for God is not a God of confusion, but of peace (*I Cor.* 14: 33).

(m) Worship is also to be edifying, for although its primary reference is Godward, it has, at the same time, an edifying influence upon believers (*Col.* 3: 16); nothing is to find a place in the worship of God which is unedifying (*I Cor.* 14: 26).

(n) In our meeting together, we are to think of one another and how we can encourage one another to love and to good deeds (*Heb.* 10: 24, 25): by our hymns, psalms and spiritual songs we should be addressing one another in our worship of God (*Eph.* 5: 19).

(o) It perhaps needs to be pointed out that the evidence of the Bible indicates that worship may influence the posture of the body, even though God's concern is with the inward attitude of the heart rather than the outward activity (*John* 4: 24).

(p) Worship is expressed by posture

(*Rev.* 5: 14; 7: 11; 19: 4; cf. *Phil.* 2: 10); the outward attitude of the body is not a matter of indifference (*Gen.* 24: 26; *Ex.* 33: 10; *I Chron.* 29: 20).

5. Worship and morality.

(a) It is important to notice that the major definitions of worship in the New Testament are all inward and ethical (*Rom.* 12: 1ff; *Heb.* 13: 15, 16; *Jas.* 1: 27).

(b) Worship has no value apart from the person who offers it (*Gen.* 4: 4, 5); Abel's faith in God as he worshipped was decisive for his acceptance (*Heb.* 11: 4); Cain's life, unlike Abel's, gave the lie to his offering (*I John* 3: 12).

(c) Worship of God must be accompanied by righteousness of life (*Ps.* 40: 6–8; *Isa.* 1: 10–17; *Amos* 5: 21–24; *Micah* 6: 6–8): the worship which the Lord requires is a matter not of sacrifices, but rather of justice, kindness, and a humble walk with Himself (*Micah* 6: 6–8).

(d) God is as concerned with the morality of His people as with their worship (*Jer.* 7: 2ff; *Mal.* 3: 4, 5): worship is not acceptable to God if we are knowingly in a wrong relationship to someone, without having sought to rectify the situation (*Matt.* 5: 23f).

(e) Worship is linked with the service of our fellowmen (*Heb.* 13: 15, 16; *Jas.* 1: 27); worship must certainly never be an excuse for passing over need (*Luke* 10: 25–37; *Acts* 3: 1–10, noting verse 1).

6. Parts of worship.

(a) Our worship should always contain praise to God for the understanding we have of His activity on our behalf (*Ps.* 27: 6); through Christ we continually offer up a sacrifice of praise to God, that is, the fruit of lips that acknowledge His name (*Heb.* 13: 15).

(b) Thanksgiving too should have a regular place in all worship (*Ps.* 136; *Jonah* 2: 9; *Eph.* 5: 20).

(c) Prayer is part of worship (*Luke* 2: 37; *I Cor.* 14: 14–16).

(d) By reason of particular circumstances, perhaps the need for guidance from God, or the necessity of making a decision, fasting alongside prayer is part of worship at times (*Luke* 2: 37; *Acts* 13: 2).

(e) Songs have a place in Christian worship (*Acts* 16: 25; *I Cor.* 14: 26; *Eph.* 5: 19; *Col.* 3: 16; *Jas.* 5: 13) for the Holy Spirit inspires a joy which expresses itself in psalms, hymns and spiritual songs (*Eph.* 5: 18, 19).

(f) We may have fragments of early Christian hymns in the New Testament (e.g. *Eph.* 4: 4–6; 5: 14; *Phil.* 2: 5–11; *I Tim.* 1: 17; 2: 5f; 6: 15f; *II Tim.* 2: 11–13; *Rev.* 4: 11).

(g) Singing must be rooted in the word of Christ, for it has as one of its purposes the indwelling of that word in us (*Col.* 3: 16).

(h) The Lord's Supper is part of Christian worship (*Acts* 20: 7; *I Cor.* 11: 23–34).

(i) Worship consists of almsgiving (*I Cor.* 16: 1, 2): our gifts can represent a fragrant offering, a sacrifice acceptable and pleasing to God (*Phil.* 4: 18).

(j) Worship includes the reading of the Scriptures (*Col.* 3: 16; *Jas.* 1: 22), and the preaching of the Word (*Acts* 20: 7; *I Cor.* 14: 19); it is to include instruction and encouragement for believers (*I Cor.* 14: 31).

(k) Christians are to seek to contribute to worship (*I Cor.* 14: 26), which means that we should always be participators rather than spectators.

7. The experience of worship.

(a) As we worship God, by means of all the different parts and aspects of worship, we desire to be in God's presence, to behold His beauty, and to have fellowship with Him (*Ps.* 27: 4; 63: 2).

(b) Worship will sometimes be a timely way of escape for us (*I Cor.* 10: 13): living in the world and making our witness there, we shall often be oppressed by the spirit of the world, and the evil prevalent in it, but our means of relief and temporary escape will be the worship of God (*Ps.* 120).

(c) Worship should be a humbling experience (*Gen.* 18: 27; *Job* 42: 5, 6; *Isa.* 6: 1–5).

(d) In worship we should draw near to God to listen (*Eccl.* 5: 1), for it may be a time when God's voice is heard in guidance (*Acts* 13: 1–3).

(e) As we worship the Lord and regain our spiritual balance, we see things more clearly and in a better light (*Ps.* 73: 17).

(f) We should not forget that worship is part of our witness to God in the world (*I Pet.* 2: 9, 10; cf. *I Cor.* 11: 26).

(g) Indeed there will be occasions when God will use the worship of His people as a powerful instrument of conviction in the lives of unbelievers who may be present (*I Cor.* 14: 24, 25).

16. PRAYER

Question: What is prayer? and how should it be exercised?

Answer: Prayer is the communion we know with God as our Father through our Lord Jesus Christ, in which we express our dependence upon Him, and ask Him for the good things He wants us to ask Him for, both for ourselves and others.

1. Defining prayer.

(a) Prayer is asking God for the good things He wants to give to His children (*Matt.* 7: 7, 11; *Luke* 11: 9, 10; *Col.* 1: 9; *Jas.* 1: 5, 6); it is sharing with Him what we or others lack (*John* 2: 3; *Jas.* 1: 5).

(b) Prayer is the offering up of our desires to God (*Ps.* 62: 8).

(c) If we know that a desire is right, we may with confidence and assurance ask for its fulfilment (*Rom.* 10: 1); if, however, we are not sure, we may bring our desire to God, in the form of a request, to which His answer may be "No" (*Rom.* 1: 10; *II Cor.* 12: 8, 9; *I Thess.* 3: 10).

(d) Prayer is the surrendering of our wills of God (*Matt.* 6: 10)—our Lord is our example here as in the Garden of Gethsemane He three times prayed the same prayer (*Matt.* 26: 39, 42, 44).

(e) Prayer is being with God, since it is not always asking but sometimes simply an expression of fellowship with God, with the desire on our part to be in His presence (*Ps.* 27: 4)—we try to be still before Him, recognising that He alone is God (*Ps.* 46: 10, 11), and we share our life with Him (*Rev.* 3: 20).

(f) Prayer is conversation with God (*Gen.* 18: 23ff; *Ex.* 5: 22; 6: 1, 10, 12, 28–30; *Deut.* 3: 23–26): God says "Seek my face!" and we reply, "Your face, Lord, 1 will seek" (*Ps.* 27: 8 cf. *Acts* 13: 1, 2).

(g) Prayer is a key to our experience of God's peace (*Phil.* 4: 6, 7), for a burden shared with God is far more than a burden halved—it is a burden lifted and carried by God (*I Pet.* 5: 7).

2. Some basic principles and rules of prayer.

(a) A first principle of prayer is that we must be in fellowship with God (*Prov.* 15: 8): reconciled to God through faith in our Lord Jesus Christ, our fellowship is with the Father and with the Son (*I John* 1: 3), and we may call God "Our Father" (*Luke* 11: 2; *Rom.* 8: 15).

(b) A second rule of prayer is the practice of obedience—by putting away sin (*Ps.* 66: 18; *I John* 1: 9), by maintaining right relationships with others (*Matt.* 5: 23, 24; *I Pet.* 3: 7), and by striving to abide in Christ (*John* 15: 7).

(c) A third rule of prayer is dependence upon the Lord Jesus Christ and His work on our behalf (*Eph.* 2: 13)—we pray in His Name (*John* 14: 13, 14; 15: 16; 16: 23, 24, 26).

(d) A fourth rule of prayer is the exercise of faith (*Heb.* 11: 6; *Jas.* 1: 6–8)—if we believe, we will receive whatever we ask for in prayer (*Matt.* 21: 22; *Mark* 11: 23, 24), and believing prayer has the assurance that we may receive beyond all our asking (*Eph.* 3: 20).

(e) A fifth rule of prayer is readiness for action, for faith and works go together (*Jas.* 2: 17): having prayed, we must be ready to be the instruments on occasions by means of which God answers our prayers (*Ex.* 14: 15; *Matt.* 9: 37, 38; cf. 10: 1 ff.).

(f) A sixth principle of prayer is the honest desire for God's will to be done, and His Name to be glorified (*Matt.* 6: 10; *I John* 5: 14; cf. *Ex.* 32: 11–13; *Matt.* 26: 39).

(g) A seventh principle of prayer is sincerity: God has no time for hypocrites who make a lot of show without reality in their hearts (*Isa.* 29: 13; *Mark* 12: 40), but He promises to be near those who call upon Him in truth (*Ps.* 145: 18).

3. Prayer's parts.

(The Bible prescribes no set order for the different parts of prayer, and our daily circumstances will dictate a varying starting point. However, there is a natural order, although not binding, which Scripture suggests.)

(a) **Adoration** consists in reverencing God in a spirit of worship (*Ps.* 89: 7, 8; *Isa.* 6: 1, 2).

(b) **Praise** concerns itself with what God is, and it gives glory to God (*Ps.* 18: 3; 145: 3).

(c) **Thanksgiving** focuses upon what God has done for us (*Phil.* 4: 6), and, no matter what our circumstances, there is always cause for thanksgiving to God (*Ps.* 126: 3; *Eph.* 1: 3; *I Thess.* 5: 18).

(d) **Confession of sin** is a vital part of prayer for the maintenance of our fellowship with God (*I John* 1: 5, 6, 9), for "he who conceals his sins does not prosper, but whoever confesses and renounces them finds mercy" (*Prov.* 28: 13).

(e) **Prayer and supplication** are separate, yet related (*I Tim.* 2: 1; *Eph.* 6: 18): prayer has regard to the needs which are always present with us (as represented in the petitions of the Lord's Prayer—*Matt.* 6: 9–13) and **supplication** has regard to specific situations where special or emergency help is required (as illustrated in Mary's petition to Jesus at the wedding in Cana—*John* 2: 3— and Mary and Martha's message to Jesus about Lazarus—*John* 11: 3).

(f) **Intercession** approaches God for others (*Col.* 4: 12): we are to pray for all men without distinction of race, nationality or social position (*I Tim.* 2: 1, 2): when they are in need or are rebellious (*Ex.* 8: 12, 30; 32: 11, 13, 32; *Num.* 14: 13–19; cf. *Jer.* 15: 1);

when they are ill (*Jas.* 5: 14); when they are unjustly treated, and perhaps imprisoned (*Acts* 12: 5; *Heb.* 13: 3); and even when they are our enemies (*Matt.* 5: 44; *Luke* 23: 34).

(g) Governments and rulers are not to be neglected in our intercession (*I Tim.* 2: 2).

(h) In praying for missionaries, for example, we should pray for their deliverance from malicious enemies, acceptance with God's people, health of mind and body, the ability to speak the right words boldly at the moment of opportunity, the turning of untoward circumstances to good, God-given opportunities for preaching Christ and progress in the establishment of the Church (*Rom.* 15: 30, 31; *II Cor.* 1: 11; *Eph.* 6: 19; *Phil.* 1: 19; *Col.* 4: 3; *II Thess.* 3: 1).

(i) **Dedication to God** and to His will must be the background to all our prayers (*Rom.* 12: 1, 2; *Heb.* 10: 7).

4. Characteristics of prayer at its best.

(a) **Reverence** (*Gen.* 18: 25, 27; *Acts* 9: 31; 10: 2; *II Cor.* 5: 11; *Heb.* 12: 28).

(b) **Humility** (*Ps.* 10: 17; *Luke* 18: 9–14; *Jas.* 4: 6).

(c) **Boldness** (*Eph.* 3: 12; *Heb.* 4: 15, 16).

(d) **In accordance with Scripture** (*I Thess.* 4: 3; *I Tim.* 2: 1–3; *I John* 5: 14, 15).

(e) **Definiteness** (*I Chron.* 4: 10; *John* 17; *Eph.* 1: 16–23; 3: 14–21; *Phil.* 1: 3–11; *Col.* 1: 9–12).

(f) **Intelligence** (*I Cor.* 14: 15; cf. *Neh.* 1: 1–11).

(g) **Earnestness** (*Luke* 11: 5–13; *Mark* 7: 27; *Jas.* 5: 17).

(h) **Persistence** (*Gen.* 32: 26; *I Thess.* 5: 17).

(i) **Submission to God** (*Matt.* 26: 39; *Mark* 14: 39; *Luke* 22: 42; *Rom.* 12: 1, 2).

(j) **Fasting** (*Neh.* 1: 4; *Matt.* 4: 2)— some situations are dealt with satisfactorily only by prayer and fasting (*Matt.* 17: 21; cf. *Acts* 14: 21–23).

5. Our chief Helper in prayer is the Holy Spirit.

(a) In the gift of the Holy Spirit (*Acts* 2: 38), God has provided a perfect Helper who is with us for ever (*John* 14: 16), and who attests to our spirits that we are children of God, helping us cry, "Abba" (*Rom.* 8: 15; cf. *Gal.* 4: 6).

(b) He prompts us to pray by bringing to our minds the words and promises of our Lord Jesus Christ (*John* 14: 26), and He urges us to pray according to the will of God which they reveal.

(c) He also prompts our concern for individuals (*Rom.* 10: 1; cf. 9: 1, 2), so that we feel it to be sin if we do not pray for them (*I Sam.* 12: 23).

(d) When the Holy Spirit excites our feelings, He also enables us to give utterance to those feelings, in the right manner—He intercedes for us according to God's will (*Rom.* 8: 26, 27).

(e) Prayer is to be in the Spirit (*Eph.* 6: 18; *Jude* 20): praying in the Spirit, we depend upon Him as we ask for the things we know to be right and in accord with God's will (*Matt.* 6: 9–13; *Luke* 11: 2–4), and the result is a renewed experience of God's peace, and an attitude of complete submission to God's will, no matter how He may choose to answer our prayers (*Phil.* 4: 6, 7; *II Cor.* 12: 7–10).

(f) We must never forget that the Holy Spirit is a Person whom we both grieve (*Eph.* 4: 30) and quench (*I Thess.* 5: 19) by sin.

(g) By the Spirit's help we can fulfil our Lord's instruction that we should always pray and not give up (*Luke* 18: 1; *Rom.* 8: 26; *I Thess.* 5: 17).

17. THE STATE

Question: What is the relationship of Christians to the state and what should be their attitude towards human authorities?

Answer: The relationship of Christians to the state is determined by the understanding the Bible gives of God's establishment of those in authority. The duty of Christians is to uphold all rightful authority and to strive to be good citizens, demonstrating by their exemplary conduct that their true citizenship is in heaven. On those infrequent occasions when the state demands an obedience contrary to God's commands, their duty then is to obey God.

1. God's establishment of those in authority.

(a) There is no authority except from God, and those that exist have been instituted by Him (*Rom.* 13: 1).

(b) God confers upon men the right to govern (*I Kings* 19: 15; *II Kings* 8: 9–13; *Jer.* 27: 6; *John* 19: 11).

(c) Men's rule is temporary, however, whereas God's rule is eternal (*Dan.* 4: 31), and He installs and removes kings (*Dan.* 2: 21), and at any moment He can bring their dominion to an end (*Dan.* 7: 12).

(d) God is like a potter who can do what He likes with the clay (*Rom.* 9: 21; cf. *Prov.* 8: 15; *Isa.* 26: 16; *Jer.* 18: 6); He can stir up the spirits of heathen kings so that they accomplish His purposes (*II Chron.* 36: 22, 23; *Ezra* 1: 1ff; *Isa.* 44: 28; 45: 1).

(e) There are various institutions of government ordained for man's common good (*I Pet.* 2: 13). (Within every people or nation, permanently settled in a geographical area, there needs to be a public authority with the power of ultimate decision which exacts obedience, and is capable of enforcing its legislative and executive measures for the protection of all, both from internal and external enemies—cf. *Acts* 17: 26).

(f) There are supreme civil authorities, whether kings, emperors, dictators, presidents or central governments (*I Pet.* 2: 13).

(g) There are also local civil authorities, such as governors and local government officials (*I Pet.* 2: 14).

(h) These different sorts of authority are God's servants for the benefit of good citizens (*Rom.* 13: 4).

(i) They are established by God to punish those who do wrong and to praise those who do right (*I Pet.* 2: 14)—they are not, therefore, a terror to good conduct but to bad (*Rom.* 13: 3).

(j) They have the right to bear the sword—that is to say, to punish, and to execute God's punishment on the evil-doer (*Rom.* 13: 4; cf. *Acts* 16: 22, 23, 33, 37; 22: 24; *II Cor.* 11: 23, 25); they are entrusted by God with the office of avenger (*I Kings* 19: 16f; *Isa.* 10: 5ff).

(k) The state, for its necessary support and maintenance, has the right to command the payment of various dues and taxes, and to expect respect and honour (*Rom.* 13: 6)—it is, in fact, God's minister in attending to such duties (*Rom.* 13:

(l) Whoever, therefore, resists the civil authorities in their God-given duties resists what God has appointed, and offenders must incur God's judgment (*Rom.* 13: 2).

170

2. The plain duty of Christians, therefore, is to uphold proper authority and to be good citizens.

(a) We are to be subject to every human institution of government (*I Pet.* 2: 13), respecting the most prominent people in the state and honouring all who hold public office (*Rom.* 13: 7), because of conscience (*Rom.* 13: 5).

(b) Our submissiveness is to express itself, whenever possible, in honest obedience to the laws and instructions of the state (*Tit.* 3: 1).

(c) We are to honour all men and in particular the supreme authority (*Rom.* 13: 7; *I Pet.* 2: 17).

(d) We are neither to curse those in authority (*Ex.* 22: 28) nor to harm them (*I Sam.* 24: 6; *II Sam.* 1: 14).

(e) We are to pray for the supreme authority, and all who are in high positions, that we and others may lead a quiet and peaceable life, godly and respectful in every way (*I Tim.* 2: 2).

(f) We are to pay taxes to the government without complaint (*Mark* 12: 13–17; *Rom.* 13: 6, 7).

(g) We are to be good citizens by speaking evil of no one, avoiding quarrelling, being gentle and showing perfect courtesy toward all men (*Tit.* 3: 2).

(h) We are to be ready for any honest work (*Tit.* 3: 1).

(i) While it is true that we hold a dual citizenship (*Phil.* 3: 20), we are given no reason whatsoever for neglecting our civil responsibilities to the state (*Rom.* 13: 1ff).

(j) Our desire to fulfil these duties is a direct consequence of our experience of God's salvation (*Tit.* 3: 1–7).

(k) For the most part at least, our duties to the state will not infringe the rights of God (*Mark* 12: 17).

3. When the state or other authorities command anything which is contrary to God's commandments, it is the duty of Christians to obey God.

(a) Rulers and civil authorities are always in danger of being intoxicated by power: they may attribute merit to themselves (*Isa.* 10: 7–11, 13f), deify themselves (*Ezek.* 28: 2–5), elevate themselves against God (*Isa.* 14: 13), and even go so far as to offend Him by blasphemy (*Dan.* 11: 36).

(b) It is as well to remember, therefore, that the authority God entrusts to men is never absolute, but it is limited by moral obligations—for example, while in the Old Testament owners were given authority over their slaves, God's law regulated its exercise by stating precisely the rights of slaves (*Ex.* 21: 1–6; 26f; *Deut.* 15: 12–18).

(c) Civil and other authorities sometimes choose to listen to the malicious accusations of enemies of the gospel who argue that Christian preaching is a political crime or that Christians are the causers of trouble (*Acts* 17: 6; cf. 19: 27; 24: 5).

(d) Religious authorities on occasion persecute Christians (*Luke* 12: 11), and in the days of the early Church it was the high priests who commanded the apostles not to speak and teach in the name of Jesus (*Acts* 4: 18; 5: 28, 40).

(e) The apostles' answer provides the classic answer when Christians are commanded to stop doing what God has plainly commanded: "We must obey God rather than men" (*Acts* 5: 29).

4. In usual circumstances, the fulfil-

171

ment by Christians of their obligations to the state will be an essential part of their Christian testimony which commends both them and the gospel to the powers that be.

(a) In Christ we are created for good works (*Eph.* 2: 10).

(b) We are urgently exhorted to bear fruit in good works (*Col.* 1: 10), to seek to do good (*I Thess.* 5: 15), and to do it for everyone (*Rom.* 15: 12; 16: 19; *Gal.* 6: 6, 10).

(c) We may rest assured that the man who does right will generally receive praise from the authorities (*I Pet.* 2: 14).

(d) We are to live in society as the servants of God (*I Pet.* 2: 16).

(e) We are to be subject to the powers that be for the Lord's sake (*I Pet.* 2: 13).

(f) By our good citizenship we are to put to silence the ignorant criticisms of foolish men (*I Pet.* 2: 15).

18. SOCIAL RESPONSIBILITY

Question: What are the principles which should guide the Christian in the exercise of social responsibility and involvement in social action?

Answer: The Christian's responsibility for society is plainly taught in the Bible, and often indirectly. Social action on behalf of any who are in need is demanded by the rule: "Love your neighbour as yourself." The description of Christians as "the salt of the earth" implies the beneficial effect their behaviour should have upon society.

1. **The pattern God Himself has set.**

(a) God gave man a body as well as a soul, and He provided for the well-being of both (*Gen.* 1: 27–30).

(b) We may say that God inaugurated social action in the provision He made for man after his disobedience—"The Lord God made garments of skin for Adam and his wife and clothed them" (*Gen.* 3: 21); and the provisions of His law underlined its importance (e.g. *Ex.* 22: 25; *Lev.* 19: 10; 23: 22; *Deut.* 15: 11; 24: 12, 14, 15).

(c) God loves the world (*John* 3: 16), and He causes His sun to rise on the evil and the good, and sends rain on the righteous and the unrighteous (*Matt.* 5: 45).

(d) God's wrath is declared against extortion, robbery, oppression, and racial discrimination (*Jer.* 22: 13; *Ezek.* 22: 23–31, especially verses 29 and 31; *Amos* 2: 6, 7).

(e) God does not forget men's dishonest dealings at the expense of the helpless (*Amos* 8: 4–14).

(f) God forbids favouritism on the grounds of class, money and privilege (*Lev.* 19: 15; *Gal.* 3: 28; *Jas.* 2: 1–13).

(g) God has shown us what is good and what He requires of us as members of society; He requires us to act justly and to love mercy and to walk humbly with Him (*Micah* 6: 8; cf. *Amos* 5: 24).

2. **God confirmed this pattern of social responsibility in the example of His Son, our Lord Jesus Christ.**

(a) Our Lord Jesus Christ went about doing good (*Acts* 10: 38).

(b) He cared for all whose need confronted Him (*Matt.* 8: 28–34; *Luke* 7: 11–17).

(c) He was friendly with outcasts (*Matt.* 9: 10–11; *Mark* 2: 15–16; *Luke* 7: 39; 15: 2; 19: 7).

(d) He healed those who were ill (*Matt.* 11: 2–6; *Luke* 7: 21).

(e) He fed the hungry (*Matt.* 14: 14–21; *Mark* 6: 30–44; *Luke* 9: 10–17; *John* 6: 1–13).

(f) He taught the importance of good works: "let your light shine before men, that they may see your good deeds and praise your Father in heaven" (*Matt.* 5: 16).

(g) He spoke of His disciples' function as light and salt in the world (*Matt.* 5: 13, 14).

3. We have the example of the early Church.

(a) The early believers had everything in common (*Acts* 2: 44).

(b) They sold their possessions and goods, and gave to anyone as he had need (*Acts* 2: 45; 4: 32, 34, 35).

(c) They sought to look after widows and others in difficulty and there were no needy persons among them as a consequence (*Acts* 4: 34; 6: 1, 2).

(d) The early churches collected gifts for the impoverished Jerusalem Christians (*Acts* 24: 17; *Rom.* 15: 26; *I Cor.* 16: 3).

4. We have the teaching of the apostles.

(a) They took up our Lord's emphasis upon the continuing debt we have to love one another—"he who loves his fellow man has fulfilled the law" (*Rom.* 13: 8; cf. *Mark* 12: 29–33; *Jas.* 2: 8).

(b) They taught that a Christian does not cease to be an earthly citizen because he has become a citizen of heaven; rather he ought to be a better citizen (*Phil.* 1: 27; *I Pet.* 2: 13–17).

(c) They instructed Christians to do good to all people, especially to those who belong to the family of believers (*Gal.* 6: 10), to be kind to each other and to everyone else (*I Thess.* 5: 15).

(d) They made it plain that Chris-tians are not to be afraid of exposing evil (*Eph.* 5: 11).

(e) They emphasised the importance of diligent work and honest dealings so that none would have just grounds for criticising believers' behaviour (*Eph.* 4: 28; *II Thess.* 3: 10–13).

5. Guidelines for Christian social involvement.

(a) We are to be good citizens (*Matt.* 17: 24–27): we have duties to the state and society as well as having a duty to God, and each must be fulfilled (*Matt.* 22: 15–22; *Rom.* 13: 1–7; *I Tim.* 2: 2; *I Pet.* 2: 17).

(b) We are to keep before us the priority of meeting man's spiritual need (e.g. *Luke* 3: 18, 19), and the unique trusteeship of the gospel our Lord Jesus Christ has committed to us (*Matt.* 28: 18–20; *I Thess.* 2: 4).

(c) By upholding the priority of the gospel, we do not neglect social action—in fact, where the gospel is genuinely received, it changes men's lives so that they influence society for good (*Luke* 19: 8; *John* 8: 11).

(d) Our commitment to the gospel, however, is not a commitment demanding callous indifference to people's material and physical needs— we must be willing to share not only the gospel but our very selves with them too (*I Thess.* 2: 8; cf. *Matt.* 25: 34–40; *I John* 3: 16–18).

(e) We are never to make our spiritual responsibilities an excuse for neglecting practical and social needs— this was the mistake of the priest and the Levite in the story our Lord told of the man who fell into the hands of robbers and who was helped by the good Samaritan (*Luke* 10: 30–37).

(f) When, however, we are involved in meeting people's material, physical and social needs, we must encourage them and ourselves to realise the importance of the right spiritual relationship with God we all need (*Mark* 2: 5, 11).

(g) We must not minimise the distinctive contribution we are able to make to social betterment by living the Christian life as we ought in all its aspects—especially within our home, among our neighbours, and at our daily employment (*Eph.* 5: 22–6: 9).

(h) As we show that we care about right relationships and that the individual counts and really matters, we make a contribution which the world desperately needs—it was in this way, for example, that Christianity brought about the freedom of slaves (cf. *Philemon*).

(i) Our primary concern should be with those social needs with which we are personally confronted day by day (*Luke* 10: 30–37; *Rom.* 15: 25, 26).

(j) When we are rightly involved in social action of any kind, we need to review periodically our involvement—and sometimes even to withdraw for a while to accomplish this review—to ensure that our proper priorities are being maintained (*John* 6: 15; *Acts* 6: 1–4).

(k) Love for God and love for man are never in conflict: loving God as we ought, we love our neighbour also (*Luke* 10: 27, 28).

19. WORK

Question: What does the Bible teach about work?

Answer: Work was an original purpose of God for man, but man's rebellion against God marred man's experience of God's purpose so that man finds his work all too often a burden rather than a pleasure.

Work is part of God's scheme for the support of the human race, and properly fulfilled it brings its own rewards. While to avoid work is folly, life is not to be filled exclusively with work—God makes provision for rest and recreation. Christians should bear witness to their faith by the quality of their work.

1. **There are many varieties of work.**

(a) Work has taken a variety of forms from the beginning of God's creation (*Gen.* 4: 2; 9: 20).

(b) The Old Testament speaks of God filling men with His Spirit, giving them ability and intelligence, with knowledge and all craftsmanship, to be metal workers, carvers and embroiderers (*Ex.* 31: 2–11).

2. **Work was an original purpose of God for man.**

(a) Man was appointed by God as His "deputy" to cooperate with Him in the continuing work of harnessing and using the resources God provides in His creation (*Gen.* 1: 27, 28).

(b) Man was commanded to subdue the earth, and to have dominion over it (*Gen.* 1: 28; *Ps.* 8: 3–8)—a command clearly implying the necessity for work.

(c) Before man's fall, we see man happily at work (*Gen.* 2: 15).

(d) The principle of work is written into the whole of God's creation (*Prov.* 6: 6–11).

(e) It is always assumed that work constitutes part of God's pattern for man (*Ex.* 20: 9, 10; *Ps.* 104: 23).

(f) Work in all its different forms is a provision of God's wisdom for mankind (*Isa.* 28: 24–26).

(g) But God is not said to have commanded man to work, and the implication is present that it was pleasure for man to work prior to the Fall (*Gen.* 2: 15; cf. 3: 17–19).

(h) God intends that man should find enjoyment in his work (*Eccl.* 5: 18–20); indeed since the Fall, there is often more pleasure in work itself than in the achievements of our work (*Eccl.* 2: 10, 11).

(i) There is no disgrace in manual work; indeed its dignity is insisted upon (*Eph.* 4: 28; *I Thess.* 4: 11)— and, of course, our Lord Jesus Christ set an example by working as a carpenter (*Mark* 6: 3).

(j) Work for all is a sign of God's blessing; sometimes unemployment in a nation may be a sign of God's judgment (*Zech.* 8).

3. Man's rebellion against God marred man's experience of God's purposes in the principle of work.

(a) The curse which followed the Fall of man was not the curse of work, but the pain and hardship connected with work by reason of the curse upon the ground (*Gen.* 3: 17–19; 5: 29).

(b) As a consequence of sin, and the disorder following in its wake, work becomes a burden all too often rather than a pleasure to man (*Gen.* 3: 17–19).

(c) Daily work can be often just pointless and empty in meaning when performed without God (*Ps.* 127: 2).

(d) There is a futile element in human work because, although the man who works may achieve something in life, his motive tends to be envy of his neighbour (*Eccl.* 4: 4).

(e) Work has sometimes been an instrument of exploitation and oppression (*Ex.* 1: 11–14; *Jas.* 5: 4–6).

(f) Men's lives can be made bitter by hard service (*Ex.* 1: 14).

4. The purpose which may be discerned behind the principle of work.

(a) The great incentive for daily work is our daily bread as the fruit of it (*Prov.* 16: 26).

(b) Daily work is the means of building the home and sustaining it (*Prov.* 24: 27).

(c) Daily work is part of God's scheme for the support of the human race (*Prov.* 27: 25–27).

(d) By our work we are to make some return to our parents (*I Tim.* 5: 4). Of course, such provision may not be necessary always, but it is a dreadful thing to work and not to provide for any member of our own family who may be in need (*I Tim.* 5: 8).

(e) Our employment is not to be merely a means of gaining things for ourselves (*Mark* 8: 36, 37).

(f) Giving to those who are not so well off as ourselves has a constant emphasis in the teaching of our Lord Jesus Christ (*Matt.* 19: 21; *Luke* 14: 13), and the early Church practised our Lord's teaching (*Acts* 2: 44, 45; 4: 32).

(g) The apostle Paul set an example of working, not only for his own support, but also for the benefit of those who were serving the Lord with him (*Acts* 20: 34); he also laid emphasis upon the provision of help for the poor (*Rom.* 15: 26, 27; *II Cor.* 8 and 9; *Gal.* 2: 10).

(h) No one should work for himself alone, but with the definite object of being able to help others (*Eph.* 4: 28), for those who are unable to work are entitled to aid.

175

5. Work, properly fulfilled, brings its rewards.

(a) Work brings the satisfaction of peaceful sleep, a benefit not to be despised (*Eccl.* 5: 12).

(b) Work, well done, is worthy of a reasonable wage (*Matt.* 10: 10; *Luke* 10: 7; *I Tim.* 5: 18).

(c) God chooses to reward men for good work, whatever their position or station in life (*Eph.* 6: 8).

(d) Diligence in daily work brings reward (*Prov.* 22: 29; 27: 23–27); whereas laziness in daily work makes the individual concerned dissatisfied (*Prov.* 13: 4).

(e) Ability eventually outruns privilege in employment, insofar that a diligent and wise employee will gain by conscientiousness what others may possess by birth or some special privilege of relationship (*Prov.* 17: 2).

6. Life is not to be all work.

(a) Work brings some reward, but too much work, or a total concern with work, can destroy its benefits (*Eccl.* 2: 10, 11, 24; 4: 6).

(b) Men can make an idol of their work and their achievements with disastrous consequences—for example, the rich fool in the parable (*Luke* 12: 16–21).

(c) Our daily work is not to be motivated by the desire to be rich for this can plunge us into ruin and destruction (*I Tim.* 6: 9, 10).

(d) It is better to have small earnings when they are gained with a restful mind, than to gain a large income by worry and anxious work (*Eccl.* 4: 6).

(e) There is great gain in godliness with contentment; and godliness, of course, acknowledges happily the principle of rest which is so clearly written into God's commandments (*I Tim.* 6: 6).

(f) The cycle of work goes hand in hand with the cycle of rest: the fourth commandment safeguards the principle that man's life is not to be all work (*Ex.* 20: 8–11).

7. The folly of avoiding work.

(a) Idleness is condemned (*II Thess.* 3: 11).

(b) The man who does not work destroys himself (*Eccl.* 4: 5).

(c) Not to have proper work to do is a man's undoing if this state of affairs arises from laziness (*Prov.* 21: 25).

(d) Idleness destroys character (*Prov.* 18: 9).

(e) God will judge the slacker, and He makes no distinction between employer and employee (*Col.* 3: 25).

(f) No one who is able to support himself is entitled to be supported by others (*II Thess.* 3: 10).

8. Employers and employees.

(a) Employers are to pay wages readily (*Lev.* 19: 13; cf. *Deut.* 24: 14, 15); and to withhold proper wages is sin in God's sight (*Jas.* 5: 4).

(b) Employers are to remember their responsibility to be fair and just to those whom they employ, never forgetting that they are to view themselves as having Christ Himself as their Heavenly Employer (*Col.* 4: 1).

(c) Employers are not to misuse the power put in their hands; and they are to forbear threatening (*Eph.* 6: 9).

(d) Employers are to be as conscientious and responsible towards those who work fo them as they expect employees to be towards employers (*Eph.* 6: 9).

(e) The Christian employee is to do his work, not with the idea of currying favour, but as a sincere expression of his devotion to the Lord (*Eph.* 6: 5, 6; *Col.* 3: 22).

(f) Whatever the Christian does, he is to put his whole heart and soul into it, as into work done for the Lord, and not for men (*Col.* 3: 23).

(g) The Christian is to know that his real reward, a heavenly one, will come from the Lord, since he is actually employed by the Lord Christ, and not just by his earthly employer (*Col.* 3: 24).

9. Christians should bear witness to their faith by the quality of their work.

(a) Knowing God through Jesus Christ makes a difference to the whole of life (*Rom.* 14: 7, 8): therefore, daily employment will be marked by this difference too.

(b) We are not to be conformed to the world's view of work, but we are to be transformed by the renewal of our mind, that we may prove what is God's will in our daily employment, as in everything else (*Rom.* 12: 2).

(c) Our daily work must be included within the sphere of the good works which God has prepared for us to do (*Eph.* 2: 10): our primary calling is to come to the Lord Jesus Christ as sinners and to believe on Him, and to be set apart for God's possession (*I Cor.* 1: 2, 9); but our secondary calling is to discover those good works for which God has both fitted and chosen us (*Eph.* 2: 8–10).

(d) The principle of our acting as salt and light in society must surely have particular reference to the sphere of our daily employment (*Matt.* 5: 13–16).

(e) We are to earn our own living (*II Thess.* 3: 12), making the maximum use of our resources and talents, whether they are large or small (*Matt.* 25: 14–30).

(f) Our daily work is to be character-ised by good behaviour (*I Pet.* 3: 16).

(g) We are to do our work quietly and efficiently (*II Thess.* 3: 12).

(h) It is important to do what may be described as "honest work" (*Eph.* 4: 28).

(i) Paul set an example of honest work by his tentmaking, and the importance of such work featured in his teaching (*Acts.* 18: 3; *I Thess.* 2: 9; *II Thess.* 3: 7–10).

(j) In all our work we are to see ourselves as serving the Lord (*Rom.* 12: 11; *Col.* 3: 22–24).

(k) Work should be an act of worship—done "as to the Lord" (*Eph.* 6: 5, 6).

(l) We must take care not to discredit the faith whether by our standards of work or by our attitude to our work (*I Thess.* 4: 11, 12).

(m) The governing attitude and principle of the whole of the Christian life is that we should do all to the glory of God, and this goal must comprehend our daily employment (*I Cor.* 10: 31).

20. LEISURE

Question: What does the Bible teach about leisure?

Answer: The principle of rest and leisure is inherent in God's institution of the Sabbath, and the fourth commandment safeguards the principle that man's life is not to be all work.

The purpose of leisure is recreation and refreshment. The knowledge that God intends all His gifts to be received, used, and rejoiced in increases the Christian's appreciation and enjoyment of leisure. In a world marred by the fall, a Christian has to exercise discernment to ensure that

177

his leisure enhances his appreciation of goodness, righteousness and truth, and genuinely refreshes him for renewed service of God in the world.

1. The basis for any consideration of the subject of leisure.

(a) Leisure is free time; time in which we are at liberty to choose our activity; the time available for other things after our daily work.

(b) The fundamental basis with which we begin and upon which we build is that everything God made is good (*I Tim.* 4: 4; cf. *Gen.* 1: 31).

(c) We must not fail to acknowledge that every good and perfect gift comes from God (*Jas.* 1: 17).

(d) God has provided in His creation satisfaction for men's bodies and gladness for men's souls (*Acts* 14: 17).

(e) God has given us a host of pursuits richly to enjoy (*I Tim.* 6: 17).

(f) The good things of God's creation are intended by God to be thankfully enjoyed by those who believe in Him and know the truth (*I Tim.* 4: 3).

(g) The creative and artistic gifts of men, as with all the other gifts given to man by God, are to be received gratefully (*I Tim.* 4: 3, 4, 5).

(h) But the fall of man means that these gifts can be abused and mis-interpreted (*I Tim.* 4: 1–5), and the principles of goodness, righteousness and truth, uniformly laid down in the Scriptures, apply (*Eph.* 5: 9).

(i) Furthermore, there is a right time for everything (*Eccl.* 3: 1–8); and there is a right and a wrong time for relaxation or leisure (*Eccl.* 10: 16, 17).

2. The essential principle behind leisure.

(a) God rested on the seventh day, after His creative activity (*Gen.* 2: 2).

(b) On the pattern and basis of God's own "rest," it would seem to have been God's purpose for man from the beginning to have one day in seven for rest and recreation (*Gen.* 2: 2, 3), for God blessed and hallowed the seventh day.

(c) The principle of rest and leisure, as necessary for man, is inherent in the institution of the sabbath (*Gen.* 2: 3; *Ex.* 20: 8–11).

(d) The fourth commandment safe-guards the principle that man's life is not to be all work (*Ex.* 20: 8–11).

(e) While the objective of the "sabbath" principle to animals is simply that of resting their bodies, for human beings the purpose is, in addition, recreation and refreshment (*Ex.* 23: 12).

(f) We need leisure and time to rest (*Mark* 6: 31).

3. The use of leisure.

(a) The early Christians chose to change from the Jewish sabbath (Saturday) to the Christian Sunday so as to combine the day of rest with the day they met together to remember Christ's death and resur-rection (*Acts* 20: 7; *Rev.* 1: 10).

(b) The principle remains that the sabbath was made for man, and not man for the sabbath (*Mark* 2: 27).

(c) Worship of the Lord on a Sunday is part of a Christian's leisure because it is something he **chooses** to do: the Lord's Day is a day when believers choose to delight themselves in the Lord; instead of following selfish and unhelpful inclinations (*Isa.* 58: 13, 14).

(d) There are many different views of pleasure and leisure: for example, it is like sport to a fool to do wrong (*Prov.* 10: 23).

(e) The writer of *Ecclesiastes* sought to put human pleasures to the test, and he found them to be meaningless (*Eccl.* 2: 1ff); men's wild pursuit of pleasure sometimes leads them into trouble (*Dan.* 5: 1ff).

(f) The leisure of a lazy man can be his undoing (*Prov.* 21: 25).

(g) Leisure is not doing nothing, but, having time at our disposal, choosing to do with it what we will. Thus, for Christian believers, one of the most profitable uses of our leisure is enjoying fellowship with God's people (*Ps.* 16: 3), and we can say, "Better is one day in your courts than a thousand elsewhere" (*Ps.* 84: 10).

(h) The believer's pleasure is in the law of the Lord, and in the works of the Lord, and this pleasure leads him to study them (*Ps.* 1: 2; 111: 2).

(i) However leisure time is utilised, it should be used positively for, if the principle behind the sabbath—so far as man's body and mind is concerned—is that of refreshment, any leisure which debilitates is unhelpful, and outside of God's purpose (*Ex.* 23: 12).

4. Principles to govern the use of leisure.

(a) Any realistic consideration of leisure recognises that the world in which we live offers many "pleasures" which compete for our attention and involvement (*I Pet.* 4: 3).

(b) We must always remind ourselves that sin offers transient pleasure; thus not every offer of pleasure is to be pursued (*Heb.* 11: 25).

(c) The desire for pleasures can be an unhelpful source of strife within ourselves (*Jas.* 4: 1), not least when they are of a purely sensuous kind (*Mark* 7: 21, 22).

(d) We are warned that in the last days men will be lovers of pleasure rather than lovers of God (*II Tim.* 3: 4).

(e) Pleasure sought for pleasure's sake proves empty and unsatisfying (*Eccl.* 2: 10, 11).

(f) Our approach to leisure, therefore, must be sober—that is to say, we must know what we are doing and why (*I Pet.* 1: 13).

(g) We have to learn to discriminate so as to refuse the evil and choose the good (*Isa.* 7: 15).

(h) The Christian knows a better way than wine and excess to obtain satisfaction and joy—the fullness of the Spirit (*Eph.* 5: 18–20).

(i) Our use of leisure time is not to be contrary to the principle of our redeeming the time (*Eph.* 5: 15, 16; *Col.* 4: 5).

(j) The time we have at our disposal, after we have done our daily work and given ourselves opportunity for rest and necessary tasks, should include fruitful labour for God—the latter is a right use of our leisure, and properly entered into proves a means of refreshment (*Phil.* 1: 22; cf. *John* 4: 6, 8, 31–34).

(k) We need to have the fact of the shortness of life brought constantly before us so that we gain a heart of wisdom to use life properly (*Ps.* 90: 12).

(l) Living in a world where entertainment is automatically assumed to have a place in men's leisure, and in his times of resting, we need to relate Christian principles to the subject. Moral considerations are as relevant to the use of leisure time as to anything else: the Christian is to seek to do all to the glory of God (*I Cor.* 10: 31).

(m) Whatever we do, we are to do everything in the name of the Lord Jesus, thanking God the Father through Him (*Col.* 3: 17); at all times we are to put on the Lord Jesus, and make no provision for the flesh, to gratify its desires (*Rom.* 13: 14).

(n) We shall often find, not least in the sphere of entertainment, that all things are lawful, but not all things are helpful (*I Cor.* 6: 12; 10: 23); we have complete liberty as Christians, but we recognise that not everything is constructive and helpful.

(o) We must not allow any pastime to make us its slave (*I Cor.* 6: 12).

(p) In our leisure, as in everything else, we should not merely go our own way, but our actions and activities should mean the good of others too (*Rom.* 15: 1–3).

(q) We are to keep in our thoughts all that is true and noble, all that is right and good, all that is lovable and attractive, whatever is morally excellent and worthy of praise—this positive and straight-forward directive provides us with tremendous scope, but with a careful yardstick to apply (*Phil.* 4: 8).

(r) Our leisure activities must not be moulded by the desires of our ignorant days, but must conform to the principle of holiness in every part of our life (*I Pet.* 1: 14–19).

(s) In our leisure activities we should abstain from the desires of our lower natures, for they are always at war with our souls (*I Pet.* 2: 11).

(t) Activities which include or tend towards licentiousness, passions, drunkenness, revels, carousing, and lawless idolatry are ruled out for the Christian (*I Pet.* 4: 3).

(u) Our former companions may think it strange that we will no longer join with them in their leisure pursuits, and accordingly say all sorts of unpleasant things about us (*I Pet.* 4: 4).

(v) Our aim to live no longer by human passions but according to the will of God will affect every use to which we put our time (*I Pet.* 4: 2), for we make it our ambition to please the Lord (*II Cor.* 5: 9), in whose presence we always find ourselves (*Ps.* 139; *Heb.* 13: 5).

2l. GUIDANCE

Question: What does the Bible teach about guidance and the will of God?

Answer: The Bible teaches that the basic secret of guidance is commitment to the will of God, both before and after it is known and discovered. The will of God in general is given to us in the instruction of the Scriptures. The particular will of God for our lives is both discovered and worked out as we present our bodies to God as a living spiritual sacrifice, and continue to do so, striving after daily obedience to His Word.

1. **The choice before us.**

(a) Human desires or the will of God? Our wishes or God's will (*I Pet.* 4: 2)?

(b) Rather than living for God's will, we have all lived much of our life according to our human desires; as Christians we should live the rest of our earthly life by the will of God (*I Pet.* 4: 2).

2. **The truth concerning our own will.**

(a) Our own will is always prone to evil; the things which our bodies and minds find congenial are often in marked contrast to what God wills for us (*Eph.* 2: 3).

(b) As Christians, we should aspire

180

not to do our own will, but God's; wanting our own will to coincide always with His (*John* 5: 30a; *Luke* 22: 42).

3. Christians find within themselves a desire for God's will.

(a) Our new life or spiritual nature demands that we seek to do God's will (*Phil.* 2: 12, 13).

(b) That we desire to follow the will of God is the result of God's grace in our life through our Lord Jesus Christ (*Eph.* 2: 8–10).

(c) God's great mercy to us, rightly considered and meditated upon, stimulates us to seek the will of God, irrespective of the cost involved (*Rom.* 12: 1).

(d) Even as our body desires food for its health, our soul requires obedience to God's will for its health (*John* 4: 34).

4. The Lord Jesus is our example of obedience to God's will.

(a) He came with the sole purpose of doing the Father's will (*Heb.* 10: 7, 9).

(b) He frequently spoke of His determination to seek not His own will but the will of the Father (*John* 5: 30a; 6: 38).

(c) Knowing the will of the Father, He spoke of it with assurance and He acted in perfect co-operation with it (*John* 6: 39, 40).

(d) At every crisis, obedience to God's will was foremost (*Matt.* 26: 42).

(e) The doing of God the Father's will was His food (*John* 4: 34).

5. Fundamental facts regarding God's will.

(a) As we consider God's will with our limited human minds, there are two parts to it: there is that which is declared or published and that which is secret or hidden. God's declared or published will includes those events which have already taken place which are revealed to be His will—for example, the death of our Lord Jesus Christ to deliver us from our sins (*Gal.* 1:4)—and the whole of His written Word in which He tells man what to do. God's secret or hidden will, through which all things are ordered and done according to His plan and decision, concerns those things which are not revealed to us (*Eph.* 1: 11).

(b) The published will of God relates to the whole of our lives: we should do **all** of it (*Col.* 4: 12); and this is God's requirement of us (*Acts* 13: 22).

(c) God's will is good and acceptable and perfect (*Rom.* 12: 2).

(d) God's will is published supremely in the Lord Jesus Christ, and the dynamic for doing it, which we so desperately need, is found in Him alone, and our union with Him (*I Thess.* 5: 18).

6. The fundamental importance of God's will in our life.

(a) What God looks for most is obedience to His will. He could say of David, "I have found in David the son of Jesse a man after my heart, who will do all my will" (*Acts* 13: 33).

(b) Obedience to the will of God is more important than mere outward profession (*Matt.* 7: 21); God requires not lip-service to His will, but action—the parable of the two sons (*Matt.* 21: 28–32).

(c) Any profession of Christ's Lordship or religious activity, without obedience to God's will, are worthless to God, and are rejected by Him (*Matt.* 7: 21–23).

(d) Obedience to the will of God is the condition and proof of a right relationship to our Lord Jesus Christ (*Matt.* 12: 50; *Mark* 3: 35).

(e) God wants us to be filled with the knowledge of His will (*Col.* 1: 9).

(f) Knowing God's will is the secret of achieving important goals: first, living as the Lord wants; secondly, doing what pleases Him; thirdly, producing in our lives all kinds of good deeds; and, fourthly, growing in our knowledge of God (*Col.* 1: 10).

7. **Examples of God's published will.** First, with regard to our salvation.

(a) It is not the will of the Father that one of those who has trusted in our Lord Jesus Christ should perish (*Matt.* 18: 14).

(b) The will of the Father is that the Son should not lose any of all those He has given Him, but that the Lord Jesus should raise them all to life on the last day (*John* 6: 39, 40).

(c) By God's will all believers are made holy through the sacrifice of the body of Jesus Christ once for all (*Heb.* 10: 10).

Secondly, with regard to our growth in holiness.

(d) The will of God for our life may be summed up in the one word "sanctification" (*I Thess.* 4: 3, 7).

(e) It is God's will that by doing good things we should silence the ignorant talk of foolish people against Christianity (*I Pet.* 2: 15).

(f) It is God's will that, as Christian believers, we should always be joyful, pray constantly, and be thankful in all circumstances (*I Thess.* 5: 16–18).

(g) It is God's will that we should appreciate our need and obligation to be filled with the Spirit at all times (*Eph.* 5: 17–20).

8. **Relating ourselves to God's will.** (a) Our purpose in life, like that of our Lord Jesus Christ, should be to do the will of the Father (*John* 6: 38).

(b) The will of God determines our place and function in the Church of Christ, and the direction of our life (*I Cor.* 12: 11; *Eph.* 2: 10).

(c) Doing the will of God means obeying the instructions given in the Word of God (*I Thess.* 4: 1, 2).

(d) We should be testing and approving what God's will is for our life (*Rom.* 12: 2).

(e) The will of God should be the determining factor in all our movements (*Rom.* 15: 32).

(f) Knowing that God's will determines the things which happen to us, we should submit to them in a Christlike manner (*I Pet.* 3: 17).

(g) There may be, therefore, a battle within us for the submission of our will to God's will (*Matt.* 26: 42) for the will of God often runs contrary to our natural feelings.

(h) In every circumstance, and in circumstances which are beyond our control, Christians may say, with confidence, "The Lord's will be done" (*Matt.* 26: 42; *Acts* 21: 14).

(i) The will of God should be sought and obeyed in small things as well as in large (*Phil.* 4: 6; *I Thess.* 5: 16–18).

9. **Discovering God's will.**

(a) When we really choose to do God's will, God never leaves us in ignorance of it (*John* 7: 17).

(b) He wishes to equip us with everything good that we may do His will (*Heb.* 13: 21).

(c) The knowledge we need of God's will does not come only from human wisdom for such so easily can make us proud (*I Cor.* 1: 20; 2: 5, 6, 13; 3: 19).

(d) Our knowledge of God's will comes from the illumination of the Holy Spirit: He gives the wisdom and understanding which enable us to know God's will (*Col.* 1: 9).

(e) The will of God in general and also on particular issues is given to us in the instruction of the Scriptures (*I Thess.* 4: 1; *Matt.* 12: 50; *Mark* 3: 35; cf. *Luke* 8: 21; *Rom.* 2: 18).

(f) The precise will of God for our individual lives, however, may be known only as we present our bodies as a living sacrifice, holy and acceptable to God (*Rom.* 12: 1, 2); to be in keeping with God's will we must dedicate ourselves to God (*II Cor.* 8: 5).

(g) This dedication involves the refusal to be conformed to this world, and the willingness for transformation of our life by the renewal of our minds (*Rom.* 12: 2).

10. Prayer has an important place both in our discovering God's will and our submission to it.

(a) The Lord Jesus Christ taught that God's will is to figure in our petitions to our Father (*Matt.* 6: 10).

(b) Our prayers should centre around our being filled with the knowledge of God's will in all spiritual wisdom and understanding, to lead a life worthy of the Lord, fully pleasing to Him, bearing fruit in every good work, and increasing in the knowledge of God (*Col.* 1: 10).

(c) Expressed another way, prayer should be directed at standing mature and fully assured in all the will of God (*Col.* 4: 12).

(d) Praying in this fashion, we may be sure that God will both hear and answer (*I John* 5: 14, 15).

(e) Prayer may be regarded as the surrendering of our wills to God's will (*II Cor.* 12: 7–10).

(f) Prayer's true motive is the desire for God's will to be done and His Name to be glorified (*John* 17: 1).

(g) All our petitions should be subject to God's will (*Rom.* 1: 10).

11. How we should do God's will when we know it.

(a) We should do what God wants with all our heart: this means doing God's will with our eye on God's approval, rather than man's (*Eph.* 6: 6).

(b) When we know God's will, we should live it out to the full (*Phil.* 1: 12–14, 22; 2: 17).

12. The practical outworking of God's will.

(a) Doing God's will means accomplishing the work He has chosen for us, whatever that may be (*John* 4: 34).

(b) Our obedience to God's will is bound to mean giving ourselves to God's people in very practical, and often costly, ways (*II Cor.* 8: 5).

(c) Doing God's will is closely associated with His working in us that which is pleasing in His sight (*Phil.* 2: 12, 13; *Heb.* 13: 21).

(d) Suffering of some kind may often be in God's will for us (*I Pet.* 4: 19); our Lord's experience is an example (*Matt.* 26: 42).

(e) Sometimes God takes something away from us that He may give it back to us for ever; but we cannot be sure that it will be so (*Philem.* 15).

(f) When God's will includes suffering, it is fundamentally important that we persist in doing right and that we should entrust our souls to our faithful Creator (*I Pet.* 4: 19).

(g) We need great patience at times to persist in doing the will of God in order to receive what God promises (*Heb.* 10: 36).

183

(h) But we may have the glorious assurance that where there is a will of God, there is a way of God: think of Joseph and Moses.

13. Finally, the blessing God's will is to us when we do it.

(a) When we do God's will we stand for ever, in marked contrast to the world around which passes away, together with all the desires we associate with the world (*I John* 2: 17).

(b) The nearest approach to heaven on earth is the doing of His will as it is done in heaven (*Matt.* 6: 10).

(c) The will of God is always identical with what is good and acceptable and perfect (*Rom.* 12: 2).

(d) When we know God's will we are in a position to choose what is right (*Rom.* 2: 18).

(e) Our spiritual life and Christian joy are fed and enriched as we are obedient (*John* 4: 34; *Ps.* 40: 8).

(f) When the will of God is the objective of our life, we discover tremendous peace (*Phil.* 4: 6, 7).

(g) As we do the will of God we receive all that He promises (*Heb.* 10: 36).

22. THE FAMILY

Question: What is the importance and function of the family?

Answer: The family begins with a husband and wife, living in a permanent marriage union, and with, generally, children as the natural consequence of that union. The principal end of the family is the procreation, preservation, and education of children which makes it the primary unit of society. The family antedates all other human relationships and societies.

1. The family requires a high view of marriage as its foundation.

(a) Marriage has its basis and norm in God's act of creation, and is the original form of human fellowship (*Mark* 10: 6, 7).

(b) When marriage takes place a fresh pattern of life is established, and a new family begins as a man leaves his own mother and father and is united to his wife, the two becoming one flesh (*Gen.* 2: 24; *Mark* 10: 8).

(c) It is good for a man to have a wife (*Gen.* 2: 18; *Prov.* 18: 22), and but one wife (*Gen.* 2: 24; *Mark* 10: 6–8; *I Cor.* 7: 2–4).

(d) A husband is the head of the wife as Christ is Head, and Saviour too, of the Church (*Eph.* 5: 23).

(e) A husband's principal duty is to love his wife (*Col.* 3: 19), and to love her as he loves himself (*Eph.* 5: 28, 33).

(f) A husband should be faithful to his wife (*Prov.* 5: 19; *Mal.* 2: 14–15), respecting her (*I Pet.* 3: 7), and avoiding all harshness or bitterness in his dealings (*Col.* 3: 19).

(g) A husband should comfort his wife (*I Sam.* 1: 8), consult her (*Gen.* 31: 4–7), and be quick to praise and show his appreciation of her (*Prov.* 31: 28, 29).

(h) A wife is the principal helper of her husband (*Gen.* 2: 18).

(i) A wife's foremost duty is submission to her husband (*Gen.* 3: 16; *Eph.* 5: 22, 24; *I Pet.* 3: 1).

(j) A wife should love (*Tit.* 2: 4), honour (*Eph.* 5: 33), and obey her husband (*I Cor.* 14: 34; *Tit.* 2: 5), always striving to be faithful to him (*I Cor.* 7: 3–5, 10).

(k) An intelligent and capable wife is a gift from the Lord (*Prov.* 19: 14), her husband's crown (*Prov.* 12: 4), and, in fact, a priceless treasure (*Prov.* 31: 10ff).

(l) Children are a gift from the Lord to a husband and wife (*Gen.* 33: 5; *Ps.* 127: 3; *I Sam.* 1: 27), and as such enhance and deepen the marriage relationship.

2. The harmony of husband and wife is essential for the well-being of a family.

(a) The fact that disharmony in any area of married life can be disastrous and detrimental to a family's welfare is one of the reasons why a Christian should seek to have a Christian partner (*I Cor.* 7: 39; *II Cor.* 6: 14).

(b) Husband and wife are to be sensitive and thoughtful of the sexual needs and demands of each other (*I Cor.* 7: 3f).

(c) For the physical relationship to cement regularly their unity and harmony, husband and wife must be faithful to one another in mind and thought as well as physically (*Matt.* 5: 27, 28).

(d) The original happiness of marriage has been sadly shattered by the corruption of the human heart (*Mark* 7: 20–23).

(e) Selfish disagreement, especially as it expresses itself in nagging, ruins harmony (*Prov.* 19: 13; 25: 24; 27: 15).

(f) Unhappy marriage brings about a total breakdown in happiness (*Prov.* 12: 4).

3. Parental duties.

(a) Parents should **love** their children (*Tit.* 2: 4), showing their love both in compassion (*Ps.* 103: 13) and in careful discipline (*Prov.* 3: 11f; *Heb.* 12: 7).

(b) Parents should **pray** for their children, praying generally for their spiritual welfare (*Gen.* 17: 18; *I Chron.* 29: 19), and specifically for

their well-being when tempted (*Job* 1: 5) or unwell (*II Sam.* 12: 16; *Mark* 5: 23; *John* 4: 46, 49).

(c) Parents should **provide** for their children (*Job* 42: 15; *Isa.* 1: 2f).

(d) They should save up for them and be prepared to spend everything they have, if necessary, for their welfare (*II Cor.* 12: 14, 15).

(e) They should know how to give good gifts to their children (*Matt.* 7: 9–11).

(f) Parents should **educate** their children (*Eph.* 6: 4), seeing themselves as their proper and primary instructors (*Prov.* 4: 1–4, 10–12).

(g) They should instruct them in God's ways (*Deut.* 31: 12–13), with the assurance that, as their children are trained up in the way that they should go, when they are old they will not depart from it (*Prov.* 22: 6).

(h) They should teach their children spiritual truth from the Scriptures, for children may share the promises of God (*Acts* 2: 39), and the Scriptures are able to make them wise for salvation through Jesus Christ (*II Tim.* 3: 15).

(i) They should teach their children most of all by example, remembering our Lord's solemn warning that if anyone causes a child who believes in Him to sin that it would be better for that person to have a millstone around his neck, and to be drowned in the depths of the sea (*Matt.* 18: 6).

(j) Parents should **discipline** their children (*Deut.* 8: 5).

(k) Children need discipline because folly is deep-rooted in their hearts (*Prov.* 22: 15; 29: 17); to neglect discipline is to throw away the family's security (*Prov.* 13: 24; 22: 6).

(l) Parental discipline, however, is to be careful and loving, and fathers in particular are instructed to be watchful lest they either discourage their children or make them resentful (*Col.* 3: 21; *Eph.* 6: 4).

(m) While discipline is never pleasant at the time, its fruits are good (*Heb.* 12: 10, 11).

(n) The experience children have of true human fatherhood should make it easy for them to appreciate God's greater Fatherhood (*Matt.* 7: 9–11; *Heb.* 12: 5–11).

4. Children's duties.

(a) Children should **love** their parents, not forgetting to be demonstrative in their love when appropriate (*Gen.* 46: 29).

(b) Children should respect their parents (*Lev.* 19: 3), honouring father and mother (*Ex.* 20: 12), and respecting too their parents' possessions as they respect other people's (*Prov.* 28: 24).

(c) To treat parents with mockery or disrespect merits condemnation (*Gen.* 27: 12; *Prov.* 30: 17).

(d) The commandment to honour parents is obligatory (*Mark* 10: 19); any instruction which cuts across it is hypocrisy and transgression (*Matt.* 15: 4–7; *Mark* 7: 10–13).

(e) Children should **obey** their parents (*Eph.* 6: 1), listening deliberately to their advice and instruction (*Prov.* 6: 20; 23: 22).

(f) The ultimate prosperity of children may greatly hinge upon their obedience to their parents (*Deut.* 4: 40; 12: 25, 28; *Ps.* 128: 1–3).

(g) Children are to strive to obey their parents in everything (*Col.* 3: 20).

(h) Children, when adults, should **provide**, where necessary, for their parents, since they have a continuing responsibility towards them (*Matt.* 15: 5, 6; *Mark* 7: 11, 12).

(i) They must learn to do what is their Christian duty, and to repay those who have brought them up (*I Tim.* 5: 4; cf. *John* 19: 26, 27).

5. The common duties of the family in which all the members need to share.

(a) **Love**—the primary duty of the members of any family is love (*I Cor.* 13; *I John* 5: 1, etc.).

(b) **Helpfulness**—the life of the family is made harmonious by deliberate co-operativeness but it is made difficult by quarrelsomeness (*Prov.* 18: 19).

(c) **Mutual forbearance**—the members of the family are to be forgiving of one another (*Gen.* 50: 17–21; *Matt.* 18: 21–22).

(d) **Submission**—all members of the family must accept the need for the proper and firm management of household life, and the necessity, therefore, for the parents to give direction (*Prov.* 31: 27; *I Tim.* 3: 4, 5).

(e) **Concern for unity**—all need to see that they contribute by their behaviour and attitudes to the unity or disunity of the family, and that unity must be the goal always (*Gen.* 45: 24; *Ps.* 133: 1).

(f) **Worship**—the worship of God together, with the home seen as a place where God's presence may be known, brings immeasurable help to the family (*Josh.* 8: 35; *I Cor.* 16: 19).

(g) **Concern for others**—the individual family unit is to look outside of itself and is to care for needy relatives, and especially grandparents (*I Tim.* 5: 3, 4), so that grandchildren become the crown of the old (*Prov.* 17: 6).

6. The Christian family has the

benefits of the gospel which add immeasurably to its happiness and security.

(a) God is known to be the Giver of every good gift the family enjoys (*Jas.* 1: 17).

(b) God's Word becomes the final authority and guide so that the family has wise and consistent direction (*II Tim.* 3: 16, 17).

(c) Parents and children are encouraged to pattern their behaviour on the kingdom of heaven (*Phil.* 1: 27; 3: 20).

(d) The Holy Spirit makes love possible and effective in the most difficult of circumstances (*II Tim.* 1: 7).

(e) Husbands love their wives after the pattern of Christ's love (*Eph.* 5: 25).

(f) Wives submit themselves to their own husbands as part of their submission to the Lord (*Eph.* 5: 22).

(g) Children obey their parents with the desire to please the Lord by so doing (*Eph.* 6: 1; *Col.* 3: 20).

(h) Elderly relatives are cared for as part of Christian duty (*I Tim.* 5: 4).

(i) Relationships within the family are seen in the context of our relationship with God: a right relationship with God demands a right relationship with those to whom we are closest (*I Pet.* 3: 7).

(j) Marriage and the family are held in the highest possible honour because God so honours them (*Heb.* 13: 4).

23. EDUCATION

Question: What does the Bible teach about education?

Answer: Education aims at developing individuals' aptitude for every kind of learning, so that they are well informed, quick to understand and qualified to serve. **Education begins in the home, and all who teach children remain delegates of those children's parents, and nothing releases parents from their basic responsibility for the teaching and discipline of their own children. The principal lesson to be taught is that the fear of the Lord is the beginning of wisdom.**

1. **Education is a subject worthy of study.**

(a) We are to attribute all that is good in this world to God (*Jas.* 1: 17): the study of everything which is good, therefore, is a worthy pursuit. Both the natural processes of the earth and the course of historical events are governed by God's wisdom (*Isa.* 28: 23–29; 31: 2); thus by a proper understanding of these things we are caused to acknowledge God more worthily.

(b) God has given man special responsibilities in His creation which demand the education of man's mind (*Gen.* 1: 28; *Ps.* 8: 5, 6, 7, 8).

(c) God has given all kinds of abilities to men which need to be discovered, drawn out, and used (*Ex.* 31: 3–5).

(d) The intellect is not to be despised: more can be done by proper education than by authoritarianism and force (*Eccl.* 9: 17, 18).

2. **The aims of education.**

(a) The first aim of education is the **imparting of understanding,** or insight (*Prov.* 4: 1, 7); and basic to this understanding or insight is the truth that "the fear of the Lord is the beginning of wisdom" (*Prov.* 1: 7).

(b) The second aim of education is **knowledge**—the person who has understanding seeks knowledge (*Prov.* 15: 14).

(c) Knowledge is gained constantly by those who have understanding, to be used at the appropriate time in the future (*Prov.* 10: 14).

(d) Knowledge helps a man to make the right and best choices (*Phil.* 1: 9, 10).

(e) The third aim is **wisdom**—that is to say, the ability to use knowledge in a way pleasing to God and helpful to man (*Prov.* 2: 1–6; 14: 33).

(f) The man who possesses wisdom does not profess to know everything, but is ever ready to take advice, and shows a willingness to learn from any who will teach him (*Prov.* 13: 10).

(g) The fact that education is not speedily achieved is generally recognised (*Dan.* 1: 4, 5): our Lord Jesus Christ is said to have grown in wisdom, as part of His human development from boyhood to manhood (*Luke* 2: 40, 52).

(h) The aims of the educative purpose may be expressed as follows: to make a man skilful in all wisdom, endowed with knowledge, understanding learning, and competent to serve (*Dan.* 1: 4).

3. **The education of children.**

(a) Children are a gift from God (*Ps.* 127: 3–5; 128: 3, 4; cf. *Gen.* 11: 30; 17: 16).

(b) Children are necessarily of limited understanding (*I Cor.* 14: 20).

(c) Children are naturally limited in their outlook (*I Cor.* 13: 11).

(d) Children are easily swayed (*Eph.* 4: 14).

(e) A basic factor in our approach springs from the knowledge that folly is bound up in the heart of a child, and this fact must always be borne in mind (*Prov.* 22: 15).

(f) Children are to be viewed not only as immature, but as sinful by nature (*Ps.* 51: 5).

(g) God-centred education should begin from the earliest days of the child's life, training the child in the way that it should go (*Prov.* 22: 6).

(h) Such education and training must include careful discipline (*Prov.* 22: 15; 29: 17).

(i) The administering of discipline is not to be abhorrent for true discipline is a mark and proof of love (*Heb.* 12: 5–11).

(j) To withhold discipline can all too easily mean setting a child's course for destruction (*Prov.* 19: 18).

(k) Education begins in the home, for parents are to give their children instruction (*Prov.* 4: 1), particularly by providing them with good precepts (*Prov.* 4: 2). We must not lose sight of the parental responsibility for the education of children: parents may delegate parts of their responsibility, but other teachers are to be regarded as their delegates.

(l) Parents are commanded to instruct their children (*Gen.* 18: 19; *Ex.* 10: 2; 12: 26, 27; 13: 14–16; *Deut.* 4: 9, 10; 6: 6–9; 11: 19; *Isa.* 38: 19).

(m) In particular, parents are to be diligent in the religious or spiritual education of their children (*Deut.* 6: 6–9), seizing the casual as well as the formal opportunities for instruction.

(n) Parents are to give their children the commands of God that they may be careful to do all the words of the law (*Deut.* 32: 46); the way of wisdom should be heard first from parents' lips, and in their parents' lives children should find living examples to follow (*Prov.* 4: 11, 12).

(o) By their actions parents are to prompt the right sort of questions

188

from their children which will enable the parents to instruct the children in the mighty redeeming acts of the Lord (*Ex.* 12: 26, 27; 13: 14–16).

(p) Education, whether provided by parents or others, requires wise teachers: the lips of the wise spread knowledge (*Prov.* 15: 7, 12).

(q) Wise teachers reprove (*Prov.* 15: 12), and are refreshing in their candour and clarity (*Prov.* 18: 4).

(r) Wise teachers have insight and discernment to recognise the character and intentions of those whom they teach (*Prov.* 20: 5), and they know how to draw out those whom they teach.

4. The requirements for success in education.

(a) To arrive at wisdom by way of understanding and knowledge, we have to begin by acknowledging that **discipline is necessary** (*Prov.* 23: 13, 14; 29: 15).

(b) Open rebuke is better than hidden (*Prov.* 27: 5).

(c) The second requirement is that **correction should be heeded** (*Prov.* 10: 17): progress comes through teachableness, and teachableness includes the readiness to accept rebuke.

(d) If an individual is often reproved, and still chooses to resist, he will suddenly be done for (*Prov.* 29: 1).

(e) To love discipline and correction is to love knowledge (*Prov.* 12: 1); the prudent heed admonition (*Prov.* 15: 5, 32).

(f) A rebuke goes deeper into a man of understanding than a hundred blows into a fool (*Prov.* 17: 10).

(g) Character benefits and is made attractive by receiving constructive criticism with genuine joy (*Prov.* 25: 12)

(h) The third requirement is that **the person under instruction should be receptive** (*Prov.* 12: 15): the wise man knows that he can always increase his learning (*Prov.* 1: 5; 18: 15).

(i) Application to work, and concentration are to be urged upon those who are under instruction (*Prov.* 23: 12).

(j) Education requires attentiveness to instruction (*Prov.* 4: 1, 13; 17: 27, 28)—wisdom is a long-term investment (*Prov.* 19: 20).

(k) The fourth requirement is that **knowledge must be practically applied** (*Prov.* 19: 27).

(l) The purpose of having an understanding mind is to be able to do successfully what has been committed to one to do in life, including the ability to discern between good and evil (*I Kings* 3: 9).

5. The value of education.

(a) Education is an adornment (*Prov.* 1: 8, 9), in that the properly educated person is attractive in character, a profitable addition to anyone's acquaintances.

(b) Education benefits the individual no end: the man who obtains wisdom loves himself (*Prov.* 19: 8).

(c) Education is satisfying, because it gives the individual hopes for a happy future (*Prov.* 23: 13–18).

(d) Education is better than material wealth (*Prov.* 16: 16): wealth can be deceptive, whereas education of the right sort foils deception (*Prov.* 28: 11).

(e) Wise speech comes from true education, and when a man can use his tongue wisely, he has overcome one of the main causes of friction and trouble in human relationships (*Prov.* 15: 7, 21; 16: 23).

(f) Goodwill on the part of all right-

189

thinking men, and success, come as the results of education arising from understanding, knowledge, and wisdom (*Prov.* 13: 15, 16; 21: 22; 24: 3–6).

6. **Basic to the whole subject of education, from the biblical viewpoint, is the truth that proper education is based upon the fear of the Lord.**

(a) Ideally, education should be God-centred (*Prov.* 1: 7; 9: 10).

(b) The purpose of God-centred education is the reverencing of God: this is the whole duty of man (*Eccl.* 12: 13).

(c) Wisdom, counsel and understanding, in the fullest sense, belong to God (*Job* 12: 13); the truly wise are those to whom God has graciously imparted wisdom (*Matt.* 12: 42; *Acts* 6: 10; 7: 10; *Jas.* 3: 17; *II Pet.* 3: 15).

(d) True wisdom stems from the fear of the Lord (*Job* 28: 28; *Ps.* 110: 10; *Prov.* 1: 7; 9: 10).

(e) As Christianity is the only true religion, and God in Christ the only true God, the only possible means of an entirely profitable education is Christian discipline and instruction (*Eph.* 6: 4).

(f) To educate fallen man, we must remember his fallen nature: he is darkened in his understanding and alienated from the life of God because of the ignorance that is in him, due to his hardness of heart (*Eph.* 4: 18).

(g) If education is divorced from God's revelation, it can soon become impoverished and unproductive (*I Cor.* 1: 17; 2: 4; *II Cor.* 1: 12), and at its worst both foolish and devilish (*I Cor.* 1: 19–25; *Jas.* 3: 15–16).

(h) Wisdom, without a reverence for God, easily becomes a source of human pride (*Isa.* 5: 21), and, having no anchor in God, it is doomed to failure (*Isa.* 19: 11–15).

(i) When men deny God, they become, in fact, futile in their thinking (*Rom.* 1: 21, 22).

(j) We need to be aware of the limitations of the intellect, even at its very best (*Eccl.* 8: 17; 12: 12).

(k) The fear of the Lord is the beginning of wisdom (*Prov.* 1: 7).

(l) Where there is a reverence for God, God is pleased to prosper the whole course of an individual's education, irrespective of the teachers who may be involved (*Dan.* 1: 17).

24. SEX

Question: What does the Bible teach about sex?

Answer: Sex is a gift of God, and is properly appreciated as we have a right understanding of marriage. As with all of God's gifts to mankind, the gift of sex can be abused. Self-knowledge, therefore, is to govern a Christian's attitude to sex; and this knowledge means the control of the thought-life and the recognition of the dignity of the Christian's body as the temple of the Holy Spirit. God's call to sanctification is the test of all behaviour between the sexes.

1. **Sex is a gift of God.**

(a) Sex is a creation of God (*Gen.* 1: 27; *Matt.* 19: 4; *I Tim.* 4: 3).

(b) Sex, as created by God, was good (*Gen.* 1: 31; *I Tim.* 4: 3, 4).

(c) God's purpose in the creation of sex was the procreation of children (*Gen.* 1: 28a): that is to say, the coming of children was intended to be always a cause of joy (*John* 16: 21).

(d) Sexual desire is one of the reasons, therefore, that men and women come together in marriage (*I Cor.* 7: 9).

(e) To fulfil this desire within marriage is right, but outside of marriage is wrong (*I Cor.* 7: 8, 9).

2. We must appreciate the importance of marriage.

(a) Marriage is a calling of God to some and not to others (*I Cor.* 7: 7, 17).

(b) Marriage has higher ends than merely the fulfilment of the sexual desire: one of its preeminent purposes is the bearing of children (*Ps.* 127: 3–5; *I Tim.* 5: 14) and their rearing in the discipline and instruction of the Lord (*Eph.* 6: 4)—for this reason among others marriage for the Christian is to be "only in the Lord" (*I Cor.* 7: 39).

(c) Marriage is further intended for the mutual help of husband and wife by means of friendship and companionship (*Gen.* 2: 18, 20).

(d) Marriage is to be entered upon not in the passion of lust but in holiness and honour (*I Thess.* 4: 4, 5).

(e) Marriage is to be received with thanksgiving, as with all of God's gifts (*I Tim.* 4: 3, 4).

(f) Marriage has special enjoyment and meaning for those who believe and know the truth of God (*I Tim.* 4: 3; *Eph.* 5: 22–23).

(g) Marriage is consecrated by the Word of God and prayer (*I Tim.* 4: 3, 4, 5).

(h) When a man and woman come together they are one flesh (*Eph.* 5: 31; note also *I Cor.* 7: 16); thus those who are married cease to have exclusive rights over their own bodies (*I Cor.* 7: 1–6).

(i) Within marriage the full enjoyment of the sexual relationship is encouraged within the bounds of self-control and holiness (*I Cor.* 7: 3–6).

(j) The marriage bond is indissoluble (*Gen.* 2: 24; *Matt.* 19: 3–9; *Mark* 10: 3–9; *Eph.* 5: 31): what God has joined together, no man should dare to put asunder (*Matt.* 19: 6).

(k) Marriage is to be held in honour by all (*Heb.* 13: 4): to violate the sanctity of marital intercourse is great wickedness and sin against God (*Gen.* 39: 9; *I Thess.* 4: 6; *Heb.* 13: 4).

3. We must also appreciate the honourableness of the unmarried state.

(a) The unmarried state is recognised to be God's call to some (*Matt.* 19: 10–12; *I Cor.* 7: 7).

(b) Celibacy or virginity is a gift of God to some, even as marriage is to others (*I Cor.* 7: 7, 17).

(c) There are definite advantages in the unmarried state so far as service for God is concerned: undivided attention to the Lord is possible in a manner which is impossible to the married (*I Cor.* 7: 32–35).

(d) The unmarried should regard themselves as married to Christ (*I Tim.* 5: 11)—their first pledge is to Him (*I Tim.* 5: 12).

4. Self-knowledge is to govern a Christian's attitude to sex.

(a) The Christian's old nature is corrupt through deceitful lusts (*Eph.* 4: 22): the lusts of the flesh are at war with the soul (*I Pet.* 2: 11), and the danger attaching to these lusts is never to be overlooked (*I Cor.* 9: 27).

(b) The Christian's new nature is in conflict with the old; and he is to live according to the new and not according to the old (*Eph.* 4: 17–24).

(c) Satan's temptations centre especially around the sexual urge (*I Cor.*

7: 5): some aspects of sex are particularly tempting and trying in youth (*II Tim.* 2: 22).

(d) The recognition of this problem inherent in man's nature means that the body is to be disciplined and subdued (*I Cor.* 9: 27).

(e) Knowledge of human nature makes plain that physical desire and attraction are often confused with love, whereas they are by no means the same (*II Sam.* 13); and physical desire, mistaken for love, once acceded to, frequently leads to lack of respect and hatred (*II Sam.* 13: 15).

(f) Of ourselves we cannot control the passion of our sinful hearts and flesh (*Rom.* 7: 19, 20, 24); only by the grace of the Holy Spirit can we overcome (*Gal.* 5: 16).

5. The control of the thought-life.

(a) Doubtless we have all sinned with regard to sex, in thought if not in deed, at some time (*John* 8: 1–9).

(b) Sin begins with the thoughts (*Mark* 7: 21; *Matt.* 5: 28).

(c) Evil thoughts, fornication, adultery, coveting, foolishness come naturally and easily to our old nature (*Mark* 7: 21).

(d) Jesus condemned as adultery of the heart the adulterous desire, even if no adulterous designs attach themselves to the desire (*Matt.* 5: 27, 28).

(e) We need to be ruthless in dealing with those things which would lead us astray sexually (*Matt.* 5: 27–30).

(f) We need to fill our thoughts with things which are honourable, just, pure, lovely and gracious (*Phil.* 4: 8), rather than occupying ourselves at all with things which are unpleasant (*Eph.* 5: 12).

6. God's warnings with regard to the misuse of sex.

(a) Men are solemnly forewarned that God will judge all who abuse sex (*I Thess.* 4: 6): the immoral and the adulterous He will judge (*Heb.* 13: 4).

(b) All who live according to human passions and not according to God's will shall give account to God who is ready to judge the living and the dead (*I Pet.* 4: 2–5).

(c) No immoral or impure person has any inheritance in the kingdom of Christ and of God (*Eph.* 5: 5, 6).

7. The Christian's body.

(a) The Christian is not to regard his body as his own—it has been bought with a price (*I Cor.* 6: 19, 20).

(b) The Christian is to have a reverence for his body: it is a temple of the Holy Spirit (*I Cor.* 6: 19).

(c) The Christian is to glorify God in his body (*I Cor.* 6: 20).

(d) The body is to be continuously presented to God as a living sacrifice (*Rom.* 12: 1).

(e) By immorality a man sins against his own body (*I Cor.* 6: 18), and against Christ (*I Cor.* 6: 15, 17).

8. Principles are laid down in the Bible to govern and guide man-woman relationships.

(a) The Christian is to know how he should behave with regard to sex whether married or unmarried (*I Thess.* 4: 3, 4, 5).

(b) The Christian's attitude to sex will surprise the non-Christian, and especially those who knew him before he became a Christian (*I Pet.* 4: 3, 4).

(c) Christians are to recognise that the fulfilment of fleshly lusts is not the most important thing in life:

more important is their heavenly citizenship (*I Pet.* 2: 11).

(d) The Christian must not be deceived by those who try to make him think that Christian standards are too high (*Eph.* 5: 6).

(e) Perfect propriety is to characterise the Christian's relationships with those of the other sex (*I Tim.* 5: 1, 2).

(f) Courtesy is to dominate the Christian man's relationship to the woman, remembering that she is the weaker vessel (*I Pet.* 3: 7; *I Tim.* 5: 2, 3).

(g) The Christian is to be wise and careful in his relationships with those of the other sex (*Eph.* 5: 15).

(h) The Christian should beware of foolishness in his approach to members of the other sex (*Eph.* 5: 15–17).

(i) The Christian should beware of silly talk or levity about sex, because such leads all too often to foolish action (*Eph.* 5: 3–5).

(j) The Christian should beware of allowing his emotions to be excessively roused—this is Paul's argument against strong drink in this very chapter (*Eph.* 5: 18).

(k) Sexual temptation is to be avoided where possible (*II Tim.* 2: 22): it is no disgrace to run away from sexual temptation—indeed it is commended (*Gen.* 39: 12; *II Tim.* 2: 22).

(l) There is to be nothing unclean in the Christian's experience of sex (*I Thess.* 4: 7).

(m) Self-control is to be exercised ruthlessly before marriage: if this is impossible, then marriage should take place (*I Cor.* 7: 9, 36)—it is recognised that the sexual urge is more powerful in some than in others (*I Cor.* 7: 8–9, 36–38).

9. The general principles of Christian conduct taught in the Bible must be applied also to sex.

(a) The Christian must not allow his attitude to sex to be governed by the moral climate of his day (*Eph.* 4: 14–21); he is not to form close associations with those who reject Christian teaching on the subject (*Eph.* 5: 7), and he must be ready to speak out against wrong views of sex (*Eph.* 5: 11).

(b) The Christian should endeavour to learn from the Scriptures what is pleasing to God with regard to sex (*Eph.* 5: 10, 17; *I Pet.* 4: 2).

(c) The Christian is called to sanctification (*I Thess.* 4: 7): his use of sex is to be consistent with holiness (*I Thess.* 4: 7).

(d) There is a right time and place for everything one needs to do (*Eccl.* 3: 1–8).

(e) There are circumstances where it is necessary to refrain from things which are right in themselves (*I Cor.* 7: 29–31).

(f) All appearance of evil in relationships between the sexes should be avoided (*I Thess.* 5: 22).

(g) Whatever the Christian would wish others to do to him, he should do to others (*Matt.* 7: 12).

(h) The Christian should not provoke others to envy by reason of some special relationship (*Gal.* 5: 26; *I Thess.* 4: 10, 11).

(i) The well-being of the Christian's soul will be a guide as to his attitude in particular situations to sex (*I Pet.* 2: 11).

(j) The Holy Spirit is given to enable the Christian to gain victory over sin in the body (*Rom.* 8: 13; *II Tim.* 1: 7; *Gal.* 5: 23): as the Holy Spirit's help is sought sincerely, His help is received (*Luke* 11: 13).

(k) The right attitude to sex is maintained as Christians are filled with the Spirit, have fellowship with one another sincerely and spiritually, and endeavour at all times and in all places to give God the thanks for His gifts (*Eph.* 5: 18–20; read these verses in the light of the earlier verses of the chapter).

25. GIVING

Question: What does the Bible teach about giving?

Answer: Giving, modelled upon the Old Testament tithe, and calculated to forward God's work by the support of His servants, is to be regular, systematic and according to how God has prospered us. However, the New Testament does not lay down the principle of the tithe, but it presupposes that our giving will more than equal the tithe because of the inward compulsion of the Holy Spirit moving us to respond to the generosity of God with similar generosity.

1. **Any consideration of Christian giving must begin with God's giving.**

(a) Every good and perfect gift comes from God the Father (*Jas.* 1: 17).

(b) When God gives, He gives with an abundant fullness, e.g. in His blessing of creation (*Gen.* 1: 22, 28; cf. *Ps.* 104), in His promises to His people (*Gen.* 17: 1–24; 22: 17; *Ex.* 1: 7, 20; 32: 13), in His bestowal of rich blessings (*Deut.* 28: 11) and in His gift of salvation (*Ps.* 5: 7; 31: 19; 51: 1).

(c) God's giving is limitless—He has given us His Son, and in His Son He gave Himself (*John* 3: 16; 1: 14; *Acts* 20: 28; *II Cor.* 9: 15).

(d) Our Lord Jesus Christ, though rich beyond all telling, became poor for our sakes, so that we through His poverty might become rich (*II Cor.* 8: 9): He gave His life as a ransom for many (*Matt.* 20: 28), and His flesh for the life of the world (*John* 6: 32, 51; cf. *Luke* 22: 19).

(e) He makes us rich with every spiritual gift (*I Cor.* 1: 5ff), with a variety of spiritual gifts (*I Cor.* 12), the gifts of His ascension (*Eph.* 4: 7–12).

(f) God's giving is part of the outflow of His love towards us (*I John* 3: 17).

(g) He gives to us that we may be in a position to give and to be generous in our giving (*II Cor.* 9: 11).

2. **Tithing was the basic pattern of giving in the Old Testament.**

(A tithe is a tenth part, and it may have to do with the ancient custom of counting by tens, a system made easy by the ten fingers and toes common to man.)

(a) The Jews were instructed to tithe their cereal and fruit crops and their livestock (*Lev.* 27: 30–33).

(b) Underlying the tithe was the basic idea that the earth is the Lord's and all that is in it (*Ps.* 24: 1).

(c) Tithing came to mean an expression of thanksgiving to God for His generosity (*Gen.* 28: 20–22).

(d) The Jews paid their tithes to the Levites (*Num.* 18: 20–24), or later to the Levites who served as priests (cf. *Heb.* 7: 5), in return for the service they rendered at the sanctuary (*Num.* 18: 21), and as compensation for their lack of landed possessions.

(e) Payment was made in Jerusalem (*Deut.* 12: 5, 6, 11, 17, 18) or each third year in their home communities (*Deut.* 14: 28–29; 26: 12).

(f) The Levites, in turn, were required to give one tenth of the tithe to the priests (*Num.* 18: 26, 28; *Neh.* 10: 38–39).

(g) In times of spiritual decline the people neglected often to pay their tithes, so that Hezekiah, for example, found it necessary to call authoritatively for their payment (*II Chron.* 31: 4–12).

(h) Nehemiah discovered a similar position of neglect (*Neh.* 13: 12).

(i) Malachi was obliged to rebuke the people for robbing God by withholding tithes and offerings (*Mal.* 3: 7–12).

(j) In the Old Testament, as in the New, giving is no substitute for justice, mercy and faithfulness (*Micah* 6: 8; *Matt.* 23: 23; *Luke* 11: 42; 18: 9–14).

(k) If we ask, Is tithing an obligation under the new covenant? the New Testament maintains an eloquent silence on the matter (for example, see *I Cor.* 9: 13).

3. **The New Testament has much to say about the characteristics of Christian giving.**

(a) It will be, pre-eminently, a reflection of God's dealings with us (*Matt.* 18: 32, 33), and an outflow of the giving of ourselves to the Lord (*II Cor.* 8: 15).

(b) It will be according to our means (*Acts* 11: 29), as God has prospered us (*I Cor.* 16: 2).

(c) At the same time it will be undeterred by our means, whether large or small, because giving will be counted a privilege (*II Cor.* 8: 3, 4).

(d) It will be regular, systematic, and without fuss or ostentation (*I Cor.* 16: 2; cf. *Matt.* 6: 2–4).

(e) It will often be costly (*Luke* 21: 4), frequently generous beyond measure (*II Cor.* 8: 2), and to the limit of our resources (*II Cor.* 8: 3)—in fact, it will set no limits (*I John* 3: 16).

(f) It will be joyful, cheerful, ungrudging, an act of the will, without external pressure, and a matter of individual determination (*Luke* 21: 4; *II Cor.* 8: 2–4, 8; 9: 5, 7).

(g) It will look for nothing in return (*Luke* 14: 12ff), and it will take every possible form (*II Cor.* 9: 11).

(h) It will be seen as one of the reasons why we go to work and earn money and have possessions—we gain in order to give away (*Eph.* 4: 28).

4. **The secret of generous giving is correct motivation.**

(a) The desire to respond to the grace and generosity of God, and our thanksgiving to God for the gift of His Son, and the love we feel for Him (*II Cor.* 8: 7–9; 9: 15).

(b) The desire to acknowledge that God Himself is our true wealth rather than the sum total of our material possessions, as the world would have us think (*Ps.* 73: 25; *II Cor.* 6: 10).

(c) The desire to be a good steward of what God has given us (*Rom.* 14: 12; *I Pet.* 4: 10f).

(d) The desire to show our love for God by love for others (*I John* 5: 1–2), as we respond to Him in good deeds by the generous use of our material resources (*I Tim.* 6: 18).

(e) The desire to help and relieve those who are in need, and especially fellow-Christians (*Acts* 11: 29; *I Cor.* 16: 1; *II Cor.* 8: 4; *Gal.* 6: 10): we share our surplus so that their deficit may be met, and on occasions vice versa (*II Cor.* 8: 14, 15; *Eph.* 4: 28; *I Tim.* 6: 18).

(f) Our desire to be faithful in supporting God's work by providing adequately and generously for the support of those who serve Christ in the gospel at home and overseas (*I Cor.* 9; *Gal.* 6: 6; *I Tim.* 5: 17).

5. There are inevitable consequences of proper giving.

(a) God is pleased by our giving (*II Cor.* 9: 7): it is a spiritual sacrifice (*Heb.* 13: 16).

(b) God more than makes up to us what we give (*II Cor.* 9: 8; *Phil.* 4: 15–19).

(c) God is thanked and praised for our giving by those who benefit from it (*II Cor.* 9: 13), and so He is glorified (*II Cor.* 8: 19).

(d) God encourages us by it too: it is a proof of our faith by our works (*II Cor.* 8: 13; *Jas.* 2: 15, 16), and evidence of God's grace at work in us (*II Cor.* 8: 1).

(e) By giving in a way which pleases God, we lay up for ourselves a good foundation for the future (*I Tim.* 6: 19).

(f) We discover too in the present a unique happiness (*Acts* 20: 35) and unexpected blessings (*Mal.* 3: 10).

26. PRIDE

Question: What is pride? and why is it sinful?

Answer: The pride we have in view is that which shows itself in our having too high an opinion of ourself. It constitutes sin because it leads us to think we can be independent of God as well as superior and often indifferent to our fellow-men.

1. The nature of pride.

(a) It comes from within our heart (*Mark* 7: 22; *Luke* 9: 46, 47): it is described as the imagination of a man's heart (*Luke* 1: 51), arrogance of heart (*Isa.* 9: 9), and the lifting up of the heart (*Ps.* 131: 1; *Dan.* 5: 20).

(b) It is our seeing ourselves as different from others in some respect, and feeling superior (*I Cor.* 4: 7); it is a false sense of our own importance (*Matt.* 26: 33; *Mark* 14: 29).

(c) It is an inappropriate love of self (*II Tim.* 3: 2), and the exaltation of self (*Luke* 18: 9–14).

(d) It is our departing from our proper position before God and our fellows (*Jude* 6), thinking of ourselves more highly than we ought to think (*Rom.* 12: 3).

2. Forms of pride.

(a) It may take the form of pride in **appearance** (*Mark* 12: 38; *I Pet.* 3: 3).

(b) It may take the form of pride in **position** or **prestige** (*Mark* 9: 33–37; *Luke* 9: 46–48; *Mark* 12: 38, 39; *I John* 2: 16).

(c) It may take the form of pride in **power** (*Lev.* 26: 19; *Ezek.* 30: 6; cf. *Acts* 8: 18, 19).

(d) It may take the form of pride in **achievements** and **success** (*II Chron.* 26: 15, 16).

(e) It may take the form of pride in **possessions** (*II Kings.* 20: 13; *Luke* 12: 13–21).

(f) It may take the form of pride in **knowledge** (*I Cor.* 8: 1) and of **intellect** (*Isa.* 5: 21).

(g) It may take the form of pride in **abilities** and **spiritual gifts** (*I Pet.* 4: 10–11; cf. *I Cor.* 12: 4ff).

(h) It may take the form of pride in **men,** and the **human relationships** we possess (*I Cor.* 3: 21).

(i) It may take the form of pride in **spiritual blessing** (*II Cor.* 12: 7).

3. The expression of pride.

(a) It expresses itself in attitudes (*Eccl.* 7: 8), in excessive self-confidence (*Matt.* 26: 33–35; *Mark* 14: 29–31; *Luke* 22: 33), in an unwillingness to take advice (*Prov.* 13: 10), in contempt for others (*Ps.* 123: 4), in presumptuous planning for the future (*Jas.* 4: 15, 16), and in arrogance (*Prov.* 8: 13).

(b) It expresses itself in our **eyes:** we may have haughty eyes (*Prov.* 6: 17; 21: 4), and such may first be demonstrated in regard to our parents (*Prov.* 30: 17).

(c) It expresses itself in our **objectives** and **ambitions:** pride always wants more of that of which it is proud (*Hab.* 2: 5), which is another way of saying that it is greedy.

(d) It expresses itself in **words** (*I Sam.* 2: 3; *Luke* 9: 46): particularly in boasting (*Isa.* 10: 12, 13), exaggeration (*Dan.* 4: 1; *II Pet.* 2: 18; *Jude* 16), and argumentativeness (*II Tim.* 2: 24, 25).

(e) It expresses itself in **actions** and **reactions:** it does not rejoice in the success of others (*I Cor.* 13: 4); it prompts anger and violence (*Gen.* 4: 6ff).

4. The effects of pride.

(a) It encourages arrogance (*Prov.* 21: 24).

(b) It inflates or puffs up (*I Cor.* 4: 6); it lifts us up to a false sense of our importance (*I Tim.* 3: 6).

(c) It brings strife in its wake (*Prov.* 13: 10; 28: 25).

(d) It breeds a false self-confidence (*Matt.* 26: 33–35; *Mark* 14: 29–31; *Luke* 22: 33).

(e) It makes us foolishly feel we can be independent of everyone, even including God (*Ps.* 10: 4; *Hos.* 7: 10).

(f) It provides a false sense of security (*Obad.* 3, 4).

(g) It leads to contempt and rejection of God's Word (*Jer.* 43: 2).

(h) It leads to self-deception (*Jer.* 49: 16); the pride of our heart deceives us (*Prov.* 26: 12; *Obad.* 3).

(i) It becomes an obstacle to our worship of God, and acceptance with Him (*Gen.* 4: 3–5; *Jas.* 4: 6).

(j) It cuts us off from God because it constitutes part of our inner defilement (*Mark* 7: 20–23).

(k) It ultimately brings both a fall (*I Cor.* 10: 12) and disgrace (*Prov.* 16: 18; cf. 18: 12).

5. Examples of pride in the Bible.

(a) The angels who did not keep their own position (*Jude* 6; cf. *Isa.* 14: 12ff).

(b) Pharaoh, who was proud in his dealings with the Israelites (*Neh.* 9: 10).

(c) Hezekiah, who was too proud to show his gratitude to God for His goodness to him (*II Chron.* 32: 25).

(d) Nebuchadnezzar, who was proud of his might and majesty (*Dan.* 3; 4: 30; 5: 20).

(e) Belshazzar, whose heart was proud in that he refused to humble himself (*Dan.* 5: 22, 23).

(f) Haman, who desired respect for himself from men (*Esth.* 3: 5).

(g) Moab, whose pride was seen in arrogance and empty boasting (*Isa.* 16: 6).

(h) Tyre, whose pride was in their achievements and their commerce (*Isa.* 23: 8, 9).

(i) Edom, whose pride misled her to feel she was not vulnerable from attack (*Obad.* 3).

(j) Babylon, whose pride led her to

be defiant against the Lord (*Jer.* 50: 29, 32).

(k) Assyria, whose pride gave her a sense of superiority over all others (*Ezek.* 31: 3, 10).

(l) Israel, whose pride was intoxicating and without justification (*Isa.* 28: 1; *Hos.* 5: 5, 9).

(m) Judah, whose pride caused her not to give glory to God (*Jer.* 13: 15, 19).

(n) The Pharisees, whose pride caused them to trust in themselves that they were righteous and to despise others (*Luke* 18: 9–14).

(o) The scribes, whose pride was seen in their delight in outward show and public acknowledgement (*Mark* 12: 38, 39).

(p) Peter, who felt he was stronger than others and able to withstand temptation (*Matt.* 26: 33–35; *Mark* 14: 29–31; *Luke* 22: 33).

(q) Herod Agrippa, who thought he could take glory to himself which was God's alone (*Acts* 12: 21–23).

(r) The Laodiceans, whose pride made them blind to their spiritual poverty (*Rev.* 3: 17).

6. The guilt of pride.

First, it causes us to sin against God.

(a) It is declared to be sin (*Prov.* 21: 4).

(b) When we are proud we have lost sight of our indebtedness to God, that we have nothing good which we have not, in fact, received (*I Cor.* 4: 7).

(c) We ascribe to ourselves the success which we really owe to God (*Judg.* 7: 2).

(d) We refuse to hear God's words and stubbornly follow our own heart's inclination (*Jer.* 13: 10).

(e) We think we can be independent of God when, in fact, the opposite is the case (*Jer.* 13: 8–11).

(f) We trust not in God but in ourselves, believing that we can build our life on what we think we can accomplish and control ourselves (*Ps.* 52: 1; 75: 4; 94: 3, 4).

Secondly, the guilt of pride is that it also causes us to sin against others.

(g) Puffed up, we favour one person against another (*I Cor.* 4: 6).

(h) Conceited, we ignore and despise those whom we think inferior to us (*Rom.* 12: 16; cf. *Luke* 18: 9).

(i) Proud, we think little of the interests of others and are often inconsiderate of them (*Ps.* 10: 2; *Prov.* 21: 24).

7. The condemnation of pride.

(a) One of the factors that should condemn pride in our own eyes is that it is Satan's pre-eminent sin (*I Tim.* 3: 6; *Rev.* 13: 5).

(b) God has no pleasure in our foolish pride (*Jer.* 13: 15; *Zeph.* 3: 11).

(c) Pride is part of those characteristics which mark men out as opposed to God (*II Tim.* 3: 2ff).

(d) God hates pride (*Amos* 6: 8; *Jer.* 13: 9) and He resists the proud (*Jas.* 4: 6; *I Pet.* 5: 5).

(e) Pride makes God's judgment inevitable (*Jer.* 13: 15–17), so that He will put an end to pride (*Ps.* 18: 27; *Isa.* 2: 12; 13: 11; 23: 9; *Jer.* 13: 9).

(f) Those who walk in pride, God is well able to abase (*Dan.* 4: 37).

8. The cure of pride.

(a) Its cure begins when we realise that there is no place at all for pride in ourselves in the presence of God (*I Cor.* 1: 29).

(b) Its cure proceeds as we see ourselves as sinners, and individually as "the worst" of sinners (*I Tim.* 1: 15), in stark contrast to how we once viewed ourselves (*Phil.* 3: 4–6).

(c) Its cure is about to be effected when we abandon all claims to self-righteousness and depend utterly and completely on Jesus Christ for both salvation and righteousness before God (*Phil.* 3: 7–11), so that we glory in Jesus Christ (*Phil.* 3: 3), and in His Cross (*Gal.* 6: 14).

(d) The cure must never be taken for granted, for the danger of pride will not be removed until we are changed perfectly into our Lord's likeness (*II Cor.* 12: 7; *Phil.* 3: 21).

(e) Pride is kept under control as we realise that the only true pride is pride of the Lord (*I Cor.* 1: 31): paradoxically, having humbled ourselves before God, we can boast in the Lord (*Jer.* 9: 23f), in His divine intervention and help in the past, and in the assurance we have of the same benefits in the future (*I Chron.* 16: 27f; 29: 11; *Ps.* 5: 11; 32: 11; 89: 17f).

(f) The cure of pride is assisted by our being mindful of the proverbs of Scripture concerning pride (*I Kings* 20: 11; *Prov.* 25: 14; 27: 1).

(g) Its cure is further assisted by our being mindful of the words of Scripture which warn against pride and encourage instead the pursuit of humility (*Jas.* 4: 6; *I Pet.* 5: 5).

(h) If we do not allow pride to be cured now, it will be finally cured at the day of judgment: God has a day reserved for the proud and lofty (*Isa.* 2: 12, 17; *Mal.* 4: 1), and His judgment is directed at the extinction of all false pride (*Dan.* 4: 37; *Matt.* 23: 12).

(i) Safety for the Christian lies in the active pursuit of humility, following the example of our Lord Jesus Christ without compromise (*Phil.* 2: 1–13).

27. WRATH

Question: What is wrath? and why is it sinful?

Answer: Wrath is our reaction of indignation and displeasure at the deeds, words or intentions of others. It is not always sinful in that wrath may be a just reaction to wrong but it is very often sinful either because selfishness prompts our anger or because our anger, though justly stirred, runs away with itself and leads us to wrong words and actions.

1. Wrath and anger.

(a) **Wrath** describes passionate rage which boils up suddenly in an angry outburst, sometimes to disappear almost as quickly, but at other times to become a lasting bitterness.

(b) **Wrath** and **anger** are almost synonymous words in the Bible. In the New Testament **wrath** comes from a Greek root which means "to boil up" or "to well up" and originally denoted violent movement. **Wrath,** therefore, indicates a rage which quickly bursts forth, often uncontrollably, and as quickly disappears. **Anger,** however, describes that angry attitude and temper which lasts and is nursed.

(c) In man wrath and anger are especially sins of the tongue (*II Cor.* 12: 20; *Jas.* 3: 3–18), but they find their place on our tongues and in our actions because they are often cherished in our hearts (*Eccl.* 7: 9; *Amos* 1: 11).

2. Wrath and anger are not always out of place and sinful.

(a) We ought to be angry when good is put aside and evil exalted, and we have examples in the Bible of just and holy anger:

  (i) Moses was angry at the Israelites' lack of trust in God (*Ex.* 16: 20), and at their apostasy in making a golden calf (*Ex.* 32: 19, 22);

(ii) David was angry at the unjust rich man about whom Nathan told him, not realising at first that it was at himself his anger was rightly directed (*II Sam.* 12: 5);

(iii) Nehemiah was angry at the abuses which had taken place in Jerusalem (*Neh.* 5: 6);

(iv) Paul's spirit was provoked to anger in Athens when he witnessed its idolatry (*Acts* 17: 16).

(b) We have evidence too of God inducing a proper anger in His people for good purposes (*Rom.* 10: 19; *II Cor.* 7: 11).

(c) Our Lord Jesus Christ was angry at men's indifference to human need (*Mark* 3: 5), and His wrath was the revelation of God's wrath.

(d) God's holy and just wrath and anger are described in the Bible in various aspects:

(i) God's wrath is **slow** (*Ps.* 103: 8; *Isa.* 48: 9; *Jonah* 4: 2; *Nah.* 1: 3);

(ii) God's wrath is **righteous** (*Ps.* 58: 10, 11; *Lam.* 1: 18; *Rom.* 2: 6, 8; 3: 5, 6; 9: 18, 20, 22; *Rev.* 16: 6, 7);

(iii) God's wrath is **perfectly controlled**—e.g. our Lord's cleansing of the temple was not done on impulse, but the night before He inspected the temple (*Mark* 11: 11).

3. **But more often than not we do wrong to be angry because of the selfish motives and attitudes which prompt our anger** (*Jonah* 4: 4).

(a) Pride—and especially hurt pride—promotes anger (*Gen.* 4: 3–5; *II Kings* 5: 11; *Esth.* 3: 5; *Dan.* 3: 13).

(b) Unwillingness to accept rebuke spurs on anger (*II Chron.* 26: 19).

(c) Jealousy kindles anger (*I Sam.* 17: 28; *Acts* 5: 17, 18).

(d) Resentment encourages anger (*Luke* 4: 28).

(e) Selfishness sparks off anger (*I Kings* 21: 4).

(f) Touchiness provides ready opportunity for anger (*Gen.* 40: 1f).

(g) Malice is the companion often of anger (*Gen.* 27: 41, 45; *Col.* 3: 8).

4. **Wrath and anger do harm and easily lead to other sins.**

(a) When we lose control of ourselves on account of wrath or anger sin crouches at the door (*Gen.* 4: 7).

(b) Like a wind or hurricane that arises swiftly or unexpectedly, or a fire that gets out of control, wrath and anger can do immeasurable harm (*Eccl.* 10: 4; *Ps.* 124: 3) and mischief (*Prov.* 6: 34; 15: 1; 16: 14), besides being overwhelming (*Prov.* 27: 4).

(c) They tear us apart (*Amos* 1: 11).

(d) They show on our face (*Gen.* 4: 5).

(e) They have physical repercussions (*Acts* 7: 54)—to harbour anger or resentment is as bad for the body as it is for the soul (*Prov.* 14: 30).

(f) They mar prayer and fellowship with God (*I Tim.* 2: 8).

(g) They spoil Christian fellowship and the life of the church (*II Cor.* 12: 20).

(h) They give the devil a foothold which he will use to his own evil advantage (*Eph.* 4: 26f).

(i) They can be the first step even to murder, and they can certainly constitute the spirit of murder for murder is only anger full-grown (*Matt.* 5: 22).

(j) They are accompanied frequently by quarrelling and harsh words (*Prov.* 15: 18; *Eph.* 4: 31).

(k) They lead often to cruelty (*Gen.* 49: 7; *II Chron.* 16: 10; *Prov.* 27: 4) and injustice (*Prov.* 14: 17; 29: 22).

(l) They issue all too often in strife and contention (*Prov.* 21: 19; 29: 22; 30: 33), violence (*Dan.* 2: 12) and murder (*Gen.* 4: 8; 49: 6; *Ex.* 2: 12; *Matt.* 2: 16–18).

5. The condemnation of wrath and anger.

(a) They *are* a characteristic of fools (*Prov.* 12: 16; 14: 17, 29; 27: 3, 4; *Eccl.* 7: 9).

(b) They provide sufficient grounds for terminating friendship, for keeping friendship with a man whose temper is uncontrolled can lead us in the same direction (*Gen.* 49: 6; *Prov.* 22: 24).

(c) They reveal the state of a man's heart (*Luke* 6: 45).

(d) They are a work of the flesh, and are opposed to God's Spirit (*Gal.* 5: 20).

(e) They never work the will of God (*Jas.* 1: 19, 20).

(f) They are an infringement of the sixth commandment (*Matt.* 5: 21, 22).

(g) They bring their own punishment (*Job* 19: 29; *Prov.* 25: 28).

(h) They are frequently an infringement of God's prerogative of judgment for wrath and anger so easily make us take judgment into our own hands (*Rom.* 12: 19).

(i) They put us in danger of God's judgment (*Matt.* 5: 22).

6. The Christian attitude to wrath and anger.

(a) We recognise wrath and anger, arising from bitterness, as belonging to the old life we once lived before our conversion, and that they are among the many things we are to put away from us (*Eph.* 4: 31).

(b) We are to be slow to be angry (*Ps.* 37: 8; *Prov.* 15: 18; 16: 32; 19: 11; *Tit.* 1: 7; *Jas.* 1: 19).

(c) Aiming at the avoidance of wrath and anger, we also try to placate those who are carried away by wrath and anger, where it is right and possible to do so (*Prov.* 15: 1, 18; 16: 32; 29: 8, 11).

(d) Our aim when anger is justifiable is neither to allow it to cause us to sin (*Eph.* 4: 26), nor to allow Satan to gain a foothold by means of it (*Eph.* 4: 27).

28. ENVY

Question: What is envy? and why is it sinful?

Answer: Envy is basically illwill occasioned by looking at someone else's superior position or advantages. It is sinful because, besides indicating discontent with God's providence, it is contrary to love for our neighbour in that love rejoices at the good of others.

1. The characteristics of envy.

(a) Envy begrudges the honour and the advantages others enjoy (*Gen.* 26: 14).

(b) It fails to see God's providence in the ordering of gifts, honours and abilities (*Deut.* 8: 17, 18; *Prov.* 30: 8, 9).

(c) It is sad at the happiness of others (*Luke* 15: 25–30).

(d) It makes us hostile to those who have never injured us (*Gen.* 37: 3, 4).

(e) It seeks the destruction of others rather than their welfare (*Matt.* 27: 18; *Mark* 15: 10).

(f) It may even break through every restraint in order to bring about the ruin of the person who is envied (*Gen.* 4: 3–8).

2. The incitement of envy.

(a) It is incited by the attractiveness and commendation given to the virtues of others (*I John* 3: 12; cf. *Gen.* 4: 3–8).

(b) It is stirred up by the success of others (*I Sam.* 18: 8, 9; *Dan.* 6: 3, 4; *Acts* 13: 45; 17: 4, 5).

(c) It is prompted by pride (*I Tim.* 6: 4, 5).

(d) It is encouraged by the existence of both bitterness (*Jas.* 3: 14) and malice (*Tit.* 3: 3) in our hearts towards others.

3. The prevalence of envy.

(a) It was behind man's first rebellion, for by means of the encouragement of envy Satan caused man to lose his enjoyment of unspoiled fellowship with God (*Gen.* 3: 1–6).

(b) It was envy which brought about the first shedding of blood in human history (*Gen.* 4: 5, 8).

(c) It is one of the evil things which is characteristic of the human heart and which marks man's defilement before God (*Mark* 7: 20–23; *Jas.* 3: 14).

(d) It is very often the explanation why people work so hard to succeed, in that they envy their neighbours and want to exceed them (*Eccl.* 4: 4).

(e) It is behind practically all coveting (*I Kings* 21: 1–4).

(f) It can fill a life in company with other sins (*Rom.* 1: 29).

4. The condemnation of envy.

(a) God hates envy (*Prov.* 3: 31, 32).

(b) Envy is a characteristic of the world, as it chooses to live without reference to God (*I Cor.* 3: 3; *Tit.* 3: 3).

(c) In terms of the great conflict there is between light and darkness, envy and jealousy belong to the darkness (*Rom.* 13: 12–13).

(d) Envy is an evidence of a corrupted mind (*Rom.* 1: 28, 29), and is a work of the flesh in contrast to the fruit of the Spirit (*Gal.* 5: 19–23).

(e) Envy is the opposite of fellowship: moved by envy, we desire to have what others have; in fellowship, however, we desire to share with others what we ourselves possess (*Mark* 14: 3–9).

(f) Envy is the opposite of love (*I Cor.* 13: 4; *I John* 3: 11, 12) so that it makes us unlike God (*I John* 4: 8).

(g) Envy makes us like Satan, whose work we further when we allow envy to rule our hearts and actions (*John* 8: 44; *I John* 3: 12).

5. The dangerous consequences of envy.

(a) It is more cruel and destructive than anger (*Prov.* 27: 4).

(b) It is like a cancer, doing harm to both the body and the mind, because it takes away our peace of mind (*Prov.* 14: 30).

(c) It ruins spiritual appetite (*I Pet.* 2: 1f) and fellowship with God (*Ps.* 66: 18).

(d) It quickly leads to insulting language (*I Pet.* 2: 1f).

(e) It breeds a destructively critical spirit (*Dan.* 6: 3, 4; *Acts* 17: 5).

(f) It gives birth to unwarranted suspicion and anger (*I Sam.* 18: 8, 9).

(g) It can give vent to itself in spiteful actions (*Gen.* 26: 14, 15).

(h) It can suddenly escalate into disorder and every kind of evil (*Jas.* 3: 16; *Gen.* 37: 11; *Acts* 7: 9): conspiracy (*Gen.* 37: 18), mockery (*Gen.* 37: 19), thoughts of murder (*Gen.* 37: 20), violence (*Gen.* 37: 23), cruelty (*Gen.* 37: 24), betrayal (*Gen.* 37: 26–28), lies (*Gen.* 37: 32) and immeasurable hurt to others (*Gen.* 37: 34).

29. LUST

Question: What is lust? and why is it sinful?

Answer: Lust is either uncontrolled, overmastering desire or desire willingly allowed to go beyond that which is lawful and legitimate. Lust is sinful because it puts pleasure before pleasing God, and it places self-gratification before the good of others.

1. **The distinction between desire and lust.**

(a) Desires—whether physical, mental, spiritual or sexual—were given by God to man at his creation and were wholly good (*Gen.* 1: 31; *I Tim.* 4: 3, 4; *Jas.* 1: 17).

(b) Sin, however, acting like a poison, mars all men's desires, and left to itself would use them to increase the corruption that is in the world (*II Pet.* 1: 4).

(c) Desire is necessary, for example, if appetite is to ensure that the body is fed (*Matt.* 4: 2), and if the human race is to be continued by procreation (*Gen.* 3: 16; *Heb.* 13: 4).

(d) Our Lord Jesus Christ had an eager desire to eat the Passover with His disciples (*Luke* 22: 15), and Paul had a desire to depart and be with Christ (*Phil.* 1: 23): these desires were wholly commendable.

(e) Our desires, however, can so easily be set on evil things and then they become lusts (*I Cor.* 10: 6).

(f) Desire becomes lust when its object is unlawful (*II Sam.* 11: 3, 4; *Ex.* 20: 14).

(g) Desire becomes lust when it gains control of us rather than our controlling it (*I Thess.* 4: 5)—thus looking becomes covetousness (*Josh.* 7: 21), eating becomes gluttony (*I Sam.* 2: 12–17), attraction leads to

mental adultery (*Matt.* 5: 27, 28), and burning sexual desire becomes immorality (*II Sam.* 11: 2, 4).

2. **The source of lust.**

(a) Desires—both good and bad—find their origin in our heart (*Ps.* 37: 4; *Matt.* 15: 19, 20; *Rom.* 1: 24, 29). (In Biblical language, the heart covers the whole inward life of a man: his thinking, feelings and will.)

(b) Lust is part of our nature as fallen men and women, and that nature may be described as being corrupt through deceitful lusts (*Eph.* 4: 22).

(c) Lust springs from the passions of our mortal bodies which demand satisfaction in unlawful, and therefore sinful ways (*Rom.* 6: 12).

(d) Lust finds its home in our flesh which pleads for the gratification of its desires (*Rom.* 13: 14; *Gal.* 5: 16).

(e) Lusts reflect the kinship of fallen men and women with the devil (*John* 8: 44).

(f) Lust is a manifestation of the sin which dwells in man and which controls him (*Rom.* 7: 7, 8).

3. **Lust's characteristics and objectives.**

(a) Lust is deceitful in that it promises happiness but it brings, in fact, misery (*Eph.* 4: 22).

(b) Lust shows itself in uncontrolled passion (*I Thess.* 4: 5) leading to sexual immorality and sometimes perversion (*Rom.* 1: 29; *Jude* 7).

(c) Lust reveals itself in covetousness whether of money (*Acts* 20: 33), other people's material possessions (*Ex.* 20: 17), or another person's body (*Prov.* 6: 25; *Matt.* 5: 28).

(d) Lust's pre-eminent stimulus is what comes to men and women through their eyes (*I John* 2: 16): Eve, for example, was tempted by what she *saw* of the tree in the midst

203

of the garden (*Gen.* 3: 6), and Achan was tempted by what he saw among the spoils of the city of Jericho (*Josh.* 7: 21).

(e) Lust finds itself stirred by what it sees, whether in the form of another person's attractiveness (*II Sam.* 11: 3, 4; *Job* 31: 1; *Matt.* 5: 28) or in terms of the pleasures of the world (*Matt.* 4: 8; *Luke* 8: 14).

(f) Lust can be stimulated by harmful friendships and bad company (*II Tim.* 2: 22).

(g) Lust keeps company with sins such as debauchery, drunkenness, orgies, carousing and idolatry (*I Pet.* 4: 3).

(h) Lust is linked often with filthiness, silly talk and levity (*Eph.* 5: 4).

(i) Lust desires our surrender to it (*I Thess.* 4: 5) through its strong enticements (*Jas* 1: 14; *Jude* 16).

(j) Lust listens only to what it wants to hear (*II Tim.* 4: 3): men who follow after their own evil desires choose to scoff at all presentations of truth which might make them uncomfortable (*II Pet.* 3: 3).

4. Lust's consequences.

(a) Lust never stands still: once conceived it gives birth to sin; and sin, when it is full-grown gives birth to death (*Jas.* 1: 15).

(b) Lust dishonours the body (*Rom.* 1: 24; *I Cor.* 6: 17–20).

(c) Lust ruins the good things of life (*II Pet.* 1: 4).

(d) Lust breeds inward conflicts and outward strife (*Jas.* 4: 1).

(e) Lust chokes the influence of God's Word in the individual's life (*Mark* 4: 19).

(f) Lust leads to transgression and offending one's brother (*I Thess.* 4: 5).

(g) Lust makes us the world's friend and God's enemy (*Jas.* 4: 4): God demands our total obedience and love from the whole heart (*Deut.* 6: 5).

(h) Lust brings upon itself the judgment of God (*I Thess.* 4: 6): it merits God's wrath (*Col.* 3: 6).

5. The antidote to lust.

(a) The only true antidote to lust is the grace of God that brings salvation and which teaches us to say "No" to ungodliness and worldly passions, and to live self-controlled, upright and godly lives in this present age while we await the return of Jesus Christ (*Tit.* 2: 11–13).

(b) Realising that the Lord Jesus gave Himself for us to redeem us from all wickedness, and to purify for Himself a people that are His very own (*Tit.* 2: 14), prompts gratitude (*Rom.* 12: 1, 2) and the desire to live for Him and not for ourselves (*II Cor.* 5: 15).

(c) We say "No," therefore, to worldly passions (*Tit.* 2: 12); we flee evil desires, if necessary, and pursue righteousness (*II Tim.* 2: 22); we put off our old self with its wrong desires and put on the new self, created to be like God in true righteousness and holiness (*Eph.* 4: 23, 24).

(d) We aim at living self-controlled lives (*Tit.* 2: 12): the godly man is not passionless, but controlled in his passions (*Gal.* 5: 23, 24).

(e) We find strength for these things from knowing that they are God's will (*I Thess.* 4: 3; *I Pet.* 4: 2f).

(f) We find power for these things by the indwelling of the Holy Spirit (*Gal.* 5: 16).

(g) We find daily encouragement from God's very great and precious promises to persevere in proving the reality of the antidote that His salvation provides against lust (*Heb.* 13: 21; *II Pet.* 1: 4).

30. GLUTTONY

Question: What is gluttony?

Answer: Gluttony is excessive eating, so that a man lives to eat rather than eating to live. It is sinful because by it a man makes a god of his stomach, and harms both his body and his usefulness to others.

1. Gluttony in general.

(a) The Greek word for "glutton" in the New Testament represents someone who eats too much (*Matt.* 11: 19; *Luke* 7: 34).

(b) Food and drink can become a foolish preoccupation of life (*Luke* 21: 34).

(c) Gluttony is greedy overindulgence in food—or eating for eating's sake (*Prov.* 23: 20).

(d) Gluttony goes beyond what is enough (*Prov.* 25: 16), in that it eats more than the body requires for satisfaction (*Ps.* 78: 29, 30); and special occasions are thought of often as a particular opportunity for excess (*Prov.* 23: 1, 2).

(e) The glutton also tends to eat too frequently, and at the wrong times (*Eccl.* 10: 16); he eats not for strength but for the enjoyment of excess (*Eccl.* 10: 17).

(f) Gluttony pays undue attention to the desire for food, and allows the desires of the flesh to dominate life (*Rom.* 13: 13, 14).

(g) Gluttony is accompanied in many instances by excessive drinking (*Prov.* 23: 20, 21), and is to be regarded as equally vicious as drunkenness (*Deut.* 21: 20; *Prov.* 23: 20).

2. The effects of gluttony.

(a) Gluttony leads to our surrender to natural appetites with their bias to excess and sin. Desires naturally characterise the body and mind of man (*Eph.* 2: 3), and because of sin those desires can often be deceitful (*Eph.* 4: 22), and Satan may endeavour to lead us astray, if he can, by the necessary appetite we have for food (*Matt.* 4: 3).

(b) Gluttony leads to lethargy and drowsiness (*Prov.* 23: 20, 21).

(c) Gluttony leads to sleep at the wrong times all too often (*Prov.* 23: 20, 21).

(d) Gluttony leads to laziness and sloth (*Eccl.* 10: 16–18).

(e) Gluttony leads to the dulling of a man's senses (*Prov.* 23: 21) so that he can become oblivious of moral and spiritual issues (*Amos* 6: 4, 7), and lacking in all spiritual alertness (*Luke* 21: 34–36).

(f) Gluttony can prove a great snare to a man because it can blunt his awareness of spiritual and moral issues (*Gen.* 25: 29–34; *Heb.* 12: 16, 17).

(g) Gluttony can lead to other associated evils (*Deut.* 21: 20; *Prov.* 23: 21; *Ps.* 141: 4), including glorying in excess (*Phil.* 3: 19).

(h) Gluttony can prove ruinous in its influence upon others (*Prov.* 28: 7; *Eccl.* 10: 16, 17).

(i) Gluttony tends to lead to a feeling of self-sufficiency and independence of God (*Deut.* 32: 15; *Prov.* 30: 8, 9; *Isa.* 22: 13).

(j) Gluttony injures health in that the body becomes fat and bloated (*Deut.* 32: 15), and may bring physical complications which could have been avoided (*Eccl.* 11: 10).

205

(k) Gluttony can be the first step to poverty (*Prov.* 23: 21).

(l) Gluttony has ruin as its end (*Phil.* 3: 19), and a self indulgent person can be described as "dead while alive" (*I Tim.* 5: 6).

(m) Esau (*Gen.* 25: 29–34), Eli's sons (*I Sam.* 2: 12–17) and the rich man called Dives (*Luke* 16: 19–31), are illustrations of some of the sad effects of gluttony.

3. The sinfulness of gluttony.

(a) Gluttony is, in effect, waste of food, and waste of food is contrary to God's intention (*Lev.* 19: 9; 23: 22; *John* 6: 12).

(b) Gluttony ignores truths and obligations God has plainly revealed. For example, the glutton forgets that it is not mere food that gives life (*Deut.* 8: 3); the glutton fails to see that God is concerned with the daily practicalities of life (*I Cor.* 10: 31), and he certainly does not seek God's blessing on his eating (*I Tim.* 4: 4, 5).

(c) Gluttony is frequently part of a hedonistic approach to life, that is to say, the theory of ethics in which pleasure is regarded as the chief good or the proper end of action (*Isa.* 22: 13; *Luke* 12: 19; *I Cor.* 15: 32).

(d) Gluttony is a form of slavery because a man makes himself a slave of food rather than a servant of God (*I Cor.* 6: 12, 13); instead of ruling his body, a man's body rules him (*Rom.* 13: 13, 14).

(e) Gluttony makes a god of food and of the stomach (*Phil.* 3: 19).

(f) Gluttony is a manifestation of worldliness, of loving the world rather than God in that lavish and expensive eating habits are something of which men can be foolishly proud (*I John* 2: 15–17; cf. *Phil.* 3: 19).

(g) Gluttony often offends the principle and commandment that we should love our neighbour as ourselves. Gluttony is frequently the sin of the person who lives only for himself (*Luke* 16: 19), so that while he eats, others whom he could help go hungry (*Luke* 16: 19, 20).

(h) Gluttony causes a man to sin against his body, forgetful of the fact that his body is a wonderful gift of God (*Ps.* 139: 14).

(i) God judges gluttony (*Num.* 11: 33, 34; *Ps.* 78: 31), and we shall all be judged for our use of the body (*II Cor.* 5: 10).

4. Correctives for the avoidance of gluttony.

(i) *A proper perspective and sense of priorities.*

(a) One day God will put an end to food and to the stomach (*I Cor.* 6: 13).

(b) There are deeper dimensions to human life than physical hunger (*Deut.* 8: 3): the food we more urgently need is that which nourishes spiritual life.

(c) The needs of the body are not as important as the requirements of the soul (*Matt.* 9: 1–8; *Mark* 2: 1–12; *I Cor.* 5: 5).

(d) God's kingdom is not a matter of eating and drinking but of the righteousness, peace and joy which the Holy Spirit gives (*Rom.* 14: 17).

(e) For the man who knows God, eating and drinking are not secular activities: whether he eats or drinks, he wants to do all to the glory of God (*I Cor.* 10: 31).

(f) True satisfaction is found neither in food nor in other physical pleasures but in doing God's will (*John* 4: 34).

(ii) *An understanding of the proper place of food in human life.*

(a) Food is a just necessity for life: every man needs to take nourishment both of proper quality and sufficient quantity to maintain his physical life and well-being (*I Tim.* 6: 8); food is meant for the stomach, and the stomach for food (*I Cor.* 6: 13).

(b) All of God's creatures depend on Him for food (*Ps.* 104: 27, 28), and we are encouraged to pray for our daily bread (*Matt.* 6: 11), and to regard it as the proper objective of our daily work (*Eccl.* 6: 7; *II Thess.* 3: 10).

(c) Food is good since God created foods to be received with thanksgiving by those who believe and know the truth (*I Tim.* 4: 4ff). He desires that we should enjoy His gifts (*I Tim.* 6: 17), for His goodness is illustrated to us in terms of the good things He has given us to eat (*Deut.* 32: 13, 14).

(d) Health, however, does not depend on living upon delicacies (*Dan.* 1: 5–16).

(e) Food should be eaten principally for the sake of maintaining strength (*Eccl.* 10: 17), and while enjoyment of eating is lawful, slavery to that enjoyment is not (*I Cor.* 6: 12).

(iii) *An appreciation of the Christian teaching concerning his body.*

(a) The body is the sphere or activity in which we do either good or evil (*II Cor.* 5: 10).

(b) The body is fearfully and wonderfully made (*Ps.* 139: 14) but sadly can be the subject of abuse (*Eccl.* 11: 10).

(c) The Christian's bodily life should be determined by what God has done for him in Jesus Christ (*Rom.* 12: 1, 2; *I Cor.* 6: 12–14, 20): the body

is not meant for lust but for the Lord (*I Cor.* 6: 13).

(d) The body is the instrument, in which, and by which, we may honour Christ (*Phil.* 1: 20).

(e) The highest dignity is given to the body in that the Christian's body is a temple of the Holy Spirit within, which he has of God (*I Cor.* 6: 19).

(f) Hence the Christian is to know how to possess, control and manage his own body in holiness and honour (*I Thess.* 4: 3, 4).

(iv) *A rightful maintenance of self-discipline.*

(a) Restraint is to be put upon a big appetite (*Prov.* 23: 2), so that enough is eaten rather than too much (*Prov.* 25: 16).

(b) Part of the fruit of the Spirit is self-control (*Gal.* 5: 23).

(c) Fasting may find a place in this self-discipline and God's people throughout the centuries have set an example of fasting: David (*II Sam.* 12: 16, 22; *Ps.* 109: 24), Esther (*Esther* 4: 16), Nehemiah (*Neh.* 1: 4), Daniel (*Dan.* 9: 3), Anna (*Luke* 2: 37), the disciples of John (*Matt.* 9: 14), Cornelius (*Acts* 10: 30), the early Christians (*Acts* 13: 2), and the apostles (*II Cor.* 6: 5; 11: 27).

(d) It is important to remember, however, that Christianity brought an end to ritual fasting (*Mark* 2: 18 22).

(e) Our Lord Himself fasted (*Matt.* 4: 2), and He made clear that certain situations are satisfactorily dealt with only by prayer and fasting (*Matt.* 17: 21).

(f) Fasting is linked, therefore, with prayer in special situations (*Mark* 9: 29): it is part of worship (*Luke* 2: 37; *Acts* 13: 1, 2) and a symbol of self-humbling before God (*Ps.* 69: 10; 35: 13).

(g) Fasting, however, is never to be a matter of display, but is to be in secret (*Matt.* 6: 16–18).

(v) *A genuine concern for the needs of others.*

(a) We avoid gluttony by exercising a proper concern for the material needs of others (*I Tim.* 6: 17, 18).

(b) We are to be generous and share our food with those who are hungry (*Prov.* 22: 9).

(c) We should discipline our intake of food so that we can assist the poor (*Isa.* 58: 6, 7).

(d) We are not to neglect the needs of people's bodies to be fed (*Jas.* 2: 16; cf. *Matt.* 25: 42).

(e) Even in the way we eat, we are to have the good of others in view before our own good (*I Cor.* 10: 31–33).

(vi) *The pursuit of the true satisfaction God intends for us.*

(a) The Christian knows that there is a better way to joy and happiness than excess in the satisfaction of his physical appetites: he is to find it in the continuous experience of God's Spirit filling his life (*Eph.* 5: 18).

(b) The Christian's "food" should be to do the Father's will (*John* 4: 34; cf. *II Cor.* 5: 9).

31. AVARICE

Question: What is avarice and why is it sinful?

Answer: Avarice is the love of money and greed for gain, the opposite of contentment. It is sinful because it is a form of idolatry in that money and what it may secure become a man's god, leading him not only to dishonour God his Creator but to neglect and abuse his fellow man.

1. **Avarice defined.**

(a) One of the principal features of human life is the amassing of earthly property (*Matt.* 6: 19ff).

(b) Avarice is the love of money and greed for gain (*I Tim.* 3: 3).

(c) Avarice means that a man never has enough (*Hab.* 2: 5).

(d) Avarice is the opposite of contentment with what a man already possesses (*Hab.* 13: 5).

(e) Avarice is not limited to material possessions: its focus, for example, can be upon power (*III John* 9) or sexual immorality (*II Pet.* 2: 14).

(f) Avarice often takes the form of covetousness (*Josh.* 7: 20, 21).

(g) Avarice is laying up treasure upon earth to the total neglect of being rich toward God (*Luke* 12: 21).

(h) Avarice can become the attitude of a whole nation in that everyone is greedy for unjust gain (*Jer.* 8: 10).

2. **How avarice manifests itself.**

Avarice manifests itself in opinions and viewpoints.

(a) *The meaning of life.* Avarice finds the meaning of life in the acquisition of money and possessions (*Luke* 12: 18, 19), encouraged by false ideas about money and what it can do.

(b) *Profit.* Avarice always keeps foremost the personal profit motive (*Tit.* 1: 11), so that each action and enterprise is looked at from the viewpoint of personal advantage.

(c) *Security.* Avarice regards wealth as the principal symbol of security (*Jas.* 5: 2, 3).

(d) *Happiness.* Avarice views wealth as the main source of happiness (*Luke* 12: 18, 19).

Avarice manifests itself in actions.

(e) *Miserliness.* Avarice can make a person stingy in his dealings with others (*Prov.* 28: 22).

(f) *Selfish luxury and pleasure.* Avarice can, on the other hand, make a man lavish in his own enjoyment of luxury and pleasure (*Jas.* 5: 5; *Luke* 16: 19).

(g) *Dishonesty.* Avarice can prompt a man to seek wealth by dishonest means (*Ezek.* 22: 27; *I Pet.* 5: 2).

(h) *Indifference to the rights of others.* The unrestricted longing for possessions can cause a man to set aside the rights of others, especially if he is in a position of power or influence (*Amos* 2: 6; *Luke* 16: 20, 21).

(i) *Division.* The desire for wealth can divide relatives and spoil relationships (*Gen.* 13: 5, 6), and particularly is this the case in families over wills (*Luke* 12: 13).

(j) *Injustice.* Greed can lead a man to become unjust, e.g. an employer giving insufficient wages in order to save himself money (*Jas.* 5: 4).

(k) *Violence.* Striving for unlawful wealth can lead to violence and even murder (*Ezek.* 22: 27; *Mic.* 6: 12).

Avarice manifests itself in attitudes of mind.

(l) *Arrogant complacency.* Wealth easily breeds a harmful complacency (*Prov.* 18: 23; 28: 11), and the false conviction that the future is in the wealthy man's hands (*Jas.* 4: 13–17).

(m) *Gloating satisfaction.* Wealth is simply hoarded often and gloated over (*Luke* 12: 18, 19; *Jas.* 5: 2, 3).

(n) *Anxiety.* Satisfied as an avaricious man may be in some respects with what he has, he will, at the same time, find that his wealth and its preservation bring anxiety (*Eccl.* 5: 12).

(o) *Discontent.* The man who loves wealth will never be satisfied by it (*Eccl.* 5: 10), and his eyes will always be greedy (*I Sam.* 2: 29; cf. 2: 12–17).

3. **The sinfulness of avarice.**

(a) *It breaks the first great commandment:* "Love the Lord your God with all your heart and with all your soul and with all your mind" (*Matt.* 22: 37).

(b) Avarice makes a man give his heart to material treasures, and to be so devoted to his possessions that he ceases to love God (*Matt.* 6: 21, 24).

(c) Avarice is a form of idolatry in that money becomes a man's god (*Col.* 3: 5).

(d) Avarice denies the truth that man's proper and true happiness is in having the Lord as God (*Ps.* 144: 15), and having Him as one's helper (*Ps.* 146: 5; *Heb.* 13: 5, 6).

(e) *It breaks the second great commandment:* "Love your neighbour as yourself" (*Matt.* 22: 39).

(f) Avarice causes men to hoard money and possessions selfishly rather than use them for personal good and the proper good of others (*Jas.* 5: 2–4).

(g) The love of money proceeds from the love of self (*II Tim.* 3: 2), and always has personal gain in view even in the discharge of the seemingly most honourable of tasks (*Tit.* 1: 11).

(h) It ravages human relationships. Greed occurs in a group of four nouns which comprehensively describe the power of sin in spoiling human relationships: wickedness, evil, greed and depravity (*Rom.* 1: 29).

(i) It hurts other people as, for example, by neglect (*Luke* 16: 19ff) or by example—for instance, if parents take the alluring road to wealth they may find their family overwhelmed by the ways of the world (*Gen.* 13: 10–13; cf. *Gen.* 19: 12–26).

(j) *Avarice is the first step to all kinds of sin* (*I Tim.* 6: 10).

(k) Greed is linked frequently in the Bible with fornication and idolatry, in that greed in one form quickly leads to greed in another, so that a man ends up worshipping the objects of his greed (*I Cor.* 5: 10f).

(l) It is behind many of the works of the flesh, all of which are in direct opposition to the will of God for man (*Gal.* 5: 19–21).

(m) It finds deceit easy in that greed may be the real motivation of what seem to be good and kind actions (*I Thess.* 2: 5; *I Pet.* 5: 2; *II Pet.* 2: 3).

(n) It is the most obvious form of worldliness, in that two of worldliness' preeminent characteristics are the desire to buy everything that appeals to man, and the pride that comes from wealth and importance: such love of the world is the opposite of love for God (*I John* 2: 15, 16).

4. The folly of avarice.

(a) The happiness and enjoyment avarice promises are often illusory (*Eccl.* 2: 8f, 26; *Luke* 19: 2).

(b) Wealth is a totally insufficient source of security for the future, because God may not give a man the opportunity to enjoy it (*Eccl.* 6: 2).

(c) Avarice loses sight of the temporary hold man has on all material possessions (*Prov.* 27: 24; *Luke* 12: 20).

(d) It forgets, too, that even man's earthly hold of them is subject to circumstances over which he has no control (*Jas.* 5: 2, 3).

(e) It brings a man into the unenviable position of not really being sure who his true friends are, although his wealth attracts many apparent friends (*Prov.* 14: 20; 19: 4).

(f) Avarice makes the big mistake of thinking that man's life consists in the abundance of his possessions (*Luke* 12: 15).

(g) Avarice neglects the fact that there are many important things money cannot do: wealth can take care of a man's burial but not his destiny thereafter (*Luke* 16: 23), so that it cannot save him from eternal separation from God; wealth of a material nature will be of no use on the day of judgment (*Isa.* 10: 3).

(h) Avarice can cost a man his eternal well-being (*Matt.* 16: 26), in that his pursuit of money leads him to forget that his greatest need is to be rich before God (*Luke* 12: 19, 20).

(i) Avarice can lead to a man possessing immense outward wealth and at the same time knowing an inner poverty (*Prov.* 28: 22).

(j) Avarice shuts a man out of God's kingdom (*Matt.* 19: 23f; *Mark* 10: 23f; *Luke* 18: 24f).

(k) Avarice brings God's judgment, in that the man who thinks all the time about getting rich will be punished (*Prov.* 21: 13; 28: 20; *Jas.* 5: 1).

(l) The proceeds of avarice will be evidence against men on the day of judgment so that wrongly accumulated wealth will prove to be a liability rather than an asset (*Jas.* 5: 3): the store of accumulated wealth becomes, in effect, a store of divine wrath from which God will draw on the day of judgment (*Jas.* 5: 3).

(m) Those whose lives are governed by avarice may be compared to cattle feasting themselves while, all unknowingly, they are living in the shadow of the day of their slaughter (*Jas.* 5: 5).

5. **Proper correctives to avarice.**

The corrective of an eternal perspective.

(a) The danger of wealth is that it may be a wealth limited to this world alone (*I Tim.* 6: 17–19).

(b) The true value of material possessions is seen when we appreciate that at the judgment of the world they will all disappear (*Rev.* 18: 11–19).

(c) Our view of wealth is determined by what we consider to be true currency (*II Cor.* 6: 10), in that there is a wealth which has nothing to do with this world's wealth (*Rev.* 2: 9).

(d) Real wealth does not consist in the abundance of our possessions but in the state of our soul, upon whether or not we are rich toward God (*Luke* 12: 15–26; cf. *Ps.* 73).

(e) The knowledge of God's salvation through Jesus Christ is more profitable than wealth and more relevant to our basic needs (*Acts* 3: 6).

(f) True wealth is spiritual wealth such as pardon (*Eph.* 1: 7), peace with God (*Rom.* 5: 1), the support of God's Spirit (*John* 14: 16) and the assurance of heaven (*John* 14: 2, 3).

(g) Christians may be poor but in fact they have everything worthwhile (*II Cor.* 6: 10; *Heb.* 10: 34).

The corrective of the Bible warnings given by way of sad examples of what avarice has caused men to do: things happened to people in the past as a warning and were then written down for our instruction (*I Cor.* 10: 11).

(h) Avarice has made men turn away from following the Lord Jesus Christ (*Matt.* 19: 22).

(i) It has made them neglect human need on their doorstep (*Luke* 16: 20).

(j) It has made them think that all is well with them when the opposite has been the case (*Luke* 12: 19).

(k) It has caused men to betray friends and commit suicide (*Matt.* 26: 15, 16; *Acts* 1: 18).

(l) It has caused men to exploit those who work for them (*Jas.* 5: 4).

(m) It has caused men to tell lies and practise deceit (*Acts* 5: 3, 4, 8).

The corrective of the genuine pursuit of Christian discipleship.

(n) Our Lord's chosen lifestyle involved the loss of any financial security (*Luke* 9: 58), and He warned His disciples against all active striving for the increase of material possessions as a means of security (*Luke* 12: 15).

(o) The Christian is not to be a lover of money (*I Tim.* 3: 3), and those who assume Christian leadership must be outstanding examples of those who neither love money nor are greedy for it (*I Tim.* 3: 3, 8; *Tit.* 1: 7).

(p) The Christian is to live with the assurance that his material needs are of concern to God and he is encouraged to bring them to God day by day as he prays (*Matt.* 6: 11; *Luke* 11: 3).

(q) The Christian's aim must be contentment (*Heb.* 13: 5).

The corrective of putting wealth to use.

(r) The Lord can make us rich (*I Sam.* 2: 7), and there is no sin in wealth providing it is acquired honourably and used wisely (*II Cor.* 9: 8).

(s) If material wealth is used rightly

211

it can add to our heavenly wealth which is much more important (*Matt.* 6: 19–21; *Luke* 12: 33, 34).

(t) Used to benefit others, our possessions are a means of showing our love not only to others but to God Himself (*I John* 3: 17).

32. SLOTH

Question: What is sloth?

Answer: Sloth is laziness and wrongful inactivity, the opposite of hard work, diligence and self-discipline. It is sinful because it abuses time, wastes life and leads to neglect of our duty to God, our fellow man, and self.

1. **Sloth's characteristics.**

(a) Sloth is laziness and disinclination to action, exertion or labour; and, persevered in, it amounts to a slow death (*Prov.* 21: 25).

(b) Sloth can be manifested in many different spheres of life: in the home (*Eccl.* 10: 18), the garden (*Prov.* 24: 30, 31), daily employment (*Prov.* 20: 4), the exercise of responsibility for others (*Isa.* 56: 9–12), and in the care of one's soul (*II Pet.* 1: 5–11).

(c) *Inactivity.* Sleep is a mark of the lazy (*Prov.* 6: 11; 19: 15; 24: 33): the lazy man gets little further than a door swinging on its hinges (*Prov.* 26: 14).

(d) *Soft options.* Sloth makes a habit of the soft choice (*Prov.* 20: 4): it encourages a man to stay at home when he ought to be out and doing (*Prov.* 22: 13).

(e) *Lack of resolution.* Sloth describes the situation of the individual who for one reason or another does not have the resolution to act: for example, he lacks discipline to get down to hard work or to begin something which needs to be done (*Prov.* 6: 6, 9, 10).

(f) *Excuses.* Sloth encourages a man to make excuses for his laziness: for example, he suggests that he is not at his best in the morning (*Prov.* 26: 14) or that he cannot do anything well if he is hurried (*Prov.* 26: 15, 16).

(g) *Pessimism.* Sloth meets difficulties everywhere (*Prov.* 15: 19), and some of them are quite exaggerated and imaginary (*Prov.* 26: 13).

(h) *A world of wishing.* Sloth causes a man to live in a world of wishing (*Prov.* 21: 25, 26): he seldom moves from the will to the deed.

(i) *Dissatisfaction.* Laziness results in dissatisfaction with life (*Prov.* 13: 4).

(j) *Conceit.* Sloth is accompanied often by conceit: a lazy man will think he is more intelligent than seven men who can give reasons for their opinions (*Prov.* 26: 16).

(k) *Blind to itself.* Sloth is sometimes completely unaware of itself (*Prov.* 26: 16); the slothful man believes his own excuses (*Prov.* 22: 13), and the shirker deceives himself into believing that he is a realist (*Prov.* 26: 13).

2. **Sloth's consequences.**

(a) Laziness has its price (*Prov.* 12: 24).

(b) *Self-indulgence.* Sloth leads to physical softness, and following the dictates of natural desires (*Prov.* 20: 4).

(c) *Untidiness of life.* Sloth breeds a general untidiness of life (*Prov.* 15: 19).

(d) *Deficient convictions.* The lazy man is too lazy to develop and possess genuine convictions (*Prov.* 26: 16); he may pretend that he is simply open-minded, although laziness is the principal cause of his lack of conviction.

(e) *Apathy.* Sloth makes a man apathetic about the most necessary duties (*Prov.* 12: 27; 26: 15).

(f) *Mischief.* Sloth leads all too easily to unhelpful and harmful activity, such as meddling in other people's affairs (*II Thess.* 3: 11) and gossip (*I Tim.* 5: 13).

(g) *Unfinished tasks and lack of achievement.* Sloth makes a man miss his opportunities: for example, failing to sow at the right time, he has no harvest to gather (*Prov.* 20: 4); he puts things beyond his reach by his laziness (*Prov.* 13: 4).

(h) *Disappointment.* Disappointment is the inevitable accompaniment of laziness (*Prov.* 13: 4; 21: 25).

(i) *Gradual deterioration.* Sloth is a creeping, spreading disease (*Prov.* 19: 15), so that a little laziness quickly becomes habitual laziness (*Prov.* 6: 10, 11).

(j) *Poverty of various sorts.* Sloth can lead to various forms of poverty (*Prov.* 6: 11), especially to material need (*Prov.* 20: 4; 21: 25) and hunger (*Prov.* 19: 15; 24: 34).

(k) *Bondage or wrongful indebtedness to others.* Sloth leads a man to bondage in that he lives at the expense of others and puts himself in their debt, frequently in a way which will prove detrimental to him (*Prov.* 12: 24).

(l) *Uselessness.* Sloth is synonymous with a somewhat expensive uselessness (*Prov.* 18: 9).

(m) *Destructiveness.* The lazy man's sluggishness eventually overwhelms him (*Prov.* 24: 30–34). When God's gifts and benefits are not properly used, they may be lost (*Luke* 19: 26).

(n) *Ruin.* A lazy man's ease is his own undoing and ruin (*Prov.* 21: 25; 24: 30, 31; *Eccl.* 10: 18).

3. Sloth's sinfulness.

The abuse of time.

(a) Sloth makes a man a bad steward of time, in that time is short (*I Cor.* 7: 29), and is to be redeemed (*Col.* 4: 5).

(b) The slothful man forgets that every day is the day the Lord has made for good purposes (*Ps.* 118: 24).

The waste of life.

(c) Human existence should mean fruitful labour (*Phil.* 1: 22).

(d) Life is to be lived with zest and purposefulness (*Col.* 3: 23).

The contradiction of God's image in which man was made.

(e) God is always working (*John* 5: 17), and His Son set us an example in that He went about doing good (*Acts* 10: 38).

(f) Our Lord's earthly life was the complete opposite of sloth: His meat was to do the Father's will (*John* 4: 34).

The neglect of duty to God, our fellowman and ourselves.

(g) By sloth we neglect to serve God with the wholeheartedness which alone satisfies Him (*Deut.* 1: 36; *Josh.* 14: 8, 9, 14; *Matt.* 25: 26).

(h) By sloth we neglect to serve our fellowman with the diligence such service requires (*Luke* 10: 30–37; 16: 19–21; *II Cor.* 8: 16).

(i) By sloth we neglect our duty to ourself in that our spiritual well-being requires diligence (*II Pet.* 1: 5), as does our usefulness by the exercise of our God-given gifts (*I Pet.* 4: 9–11).

4. Correctives to sloth.

A Christian understanding.

(a) Sloth is contrary to Christian instruction (*II Thess.* 3: 6), and the

213

apostles set a deliberate example of avoiding all idleness (*II Thess.* 3: 7, 8).

(b) The Christian is not to flag in zeal but rather is to be aglow with the Spirit in his service of the Lord (*Rom.* 12: 11).

(c) The Christian is to make good use of the time between now and the Lord's second advent (*Matt.* 25: 1–30), making sure that he fulfils the ministry the Lord has given to him (*Col.* 4: 17).

(d) The Christian is to serve the Lord in newness of spirit (*Rom.* 7: 6).

A proper stewardship of time.

(e) There are many evil pressures encouraging the misuse of time, so that proper stewardship is all the more important (*Eph.* 5: 16).

(f) The shortness of life's opportunities should make us wise in the use of our time (*Ps.* 90: 12).

(g) There is a right time for everything (*Eccl.* 3: 1ff).

An appreciation of the purpose of life.

(h) Whatever our hands find to do, we should do with all our might (*Eccl.* 9: 10).

(i) We may be sure that God has a programme of good works for us to fulfil at every stage of our life (*Eph.* 2: 10).

A proper place for, and control of, sleep and relaxation.

(j) Restful sleep is a gift from God (*Ps.* 127: 2), and it is intended that sleep should be the reward of a diligent worker (*Eccl.* 5: 12).

(k) Our Lord practised retirement from activity (*Matt.* 14: 13, 23), and called upon His disciples to do the same (*Mark* 6: 31).

(l) There is a right and wrong time both for sleep and relaxation and wisdom knows the difference (*Eccl.* 10: 16, 17).

An understanding of the place of diligence in right living.

(m) The ant is an example of diligence: ants have no leader, chief, ruler, but they store up their food during the summer, getting ready for winter (*Prov.* 6: 6, 7).

(n) Diligence is necessary if we would gain understanding and wisdom (*Prov.* 17: 24).

(o) Diligence should characterise our activity no matter how uncertain we are of the future (*Eccl.* 11: 6).

(p) All the responsibilities which come to us in life are to be exercised diligently (*Rom.* 12: 8; *Col.* 3: 17).

(q) Diligence brings its own reward and wealth (*Prov.* 13: 4; 12: 27).

33. LOVE

Galatians 5: 22: "The fruit of the Spirit is love."

Question: What is the love required of us?

Answer: The love required of us is a totally unselfish love, a matter of will and action, expressed in service of the unworthy as much as of the worthy, based upon the pattern of the love set forth in the Cross of our Lord Jesus Christ.

1. God is the source of love.

(a) Love comes from God (*I John* 4: 7).

(b) God is love (*I John* 4: 8, 16), and is called "the God of love" (*II Cor.* 13: 11).

(c) Love characterises every aspect of God's relationship to His people (*Hos.* 2: 19).

(d) God has demonstrated His love to us: He sent His one and only Son into the world (*Rom.* 8: 32; *Col.* 1:

214

13)—He sent Him to be the atoning sacrifice for our sins (*John* 3: 16; *Rom.* 5: 8; *Gal.* 2: 20; *I John* 4: 9, 10).

(e) God the Father has lavished the greatest possible love upon us as believers by letting us be called God's children (*Eph.* 1: 4; *I John* 3: 1; *Jude* 1).

(f) We both know and rely upon the love God has for us (*I John* 4: 16).

(g) God has given us the Spirit of love to indwell us (*Gal.* 5: 22; *II Tim.* 1: 7).

(h) God has poured out His love into our hearts by the Holy Spirit (*Rom.* 5: 5)—His love holds us captive (*II Cor.* 5: 14).

(i) Our love for God is the response of gratitude (*Luke* 7: 47; *I John* 4: 19).

(j) We are to show to the world that we are God's children, and Christ's disciples, by the display and practice of love (*John* 13: 35; *I John* 3: 14; 4: 7).

(k) The love of Christ's people for others for His sake is something quite different from the love with which the world is familiar (*John* 13: 34).

2. The priority of love.

(a) Love has priority over spiritual gifts (*I Cor.* 13: 1–3).

(b) To be specific, love has priority over the gift of tongues (*I Cor.* 13: 1).

(c) Love has priority over the gift of prophecy (*I Cor.* 13: 2).

(d) Love has priority over the gift of knowledge and teaching (*I Cor.* 13: 2, 8)—knowledge without love so easily puffs a man up with a sense of his own importance (*I Cor.* 8: 1).

(e) Love has priority over the special gift of faith that can accomplish miracles (*I Cor.* 13: 2; cf. 12: 29; *Mark* 11: 22f).

(f) Love has priority over the special gift of generous giving (*I Cor.* 13: 3; cf. *Rom.* 12: 8).

(g) Love has priority over complete dedication to an ideal, even if that dedication involves death for its sake (*I Cor.* 13: 3).

(h) Love's priority is seen in that it is to be the aim of *all* believers, whereas this is not true of God's other gifts (*I Cor.* 14: 1; cf. 12: 27–31).

(i) Besides being part of the fruit of the Spirit, love takes first rank among that fruit (*Gal.* 5: 22; cf. *Rom.* 15: 30; *Col.* 1: 8; 3: 14).

(j) Love's priority is seen in that our Lord has given love as a new commandment (*John* 13: 34; *John* 4: 21): it is one of the first commandments we receive after we have come to faith in the Lord Jesus (*I John* 3: 23; cf. *Matt.* 28: 20).

(k) Love is the one perpetual debt we owe to one another (*Rom.* 13: 8).

(l) Its priority is all the greater when we realise that the true love we express to others is really love expressed to Jesus Christ Himself (*Matt.* 25: 33ff).

3. The foremost characteristics and activities of love.

(a) Patience (*I Cor.* 13: 4).

(b) Kindness (*I Cor.* 13: 4): love strives to be honest (*Mark* 10: 21), and in speaking the truth endeavours to do so without offence (*Eph.* 4: 15).

(c) Joy (*I Cor.* 13: 6).

(d) Forbearance (*I Cor.* 13: 7): love makes allowances for people (*Eph.* 4: 2), and covers over a multitude of sins (*I Pet.* 4: 8).

(e) Faith: the outflow of genuine faith is love (*Gal.* 5: 6; *I Thess.* 3: 6; 5: 8; *I Tim.* 1: 14).

(f) Hope (*I Cor.* 13: 7).

(g) Endurance (*I Cor.* 13: 7), after

the pattern of our Lord's love for His disciples (*John* 13: 1).

(h) Service: love is active in good works (*Heb.* 10: 24), prompt in willing service (*Gal.* 5: 13), and anxious to fulfil God's law towards a neighbour (*Rom.* 13: 10).

(i) Generosity (*II Cor.* 8: 8–12, 24): love goes out of its way to share and meet another's need (*I John* 3: 17).

(j) Constructiveness: love builds up (*I Cor.* 8: 1), unites believers (*Col.* 2: 2), and binds all other virtues together in perfect unity (*Col.* 3: 14).

(k) Reflective of God's love: love shows kindness even to its enemies (*Matt.* 5: 44, 45; *Luke* 6: 27, 35), always endeavouring to show to others the love the Lord Jesus has shown to us (*John* 13: 34).

4. The opposites of love.

(a) Jealousy (*I Cor.* 13: 4).

(b) Boastfulness (*I Cor.* 13: 4).

(c) Arrogance (*I Cor.* 13: 5).

(d) Rudeness (*I Cor.* 13: 5).

(e) Selfishness (*I Cor.* 13: 5).

(f) Irritability (*I Cor.* 13: 5).

(g) Resentment (*I Cor.* 13: 5).

(h) Maliciousness (*I Cor.* 13: 6).

(i) Hatred (*I John* 3: 11–18).

5. The consistent aims and objectives of love.

(a) Love aims at growth. (*Phil.* 1: 9), that it may abound, increase and overflow (*I Thess.* 3: 12; *II Thess.* 1: 3).

(b) Love aims at being nonselective in its objects and to love all in the same way (*Phil.* 2: 2)—Christian love loves all other Christians as brothers and other men as neighbours (*Gal.* 6: 10).

(c) Love aims at sincerity and genuineness (*Rom.* 12: 9; *II Cor.* 6: 6; *I Pet.* 1: 22; *I John* 4: 18).

(d) Love aims at consistency: its objective is to *walk* in love (*Eph.* 5: 2); it wants to be unfailing (*I Pet.* 4: 8).

(e) Love aims at building others up in the things of God (*I Cor.* 8: 1), with no thought of self-interest (*Rom.* 15: 1–4).

(f) Love's objective is to follow the pattern of Christ's love even if that means great personal sacrifice (*John* 13: 34; *Eph.* 5: 2, 25, 28).

(g) Love's objective, therefore, is to mix love with every action (*I Cor.* 16: 14).

6. The permanence of the priority of love.

(a) It is basic to all Christian ethics (*I John* 2: 7).

(b) It remains the principal test of a Christian profession (*I John* 2: 9, 10; cf. *John* 13: 35).

(c) It never ends (*I Cor.* 13: 8).

(d) When spiritual gifts pass away, and are unnecessary, love will remain (*I Cor.* 13: 8–12).

(e) Faith, hope and love are the principal priorities of the Christian life, but the greatest of these is love (*I Cor.* 13: 13).

34. JOY

Galatians 5: 22: "The fruit of the Spirit is . . . joy."

Question: What is the joy required of us?

Answer: The joy required of us is not the seldom found result of an agreeable set of circumstances but an inward joy springing up within us, irrespective of what our difficulties may be. It is a gift of God through our Lord Jesus Christ, and is one of the principal consequences of the experience of salvation.

1. Defining joy.

(a) Joy is virtually synonymous with gladness or delight (*Matt.* 5: 12; *Luke* 1: 14), and has to do with a man's heart (*Ps.* 16: 9; 33: 21; *Acts* 2: 26, 46; 14: 17) or soul or spirit (*Luke* 1: 47), that is to say, his innermost being (*John* 7: 38).

(b) God Himself is the author of the joy a man's heart or soul needs to know (*I Thess.* 3: 9), and it is His gift to believers (*Rom.* 15: 13).

(c) Christian joy has God as its object (*Ps.* 9: 2; 33: 21; 149: 1; *Joel* 2: 23)—God Himself becomes our exceeding joy (*Ps.* 43: 4).

(d) Joy focuses its attention on the contemplation of God—His power, His holiness and His mercy (*Luke* 1: 49, 50)—and on His habitual acts (*Luke* 1: 51–53); it finds its rest in God's character and attributes (*Rev.* 19: 6, 7).

(e) Christian joy is always joy in God's saving acts (*Isa.* 44: 23)—His salvation is its supreme joy (*Rev.* 19: 7).

(f) The distinctive feature of Christian joy is that it is joy in God through our Lord Jesus (*Rom.* 5: 11; cf. *I Cor.* 1: 31; *Phil.* 3: 3; 4: 4, 10)—in fact, He has been the anticipated joy of the ages in that Abraham and others rejoiced at the thought of seeing His day (*John* 8: 56; cf. *I Pet.* 1: 10–12).

(g) God the Holy Spirit conveys this joy in Christ to the individual believer's soul (*John* 7: 38; cf. *Luke* 10: 21; *Rom.* 14: 17; *I Thess.* 1: 6; *Gal.* 5: 22)—a joy which is a foretaste of heaven (*I Pet.* 4: 13; *Jude* 24).

(h) Christian joy is a *secure* joy: since it does not find its source in man, man cannot take it away (*John* 16: 22).

(i) Christian joy is a *glorious* joy for it already has something of heaven's touch upon it (*I Pet.* 1: 8).

(j) Christian joy is an *inexpressible* joy since it is incapable of declaration by words (*I Pet.* 1: 8).

(k) Christian joy is an *everlasting* joy (*Isa.* 35: 10; 51: 11).

2. Defining some of the foundations of Christian joy.

(a) Christian joy is the joy which the gospel of our Lord Jesus Christ provides (*Luke* 2: 10, 11; *I John* 1: 1–4; *I Thess.* 1: 6): for example, the joy of being found by the Heavenly Father through the Good Shepherd (*Luke* 15), or the joy of finding Christ and His kingdom as a treasure without price (*Matt.* 13: 44, 45).

(b) Christian joy is the joy of faith (*Ps.* 33: 21; *Acts* 16: 34; *Phil.* 1: 25)—faith and joy in a crucified (*Gal.* 2: 20; 6: 14), risen (*Matt.* 28: 8; *John* 16: 20, 22) and ascended Saviour (*Luke* 24: 50–53), whom we have not yet seen, but believing in Him we are filled with joy (*I Pet.* 1: 8).

(c) Christian joy is the joy of salvation (*Ps.* 51: 14; *Isa.* 35: 10; 51: 11; *Hab.* 3: 18; *Acts* 8: 39; 13: 48), with the particular joys that salvation brings of forgiveness (*Ps.* 51: 1–12; cf. *Eph.* 1: 7), reconciliation to God (*Rom.* 5: 11), justification through faith (*Rom.* 5: 1, 2), and acceptance with God (*Jude* 24).

(d) Christian joy is the joy of a new life (*Rom.* 6: 4; *II Cor.* 5: 17; cf. *Luke* 19: 6–9).

(e) Christian joy is the joy of fellowship with the Father and with His Son Jesus Christ (*I John* 1: 3, 4; cf. *John* 14: 21, 23).

(f) Christian joy is the joy of fellowship with one another (*Ps.* 133: 1;

II Cor. 2: 2) because that fellowship is based on fellowship with the Father and the Son (*I John* 1: 1–7).

(g) Christian joy is the joy of future and certain glorious prospects—of rewards (*Matt.* 5: 12; 25: 21, 23), but most of all of the hope of the glory of God (*Rom.* 5: 2) and sharing in our Saviour's triumph (*Heb.* 12: 2; cf. *Phil.* 2: 9–11; *II Tim.* 2: 11, 12).

(h) One important way of defining Christian joy is that it is Jesus Christ's joy in us (*John* 15: 11).

3. The joy our Lord Jesus Christ exhibited.

(a) He possessed a full and unique joy (*John* 15: 11; 17: 13).

(b) His joy expressed itself in praise and thanksgiving (*Luke* 10: 21).

(c) He was full of joy through the Holy Spirit (*Luke* 10: 21).

(d) His joy was to do the Father's will (*Ps.* 40: 8; *John* 4: 34).

(e) He endured the Cross, despising the shame, for the joy that was set before Him (*Heb.* 12: 2).

(f) His prayer for His disciples to His Father was that they should have the full measure of His joy within them (*John* 17: 13).

(g) Christian joy at its best, therefore, is the Lord Jesus sharing His joy with us to the full as He completely shares our life (*John* 17: 13; cf. 14: 21, 23; *Rev.* 3: 20).

4. How joy expresses itself.

(a) It expresses itself in contentment and pleasure in ordinary everyday things (*Acts* 2: 46) because God is recognised as the source and author of all that is good and all in which we can rejoice (*I Thess.* 3: 9; *I Tim.* 4: 4; 6: 17; *Jas.* 1: 17).

(b) It expresses itself in praise and thanksgiving (*Ps.* 27: 6; 33: 1; *Luke* 1: 46, 47; 10: 21; *Acts* 2: 46, 47; *Rev.* 19: 7).

(c) It expresses itself in singing (*Ps.* 5: 11; 9: 2; 84: 2; *Isa.* 12: 6; 35: 10; 44: 23; 49: 13) as the Holy Spirit aids that expression through psalms, hymns and spiritual songs (*Eph.* 5: 18, 19).

(d) It expresses itself in confidence in God and in His supplies of strength (*Neh.* 8: 10), so that Christian joy not only survives difficult circumstances but almost seems to thrive on them (*Matt.* 5: 12; *Acts* 5: 41; *Col.* 1: 11), because of the joyful perspective of faith that God uses every difficulty and obstacle to mature and perfect the development of the character of His Son in us (*Rom.* 5: 3; *Heb.* 12: 11; *Jas.* 1: 2).

(e) Joy expresses itself in confident prayer (*John* 16: 24).

(f) Joy expresses itself in Christian fellowship (*Rom.* 12: 15; *II Tim.* 1: 4; *II John* 12).

(g) Joy expresses itself in generous giving (*II Cor.* 8: 2).

5. The maintenance of the Christian's joy.

(a) There is no doubt that God intends that it should be maintained (*I Thess.* 5: 16), and outward trials (*I Pet.* 1: 6), and earthly considerations which affect ordinary human happiness (*Hab.* 3: 17, 18; *Ps.* 73: 25, 26; *Phil.* 4: 11–13; *II Cor.* 6: 10; *Heb.* 13: 5, 6) should make no difference since the One in whom our joys are found is always the same (*Heb.* 13: 8).

(b) Joy is maintained as faith grows (*Phil.* 1: 25).

(c) Joy is maintained as hope abounds (*Rom.* 15: 13): we are ever to have before us our living hope (*I Pet.* 1: 3) and the prospect of our sharing Christ's glory (*I Pet.* 4: 13).

(d) Joy is maintained as identification with the Lord Jesus is practised (*I Pet.* 4: 13; cf. *Col.* 1: 24).

(e) Joy is maintained as we continually rediscover the perfection of God's peace through the exercise of prayer (*Ps.* 34: 5; *John* 16: 24; *Rom.* 15: 13; *Phil.* 4: 6, 7).

(f) Joy is maintained as we honestly face the obstacles. Joy is maintained as we are filled with the Holy Spirit day by day (*Acts* 13: 52; *Eph.* 5: 18–20).

6. Obstacles and impediments to Christian joy.

(a) Failure to progress in the faith (*Phil.* 1: 25).

(b) Neglect of practical righteousness (*Rom.* 14: 17; cf. *Matt.* 5: 6).

(c) Omitting to seek peace in human relationships with diligence (*Rom.* 14: 17; cf. *Matt.* 5: 9).

(d) Breakdowns in loving each other as commanded by our Lord Jesus Christ (*John* 15: 10–12).

(e) Unbelief (*Phil.* 1: 25; *I Pet.* 1: 6, 7).

(f) Disobedience (*John* 15: 10, 11).

(g) The neglect of prayer (*John* 16: 24).

(h) Broken fellowship with God and His people in any way (*I John* 1: 1–7).

(i) Unconfessed sin (*Ps.* 51: 3, 8, 9, 12; *I John* 1: 1–10).

(j) All that grieves the Holy Spirit (*Eph.* 4: 30), for His ministry is the key to our experience of our Saviour's joy.

35. PEACE

Galatians 5: 22: "The fruit of the Spirit is . . . peace."

Question: What is the peace required of us?

Answer: The peace required of us is peace in the sense of peaceableness. The peaceableness, however, is the direct consequence of our discovery of peace with God through our Lord Jesus Christ, and the disposition this new relationship with God brings.

1. **The priority of peace with God, and the way to it.**

(a) The world has lost true peace because of man's sin: there is no peace for the wicked (*Isa.* 48: 22; 57: 21).

(b) Fallen rebellious man does not know the way of peace (*Rom.* 3: 17).

(c) When we lack peace, we soon forget what real happiness is like (*Lam.* 3: 17).

(d) God alone can give His creatures true peace (*Ps.* 4: 8).

(e) In order to provide peace for His creatures, God had to make the great provision of a Saviour (*Luke* 2: 9–14).

(f) No peace with God was possible without the just demands of His wrath against sins being satisfied, and God accomplished this by the death of His Son upon the Cross for our sins (*Rom.* 5: 1; *Col.* 1: 20).

(g) Christians are those who, like all men by nature, were once enemies of God, but whom God has reconciled to Himself (*Rom.* 5: 11; *Eph.* 2: 16).

(h) The Lord Jesus Christ, therefore, came into the world to guide our feet into the way of peace (*Luke* 1: 79), and His saving work is the sole foundation of our peace (*Eph.* 2: 14–17).

(i) Justified by faith, we have peace with God through our Lord Jesus Christ (*Rom.* 5: 1)—peace follows upon faith (*Mark* 5: 34; *Luke* 7: 50; *Rom.* 15: 13).

(j) Peace, therefore, is completely inseparable from the experience of

God's grace in Christ (*Gal.* 1: 3; *I Thess.* 1: 1)—it is through God's steadfast love and mercy that we can know true peace (*Jer.* 16: 5).

(k) Peace is God's free gift to His people (*Num.* 6: 26), and He delights in their enjoyment of peace (*Ps.* 35: 27; 147: 14).

(l) God's peace is like a river (*Isa.* 48: 18); it is a peace which passes understanding (*Phil.* 4: 7).

(m) The Lord Jesus Christ, our Saviour and Lord, is the Guarantor and Guardian of our peace (*Isa.* 9: 6), and He can give us peace at all times and in many different ways (*II Thess.* 3: 16).

(n) His peace is quite different from that which the world provides, for it can quiet troubled hearts and dismiss anxious fears (*John* 14: 27).

(o) Obedience to God, and in particular to His commandments, is a key to the maintenance of our experience of God's peace (*Ps.* 119: 165; *Isa.* 48: 18).

(p) The active pursuit of righteousness is a second condition of the maintenance of our peace (*Ps.* 85: 10; *Rom.* 12: 17, 18).

(q) The third condition is maintained fellowship with God (*Ps.* 73: 21–28), especially as that fellowship expresses itself in prayer (*Phil.* 4: 6, 7).

(r) The peace we know with God, and from God, brings the obligation to know too the peace between man and man which was one of the purposes for which our Lord Jesus Christ died (*Eph.* 2: 14).

2. The peaceableness which flows from finding our peace with God and the peace He gives.

(a) When we lack peace with God, and thus peace within, we also lack peace in our personal relationships (*Jas.* 4: 1–4).

(b) Finding in our Lord Jesus peace with God, however, we also find a meeting place and concord with one another, whatever may have been our divisions of race, colour, class or circumstances beforehand (*Eph.* 2: 14).

(c) Peace or peaceableness is part of the outflow of spiritual and eternal life (*Rom.* 8: 6).

(d) Peaceableness is a consequence of having the salt of the gospel in our life (*Mark* 9: 50)—all our relationships are significantly affected for the good (*Rom.* 14: 17, 19).

(e) Peaceableness is the outworking of love (*Col.* 3: 14, 15; *I Thess.* 5: 13), and love is not easily provoked (*I Cor.* 13: 5).

(f) Reconciled to God, we are able to benefit from God's heavenly wisdom, and peaceableness is a fundamental aspect of that wisdom (*Jas.* 1: 5; 3: 17, 18).

(g) Reconciliation to God brings a commitment to righteousness (*I Pet.* 2: 24), and peace is the normal fruit and gift from God of persevering in doing the right thing (*Rom.* 14: 17; *Jas.* 3: 18; cf. *Isa.* 32: 17).

(h) Reconciliation to God is synonymous with membership of God's family, and God carefully disciplines the characters of His spiritual children to make them more peaceable (*Heb.* 12: 11).

(i) Filled with the Spirit (*Eph.* 5: 17)—a further great gift of reconciliation—we develop His fruit of peaceableness in our characters (*Gal.* 5: 22; *Rom.* 8: 6).

(j) Peaceableness is a fundamental aspect of the kingdom of God (*Rom.* 14: 17), so much so that the Lord

Jesus said, "Blessed are the peacemakers" (*Matt.* 5: 9).

3. The expression of peaceableness.

(a) Peaceableness expresses itself in the determination to maintain a clear conscience (*I Pet.* 3: 10–16), and this resolve involves the regular and genuine pursuit of practical righteousness (*Heb.* 12: 14)—peacemakers so sow peace that they raise a harvest of righteousness (*Jas.* 3: 18).

(b) Peaceableness expresses itself in the active pursuit of good works (*Jas.* 3: 17), even in the face of opposition from those who regard themselves as our enemies (*Matt.* 5: 43–48; *I Pet.* 2: 20; 3: 13, 14).

(c) Peaceableness expresses itself in forbearance (*II Tim.* 2: 22, 24) mercifulness (*Jas.* 3: 17) and gentleness (*I Pet.* 3: 15; *Tit.* 3: 2), especially where correction has to be given by us (*II Tim.* 2: 22, 25).

(d) Peaceableness expresses itself in courtesy (*Tit.* 3: 2), considerateness (*Jas.* 3: 17), kindliness (*II Tim.* 2: 22, 24), and respect to all without discrimination or prejudice (*I Pet.* 3: 15).

(e) Peaceableness expresses itself in the active pursuit of peace, even if it means relinquishing our rights (*Gen.* 13: 8; 21: 22–24)—although that does not mean pretending problems do not exist but rather dealing with them peaccably (*Gen.* 21: 25ff).

(f) Peaceableness expresses itself by coming between contending parties and trying to make peace (*I Sam.* 25: 18–35; *Matt.* 5: 9).

(g) Peaceableness expresses itself particularly in the words and language we employ (*Prov.* 18: 6, 7), seeking that its words should be righteous (*Prov.* 16: 13), wise (*Prov.* 25: 11, 12), calm (*Prov.* 15: 1; 17: 27), and sometimes very few (*Prov.* 11: 12, 13).

(h) Peaceableness expresses itself in the home (*Prov.* 17: 1), for a lack of peace there brings misery (*I Sam.* 1: 3–7).

(i) Peaceableness in marriage has as its secret the concentration of each partner upon his or her duties to the other rather than what he or she may expect from the other as his or her rights (*Eph.* 5: 22, 25).

(j) Peaceableness for parents means being sensitive and realistic in their demands and expectations of their children (*Eph.* 6: 4).

(k) Peaceableness within the church fellowship means striving always for peace and agreement (*Col.* 3: 15; *I Thess.* 5: 13; *Heb.* 12: 14).

4. Appreciating peaceableness by identifying its opposites.

(a) Envy (*Prov.* 14: 30; *Gal.* 5: 21; *I Tim.* 6: 4; *Jas.* 3: 14, 16, 17).

(b) Jealousy (*Mark* 10: 37, 41; *II Cor.* 12: 20; *Gal.* 5: 20; *Jas.* 3: 16, 17).

(c) Pride and conceit (*Gen.* 4: 5; *Ps.* 131: 1; *Jas.* 4: 1–6).

(d) Arrogance (*II Cor.* 12: 20).

(e) Selfish ambition (*Jas.* 3: 14, 16, 17).

(f) False loyalties (*I Cor.* 1: 10–12).

(g) Uncontrolled desires (*Jas.* 4: 1, 2), such as coveting (*Jas.* 4: 2).

(h) Hatred (*Gal.* 5: 20).

(i) Uncontrolled behaviour, especially that brought about by drunkenness (*Esth.* 1: 12; *Gal.* 5: 21; *I Tim.* 3: 3).

(j) The desire for vengeance (*Esth.* 2: 21).

(k) Harshness (*Prov.* 15: 1).

(l) Evil-speaking, gossip and malicious talk (*II Cor.* 12: 20; *I Tim.* 6: 4; *Tit.* 3: 2; *I Pet.* 3: 10–12).

(m) Unhealthy interest in controversies and arguments (*I Tim.* 6: 4; *II Tim.* 2: 23).

(n) Quarrelling (*I Cor.* 1: 11; *II Cor.* 12: 20; *I Tim.* 3: 3; 6: 4; *Tit.* 3: 2).

(o) Factions, dissensions, and conspiracy (*Esth.* 2: 21; *II Cor.* 12: 20; *Gal.* 5: 20).

(p) Some activities lead to peace, and others do not (*Luke* 19: 42; *Rom.* 14: 19): those which lead to peace are to be pursued, and those which do not are to be fled from without debate (*II Tim.* 2: 22).

5. The fundamental importance of peaceableness.

(a) God is slow to anger (*Jonah* 4: 2), and His spiritual children should be the same (*Matt.* 5: 9).

(b) Peaceableness characterised the life and ministry of our Saviour (*Zech.* 9: 9; *Matt.* 21: 3; *John* 12: 14, 15), and His mind is to be in us (*Phil.* 2: 5), and His example ever before us (*I Pet.* 2: 21).

(c) God the Holy Spirit would have peaceableness as one of His pre-eminent fruits in our life (*Gal.* 5: 22).

(d) Our experience of spiritual joy is intimately linked with our pursuit of righteousness and peace (*Rom.* 14: 17).

(e) Furthermore, a tranquil mind gives physical health (*Prov.* 14: 30).

(f) Peaceableness is one of the conditions of God's presence and of His blessing upon us (*II Cor.* 13: 11)—and often we shall find Him making up to us in spiritual peace what we may appear to have lost in preserving neighbourly peace (*Gen.* 13: 14–18; *I Pet.* 3: 9).

(g) The body of Christ, the Church, can function properly only as it knows peace (*I Cor.* 14: 33): without peace there can be no mutual edification (*Rom.* 14: 19).

(h) Peaceableness helps to bind God's people together in unity (*Eph.* 4: 3).

(i) Peaceableness is sometimes used by God to win surprising victories, victories which might not have been won in any other way (*Prov.* 25: 15; *I Sam.* 24: 17; *I Pet.* 3: 15, 16).

(j) Peaceableness is a matter for active pursuit in the Christian life (*I Pet.* 3: 12).

36. PATIENCE

Galatians 5: 22: "The fruit of the Spirit is . . . patience."

Question: What is the patience required of us?

Answer: Of the two Greek words translated often as patience, that chosen to describe this aspect of the fruit of the Spirit is the one used of God's patience, forbearance and steadfastness. It particularly expresses restraint in the face of opposition. Our patience, like God's, is to be the outflow of love, shown to everyone, and demonstrated most of all in forgiveness. The patience God has shown to us is to be reflected directly in the patience we show to others.

1. **God is patient.**

(a) Patience was part of God's amazing revelation of His character to His people in the Old Testament (*Ex.* 34: 6; *Num.* 14: 18); it was a fact of certain knowledge among them (*Jonah* 4: 2).

(b) The same truth concerning God's patience is presented to us in the New Testament (*Rom.* 9: 22; *I Tim.* 1: 16; *I Pet.* 3: 20; *II Pet.* 3:

15): He is rich in patience (*Rom.* 2: 4).

(c) God's patience has been seen throughout the history of mankind, most of all in His dealings with Israel (*Judg.* 3: 7, 9, 12, 15; *Rom.* 10: 21), in spite of all her spiritual adultery and backsliding (*Hos.* 2: 14–23; *Amos* 4: 6–11).

(d) God's patience is regularly linked with His constancy (*Num.* 14: 18; *Ps.* 86: 15; *Jonah* 4: 2), goodness and forbearance (*Ex.* 34: 6; *Rom.* 2: 4).

(e) God's patience is not in opposition to His righteous wrath: His patience means that His wrath's operation is postponed until something takes place in man which justifies the postponement; if, however, a change does not take place, then wrath executes its judgment (*Num.* 14: 18).

(f) God's patience allows the development of either obedience or disobedience, resulting either in deliverance or destruction (*I Pet.* 3: 20); and the potential of wrath necessarily increases with the patience shown (*Rom.* 9: 22).

(g) God's patience is seen in that He waits to be gracious to us (*Isa.* 30: 18).

(h) It is plain, therefore, that God's patience should lead men to repentance (*Rom.* 2: 4), and they should be urged not to abuse God's patience and the opportunity it gives for finding salvation (*II Pet.* 3: 15).

(i) We may find God's patience difficult to understand, particularly when the implementation of His justice seems to be delayed (*Jer.* 15: 15); one of the reasons for this problem in our minds is our very human concept of time (*II Pet.* 3: 8).

(j) We are called to be like God in all His attributes which can be shared by us, and this includes, therefore, His patience (*Matt.* 5: 48).

2. God has given us examples of patience.

(a) The foremost example is our Lord Jesus Christ who displayed amazing patience with His disciples: in their slowness to understand (*Mark* 4: 10–20); in their earthly mindedness (*Mark* 10: 35–45), and in their desertion of Him in His hour of need (*Matt.* 26: 56; *Mark* 16: 7; *John* 11: 15–19).

(b) The supreme example of His patience was His conduct in His trial and crucifixion (*Matt.* 26: 59–68; 27: 29–50; *I Pet.* 2: 21–25).

(c) His continuing patience is seen in His present dealings with men: Paul knew himself to be an example of Christ's waiting patience which bore with him as a persecutor until it won him over—a waiting patience which continues towards men to this day (*I Tim.* 1: 13–16).

(d) Abraham (*Gen.* 22: 17, 18; *Heb.* 6: 15), Job (*James* 5: 11), the prophets (*Jas.* 5: 10), and so many of our spiritual forefathers are examples to us of patience (*Heb.* 11: 13); and the things that happened to them are object lessons to help us (*I Cor.* 10: 11).

(e) The example of patience the apostle Paul was to Timothy helps us also (*II Tim.* 3: 20).

3. The patience God has shown to us is the patience we are to show to others.

(a) The pattern of God's dealings with us is to be the pattern of our dealings with others (*Luke* 6: 36; *Matt.* 5: 7).

(b) Our patience must most of all be shown in forgiveness (*Matt.* 18: 23–35).

223

(c) Our patience must be the expression of love (*I Cor.* 13: 4).

(d) Our patience is to be evident in our relationships to everyone, whether we are warning, encouraging or supporting them (*I Thess.* 5: 14).

4. The necessity of patience.

(a) It is essential to a life worthy of our calling as Christians, enabling us to preserve the unity the Spirit gives, for patience encourages that peace which binds us together (*Eph.* 4: 1–3; *Col.* 1: 11).

(b) It is an essential part of the Christian's spiritual "dress" or "clothing" (*Col.* 3: 12).

(c) It is a necessary condition of claiming God's promises (*Heb.* 6: 12).

(d) It is a priority in the teaching of and preaching to others (*II Tim.* 4: 2).

(e) It is a key to victory in the battle against the world, the flesh and the devil (*I Pet.* 2: 11; 5: 8–10; see the repeated use of the verb "stand" in *Eph.* 6: 11, 13, 14).

(f) It is an essential part of the Christian's testimony, when persecuted or unjustly treated, that he patiently refuses to retaliate (*I Pet.* 2: 18–23; 3: 13, 14).

5. The rewards of patience.

(a) It can bring people to an experience of salvation (*II Pet.* 3: 15).

(b) It gains its end in fruitfulness (*Jas.* 5: 7).

(c) It adds beauty to character (*Gal.* 5: 22).

(d) It marks us out as true servants of God (*II Cor.* 6: 6).

6. The achievement of patience.

(a) First and foremost, we must focus our attention upon the example God has given us in His Son Jesus Christ (*Heb.* 12: 1–3).

(b) We should pray for patience, being realistic in facing up to the challenges to our patience (*Col.* 1: 11).

(c) We are to make it a deliberate objective (*Col.* 3: 12).

(d) As we grow in grace, and in the knowledge of our Lord Jesus Christ (*II Pet.* 3: 18), so the fruit of the Spirit will grow, which includes patience.

37. KINDNESS

Galatians 5: 22: "The fruit of the Spirit is . . . kindness."

Question: What is the kindness required of us?

Answer: The kindness required of us is the outflow of love in goodness and forgiveness, after the pattern of God's kindness to us. Such kindness is sympathetic, down-to-earth in practical concern and help, and uninfluenced by either the merits or gratitude of those to whom it is extended.

1. The nature of kindness.

(a) Kindness is linked with tenderheartedness (*Eph.* 4: 32); it follows upon compassion in the spiritual garments believers are to wear (*Col.* 3: 12).

(b) Kindness is love in action (*Eph.* 2: 7; 4: 32; *Tit.* 3: 4).

(c) Kindness is the reaction of love with goodness towards those who may ill-treat it (*I Cor.* 13: 4): it is goodness in action (*II Cor.* 6: 6).

(d) Kindness is love in practice, doing good to others (*Luke* 6: 35).

(e) Kindness is almost synonymous with forgiveness (*Eph.* 4: 32; *Col.* 3: 12, 13).

(f) Kindness is uninfluenced by the

gratitude or ingratitude of those to whom it is extended; it does not stop when it gets no return (*Luke* 6: 32–35).

2. The declared opposites of kindness.

(a) Bitterness (*Eph.* 4: 31, 32).

(b) Anger (*Eph.* 4: 31, 32).

(c) Insults (*Eph.* 4: 31, 32; *I Pet.* 2: 1–3).

(d) Hateful feelings of any sort (*Eph.* 4: 31, 32).

(e) Lying (*I Pet.* 2: 1–3).

(f) Hypocrisy (*I Pet.* 2: 1–3).

(g) Jealousy (*I Pet.* 2: 1–3).

3. The fundamental example of kindness.

(a) God Himself is the supreme example of kindness: His kindness never fails (*Ps.* 118: 1–14, 29), and we are instructed to consider it well (*Rom.* 11: 22).

(b) God is rich in kindness, a truth displayed in His tolerance and patience to the ungrateful and the wicked (*Rom.* 2: 4; *Luke* 6: 35).

(c) God's kindness is seen in the way in which God delays the Judgment, giving men an opportunity for repentance (*Rom.* 2: 4).

(d) Salvation is the fruit of God's kindness exercised through our Lord Jesus Christ (*Tit.* 3: 4): not only has He saved us from the punishment of sin but He has raised us up with Christ and made us to sit with Him in the heavenly places (*Eph.* 2: 4–6).

(e) Furthermore, in the ages to come, He is going to show the immeasurable riches of His grace towards us in Christ Jesus, so that Christians are examples of how very, very rich God's kindness is (*Eph.* 2: 7).

(f) Everything the Lord Jesus Christ said and did revealed the kindness of God: when He said, "My yoke is easy," He used the adjective derived from the noun "kindness" used in Galatians 5: 22. The burdens He puts upon us when we become His disciples are never too much for us; to serve Him is to find ourselves experiencing His kindness (*Matt.* 11: 30).

(g) God's kindness does not come to an end (*Ruth* 2: 20).

(h) Men should not presume, however, upon God's kindness (*Rom.* 2: 4), for His kindness provides no evidence that He will not punish the guilty (*Rom.* 11: 22); rather God's kindness should lead men to repentance (*Rom.* 2: 4).

4. The outworkings of kindness (*Luke* 6: 35).

(a) Kindness means loving our enemies, and doing good to those who hate us (*Luke* 6: 27).

(b) Kindness involves blessing those who curse us, and praying for those who mistreat us (*Luke* 6: 28).

(c) Kindness means that if anyone hits us on one cheek, we let him hit the other one too; if someone takes our coat, then we let him have our shirt as well (*Luke* 6: 29).

(d) Kindness finds expression by giving to everyone who asks us for something, and when someone takes what is ours, not asking for it back (*Luke* 6: 30).

(e) Kindness works by doing to others just what we want them to do for us (*Luke* 6: 31).

(f) Kindness is not loving only the people who love us but loving our enemies and doing good to them, lending and expecting nothing back (*Luke* 6: 32–36).

(g) Kindness refrains from judging others (*Luke* 6: 37).

(h) Kindness is marked by generous giving (*Luke* 6: 38).

(i) Where kindness is at work, after the pattern of our Lord Jesus Christ, people are not chafed, irked or galled unnecessarily; burdens are not unsympathetically placed upon them (*Matt.* 11: 30).

(j) Where kindness is really at work, its expressions are the same to all men, even when the person showing kindness may himself be under strain (*II Cor.* 6: 6).

5. The necessity of kindness in the Christian.

(a) God requires kindness to others: it is a condition of pleasing Him, and of walking humbly with Him (*Micah* 6: 8), and without it the Lord has a controversy with us (*Hos.* 4: 1).

(b) Kindness is a proof of our new birth, in the possession of the divine nature, for in genuine kindness we reveal the same attitude as our heavenly Father (*Luke* 6: 27, 35).

(c) Kindness is a characteristic of the new man which is renewed in knowledge after the image of its creator (*Col.* 3: 10); it is an essential part of the spiritual clothing of God's people to be put on deliberately (*Col.* 3: 12).

(d) Kindness is one of the marks of God's servants (*II Cor.* 6: 6).

(e) Kindness also has a converting power (*Rom.* 2: 4; *Luke* 22: 61, 62; cf. *I Pet.* 2: 12).

(f) The measure of kindness we use towards others is the one we may expect God to use towards us (*Luke* 6: 38).

38. GOODNESS

Galatians 5: 22: "The fruit of the Spirit is . . . goodness."

Question: What is the goodness required of us?

Answer: When we affirm that God is good, we are declaring that He is all that He as God ought to be. The goodness required of us is that we should always strive to live as the members of God's family ought to live, with high moral standards and the active practice of good works. The basic content of the Christian's life is to be goodness.

1. God's goodness.

(a) God is good (*II Chron.* 30: 18; *Ps.* 86: 5; 106: 1; 107: 1; 118: 1), and He alone is worthy of that description (*Matt.* 19: 17; *Mark* 10: 18).

(b) His goodness is seen in that His steadfast love endures for ever (*I Chron.* 16: 34).

(c) His goodness is displayed in His creation (*Gen.* 1: 4, 10, 12, 18, 21, 25, 31; *I Tim.* 4: 4).

(d) His goodness is demonstrated in all His works (*Ps.* 104: 24–31; 119: 68; *Acts* 14: 17).

(e) His goodness is witnessed by His gifts (*Neh.* 9: 20; *Ps.* 85: 12; *Luke* 1: 53; 11: 13; *Jas.* 1: 17).

(f) The commandments and directions God gives are good (*Ps.* 119: 39; *Mark* 3: 4; *Rom.* 7: 12; *Heb.* 6: 5).

(g) God's promises are good (*I Kings* 8: 56), not least in the salvation (*Heb.* 9: 11; 10: 1) and hope (*II Thess.* 2: 16) He grants to those who believe on His Son Jesus Christ.

(h) God's message to mankind in Jesus Christ is *good* news (*Rom.* 10: 15).

(i) God's will and purposes for our lives are good (*Ps.* 84: 11; *Rom.* 12: 2) and the work He begins in Christians' lives at their new birth is "a good work" (*Phil.* 1: 6).

(j) Even when God needs to discipline Christians it is always for their good (*Ps.* 119: 67, 71; *Heb.* 12: 10).

(k) There is no limit to God's goodness and the good He gives to His spiritual children in Christ (*Rom.* 8: 32; *Eph.* 1: 3).

(l) Goodness finds its model and example in our Lord Jesus Christ (*I Pet* 2: 19–24), who is the visible image of the invisible God (*Col.* 1: 15): He went about doing good (*Acts* 10: 38).

2. God's goodness teaches us truth about ourselves.

(a) Goodness is the test of a man's life (*Matt.* 7: 15–20; *Luke* 6: 43–45), and God judges everyone by the same standard of goodness (*Rom.* 2: 10, 11).

(b) By nature no one consistently does good (*Rom.* 3: 12): evil things rather than good things are the more natural fruit of human lives (*Matt.* 12: 34).

(c) The more we know ourselves, the more we know that good does not naturally dwell in us (*Rom.* 7: 18).

(d) Even though we may possess the desire to do good, we are not able to do it; instead of doing the good we want, we find ourselves doing the evil we do not want to do (*Rom.* 7: 18, 19).

(e) The call God gives to salvation, therefore, is not based upon man's goodness but entirely upon God's grace (*Rom.* 9: 11, 12; *Eph.* 2: 8): God has shown how much He loves us in that while we were still sinners the Lord Jesus Christ died for us (*Rom.* 5: 7, 8).

(f) God's goodness should make us continually thankful (*Ps.* 118: 29), so that we recognise that the only

proper response to it is the offering of ourselves to Him (*Rom.* 12: 1).

(g) Real goodness begins when we hear God's message of salvation, retain it in a good and obedient heart, and persist until fruit is born (*Luke* 8: 8, 15)—the fruit of the Spirit which includes goodness (*Gal.* 5: 22, 23).

3. Defining goodness.

(a) Goodness is to do justice, love kindness and to walk humbly with God (*Micah* 6: 8).

(b) Goodness is genuine obedience to the law of God (*Ps.* 34: 14ff; 37: 27).

(c) Goodness is the outflow of love (*Gal.* 5: 22; *I Cor.* 13).

(d) Goodness is the putting aside of our own will and pleasure so as to please our neighbour for his good in order to build him up in the faith (*Rom.* 15: 2).

(e) Goodness is the opposite of evil (*I Thess.* 5: 15; *I Pet.* 3: 11; *III John* 11), disobedience (*Tit.* 1: 16), selfishness (*Rom.* 2: 7, 8) and hypocrisy (*Jas.* 3: 17).

(f) Goodness always helps rather than harms (*Luke* 6: 9; *Acts* 9: 36), delights in giving rather than receiving (*Matt.* 7: 11; *Acts* 20: 35; *II Cor.* 9: 8), and concerns itself with the need that requires to be met rather than with the merits of the person in need (*Luke* 6: 33; *Gal.* 6: 10).

(g) Real goodness is consistent goodness (*Tit.* 2: 10), flowing from a life full of the Holy Spirit and of faith (*John* 7: 38, 39; *Acts* 11: 24).

4. Goodness in us is the fruit of the Spirit.

(a) The word translated "goodness" in "the fruit of the Spirit" (*Gal.* 5: 22) conveys the idea of moral excellence and belongs with righteousness and

227

truth to "the fruit of light" (*Eph.* 5: 9).

(b) The fruits of the Christian life are all fruits of goodness (*Matt.* 7: 17–20).

(c) Born again by God's Spirit into God's family, we find within ourselves new desires after goodness (*II Thess.* 1: 11).

(d) Goodness is a reflection of our heavenly Father's character being reproduced in us (*Matt.* 5: 45; *III John* 4, 11).

(e) Practical goodness is part of the transformation to be expected of converted men and women (*Eph.* 4: 28).

(f) Christians should be full of goodness (*Rom.* 15: 14), being wise about what is good but innocent about what is evil (*Rom.* 16: 19).

(g) Goodness is essentially living and behaving in the world as true servants of God (*I Pet.* 2: 15, 16).

(h) One of its principal demonstrations is in the general principle of submission to others: to civil authorities (*I Pet.* 2: 13–17), to employers (*I Pet.* 2: 18–25), of wives to husbands (*I Pet.* 3: 1–6), of children to parents (*Eph.* 6: 1, 2), and to one another (*Eph.* 5: 21; *I Pet.* 3: 8).

(i) Goodness responds to opposition and suffering with patience (*I Pet.* 2: 20), and does not allow anything to put it off from pursuing the right course (*I Pet.* 3: 6).

(j) Goodness on the part of Christians is God's chosen answer to men's unjust opposition to Christian witness (*I Pet.* 2: 15; 3: 1ff).

(k) Our lives are meant to bear fruit in every good work (*Col.* 1: 10).

5. **Goodness and good works.**

(a) True religion and good works go together (*I Tim.* 2: 10; *Matt.* 5: 16).

(b) Good works have no place in the obtaining of salvation (*Eph.* 2: 9; *Tit.* 3: 5), but they are a principal evidence of the experience of salvation (*Jas.* 2: 17): we are born again to do good works God has planned (*Eph.* 2: 10).

(c) Works cannot be divorced from words (*II Thess.* 2: 17), and goodness manifests itself in speech (*Matt.* 12: 34; *Luke* 6: 45; *II Thess.* 2: 17)— speech that builds up (*Eph.* 4: 29) and avoids speaking evil (*Tit.* 3: 1, 2).

(d) Goodness never pays back wrong for wrong but always tries to be kind (*I Thess.* 5: 15), not only to fellow-Christians but to everyone (*Gal.* 6: 10).

(e) Our income is intended to enable us to be rich in good works (*I Tim.* 6: 17, 18), so that there should be a harvest of good works in our lives as we wisely use what God has given (*II Cor.* 9: 8–10).

(f) Goodness is displayed in all kinds of good deeds such as bringing up children well, showing hospitality, doing menial tasks for others, helping those in trouble, and being available to do good whenever the opportunity presents itself (*I Tim.* 5: 10; *Tit.* 3: 1).

(g) Good works do not have to be forced upon goodness; rather they are spontaneous and willing (*Philem.* 14).

(h) God has provided the Scriptures so that by the instruction they provide we may be thoroughly equipped for every good work (*II Tim.* 3: 17), for the wisdom they impart from above ensures a harvest of good deeds (*Jas.* 3: 17).

(i) God provides strength and encouragement to persevere in good works (*II Thess.* 2: 17; *Heb.* 13: 20, 21).

(j) Good works honour God: they make the teaching about God our Saviour attractive in the eyes of the world (*Tit.* 2: 10), and they compel men to praise our Father in heaven (*Matt.* 5: 16).

(k) It is not surprising, therefore, that the Christian should be eager to do good (*I Pet.* 3: 13).

39. FAITHFULNESS

Question: What is the faithfulness required of us?

Answer: Faithfulness is our proper response to God's faithfulness, and an outworking of living faith in Jesus Christ. Faithfulness is loyalty, reliability and dependability. It expresses itself in unswerving loyalty to God at any cost. It means fulfilling our duties and responsibilities to others, irrespective of how convenient or easy these obligations may be. Faithfulness is the principal virtue our Lord Jesus Christ chooses to reward.

1. **Faithfulness is an outstanding feature of God's character** (*Isa.* 49: 7; *I Cor.* 1: 9; 10: 13).

(a) He is the faithful God who keeps covenant and steadfast love with those who love Him and keep His commandments (*Deut.* 7: 9).

(b) He cannot lie (*Num.* 23: 19; *Tit.* 1: 2).

(c) His faithfulness is unfailing (*II Tim.* 2: 13), great (*Lam.* 3: 23) and incomparable (*Ps.* 89: 8).

(d) His faithfulness is determined (*Ps.* 89: 33), immeasurable (*Ps.* 36: 5), certain (*Ps.* 89: 2; *Isa.* 54: 10), and everlasting (*Ps.* 119: 90).

(e) His faithfulness is revealed in nature's order and balance (*Gen.* 8: 22; *Jer.* 33: 20–22).

(f) His faithfulness shows itself in the fulfilment of His promises to His people (*Josh.* 21: 43; *Ezek.* 37: 11–14; *Isa.* 25: 1).

(g) His faithfulness has been gloriously expressed to us in our Lord Jesus Christ (*John* 1: 14; 13: 1; 14: 6; *Rev.* 19: 11).

2. **Faithfulness is an essential aspect of Christian character.**

(a) It is part of the fruit of the Spirit, and that fruit is the sum of Christian character (*Gal.* 5: 22, 23).

(b) Character is the test of a man's religion (*Matt.* 7: 15–20; *Luke* 6: 43–45), and is the one thing we cannot borrow, lend or escape for it is the real "us" (*Prov.* 9: 12; cf. 14: 10).

(c) Faithfulness arises from what a man is through and through—it does not occur accidentally (*Luke* 16: 10).

(d) The general principle holds true with regard to faithfulness that as a man thinks in his heart so he is (*Prov.* 23: 7).

(e) Faithfulness needs to be gloried in, and meditated upon in the heart, if it is to show itself in conduct (*Prov.* 3: 3).

(f) Faithfulness should extend to every aspect of life (*I Tim.* 3: 11).

(g) The person who is faithful in very little will be found faithful also in much (*Luke* 16: 10).

(h) Without faithfulness our characters are deficient of an essential quality (*Jas.* 1: 2–4).

(i) Christian character, however, is not produced in a moment (*Rom.* 5: 4): many of the testings which God permits, He overrules so as to develop faithfulness on our part (*Jas.* 1: 2ff).

3. **Faithfulness has relevance to our speech and our general use of words.**

(a) Faithful speech is honest, direct, and unambiguous (*Matt.* 5: 37);

when we say either "Yes" or "No" we must mean what we say (*II Cor.* 1: 18).

(b) Faithful speech is strictly truthful and avoids exaggeration (*Jas.* 5: 12).

(c) Faithful speech is the opposite of lying, false witness and evasive speech (*Prov.* 14: 5; *Hos.* 4: 1, 2).

(d) Faithful speech rebukes when such is necessary, but with kindness and love (*Ps.* 141: 5; *Prov.* 27: 6).

(e) It is not enough to protest loyalty with our lips and then to deny it by conduct (*Prov.* 20: 6).

(f) Since it is characteristic of God to be always faithful to His promises, so must we be faithful to the promises we make (*Heb.* 10: 23; *Matt.* 5: 48; *II Cor.* 1: 17–20).

4. Faithfulness is to mark our relationship to God.

(a) Genuine faith in God must always lead to faithfulness to Him (*Hab.* 2: 4).

(b) God requires our total loyalty (*Luke* 16: 13), and our foremost expression of faithfulness must be to Him (*Acts* 11: 23).

(c) Faithfulness itself, even more than the fruits of faithfulness, is that for which God looks (*Matt.* 24: 20–23), and if it is absent He has a controversy with us (*Hos.* 4:

(d) Christians are called of God to show faithfulness to Jesus Christ His Son (*Eph.* 1: 1; *Col.* 1: 2), a faithfulness which must be steadfast and continuing (*Acts* 11: 23).

(e) We are to be faithful in doing the will of God no matter what the obstacles (*Heb.* 10: 36), even in the face of death (*Rev.* 2: 10).

(f) Our faithfulness is precious to God (*I Pet.* 1: 7), and it causes us to find favour and good repute in His sight (*Prov.* 3: 4).

(g) Faithfulness is also a condition of our growing in the knowledge of God (*Hos.* 2: 20).

(h) Our faithfulness to God is very much influenced by our appreciation of His faithfulness to us (*Heb.* 10: 23).

(i) Fortunately, our occasions of faithlessness do not nullify the faithfulness of God (*Rom.* 3: 3; *II Tim.* 2: 13); God is willing to heal our faithlessness when we return to Him in repentance (*Hos.* 14: 4).

5. Faithfulness is to mark all our other relationships.

A. Husbands and wives.

(a) **Husbands** should be completely faithful to their wives (*Prov.* 5: 15–20; *I Tim.* 3: 2, 12), a faithfulness which should extend to their thoughts (*Ex.* 20: 17; *Matt.* 5: 27, 28).

(b) A faithful husband loves his wife as he loves his own body (*Eph.* 5: 28), and finds his satisfaction in her (*Prov.* 5: 15).

(c) A faithful husband treats his wife with consideration, bestowing honour upon her as the weaker vessel (*I Pet.* 3: 7).

(d) A faithful husband strives to love his wife as Christ loves the Church (*Eph.* 5: 25ff).

(e) **Wives** are to be consistently faithful to their husbands' interests (*Prov.* 31: 12).

(f) A faithful wife helps her husband play his part in the community (*Prov.* 31: 23).

(g) A faithful wife can be completely trusted by her husband (*Prov.* 31: 11), and her affection for him will fill him with delight at all times (*Prov.* 5: 19).

(h) A faithful wife is her husband's pride and joy (*Prov.* 12: 4).

B. Parents and children.

(a) Faithful **parents** recognise that their children must never have precedence over discipleship of the Lord Jesus (*Mark* 10: 29; *Luke* 18: 29; *Matt.* 19: 29; cf. *I Sam.* 2: 20, 29; *Heb.* 11: 17).

(b) Faithful parents are careful in the training of their children, recognising that the course their children adopt in later life depends upon the training they initially receive at home (*Prov.* 22: 6), and so they give their children instruction and good precepts from their earliest age (*Prov.* 4: 1–4).

(c) Faithful parents diligently discipline their children because they love them (*Prov.* 13: 24).

(d) Faithful parents not only teach their children the way of wisdom but they lead them in the paths of uprightness (*Prov.* 4: 11), conferring upon them for life the benefit of godly example (*Prov.* 20: 7).

(e) Faithful parents teach their children about the past dealings of God with His people, appreciating their responsibility for the generations which are to follow (*Ps.* 78: 5, 6).

(f) Faithful **children** obey their parents on the strength of the commandment, "Honour your father and mother" (*Eph.* 6: 2; *Ex.* 20: 12).

(g) Faithful children listen to their father and do not despise their mother when she is old (*Prov.* 23: 22).

(h) Faithful children do not regard the property of their parents lightly, and avoid the snare of imagining that what is wrong outside the family is permissible within it (*Prov.* 28: 24).

(i) Faithful children appreciate that they have duties as well as rights: they are careful, therefore, in their treatment of their parents, and make necessary provision for them (*Prov.* 19: 26).

C. **Employers and employees.**

(a) Faithful **employers** do not withhold proper wages (*Jas.* 5: 4).

(b) Faithful employers are conscientious and responsible towards those who serve them as they expect them to be in turn towards them (*Eph.* 6: 9).

(c) **Employees** are to be faithful to their employers (*Tit.* 2: 10).

(d) A faithful employee does not pilfer (*Tit.* 2: 10); rather, he should be so reliable, for example, in handling money entrusted to him, that he does not need to be checked up upon (*II Kings* 12: 15).

(e) A faithful employee is never rude or insolent to his employer (*Tit.* 2: 10).

(f) A faithful employee renders to his earthly employer service as if it were to the Lord Jesus Christ Himself (*Eph.* 6: 5–8), and in this way, by his behaviour at work, he commends the gospel to others (*Tit.* 2: 10).

D. **Christian fellowship.**

(a) We are to be faithful brothers and sisters to one another because of our common relationship to the Lord Jesus Christ (*Col.* 1: 2).

(b) We must, for example, be always eager to believe the best of one another (*I Cor.* 13: 7).

(c) Where wrong needs to be put right, we must be faithful in speaking the truth to one another in love (*Prov.* 27: 6; *Eph.* 4: 15, 25).

(d) We must stand by one another, even when trouble may result (*Heb.* 10: 33).

(e) We must be faithful in our exercise of the gift of hospitality (*III John* 5).

(f) We must serve one another all the better because of our relationship in Christ (*I Tim.* 6: 2).

231

(g) To be faithful to one another we must make time, and seize opportunities, to meet with other Christians so as to encourage and help one another (*Heb.* 10: 25).

(h) We must be faithful to the spiritual leaders God gives us, so that they may fulfil their task joyfully and not sadly (*Heb.* 13: 7; *I Thess.* 5: 12, 13).

6. Faithfulness also finds expression in our service of God, and the use to which we put all He has given us.

(a) Faithfulness is a primary qualification for service and office in the body of Christ, the Church (*I Tim.* 3: 11; *II Tim.* 2: 2).

(b) God is to be served with faithfulness (*Josh.* 24: 14; *Matt.* 24: 45; *Heb.* 3: 1, 2, 5, 6): we cannot serve two masters (*Luke* 16: 13).

(c) God entrusts us with a stewardship and it is required of stewards that they should be found faithful (*I Cor.* 4: 2).

(d) If, for example, our service is the communicating of God's Word in any way, we are to speak that Word faithfully, as in the sight of God (*Jer.* 23: 28; *II Cor.* 2: 17), renouncing all that is underhand or insincere (*II Cor.* 4: 2), and ensuring that we pass God's Word on accurately and faithfully (*Josh.* 11: 15; *Acts* 20: 27).

(e) We are to serve God faithfully by maintaining and upholding the faith (*II Tim.* 4: 7), earnestly contending for the faith which was once for all delivered to God's people (*Jude* 3).

(f) Whatever service we render to others, we are to render it faithfully (*III John* 5).

(g) We serve God faithfully as we use our money and material possessions in the interests of His kingdom (*Luke* 16: 11), recognising that all we own is a gift from Him (*I Chron.* 29: 14).

7. Faithfulness has great importance in respect of the rewards our Lord Jesus Christ wants to give.

(a) The Lord rewards every man for his faithfulness (*I Sam.* 26: 23).

(b) The true standard of reward is faithfulness to opportunity rather than length, honour or seeming importance of service (*Matt.* 20: 1–16).

(c) The Lord knows the truth about our faithfulness (*Rev.* 2: 13, 19).

(d) A faithful individual will abound with blessings (*Prov.* 28: 20).

(e) The Lord Jesus will reward His faithful servants on His return (*Matt.* 24: 46): equal gifts, if used with unequal faithfulness, will be unequally rewarded (*Luke* 19: 12–27); unequal gifts, used with equal faithfulness, will be equally rewarded (*Matt.* 25: 14–30).

(f) A crown of righteousness awaits the servants of Christ who have kept the faith and been faithful in service (*II Tim.* 4: 7, 8): significantly, those who are described as being in the closest proximity to the Lord Jesus Christ in heaven are described as those who have proved themselves faithful (*Rev.* 17: 14).

(g) We should be watchful concerning our faithfulness, lest we lose our reward (*II John* 8).

8. The Bible provides us with many examples of faithfulness.

(a) Abraham was found faithful in his heart to the Lord (*Neh.* 9: 8; *Gal.* 3: 9).

(b) Moses was faithful to the tasks God committed to him of caring for God's people (*Num.* 12: 7; *Heb.* 3: 2, 5).

232

(c) Joseph was faithful to his Egyptian master at great cost to himself (*Gen.* 39: 7ff) and then also to the keeper of the prison (*Gen.* 39: 22, 23).

(d) David was faithful to Saul in spite of all the injustices he suffered at his hands (*I Sam.* 22: 14).

(e) Daniel was faithful both to the Lord and to his earthly employer, the king of Babylon (*Dan.* 6: 4, 10).

(f) Shadrach, Meshach and Abednego were outstanding examples of faithfulness to God as they obeyed His commandment (*Dan.* 3: 28; *Ex.* 20: 5).

(g) Ruth's answer to Naomi is a classic example of faithfulness (*Ruth* 1: 16, 17).

(h) Paul sought to be faithful in not holding back any truth God wanted His people to receive from him (*Acts* 20: 20, 27).

(i) Silvanus, or Silas, was a faithful brother in his service of both Peter (*I Pet.* 5: 12) and the apostle Paul (*Acts* 15: 40; *I Thess.* 1: 1).

(j) Onesimus was a Christian who was faithful in his relationship to his fellow-Christians (*Col.* 4: 9).

(k) Tychicus was faithful in serving others for Christ's sake (*Eph.* 6: 21).

(l) Timothy was faithful to the apostle Paul in the tasks delegated to him (*I Cor.* 4: 17; *Phil.* 2: 19–24).

(m) Antipas was faithful in his witness to the Lord Jesus even though it meant martyrdom (*Rev.* 2: 13).

(n) The recollection of the witnesses of the faith and those who have been faithful in the past inspires us to faithfulness (*Heb.* 11; 12: 1, 2).

(o) We do well to imitate the faith and faithfulness of godly leaders who have both helped us and have been an example to us in the past (*Heb.* 13: 7).

10. **Faithfulness may bring its own costly consequences.**

(a) Faithfulness may bring reproach and persecution as it did to our Lord Jesus Christ (*Rom.* 15: 3).

(b) There is great blessing, however, in hardship or persecution which comes as a result of faithfulness (*Matt.* 5: 11, 12).

(c) Even our lives may be put in jeopardy by faithfulness (*Dan.* 3: 16–19; *Rev.* 2: 13).

(d) But suffering on account of faithfulness to God, and to others because it is God's will, will bring its own experience of God's help (*II Tim.* 1: 8), and it is, of course, only by God's help that faithfulness can be achieved (*I Cor.* 7: 25).

40. MEEKNESS

Galatians 5: 22, 23: "The fruit of the Spirit is . . . meekness" (A.V.).

Question: What is the meekness required of us?

Answer: The meekness required of us is an inward attitude which enables us to be in a position of submission to the will of God, irrespective of difficulty, and to treat others with gentleness, humility, courtesy, and considerateness. (Meekness is not a commonly appreciated or admired quality, for, in its contemporary use, it carries a suggestion of spinelessness. **Gentleness** is the alternative in many modern translations (e.g. R.S.V., N.I.V.), but it is not completely satisfactory. Aristotle defined meekness as the happy medium between excessive anger and excessive angerlessness. Gentleness, humility, courtesy, considerateness and meekness—put together—

233

best express the Greek word *prautēs*.)

1. The nature of meekness.

(a) Meekness is part of love's outflow (*I Cor.* 4: 21).

(b) It is frequently linked in the New Testament with patience and forbearance (*II Cor.* 10: 1; *Eph.* 4: 2; *Col.* 3: 12, 13), and also with humility (*Matt.* 11: 29; *Eph.* 4: 2; *Col.* 3: 12).

(c) It is a gift of the Spirit, and a fruit of the wisdom from above which God gives (*Jas.* 3: 13).

(d) It is a duty laid upon us by God as an essential part of the life to which He has called us in Christ (*Eph.* 4: 2; *Col.* 3: 12).

(e) Meekness may be thought of as part of the Christian's essential clothing (*Col.* 3: 12), which he must never be without (*Tit.* 3: 2).

(f) **Submission to the will of God** is the most important aspect of meekness (*Jas.* 4: 10; *I Pet.* 5: 6).

(g) Meekness strives to choose God's will before self-will (*Mark* 14: 36; *Matt.* 26: 39; *Luke* 22: 42).

(h) Even if submission to God means being regarded as the scum of the earth, meekness accepts obedience to God's will, and strives to act in a manner pleasing to God (*I Cor.* 4: 13)—cf. the example of Stephen (*Acts* 7: 60).

(i) Meekness cries to God in prayer, and reverently accepts His answer whatever it may be (*Heb.* 5: 7).

(j) Meekness goes hand in hand with triumphant waiting upon God (*Ps.* 147: 6; 149: 4; *I Pet.* 2: 21–23)—it causes a man to counsel himself, "Be still before the Lord, and wait patiently for Him" (*Ps.* 37: 7).

(k) Meekness discovers the unique peace that comes from submission to God's will (*Ps.* 131: 1, 2).

(l) Mary is an example of meekness before God: "I am the Lord's servant . . . May it be to me as you have said" (*Luke* 1: 38).

(m) Consideration for others is the second most important aspect of meekness—humble before God, we learn to be gentle in our dealings with others (*I Pet.* 5: 5, 6).

(n) Meekness is synonymous with universal courtesy (*Tit.* 3: 2).

(o) Meekness is unassuming (*Zech.* 9: 9; *Matt.* 21: 5) and makes us approachable (*Matt.* 11: 29).

(p) Meekness is a mark of a servant of God (*Isa.* 42: 1ff; 53: 6f; *II Tim.* 2: 24, 25), of someone who genuinely strives to walk in the Lord Jesus Christ's footsteps (*I Pet.* 2: 21–24).

(q) Meekness is much more concerned to serve God than to advance personal status (*Num.* 12: 3; *Phil.* 2: 5ff).

(r) Meekness is an indispensable characteristic of the ideal teacher (*Matt.* 11: 29; *II Tim.* 2: 25).

(s) It is also an indispensable factor in the exercise of discipline (*I Cor.* 4: 21), and in the spirit in which the erring or wayward Christian is to be sought out and brought back into fellowship (*Gal.* 6: 1).

(t) Moses exhibited meekness to a remarkable degree, more than all his contemporaries (*Num.* 12: 3), and, significantly, he was described by God as His true servant (*Num.* 12: 7).

2. The meekness of our Lord Jesus Christ.

(a) Meekness was a promised characteristic of the Messiah in the Old Testament prophecies (*Isa.* 42: 1ff; *Zech.* 9: 9).

(b) Meekness was, in fact, one of the foremost characteristics which our Lord Jesus Christ exhibited during

His earthly life (*II Cor.* 10: 1), and was part of His own self-description (*Matt.* 11: 29).

(c) **Submission to the will of God the Father** was an important aspect of our Lord's meekness (*Heb.* 10: 7).

(d) His food was to do the will of the Father and to finish His work (*John* 4: 34).

(e) His submission was epitomised in the Garden of Gethsemane when He prayed, "Not my will, but yours be done" (*Luke* 22: 42).

(f) It was also displayed in His submission to the wrongs inflicted upon Him as He discharged His ministry as God's suffering Servant: "He was oppressed, and He was afflicted, yet He opened not His mouth" (*Isa.* 53: 7); He did "not shout or cry out, or raise his voice in the streets" (*Isa.* 42: 2).

(g) When insults were hurled at Him, He did not respond with retaliation; His response was simply to entrust Himself to Him who judges justly (*I Pet.* 2: 23).

(h) But the second important aspect of our Lord's meekness was **His consideration for others,** and especially His unassertiveness and His tenderness to the weak and inadequate (*Isa.* 42: 2, 3)—e.g. His dealings with the Samaritan woman (*John* 4), the woman taken in adultery (*John* 8: 1-11), and Zacchaeus (*Luke* 19: 1 10).

(i) He encouraged men and women to come to Him precisely because of His meekness (*Matt.* 11: 29).

(j) His consideration for the disciples was marked: for example, He was concerned for them when they were tired (*Mark* 6: 31), and when they were troubled and needed comfort (*John* 14: 1ff).

3. **Meekness may be better understood by appreciating some of the opposite features of human behaviour with which it is contrasted.**

(a) Self-assertiveness or arrogance (*I Pet.* 3: 15).

(b) Jealousy and selfish ambition (*Jas.* 3: 13, 14).

(c) Quarrelsomeness (*Isa.* 42: 2; *Matt.* 12: 19; *II Tim.* 2: 24, 25).

(d) Self-justification and self-defence (*Isa.* 42: 2; *Matt.* 12: 19).

(e) Resentment (*II Tim.* 2: 24, 25).

(f) Abrasiveness (*Matt.* 11: 29, 30).

(g) Anger (*Jas.* 1: 20, 21).

(h) Violence and being warlike (*Matt.* 21: 5).

(i) Aggressiveness (*I Cor.* 4: 21).

(j) Unnecessary sternness in the application of discipline (*I Cor.* 4: 4, 21; *II Tim.* 2: 25).

4. **The practice and expression of meekness.**

(a) Its practice is to be continuous, like the wearing of clothes (*Col.* 3: 12); it is to be actively pursued (*I Tim.* 6: 11).

(b) It expresses itself in believing submission to God's will, even when it cannot understand what God may be doing (*Job* 1: 21; *Acts* 20: 22-24; 21: 10-14; *I Pet.* 4: 19).

(c) It expresses itself in submissive listening and obedience to the instruction of God's Word, even if that obedience involves the acceptance of rebuke and the need for repentance (*Jas.* 1: 21).

(d) It expresses itself in respect for all people, not for whom or what they are, or what their attitude may be in return (*Tit.* 3: 2; *I Pet.* 3: 15).

(e) It expresses itself in restraint when provoked (*II Tim.* 2: 25).

(f) When authorities or others ask

for an account of the Christian's profession of faith, it is to be given with meekness, even though injustice which has been suffered might prompt indignation or hurt (*I Pet.* 3: 16).

(g) It expresses itself in tenderness in dealing with those who need to be corrected (*Isa.* 42: 3; *II Tim.* 2: 25), correcting them without arrogance, impatience or anger, and endeavouring to give no unnecessary offence (*Gal.* 6: 1).

(h) It expresses itself in accepting the example of the Lord Jesus as the only acceptable norm for obedience to God and service of man (*II Cor.* 10: 1; *Phil.* 2: 5ff).

5. **The importance of meekness.**

(a) Meekness finds its place among the Beatitudes: "Blessed are the meek, for they will inherit the earth" (*Matt.* 5: 5).

(b) Meekness makes us true helpers of others after the pattern of our Lord Jesus Christ (*Matt.* 11: 29), for rather than antagonising people we may win them over to what is right by love's expression through meekness (*II Tim.* 2: 25).

(c) Meekness is a necessary condition for knowing God's guidance (*Ps.* 25: 9).

(d) Meekness is a condition of receiving God's blessing (*Ps.* 37: 11).

(e) The Lord causes meekness to prosper—He adorns the humble with victory (*Ps.* 149: 4).

(f) While it may be a mystery and a paradox to the unbelieving world, meekness is a secret of happiness (*Ps.* 37: 11; *Matt.* 5: 5).

41. SELF–CONTROL

Galatians 5: 22, 23: "The fruit of the Spirit is . . . temperance (self-control)."

Question: What is the temperance or self-control required of us?

Answer: Temperance (the Authorised Version translation) gives the wrong impression of self-control. The self-control required of us is self-mastery, so that through the help of the Holy Spirit, we are not under the power or dominion of any sin or habit, but we willingly use our Christian freedom to serve Christ by serving others. It is different from the rest of the fruit of the Spirit because it is neither Godward nor manward in its primary emphasis, but more properly selfward.

1. **Areas in which self-control is most obviously relevant.**

(a) In fact, self-control is relevant to **the whole of human life** (*I Thess.* 5: 6, 22).

(b) **Eating** (*Prov.* 23: 20; 25: 16).

(c) **Drinking** (*Eccl.* 10: 17; *Rom.* 13: 13)—drunkenness leads to uncontrolled actions and excess (*Eph.* 5: 18).

(d) **Sex** (*Tit.* 2: 5): the sex instinct is a good gift of God which is built into man but is meant to be exercised in marriage alone (*Mark* 10: 7), and even there it is a precious benefit to be enjoyed in a manner consistent with self-control (*I Cor.* 7: 1–6).

(e) The exercise and satisfaction of human desires (*I Pet.* 2: 11; 4: 4; cf. *Matt.* 14: 4; *Mark* 6: 18), and the enjoyment of human **pleasures** (*Matt.* 14: 6, 7; *Mark* 6: 21, 22).

(f) Occasions of **temptation** (*Mark* 14: 37–40, 66–72): sometimes the self-controlled Christian will know that the wisest course will be to flee from it (*II Tim.* 2: 22; *Jas.* 1: 14).

(g) **The estimate we have of ourselves,** and the exercise of **pride** (*Rom.* 12: 3, 16; cf. *Phil.* 2: 3).

236

(h) **Weaknesses of temperament**—for example, a man's tendency to be cowardly (*Mark* 6: 26; *Matt.* 14: 9; *II Tim.* 1: 7).

(i) **The expression of our feelings:** for example, if insulted it is the fool who shows his irritation straightaway; whereas it is the prudent, self-controlled man, who keeps his feelings out of sight (*Prov.* 12: 16).

(j) **Temper** (*Ps.* 37: 8; *Eph.* 4: 26; *I Thess.* 5: 14).

(k) **The use of the tongue** (*Matt.* 14: 7; *Mark* 6: 22, 23; *I Tim.* 3: 8; *Jas.* 3: 1, 2), and in the promises we may make (*Ex.* 8: 8, 15; *Eccl.* 5: 2; *Matt.* 14: 7; *Mark* 6: 22, 23).

(l) Resistance to worldly pressures to live with a wholly **materialistic outlook** (*I Tim.* 6: 6–10): it is only by self-control that we can avoid the sin of coveting (*Acts* 20: 33; *Rom.* 7: 7; 13: 9), and ensure that our treasure is in heaven rather than on earth (*Matt.* 6: 19, 20; cf. *John* 6: 27).

(m) The use of **time** (*Eccl.* 3: 1ff; *Eph.* 5: 15, 16; *Col.* 4: 5).

(n) **Spiritual experience:** our calling to freedom must not mean indulgence of our sinful nature (*Gal.* 5: 13); our spiritual joy and exuberance must not lead to excess (*Eph.* 5: 18–20); and our exercise of spiritual gifts must not be selfish but for the edifying of the whole body of Christ (*I Cor.* 14: 12, 26–33, 40).

2. **Opposites of self-control.**

(a) **Undisciplined living** with all its sad consequences (*Prov.* 21: 25; 26: 14; *Eccl.* 10: 18; *I Pet.* 1: 13, 14; 4: 3, 4).

(b) **Sexual immorality, impurity and licentiousness** (*Gal.* 5: 10)—all illustrations of a lack of control of the body and its sexual appetites.

(c) **Idolatry,** of which covetousness is a form (*Gal.* 5: 20; *Col.* 3: 5)—a lack of control over our eyes and coveting, and a lack of discipline with regard to the acquisitive spirit encouraged by society (*I John* 2: 15, 16).

(d) **Hatred, jealousy, and envy** (*Gal.* 5: 20, 21)—all failures to control the wrongful feelings which our sinful nature prompts.

(e) **Discord, selfish ambition, dissensions and factions** (*Gal.* 5: 20)—these all arise from the failure to control self and its display in forceful and selfish feelings or points of view.

(f) **Fits of temper** (*Gal.* 5: 20)—failure to control our anger and our tongue.

(g) **Drunkenness and orgies** (*Gal.* 5: 20)—failure to control thirst and the desire for pleasure.

3. **What self-control means in practice.**

(a) It is essentially self-mastery or dominion over oneself (*Rom.* 6: 13, 14), leading to an orderly life (*Eph.* 5: 15).

(b) It means coming to terms with the truth about ourselves and our flesh: our flesh is weak (*Mark* 14: 38; *Rom.* 6: 19; 8: 1), sinful (*Rom.* 8: 3), and always looking for an opportunity to have its fling (*Rom.* 13: 14; *Gal.* 5: 13).

(c) It means making our body our slave rather than allowing it to be our master (*I Cor.* 9: 27).

(d) It means being sufficiently honest with ourselves to appreciate that self-discipline must begin with our mind and our thoughts (*I Pet.* 1: 3; *Phil.* 4: 8; cf. *Matt.* 5: 28).

(e) It means having before us clear goals, so that we live our lives with purpose and a clear sense of direction (*I Cor.* 9: 24–27).

237

(f) It means having an eye to the good of others as well as our own: our Christian freedom is not to please ourselves but to choose to please others for their good, following the example of our Lord Jesus (*Rom.* 15: 1–3).

(g) It means recognising the place of watchfulness (*Matt.* 26: 41; *Mark* 14: 38) and not overestimating our strength (*I Cor.* 10: 12).

(h) It means recognising the place of prayer, and giving time to it (*Matt.* 26: 41; *Mark* 14: 38; *I Pet.* 4: 7).

(i) It means honest and drastic action often with regard to the known sources of temptation (*Matt.* 5: 29; 18: 8, 9; *Mark* 9: 43–47), giving no room for the gratification of the desires of our sinful flesh (*Rom.* 13: 14)—in other words, the readiness to say "No" to ungodliness and worldly passions (*Tit.* 2: 12).

(j) It means being like an athlete in our approach to life (*I Cor.* 9: 25; *II Tim.* 2: 5).

(k) It means perseverance (*II Pet.* 1: 6).

(l) It means being inwardly strong through the resources of Jesus Christ (*Phil.* 4: 13; *II Tim.* 1: 7; 2: 1).

4. The necessity and priority of self-control.

(a) It is an essential part of godliness which, sadly, will be despised in the last days (*II Tim.* 3: 2–4).

(b) It is an essential qualification for holding office in the Church of God (*I Tim.* 3: 2; *Tit.* 1: 8).

(c) It is linked with righteousness (*Acts* 24: 25), one of the principal priorities of Christian living (*I Pet.* 2: 24).

(d) It is part of our present experience of God's salvation (*Tit.* 2: 12, 13).

(e) It is the climax of the fruit of the Spirit (*Gal.* 5: 23), and is relevant to every age-group (*Tit.* 2: 2, 5, 6, 12).

(f) It is part of the freedom to which our Lord Jesus Christ calls us (*John* 8: 36; *Gal.* 5:1, 13)—a freedom purchased at tremendous cost (*Gal.* 3: 13).

(g) Without self-control we are easy prey for Satan (*I Cor.* 7: 5; *Eph.* 4: 26).

(h) Without self-control we may bring harm to others as well as to ourselves (*Mark* 6: 20, 21–28; cf. *II Sam.* 11: 1–5, 17; 12: 15).

(i) It is essential if we are to maintain and safeguard the value of our Christian testimony and service of the Lord Jesus (*I Cor.* 9: 25–27).

(j) It is part of our conformity to the likeness of our Lord Jesus Christ (*Rom.* 8: 29): His whole life was disciplined so as to fulfil the Father's will (*Luke* 9: 51; *John* 4: 34); He was disciplined in prayer (*Mark* 1: 35; *Luke* 11: 1), before temptation (*John* 6: 15; *Luke* 22: 39–46), and in the face of extreme ill-treatment (*I Pet.* 2: 23).

(k) We shall be judged with regard to our exercise of self-control (*Acts* 24: 25; *I Cor.* 9: 25).

42. CHRISTIAN DISCIPLESHIP

Question: What is Christian discipleship?

Answer: Christian discipleship is our response to the call of Jesus Christ to follow Him. It involves a counting of the cost and a total commitment to Jesus Christ, so that the whole of our life is given to seeking first God's kingdom and His righteousness.

1. The cost and conditions of discipleship.

238

(a) "Disciple," the Greek word for "apprentice" or "learner," is the word used most often in the New Testament—in fact, some 250 times—to describe members of Christ's kingdom (*Luke* 11: 1; 14: 26ff).

(b) Disciples of the Lord Jesus were not called "Christians" until the establishment of the church in Antioch (*Acts* 11: 26), and then it was but a nickname.

(c) Discipleship constitutes our answer to the call of Jesus Christ to follow Him (*Matt.* 4: 19; *Mark* 1: 17; 2: 14; 10: 21; *Luke* 9: 59; *John* 1: 43), in the light of His death and resurrection on our behalf (*Matt.* 28: 18–20; *Acts* 9: 1–22; *Rom.* 12: 1, 2; *Phil.* 3: 1–11).

(d) No one, however, should be allowed to embark upon discipleship without first appreciating the cost (*Matt.* 19: 21; *Luke* 18: 22)—our Lord went to great trouble to underline its demands (*Luke* 14: 25–33).

(e) The love we have for people, and the desire we may have that they should become disciples, must not mean that we neglect to make them count the cost (*Mark* 10: 21).

(f) The basic principle is that no man can serve two masters; if he tries to do so, the results are bound to be unfortunate (*Matt.* 6: 24; *Luke* 16: 13).

(g) For some, the cost may relate particularly to wealth, since discipleship involves the abandonment of every idol that would take Christ's place in a person's life (*Matt.* 19: 21; *Mark* 10: 21; *Luke* 18: 22).

(h) The home is not to assume priority over discipleship of Christ (*Luke* 18: 28ff).

(i) Discipleship begins with **a renunciation,** and it is not intended that the act of renunciation should be left until later (*Matt.* 19: 21; *Mark* 10: 21; *Luke* 18: 22).

(j) Looking back is no more possible for the disciple than it is for someone who flees persecution (*Luke* 17: 31f; cf. *Gen.* 19: 17, 26), or for the man who has put his hand to the plough (*Luke* 9: 62; cf. *I Kings* 19: 20f), or for the athlete who does not look back at the ground he has covered but at the finishing tape ahead (*Phil.* 3: 13f).

(k) Discipleship means, secondly, **a sincere acknowledgement of the Lordship of Christ** (*Matt.* 7: 21–23; *Luke* 6: 46; 13: 26–27).

(l) Discipleship means, thirdly, **a life of devotion to Christ**—the relationship we have to Him supercedes every other relationship (*Matt.* 12: 49, 50; *Mark* 3: 34, 35; *Luke* 8: 21).

(m) Devotion to Christ may bring reproach from men but it is something of tremendous value to Him (*Matt.* 26: 10; *Mark* 14: 6).

(n) Discipleship means, fourthly, **the acceptance of the principle of dying to self** (*John* 12: 23–26).

(o) Our Lord Jesus Christ set a pattern for all disciples to follow: the man who loves his life will lose it, but the man who is willing to act as if he hates his life, out of allegiance to Christ's cause, will keep it for eternal life (*Matt.* 10: 39; 16: 25; *Mark* 8: 35; *Luke* 9: 24; 17: 33; *John* 12: 25).

(p) Only when this principle of dying to self is genuinely accepted can there be a true readiness for tribulation and persecution (*Matt.* 5: 10–12; *Mark* 9: 49; cf. 8: 34–37).

(q) Only when the disciple is willing to die daily to himself will he be ready to serve others for Christ's sake without reservation or personal choice (*Matt.* 20: 26, 27; *Mark* 10: 43, 44).

(r) Discipleship means, fifthly, **the discipline of instruction** (*Matt.* 10: 24, 25; *Luke* 6: 40).

(s) Discipleship means doing the will of the Father, and to this end the Word of God must be both listened to and obeyed (*Matt.* 12: 49, 50).

2. The proof of discipleship.

(a) The proof of which our Lord spoke most often is the proof of **obedience** (*Matt.* 7: 21, 24–27; 12: 50; *Mark* 3: 35; *Luke* 6: 46–49; 8: 21; 11: 28).

(b) It is by our obedience to Christ that we show our love for Him, so that disobedience is synonymous with an absence of love (*John* 14: 21, 24).

(c) True obedience to Christ will frequently incur the world's hatred (*John* 15: 17–27).

(d) The proof of discipleship is seen often, therefore, in the correspondence between the world's reaction to the ministry of Christ's disciples and the reaction our Lord Himself received in the course of His own ministry as He obeyed the Father (*John* 15: 20).

(e) **Fruitfulness** is picked out as a proof of discipleship (*John* 15: 8)—there are different levels of fruitfulness (*Matt.* 13: 8, 23; *Mark* 4: 8, 20; *Luke* 8: 8, 15), and it does not happen all at once (*Luke* 8: 14, 15).

(f) When disciples abide in Christ by means of obedience, they become spiritually fruitful (*John* 15: 5), so that fruitfulness becomes a legitimate test of any profession of discipleship (*Matt.* 12: 33; *Luke* 6: 43, 44).

(g) Chastisement—or bearing in mind the picture of fruit, pruning— is a necessary part of the discipleship calculated to make us more profitable to God (*John* 15: 2).

(h) **Love** is a proof of discipleship (*John* 13: 34f).

(i) Love for God is the substance of the first summary of the commandments, and love for others the substance of the second (*Matt.* 22: 36–39; *Mark* 12: 28, 31; *Luke* 10: 27).

(j) The love disciples exhibit is to go beyond the limits of ordinary human love (*Matt.* 5: 46, 47; *Luke* 6: 32–35).

(k) **An obvious awareness of privilege** is another proof of discipleship, since we quickly learn that we did not choose Christ but that He chose us (*John* 15: 16).

(l) Over all the work of disciples there stands, in effect, the principle: having paid nothing for what they receive, they charge nothing for what they do (*Matt.* 10: 8; *Acts* 3: 6; 20: 33ff; cf. *Rom.* 1: 5).

(m) **Humility** is a further proof of discipleship (*Mark* 9: 35; cf. *Matt.* 11: 28ff; *Phil.* 2: 5–11).

(n) Greatness in the sight of God involves humble service (*Mark* 9: 35): it expresses itself in the willingness to take upon ourselves the function and attitude of a servant (*Matt.* 20: 26; *Mark* 10: 43; *Luke* 22: 26).

(o) Our Lord warned against the desire for status (*Luke* 14: 11; cf. *Mark* 10: 15f).

(p) Like a child, we should know how lowly we really are (*Matt.* 18: 1–5).

(q) Disciples, desiring to walk in Christ's footsteps, willingly wash one another's feet (*John* 13: 14).

(r) A final proof of discipleship is **faithfulness**—the one who stands firm to the end is the man who shall be saved (*Matt.* 24: 13).

(s) The parables of the talents and pounds emphasise the need for faithful service during this present period of history, prior to the Lord's return (*Matt.* 25: 14–30; *Luke* 19: 12–27).

3. The aims of discipleship.

(a) Perhaps the principal, all-comprehending aim, is simply Christlikeness of character (*Matt.* 10: 24, 25; *Luke* 6: 40), the character outlined in the Beatitudes (*Matt.* 5: 3–10); and summed up in the fruits of the Spirit (*Gal.* 5: 22, 23).

(b) The aim of discipleship is to share in the work of the Lord Jesus whether in terms of what we **are**—for example, as salt (*Matt.* 5: 13) and light (*Matt.* 5: 14ff)—or in terms of what we are to **do**—for example in catching men (*Luke* 5: 10), harvesting the spiritual harvest (*Matt.* 9: 37; *John* 4: 35–38), preaching the kingdom of heaven (*Matt.* 10: 5ff), serving others with the spirit of a servant (*John* 13: 1ff), and making disciples (*Matt.* 28: 19, 20).

(c) The aim of discipleship is to glorify the Father on earth by finishing the work He has given us to do (*Matt.* 5: 16; *John* 17: 4).

(d) The aim of discipleship is to express such unity among disciples that the world knows that the Father sent the Son into the world to show His love (*John* 10: 16; 17: 20–23).

(e) In essence, the aim of discipleship is to bear witness to our Lord Jesus Christ (*Luke* 24: 48; *Acts* 1: 8), and to His total pre-eminence in God's purposes, both in creation or redemption (*Acts* 3: 20, 21; *Col.* 1: 15–20).

4. The benefits of discipleship.

(a) First, a spiritual relationship to God through His Son Jesus Christ (*Mark* 3: 32–35)—eternal life is to know God the Father and Jesus Christ whom He sent (*John* 17: 3).

(b) Secondly, a personal attachment to Christ which shapes the whole of life (*Mark* 2: 18ff; *John* 21: 19, 22)—we are one with Him in His death, resurrection and ascension (*Rom.* 6: 1–4; *Eph.* 2: 6, 7).

(c) Thirdly, a discovery of God's purpose for life (*Rom.* 12: 1, 2; *II Cor.* 5: 9, 15).

(d) Fourthly, a sharing of a wonderful fellowship (*Mark* 3: 13, 14; *Luke* 12: 32; *Acts* 1: 14; 2: 42; *I Pet.* 5: 9, 13).

(e) Fifthly, a learning of the way to joy—the Beatitudes, for example, emphasise that the disciple possesses the secret of true happiness or joy (*Matt.* 5: 3–10).

(f) Joy is the result of discovering the kingdom of heaven (*Matt.* 13: 44).

(g) The disciple's joy is not in what he has achieved himself, but in what God has done for him through His Son (*Luke* 10: 20).

(h) Our Lord Jesus desires that His own joy should be in His disciples, and that their joy should be full (*John* 15: 11; 17: 13).

(i) Sixthly, a freedom from the besetting worries of human existence: as we seek first God's kingdom and His righteousness, food, clothing, housing and all we need besides will be given us in addition, without our needing to be anxious about them (*Matt.* 6: 33–34).

(j) Seventhly, a joyful anticipation of heaven (*John* 14: 1ff; 17: 24), and the recompense the Lord Jesus will give His faithful disciples (*Matt.* 16: 27).

(k) As our Lord Jesus was not of this

241

world, so too disciples are no longer of this world; as He was exalted because of His faithful obedience, so His faithful disciples shall be exalted (*II Tim.* 2: 12)—none can measure the joy of the disciples' spiritual inheritance (*I Pet.* 1: 4; cf. *Ps.* 16: 11).

43. OBEDIENCE

Question: What does the Bible teach concerning obedience?

Answer: Obedience is doing everything God commands, of which our Lord Jesus Christ is the perfect example. The Christian life begins with obedience and continues by means of it. It is the proof both of new birth and discipleship, and it constitutes the secret of the happiness the Christian enjoys, no matter how costly that obedience may be.

1. **The Bible defines obedience.**

(a) Obedience is doing everything God commands (*Ex.* 19: 5; *Deut.* 5: 10; *Josh.* 22: 2; *Jer.* 7: 23).

(b) The Scriptures, God's Word, are to be the rule of our whole life (*II Tim.* 3: 16, 17).

(c) Obedience is our practical response to the Word of God (*Matt.* 13: 23; *Gal.* 5: 7; *Jas.* 1: 22–25).

(d) Christian obedience is our coming to Christ, hearing His words, and putting them into practice (*Luke* 6: 47; *John* 8: 51).

(e) Obedience is closely associated with a sensitive conscience, which is constantly educated and informed by the Holy Spirit by means of the Scriptures, and is consistently obeyed (*Acts* 23: 1; 24: 16; *II Cor.* 1: 12; *II Tim.* 1: 3).

(f) Obedience is synonymous with walking with God (*Gen.* 6: 9) and loving God (*I John* 5: 2).

2. **Our Lord Jesus Christ is the perfect example of obedience.**

(a) Obedience was the foremost characteristic of His earthly life (*Heb.* 10: 7).

(b) He obeyed the Father's commands and remained in His love (*John* 15: 10).

(c) His perfect obedience in accepting even death (*Phil.* 2: 8) made possible our acceptance with God and our fellowship with Him as we believe in Him as the Son of God and Saviour (*Rom.* 5: 15–19).

(d) His obedience to the Father should be the pattern of ours (*John* 15: 10).

3. **Obedience has an important place both in the beginnings of the Christian life and in its continuance.**

(a) Under the New Covenant obedience is God's gift to enable His people to enjoy His favour, rather than a necessary condition to be achieved before His favour may be enjoyed (*Jer.* 31: 33; 32: 40).

(b) The Christian life begins with obedience (*John* 6: 29; *Acts* 26: 19; *I Pet.* 1: 22), having as its first object the form of teaching presented in the gospel (*Rom.* 6: 17), summarised in the words, "Repent and believe the gospel" (*Mark* 1: 15; *Acts* 2: 38).

(c) Discipleship begins with an act of obedience (*Matt.* 9: 9; *Mark* 2: 14).

(d) We are chosen, redeemed and sanctified with our obedience to Jesus Christ in view (*I Pet.* 1: 2).

(e) It is as a result of our new relationship to God by new birth that we are called upon to obey Him (*I Pet.* 1: 14).

(f) Obedience is God's work in us, as a consequence of the new birth, for God works in us to will and to act

242

according to His good purpose (*Phil.* 2: 13, 14).

4. The priority of obedience.

(a) Obedience has from the beginning of creation been an indispensable obligation, since God has every right to command His creatures, and has made known His requirements (*Gen.* 2: 15–17).

(b) The results of Adam's failure to obey indicate its priority: by his failure to obey the whole of mankind was involved in guilt, condemnation and death (*Rom.* 5: 19; *I Cor.* 15: 22).

(c) The Old Covenant required obedience as a condition of God's favour (*Ex.* 19: 5; *I Kings* 3: 14; *II Kings* 21: 8; *Neh.* 1: 5).

(d) Obedience sums up our whole duty to God (*Deut.* 10: 12, 13; *Eccl.* 12: 13) and is commanded (*Deut.* 13: 4; *Ps.* 119: 4).

(e) Obedience is more important than isolated acts of service to God, religious observances and externals (*I Sam.* 15: 22; *I Cor.* 7: 19).

(f) Obedience is the mode of practice by which we please God (*I John* 3: 22).

(g) Where obedience to God clashes with obedience to man, God is to be obeyed rather than man (*Acts* 5: 29).

(h) Obedience is the condition of our dwelling in our Lord Jesus Christ's love (*John* 15: 10), and enjoying a personal relationship to Him (*Matt.* 12: 50).

(i) Obedience is a prerequisite of unbroken fellowship with the Father and the Son (*John* 14: 23–24; *I John* 1: 3, 7).

(j) Obedience is the means of our growing in holiness (*Luke* 1: 6).

(k) Obedience is the perfecting of our love for God (*I John* 2: 5).

5. Practical implications of obedience.

(a) Obedience involves devoting ourselves to the study and observance of God's Law (*Ezra* 7: 10).

(b) Obedience demands a change in the pattern of our life compared with what it was before our conversion (*I Pet.* 1: 14): obedience to God is opposite to the service of sin (*Rom.* 6: 17).

(c) Obedience includes loving God's children (*I John* 5: 2).

(d) Obedience requires holiness in all we do (*I Pet.* 1: 15, 16).

(e) Obedience results in practising the humility our Lord Jesus exemplified (*John* 13: 12–17; *Phil.* 2: 5–8).

(f) No matter how difficult or complicated a problem or a decision, the first course of action to be followed is that of obedience to God (*Phil.* 2: 12, 13).

(g) Obedience to God demands obedience within family relationships: subjection to one another out of reverence for Christ (*Eph.* 5: 21); the subjection of a wife to her husband (*Eph.* 5: 22); and the obedience of children to their parents (*Eph.* 6: 1–3).

(h) Obedience to God expresses itself in obedience within the fellowship of the local church, as we follow the direction of our spiritual teachers (*Phil.* 2: 12), and as we obey our spiritual leaders (*Heb.* 13: 17).

(i) Obedience to God includes rendering the obedience He commands to the governing authorities (*Matt.* 22: 21; *Rom.* 13: 1f, 6, 7; *I Pet.* 3: 13, 14; *Tit.* 3: 1).

6. Characteristics of obedience.

(a) Obedience recognises God's supreme authority to command (*I Sam.* 3: 10; *Acts* 9: 6).

243

(b) Obedience springs from a delight in the law of the Lord and meditation on it (*Ps.* 1: 2; 119: 104, 105, 129).

(c) Obedience is diligent (*Heb.* 6: 11) and persevering (*Heb.* 10: 36).

(d) Obedience is rendered even when apprehension concerning the results of that obedience exist (*Acts* 9: 10–19).

(e) Obedience is precise and whole-hearted (*Matt.* 6: 24; *John* 15: 14).

(f) Obedience, once practised, is taught and communicated to others (*Matt.* 5: 19).

7. The significance of obedience when found in the life of an individual.

(a) Obedience is the proof of discipleship (*John* 10: 27), and is never burdensome to the true believer (*I John* 5: 3).

(b) Obedience results from spiritual birth (*Eph.* 2: 10).

(c) Obedience proves the reality of our knowledge of God (*I John* 2: 3).

(d) Obedience demonstrates our love for God (*Dan.* 9: 4; *John* 14: 15, 23, 24; *II John* 6).

(e) Obedience indicates that we dwell in Christ and that He dwells in us (*I John* 2: 6; 3: 24).

(f) Obedience provides a measure of our fruitfulness as Christians (*Matt.* 13: 23; *Mark* 4: 20; *Luke* 8: 15; *John* 15: 10, 14, 16).

(g) Obedience marks us out as faithful (*Rev.* 12: 17).

7. Obedience's incentives.

(a) Faith prompts and sustains obedience (*Heb.* 11: 8), with right views of Christ constituting our secret of faith (*Heb.* 12: 2).

(b) Meditation upon the value of our Lord's friendship encourages obedience (*John* 15: 14).

(c) The consideration of God's goodness stimulates obedience (*I Sam.* 12: 24; *Ps.* 26: 3; *Rom.* 12: 1).

(d) The knowledge of the certain rewards of obedience serves to energize obedience: happiness (*Luke* 11: 28; *Jas.* 1: 25); joy (*John* 15: 1–11); God's blessing (*Mal.* 3: 10–12); confidence before God in prayer (*I John* 3: 21, 22); spiritual stability (*Luke* 6: 46–49); everlasting life (*John* 8: 51; *Rev.* 2: 10) and a graciously generous reward (*Matt.* 6: 24; *John* 12: 26).

44. CHRISTIAN WITNESS

Question: What is Christian witness? Answer: Christian witness is the privilege and duty which arises from the experience of God's salvation in Jesus Christ. Commanded by God, and worldwide in its scope and intention, its purpose is to set forth God's saving acts in the death and resurrection of our Lord Jesus Christ, in accordance with the Scriptures, and in dependence upon the Holy Spirit.

1. Witness is both a privilege and a duty arising from the experience of God's salvation.

(a) Witness is the spontaneous and natural consequence of an experience of our Lord Jesus Christ's power (*Mark* 5: 20; *Luke* 8: 39; *John* 4: 29, 30).

(b) Those who love God's salvation delight to say "The Lord be exalted" (*Ps.* 40: 16).

(c) A sense of compulsion lies behind Christian witness—we cannot help speaking about what we believe and know about Jesus Christ (*Acts* 4: 20; *II Cor.* 4: 13).

(d) Christ's love compels us to witness (*II Cor.* 5: 14).

(e) Reconciled to God, through the

atoning work of Christ, we find ourselves entrusted with the message of reconciliation (*II Cor.* 5: 18, 19).

(f) Christian witness finds its impetus in the personal experience of salvation (*Isa.* 12: 2–4; *II Tim.* 1: 11, 12).

2. Witness is expected, and commanded by God.

(a) All who know, believe and understand that the Lord is both God and Saviour are commissioned to be His witnesses (*Isa.* 43: 10, 11).

(b) Testimony to the Lord Jesus Christ is to be given without shame (*Luke* 12: 8, 9; *II Tim.* 1: 8).

(c) The Word of life is to be held out by all Christians (*Phil.* 2: 16).

(d) Witness is to be given courageously and fearlessly (*Phil.* 1: 14).

(e) This witness, however, is to be given with gentleness and with respect for the individuals to whom it is addressed (*I Pet.* 3: 15).

(f) At any time, as opportunity provides, we are to be ready to witness (*I Pet.* 3: 15); if we do not aim at witnessing at every proper opportunity, as commanded (*Col.* 4: 5), we shall probably not witness at all (*Eccl.* 11: 3, 4).

(g) Our witness should be consistent and continuous, for the success which may attend it can never be predicted (*Eccl.* 11: 6; *Heb.* 10: 23).

(h) Our witness should be clear—like a city on a hill (*Matt.* 5: 14)—and effective—like salt (*Matt.* 5: 13).

(i) Restraint should be removed from our lips when there is opportunity for witness (*Ps.* 40: 9).

(j) To conceal our testimony to God's faithfulness and salvation is sinful (*Ps.* 40: 10).

3. Witness is to be world-wide in its scope and concern.

(a) Witness should begin with our family and our immediate acquaintances (*Mark* 5: 19; *Acts* 16: 31).

(b) Ideally, corporate Christian witness should have a repercussive and spreading effect throughout a whole neighbourhood and area (*I Thess.* 1: 8).

(c) In fact, the scope of Christian witness is to be the world (*Isa.* 12: 2–4; *Acts* 1: 8), and it is God's ordained means of spreading the gospel to all creation (*Matt.* 28: 19, 20).

4. Witness cannot be separated from the life and conduct of the individual Christian and the local church.

(a) Witness of life and speech go together but there is a sense in which the witness of life must come first (*Phil.* 2: 15, 16; *I Pet.* 3: 1, 2).

(b) Witness must be confirmed by the evidence of a cleansed life (*Ps.* 26: 6, 7; 51: 1–19).

(c) The truth of Christian witness is substantiated by the good effects it has upon men's lives (*I Cor.* 1: 6) in distinctive Christian character and conduct (*Matt.* 5: 13).

(d) Good conduct, in spite of provocation and opposition, constitutes essential Christian witness (*I Pet.* 2: 12).

(e) The witness of the life must support the witness of the lips (*I Thess.* 1: 7, 8; *I Pet.* 3: 1).

(f) The corporate life of God's people—especially in their display of Christian love—is fundamental to their witness (*Phil.* 2: 14–16; *I Pet.* 1: 22; 2: 9).

5. Witness is, nevertheless, primarily that of word or speech.

(a) Christian witness requires the witness of words (*I Pet.* 3: 15).

(b) With the great end of redemption

as the confession "Jesus Christ is Lord," it is clearly our duty to bear testimony to this truth now (*Phil.* 2: 11).

(c) Witness involves this confession of the mouth that "Jesus is Lord" (*Rom.* 10: 9), a confession we are to make before the world (*Matt.* 10: 32; *Luke* 12: 8).

(d) In giving witness we speak of the glory of God's kingdom and we tell of His might (*Ps.* 145: 11), and how both are made known to us so wonderfully in Jesus Christ (*Acts* 8: 12).

(e) The witness of words cannot help but often find expression in song (*I Chron.* 16: 8, 9; *Ps.* 9: 11; 18: 49; 40: 3; *Isa.* 12: 4, 5; *Eph.* 5: 19).

6. Witness requires the power of the Holy Spirit to be effective.

(a) Power for witness is given by God (*Acts* 1: 8; *Rev.* 4: 8, 31).

(b) Witness needs not only words, but the power of the Holy Spirit to give those words strong conviction (*I Thess.* 1: 5).

(c) Effective witness depends completely on the enduement and power of the Holy Spirit (*Luke* 24: 48, 49; *I Cor.* 12: 3).

7. The central subject of witness is what God has achieved through the work of His Son, the Lord Jesus Christ.

(a) Witness is the making known of God's deeds among the people (*I Chron.* 16: 8; *Ps.* 9: 11; *Isa.* 12: 4; *Jer.* 51: 10; *Mark* 5: 19; *I Pet.* 2: 9–10).

(b) At its simplest, witness is proclaiming how much Jesus has done for sinners (*Mark* 5: 19, 20; *Luke* 8: 39).

(c) It is the proclaiming of the good news of Jesus Christ (*I Cor.* 1: 6; 15: 15; *I John* 1: 1–4).

(d) It centres around the death of Christ, His resurrection from the dead, and the message of light and life which springs from these saving events (*Acts* 26: 23; *I Cor.* 15: 1–4).

(e) Central to all that is stated is the message of Jesus Christ and Him crucified (*I Cor.* 2: 2; *Gal.* 6: 14).

8. What God has achieved through the work of His Son, Jesus Christ, is described in the Bible as "the Word of God."

(a) The good news of Christ is identical with the Word of the Lord which abides for ever (*I Pet.* 1: 25); the gospel of salvation through Christ is the Word of truth (*Eph.* 1: 13).

(b) All Scripture is inspired by God and is able to make men wise for salvation through faith in Jesus Christ (*II Tim.* 3: 15, 16).

(c) The principal theme of the whole of the Word of God is that Christ, the Messiah, had to suffer and then to rise again on the third day, and that through what He accomplished repentance and forgiveness may be preached to men (*Luke* 24: 45–47).

(d) This fact explains the early Church's concern to preach the Word of God with boldness (*Acts* 4: 4, 29, 31).

(e) Preaching the Word was the priority of the early Church (*Acts* 6: 2, 4), in that the whole evangelistic programme of the early Church is summed up in expressions relating to the preaching of the Word of God (*Acts* 13: 5, 7, 44, 46, 48, 49; 14: 25; 15: 7; 15: 35, 36; 16: 6, 32; 17: 11, 13; 18: 11; 19: 10).

(f) The progress of the early Church in witness is described in terms of the spread of the Word of God (*Acts* 6: 7; 12: 24; 19: 20).

(g) Witness and evangelism go forward as the Word of the

Lord spreads on and is honoured (*II Thess.* 3: 1).

(h) To preach the Word of God is to preach Christ, for He is the Incarnate Word of God (*John* 1: 1; *Rev.* 19: 13)—by Him God has spoken to men (*Heb.* 1: 2), and all the Scriptures speak of Him (*Luke* 24: 27).

(i) It was for the Word of God and the testimony they maintained that the martyrs were slain (*Rev.* 6: 9).

9. Christian witness, therefore, is according to the Word of God and from the Word of God.

(a) Christian witness is the declaration of God's attested truth (*Luke* 24: 44–45; *I Cor.* 2: 1).

(b) It begins with the great proclamation that God has spoken (*Heb.* 1: 1), first, in the Old Testament (*Heb.* 1: 1), and secondly, in a unique and final manner by His Son Jesus Christ (*Heb.* 1: 2).

(c) Christian witness to the Lord Jesus Christ is according to the pattern of sound teaching given us in God's Word (*II Tim.* 1: 8, 13).

(d) Christian witness emphasises that everything that happened in the life of the Lord Jesus Christ was in accord with the Old Testament Scriptures (*Acts* 26: 22, 23; *I Cor.* 15: 3, 4; *Heb.* 1: 1–4, 5–13).

(e) Christian witness bears testimony to what the Scriptures declare concerning the death and resurrection of Jesus, and the repentance and forgiveness to be preached in consequence (*Luke* 24: 46, 47).

(f) Christian witness consists of teaching and preaching (*Acts* 5: 42; 15: 35) so that the Word of God is presented in its fullness (*Col.* 1: 25). The facts having been taught (*II Cor.* 5: 17, 18, 19), the appeal by preaching can be made to men's will, "Be reconciled to God" (*II Cor.* 5: 20).

(g) Christian witness, therefore, is not a matter of fine words or human cleverness, but rather the simple declaration of God's Word (*I Cor.* 2: 1), so that the hearers may confirm the truth of what has been said by their private examination of the Scriptures (*Acts* 17: 11).

(h) Christian witness may be summed up as bearing witness to the Word of God and the testimony of Jesus Christ (*Rev.* 1: 2).

10. Christian witness requires a recognition of the carefulness with which the Word of God should be handled and used.

(a) We must handle the Word of God honestly, always refusing to use deception, or to distort it (*II Cor.* 4: 2).

(b) As we witness by setting forth the truth plainly, we commend ourselves to every man's conscience in the sight of God (*II Cor.* 4: 2).

(c) The Word of God is the Spirit's sword (*Eph.* 6: 17).

(d) It is the instrument God uses to bring spiritual life to men and women (*Jas.* 1: 18; *I Pet.* 1: 23).

11. Our witness is inevitably and vitally linked with our knowledge of, and obedience to, God's Word.

(a) We are to be instructed in the Word (*Acts* 2: 42; *Gal.* 6: 6).

(b) By constant use of the Scriptures, we should be skilful in our use of them (*Eph.* 6: 17; *Heb.* 5: 13, 14).

(c) We should do our best to present ourselves to God as those who are approved, workmen who do not need to be ashamed, and who correctly handle the Word of truth (*II Tim.* 2: 15).

(d) We are to let the Word of God dwell in us richly (*Col.* 3: 16).

(e) When the Word of God is at work in our lives we impart it to others (*I Thess.* 2: 13; cf. 1: 7, 8).

12. **The Holy Spirit adds His power to the Word of God when it is proclaimed faithfully.**

(a) The secret of witnessing to the Word of God with boldness and effectiveness lies in being filled with the Spirit (*Acts* 4: 31).

(b) Desiring above everything else to witness to our Lord Jesus Christ, the Holy Spirit delights to bear witness to the Word of God's grace in Christ when it is faithfully declared (*John* 15: 26; *Acts* 14: 3).

(c) As genuine witness to Christ is given, according to the Word of God, the Holy Spirit adds His own spiritual power to it (*I Cor.* 2: 4).

(d) When the Holy Spirit does this, faith is awakened by the message which comes through the Word of God (*Rom.* 10: 17), and as the Word of God is received, those who receive it are brought to living faith in Christ and membership of His Church (*Acts* 2: 41; cf. 2: 22–36).

(e) The confidence of Christian witness, therefore, is not in plausible words or subtle argument but in the power of the Word of God and the Holy Spirit (*I Cor.* 2: 1–5).

46. PERSONAL EVANGELISM

Question: How are we to fulfil our responsibilities in personal evangelism?

Answer: We are to see ourselves as workers together with God, understanding what is His work in bringing a person to saving faith in Jesus Christ, and what is our part.

As we present the gospel to all to whom God gives us the opportunity, we are to look expectantly for such evidence of the Holy Spirit's activity in their lives as the Bible leads us to expect.

1. **Essential truths should influence all our thinking and acting when endeavouring to lead others to faith in our Lord Jesus Christ.**

(a) Such activity is pleasing to God: there is more joy in heaven over one sinner that repents than over ninety-nine who need no repentance (*Luke* 15: 7).

(b) It is by means of this activity that the Christian Church grows and multiplies (*Acts* 2: 47; 6: 7; 9: 31; 12: 24).

(c) The New Testament assumes that all Christians will be ready to engage in making the gospel known to others (*Matt.* 28: 19; *Phil.* 2: 15, 16; *Col.* 4: 5; *I Pet.* 3: 15).

(d) To endeavour to lead others to Christ is part of loving our neighbour as ourself (*Luke* 10: 27; *II Cor.* 5: 14; *John* 1: 40ff).

(e) We know that it is not God's will for any to perish but for all to come to repentance (*II Pet.* 3: 9).

(f) We are in conflict all the time with the devil while we endeavour to do this task (*Eph.* 6: 12): he has blinded the minds of unbelievers, to keep them from seeing the light of the gospel of the glory of Christ (*II Cor.* 4: 4). We do not despair, however, for we know that the work is God's (*I Pet.* 1: 2; *Acts* 16: 14; *Gal.* 1: 15, 16).

(g) We are workers together with God in this task (*II Cor.* 6: 1; *I Cor.* 3: 5–9).

(h) We work not for time but for eternity (*Dan.* 12: 3).

(i) Our supreme motive is the glory of God (*I Cor.* 1: 30, 31).

2. We must be clear as to what God alone can do, and what we, therefore, cannot do.

(a) Conviction of sin is the work of God the Holy Spirit (*John* 16: 8).

(b) God alone can give repentance to men (*Acts* 5: 31; 11: 18)—it is His gift.

(c) Only God can draw men and women to Christ (*John* 6: 44).

(d) God alone can reveal Jesus (*Acts* 9: 3, 4; *II Cor.* 4: 6).

(e) It is God's unique prerogative to bring about new birth (*John* 1: 13; 3: 3, 5).

3. We must be clear as to what God requires of us by way of preparation for this work.

(a) We need an awareness of our own dependence upon the Lord Jesus for salvation (*Gal.* 2: 20b; *I Tim.* 1: 15).

(b) We must know the Scriptures.

(i) They alone equip us effectively (*II Tim.* 3: 17).

(ii) Only the Scriptures contain the truth men need in order to be saved (*II Tim.* 3: 15).

(iii) The Scriptures bring about conviction of sin (*Acts* 2: 37).

(iv) By the Spirit's power, the Scriptures bring regeneration (*I Pet.* 1: 23).

(v) The Scriptures are the means the Spirit uses to give saving faith (*Rom.* 10: 17).

(vi) To help people by means of the Scriptures requires diligent study and growth in understanding on our part (*II Tim.* 2: 15).

(c) We need an understanding of the desperately urgent plight of men without Christ (*Matt.* 9: 36).

(i) They are lost (*Luke* 19: 10).

(ii) Their need should touch our emotions (*Acts* 20: 31).

(d) We must be in earnest when we engage in this work.

(i) We should know great sorrow and unceasing anguish in our hearts for men without Christ (*Rom.* 9: 1, 2).

(ii) We should long in our hearts for the salvation of others (*Rom.* 10: 1).

(e) The whole of our life needs to be open before God, and cleansing should be sought for all known sin (*II Tim.* 2: 20, 21; *Ps.* 51: 10, 12, 13).

(f) We must be filled with the Holy Spirit (*Eph.* 5: 18; *Acts* 6: 5; cf. 8: 12, 29, 39, 40; *I Cor.* 2: 4).

4. We must be clear as to what God requires of us by way of co-operation in this work.

(a) Although the work of conversion is essentially God the Holy Spirit's work, He calls us to work with Him in achieving it (*Acts* 26: 18).

(b) God has given us all that is necessary for performing the task: the authority of Jesus, His commission to preach, the message of salvation (symbolised in baptism), the commandments of Jesus; and His presence by the Spirit (*Matt.* 28: 18–20).

(c) Our responsibility is to make known the Word of God (*Acts* 16: 14; *Rom.* 10: 14–17).

(d) We should endeavour to make it known to all men without being influenced by any kind of prejudice (*Gal.* 6: 10; cf. *Luke* 14: 21–23; *I Cor.* 1: 26–29).

(e) We should urge men to seek God (*Luke* 13: 24, 25; *Isa.* 55: 6, 7), to repent (*Matt.* 4: 17; *Acts* 17: 30), to be converted (*Matt.* 18: 3), and to believe on the Lord Jesus Christ (*Acts* 16: 31).

(f) In doing these things we must be willing to show them real and genuine friendship, which will often be costly in time, energy and many other things (*Luke* 10: 29, 33–35; *II Tim.* 2: 10).

(g) We are to be ready to do this work at any time and anywhere.

(i) This work begins where we are and extends to wherever God may call us (*Acts* 1: 8).

(ii) Whether in our homes (*Acts* 18: 26) or in public places (*John* 4: 7–26; *Acts* 17: 17), on board ship (*Acts* 27: 24, 25) or in prison (*Acts* 16: 30, 31; *Phil.* 1: 12, 13; 4: 22), in the open air (*Acts* 16: 13, 14) or from house to house (*Acts* 20: 20), we are to be ready to make Christ known.

(h) We co-operate with God by means of prayer.

(i) James tells us that we have not because we ask not (*Jas.* 4: 2).

(ii) The reality of our concern will be seen in our prayers for the salvation of others (*Rom.* 10: 1).

(iii) We may ask God to do the things which He alone can do (*Acts* 4: 29, 30).

5. **We need to be clear as to the essential facts of the gospel which must be made known before any response should be anticipated.**

(1) **The gospel which has to be understood.**

(a) The appointed time, concerning which the prophets in the Old Testament had spoken and to which the people of God had looked forward, has come. Through Christ God has visited and redeemed His people (*Acts* 2: 16–21).

(b) This act of God, intervening in human history, is to be seen in the life of Jesus Christ, the Messiah, sent by God, rejected, put to death by men, and raised up by God on the third day (*Acts* 2: 32, 36).

(c) By His death and resurrection Jesus Christ has conquered sin and death and opened the kingdom of heaven to all believers. In no one else is salvation to be found (*Acts* 4: 12).

(d) The proofs of God's present power in the world are to be found in the fact of the resurrection and the evidences of the Holy Spirit's working in the Church (*Rom.* 1: 4; *Eph.* 1: 19, 20; *Acts* 4: 33).

(e) This is but the beginning of God's kingdom. Christ will come again as Judge, and God's kingdom will be finally established (*Acts* 3: 20, 21; 17: 30, 31; *II Thess.* 1: 7–10).

(f) Therefore all men everywhere should repent and be baptised in the name of Jesus the Messiah for the forgiveness of their sins, and thus receive the gift of the Holy Spirit (*Acts* 2: 38).

(2) **Fundamental to a person's understanding of the gospel is appreciation, therefore, of at least the following truths:**

(a) Christ's coming and death were part of God's eternal plan and were no accident (*Acts* 2: 23; *I Pet.* 1: 20).

(b) Jesus is the Christ, the Son of God (*John* 20: 31; *Acts* 8: 37).

(c) Christ's purpose in coming into the world and in dying upon the cross was to save sinners (*Gal.* 2: 20; *I Tim.* 1: 15).

(d) Christ's resurrection was God the Father's declaration of Christ as His Son and evidence of His satisfaction with His work (*Rom.* 1: 4).

(e) To enter into the benefits of Christ's work—to know forgiveness, the gift of God's Spirit and a place in

His kingdom—repentance and open confession of Christ are required (*Acts* 2: 38).

(f) A Christian recognises his personal sinfulness (*Rom.* 7: 24; *I Tim.* 1: 15).

(g) A Christian knows his personal indebtedness to Christ in that He gave His life a ransom for him (*Mark* 10: 45; *Gal.* 2: 20; *I Pet.* 2: 24).

(3) The benefits promised by the gospel.

(a) Reconciliation with God (*II Cor.* 5: 18–21).

(b) Justification (*I Cor.* 1: 30; 6: 11).

(c) Deliverance from condemnation (*John* 3: 18; *Rom.* 8: 1; *I Cor.* 11: 32).

(d) Belonging to the people of God (*Acts* 2: 41, 47; *I Cor.* 1: 2; 6: 1, 2; 16: 1, 15; *I Pet.* 2: 4–10).

(e) Membership of the kingdom of God (*I Cor.* 6: 10; *Col.* 1: 13).

(f) The gift of the Holy Spirit (*Acts* 2: 38; *I Cor.* 2: 12; 6: 19).

(g) Eternal life (*John* 3: 16; 11: 25, 26).

(h) The resurrection of the body (*I Cor.* 6: 14; 15: 53, 57).

6. We need to adhere to the principles which are always to govern our presentation of the gospel.

(a) We act towards people in the light of what the Bible says about the unconverted and unregenerate.

(i) They are dead in trespasses and sins (*Eph.* 2: 1).

(ii) Their unbelieving minds are blinded by Satan (*II Cor.* 4: 4).

(iii) They are lost (*Luke* 19: 10).

(iv) They are slaves of sin (*John* 8: 34).

(b) We are always to think of the other person's good rather than of our own (*I Cor.* 10: 33).

(c) We are to be direct and straightforward in our presentation of the gospel and its demands, never allowing our presentation of the truth to be influenced by people's reactions (*II Cor.* 4: 2).

(d) We are to be direct and forthright in speaking of sin (*Acts* 24: 25; *Mark* 7: 20–23).

(e) We are to aim at speaking clearly to people, i.e. in terms which they can understand (*Col.* 4: 4).

(f) Gentleness and respect are to characterise our words (*I Pet.* 3: 15; *Col.* 4: 6).

(g) Love, in all its aspects, is to be dominant in our approach (*I Cor.* 13).

(h) We are to deal with people from the Scriptures (*II Tim.* 3: 15; *Acts* 8: 30–35), our confidence being not in our skill of presentation but in the power of God's truth (*I Cor.* 2: 1, 2, 4), knowing that the word of the Cross will be the power of God to those who are to be saved (*I Cor.* 1: 18).

(i) We are to act in the assurance that if a person really seeks God, he will find Him (*Matt.* 7: 7, 8; *Acts* 10: 1–8, 30–33, 44–48).

(j) We are not to hesitate to give our personal testimony (*I Pet.* 3: 15; *Acts* 22: 6–11; 26: 12–18; *I Tim.* 1: 15).

(k) We are to depend all the time upon God the Holy Spirit.

(i) We need to be sensitive to His promptings (*Acts* 16: 6, 7), and there may be occasions when He urges us to be very direct in our approach (*Acts* 8: 30).

(ii) The work we do is valuable only as it is done in the demonstration and power of the Holy Spirit (*I Cor.* 2: 4).

(iii) If the Holy Spirit is at work, we know that He will complete His work (*Phil.* 1: 6).

7. There are certain things we are to look for in dealing with people whom we would lead to Christ.

(a) Conviction of sin (*Acts* 2: 37).

(b) An awareness of God's holiness (*Isa.* 6: 5; *Luke* 5: 8).

(c) The deflation of pride (*Jas.* 4: 6).

(d) A submission to what God says (*Jas.* 4: 7).

(e) A resistance to those considerations which would turn aside a person from having dealings with God (*Jas.* 4: 7).

(f) Readiness to use the means God has given us of drawing close to Him (*Jas.* 4: 8).

(g) Eagerness to hear the Word of God (*Acts* 16: 14).

(h) Prayer (*Acts* 9: 11; 10: 2; *Jas.* 4: 8).

(i) Changing attitudes, habits and actions (*Jas.* 4: 8).

(j) Sorrow for sin (*Jas.* 4: 9).

(k) A humility before God (*Jas.* 4: 10).

(l) When these things are present we may be sure that God is at work in people's lives and we may encourage them to call upon the name of the Lord Jesus for salvation (*Rom.* 10: 13), knowing that He will lift them up (*Jas.* 4: 10).

46. THE MISSIONARY TASK AND MISSIONARY MOTIVES

Question: What is the missionary task, and what are the considerations and motives which demand our involvement in missionary enterprise?

Answer: The missionary task is to make disciples of all nations. The Bible presents many motives for supporting and engaging in missionary work, prominent among which are concern for God's glory, obedience to our Lord's commission, the desperate need of men without Christ, the adequacy and purpose of the atonement, and the coming again of our Lord Jesus Christ.

The Missionary Task

1. Our Saviour's commission to us is to make disciples of all nations (*Matt.* 28: 19, 20).

(a) As the ministry of reconciliation is exercised (*II Cor.* 5: 18–20), and the fragrance of the knowledge of Christ is spread everywhere (*II Cor.* 2: 14), men and women will receive the gospel, take their stand upon it, hold it fast, and be saved by it (*I Cor.* 15: 1–11); they are then to be made into true disciples (*Matt.* 28: 19).

(b) The most common description of Christians in the Acts of the Apostles is "disciples" (*Acts* 6: 2, 7).

(c) The task of missions is to make disciples (*Acts* 14: 21), that is to say, to secure the obedience of men and women in word and deed to Christ (*Acts* 6: 7; *Rom.* 15: 18; cf. *Acts* 8: 36–39; 9: 18).

2. The whole world, therefore, is our concern.

(a) Starting from home to the ends of the earth is our sphere of operation (*Acts* 1: 8).

(b) The scope of our endeavours is to take in "all who are far off" (*Acts* 2: 39).

(c) The world is to be thought of as a plentiful harvest field (*Luke* 10: 2).

(d) Pentecost was an illustration of the scope of missions: everyone—no matter what his nationality—heard the good news of Christ in his own tongue (*Acts* 2: 6–11).

(e) Our commission is to preach the gospel to every creature, no matter what human barriers and prejudices

252

have to be overcome in the process (*Acts* 10: 1–48, and especially 10: 28, 34).

(f) The obligation that is upon us is to preach the gospel to all (*Rom.* 1: 14, 15; *Luke* 10: 5, 6).

3. Priorities have to be determined and recognised in the furtherance of the missionary task.

(a) Our Lord's primary attention, for example, was directed towards the Jews (*Matt.* 10: 5, 6), although this in no way implied that the gospel was not to go to the Gentiles: it was merely a question of priorities in the early days.

(b) Those among the Jews who had not heard His message were a priority to our Lord (*Mark* 1: 37, 38; *Luke* 4: 42, 43).

(c) The aim of missions must always be to preach the gospel where the name of Christ is as yet unknown (*Rom.* 15: 20).

4. The conversion of whole families is to be a priority in missionary work.

(a) The household is to be the objective (*Luke* 10: 5): if we aim only at the children, we delay the founding of the church for a generation.

(b) The conversion of whole households is to be looked for and expected (*Acts* 10: 24, 33, 44; 16: 15, 31–34; 18: 8).

(c) The first church in a place may well be a house-church (*Acts* 16: 14, 15; *Philem.* 2).

Missionary Motives

5. The glory of God.

(a) Our desire is to be that God should be glorified in all things (*I Pet.* 4: 11).

(b) Our concern for God's glory should be a consuming passion (*John* 2: 17).

(c) Our chief purpose in life is to glorify God (*I Cor.* 10: 31).

(d) The great end of the plan of redemption is the glory of the Father (*Phil.* 2: 11; *Eph.* 1: 6, 14).

(e) God is glorified when men are caused to praise Him (*Ps.* 50: 23)— for no reason do men praise Him more than for His salvation (*Luke* 2: 10–14, 20).

(f) God is glorified when redeemed men and women bring glory to God for His mercy to them (*Rom.* 15: 8–12).

(g) Our Lord Jesus glorified the Father on earth, having accomplished the work which the Father gave Him to do (*John* 17: 4)—we should have the same objective.

6. The command of our Lord Jesus Christ.

(a) We are to go into all the world and preach the gospel to every creature (*Mark* 16: 15).

(b) We are to go and make disciples of all nations (*Matt.* 28: 19).

(c) This was the final command of our Lord Jesus which He gave with impressive authority (*Matt.* 28: 18).

7. The trust which the gospel is in itself.

(a) The gospel is a trust (*I Thess.* 2: 4).

(b) Its value cannot be overestimated (*Gal.* 1: 8, 9).

(c) It is a ground of universal joy, and it demands to be proclaimed (*Luke* 2: 10, 11, 17).

(d) The message of God's love is so great (*John* 3: 16) that it must not be kept secret.

8. The experience we ourselves have of salvation.

(a) Knowing the joy of God's salvation, we feel compelled to teach

253

transgressors God's ways, and to cause sinners to return to the Lord (*Ps.* 51: 12, 13).

(b) Our experience of God's salvation puts us under an obligation to declare it to others (*Rom.* 1: 14–16).

9. The constraint of Christ's love.

(a) Knowing Christ's love for us, we find ourselves motivated by His love for others to reach them with the gospel (*II Cor.* 5: 14).

10. The need of those who are without Christ.

(a) Men and women without Christ are without hope and without God in the world (*Eph.* 2: 12).

(b) They do not know God, and their lives are governed by their passions (*I Thess.* 4: 5).

(c) Their main concerns are what to eat, drink and wear, not knowing the love of a heavenly Father (*Matt.* 6: 32; *Luke* 12: 30).

(d) They are often led astray to dumb idols (*I Cor.* 12: 2).

(e) The sorrows of those without Christ are multiplied because of the false gods they follow (*Ps.* 16: 4).

(f) They are spiritually blind and imprisoned (*Isa.* 42: 7).

(g) Compassion for the harassed souls of men is a great missionary motive (*Matt.* 9: 36).

(h) It is part and parcel of loving our neighbour as ourself (*Luke* 10: 27).

11. The adequacy of the atonement.

(a) Christ is the propitiation for our sins, and not for ours only but also for the sins of the whole world (*I John* 2: 2).

(b) The death of Christ was not for the Jewish nation only, but to gather into one the children of God who are scattered abroad (*John* 11: 52).

(c) By His blood Christ ransomed men for God from every tribe and tongue and people and nation, and He has made them a kingdom and priests to God (*Rev.* 5: 9, 10).

12. The revealed and declared purposes of God concerning the Church.

(a) God's purpose from the beginning has been to bless all the nations of the earth through the obedience of Abraham (*Gen.* 22: 17, 18).

(b) His purpose is that all nations shall flow to Zion (*Isa.* 2: 2).

(c) Throughout the Scriptures God has given assurance of His purpose to call the heathen to faith in Himself (*Mal.* 1: 11).

(d) His purpose is to take out of all peoples a people for His name (*Amos* 9: 11, 12; *Jer.* 12: 15f; *Isa.* 45: 22; *Acts* 15: 14–18).

(e) The Father has promised the nations as His Son's inheritance (*Ps.* 2: 8).

(f) The knowledge that God is going to call men and women to Himself is a powerful motive (*Acts* 2: 38, 39; 18: 9, 10).

13. The desire to please Christ, and to receive His commendation.

(a) It is right for us to want Christ to see of the travail of His soul and to be satisfied (*Isa.* 53: 11).

(b) In communicating the gospel our desire is to please God who tests our hearts (*I Thess.* 2: 4).

(c) The parables of the pounds and the talents encourage us to work for the commendation of our Master, in fulfilling the great task He has assigned to us (*Luke* 19: 11–27; *Matt.* 25: 14–30; cf. *II Cor.* 10: 18).

(d) Knowing what it means to fear the Lord, and to want to please Him, we try to persuade men (*II Cor.* 5: 11).

14. The judgment which is to come.

(a) The fact that Christians must stand before the judgment seat of

Christ too is not to promote fear but the desire to please Him now, so that they may be pleasing to Him then (*II Cor.* 5: 9, 10).

(b) The certainty of judgment is a great incentive to urgent preaching (*II Tim.* 4: 1, 2; *II Cor.* 5: 11).

(c) The judgment will be a time of misery for those who have rejected the Lord Jesus Christ (*Rev.* 1: 7; *II Thess.* 1: 8, 9).

(d) Those who have disobeyed the truth and obeyed wickedness will experience the wrath of God and eternal punishment (*Rom.* 2: 8; *Jude* 15; *Rev.* 20: 15).

15. The return of the Lord Jesus Christ.

(a) The coming of the Lord is a missionary motive because the gospel is to be preached to all nations and throughout the whole world as a testimony to all nations, before the end (*Mark* 13: 10; *Matt.* 24: 14).

47. MISSIONARY WORK

Question: What governing concept should we have of missionary work?

Answer: Missionary work is essentially God's work, by which our Lord Jesus Christ's ministry and work are continued, and in which He requires our active co-operation and hard work.

1. Missonary work is the Lord's work.

(a) God assigns the workers (*I Cor.* 3: 5).

(b) God gives the spiritual increase (*I Cor.* 3: 7).

(c) God makes the appeal through His ambassadors (*II Cor.* 5: 20).

(d) God shines into the hearts of men and women with the light of the gospel (*II Cor.* 4: 6, 7).

(e) God calls men and women to faith in His Son (*Acts* 2: 39).

(f) God opens the hearts of individuals so that they give heed to the message of the gospel (*Acts* 16: 14).

(g) God gives to men and women the gift of repentance unto life (*Acts* 11: 18).

(h) God opens the door of faith to individuals (*Acts* 14: 27; cf. 15: 4, 12).

(i) The Lord adds day by day those who are being saved (*Acts* 2: 47).

(j) The task of missions is to work together with God (*II Cor.* 6: 1).

2. Missionary work is the continuation of Christ's ministry and work.

(a) The Church is to continue what the Lord Jesus began to do and teach (*Acts* 1: 1–3; *Luke* 10: 16).

(b) While the whole emphasis is to be upon teaching and preaching, a concern for the whole man is to be shown by missions (*Luke* 10: 9).

(c) This fact implies that there is a place for the healing ministry in missions, but such a ministry must be clearly administered in the name of Jesus Christ (*Acts* 4: 9, 10).

3. The example and principles established by our Lord Jesus should be followed carefully.

(a) Certain fundamental principles were laid down in the sending out of the twelve (*Mark* 6: 8–13; *Matt.* 10: 1, 5–14; *Luke* 9: 1–6), as too in the sending out of the seventy (*Luke* 10: 1–12).

(b) There are occasions in the Acts of the Apostles where we can see Paul following the pattern set by our Lord (*Acts* 13: 51; 18: 6).

4. Missionaries are God-appointed.

(a) The Lord appoints His messengers (*Luke* 10: 1).

(b) The Lord assigns the tasks to which they are called (*I Cor.* 3: 5).

255

(c) The Lord chooses His particular instruments for His particular tasks (*Acts* 9: 15, 16).

(d) The Lord tells the churches the individuals to be set apart for the work to which He has called them (*Acts* 13: 2).

5. God gives specific commissions to individuals to fulfil.

(a) Peter was entrusted, for example, with the gospel to the circumcised, and Paul with the gospel to the Gentiles (*Gal.* 2: 7–9; *Acts* 22: 17–21).

(b) Some may be assigned to planting, others to watering; some to laying foundations, others to building upon foundations already laid (*I Cor.* 3: 5–10).

6. Missionary work is a matter of partnership.

(a) First, it is to be undertaken in partnership with God (*I Cor.* 3: 7, 9; *II Cor.* 6: 1).

(b) Secondly, it is to be undertaken in partnership with other missionaries, and other missions (*Gal.* 2: 9; *I Cor.* 3: 7–10; *Luke* 10: 1; *Acts* 20: 4; *Rom.* 16: 1–4).

(c) Thirdly, it is to be undertaken in partnership with the local church or churches (*Phil.* 1: 5).

(i) The church is to be regarded as the sending or directing agency under the guidance of the Holy Spirit (*Acts* 13: 2, 3);

(ii) Missionaries are to be commended to the grace of God by the church which confirms the missionaries' call (*Acts* 14: 26);

(iii) The whole church is to be concerned in the missionary enterprise of its members (*Acts* 15: 22, 25), with all its members involved and interested in all that God does with and through them (*Acts* 14: 27);

(iv) Missionaries are to work in close partnership with the church or churches which, under God, send them forth (*Acts* 14: 26);

(v) Missionaries have a responsibility to report to the churches what God has done with them and through them (*Acts* 15: 4, 12; cf. *Acts* 14: 27).

7. Different contributions are necessary in missionary endeavour.

(a) There are varieties of gifts, service and working, but it is the same God who inspires them all in every one (*I Cor.* 12: 4–6).

(b) Some missionary work is foundation laying, while other is building upon a foundation already laid (*I Cor.* 3: 10).

(c) Some missionary work is planting, while other is watering that which another has planted (*I Cor.* 3: 8).

8. Missionary work requires hard work and often suffering.

(a) A harvest field requires labourers (*Luke* 10: 2).

(b) "Labour" is a term frequently used by Paul to describe missionary enterprise (*Phil.* 1: 22; *II Cor.* 11: 23; *Phil.* 2: 30; cf. *Acts* 15: 38).

(c) Missionary work involves identification and accommodation to other people and their ways (*Luke* 10: 8; *I Cor.* 9: 19–23).

(d) Missionary work means sacrifice, hardship and suffering (*II Cor.* 4: 7–18; 11: 23–29; 6: 3–10; cf. *Acts* 9: 16).

(e) Missionary work often meets with great opposition, sometimes because it conflicts with vested interests: the gospel is to be proclaimed nevertheless (*Acts* 16: 19–24; *I Thess.* 2: 2).

(f) Opposition is to provide no

256

hindrance to our fulfilment of the task (*Luke* 10: 3).

(g) We should be willing to endure anything for the sake of winning the elect (*II Tim.* 2: 10).

48. MISSIONARY STRATEGY

Question: What are the first principles of missionary strategy?

Answer: The first principles of missionary strategy are the divine wisdom in choosing the foolishness of preaching, and the priority, therefore, of the teaching and preaching of the Word of God for the birth and consolidation of witnessing churches.

1. **The divine wisdom in choosing the foolishness of preaching.**

(a) While to us who are being saved the cross is the power of God, to those who are perishing the preaching of the cross is utter foolishness (*I Cor.* 1: 18).

(b) It pleases God through the folly—in the world's eyes—of what is preached through the gospel, to save those who believe (*I Cor.* 1: 21).

(c) Human ways of thinking may be quite contrary to God's strategy (*I Cor.* 1: 26–31).

(d) We are reminded that missionary work is carried on, not according to earthly, material considerations but according to eternal considerations (*II Cor.* 4: 16–18).

2. **The concept of progress which should be uppermost is the growth and multiplication of the Word.**

(a) The main task of missions is to proclaim the Word (*Acts* 17: 10–13), to deliver the essential truths (*I Cor.* 15: 3), so that hearing the preaching of Christ, men and women may come to faith (*Rom.* 10: 14–17).

(b) Missionary progress is to be thought of in terms of the growth and increase of the Word of God (*Acts* 6: 7; 12: 24; 19: 10, 20).

(c) In seeking prayer for himself and his fellow-missionaries, Paul significantly urged his friends, "Pray for us, that the Word of the Lord may speed on and triumph, as it did among you" (*II Thess.* 3: 1, R.S.V.).

3. **Missionary endeavour must concentrate on teaching the Word.**

(a) Our task is to teach disciples all that the Lord Jesus has commanded disciples to observe (*Matt.* 28: 19, 20).

(b) Fulfilling the task of teaching disciples all that the Lord Jesus Christ has commanded disciples to observe involves, of necessity, providing disciples with the Scriptures in their own tongue (*Matt.* 28: 19, 20).

(c) The emphasis of the apostles was clearly upon teaching:

(i) The Jewish authorities directed their opposition at the apostles' speaking and *teaching* in the name of Jesus (*Acts* 4: 18);

(ii) Miraculously released from prison, Peter and John were found in the temple again *teaching* the people (*Acts* 5: 25);

(iii) The apostles taught in Jesus' name so effectively that the opposing authorities said that they had filled Jerusalem with their *teaching* (*Acts* 5: 28);

(iv) Every day in the temple and at home the apostles did not cease *teaching* and preaching Jesus as Christ (*Acts* 5: 42);

(v) Following the Conference at Jerusalem, Paul and Barnabas returned to Antioch and stayed there, "where they and many others *taught* and preached the Word of the Lord" (*Acts* 15: 35);

(vi) Having received the assurance from the Lord that He was calling out many people, Paul continued in Corinth for eighteen months, *"teaching* them the Word of God" (*Acts* 18: 11);

(vii) At the end of the Acts of the Apostles we find Paul confined to his lodgings, but he "preached the kingdom of God and *taught* about the Lord Jesus Christ" (*Acts* 28: 31).

(d) A right balance is clearly necessary between teaching and preaching (*Acts* 8: 5, 25, 35, 40; 15: 35; 28: 31).

(e) The apostolic pattern was to deliberately entrust Christian teaching to faithful men who, in turn, would be able to teach others also (*II Tim.* 2: 2).

4. Witness should be established in key centres.

(a) In the Mediterranean, Paul operated from Antioch, the third city of the Roman empire (*Acts* 11: 25–30; 12: 25; 13: 1–3; 14: 24–28).

(b) Paul spent three years in Corinth, which was one of the largest commercial centres of the Roman Empire (*Acts* 18: 1–18).

(c) He had a long stay in Ephesus, the capital of the province of Asia and the centre of trade for Asia Minor (*Acts* 19: 1–41).

(d) Missionary work is clearly to take in the villages and the rural areas with the cities and towns (*Luke* 10: 1; *Mark* 1: 35–39; *Acts* 8: 5, 25, 40).

(e) Key cities and centres, however, are the obvious starting point in any new area: when, for example, the gospel came to Europe, the first preaching point was "Philippi, a Roman colony and the leading city of that district of Macedonia" (*Acts* 16: 12).

5. A simple course of strategy should be followed.

(a) Work should begin with those who are most disposed to listen, with the intention of working out into the community from such:

(i) Thus, in a Jewish situation, the apostles preached first of all in the temple (*Acts* 5: 20, 25), and Paul's first approach where there were any Jews in the community was to seek to preach the gospel in the synagogue (*Acts* 9: 20; 13: 5; 17: 1, 2, 10, 17; 18: 4, 5).

(ii) Where there was no synagogue, Paul's first approach was to seek to preach to any who sought to follow the Jewish religion, although perhaps not Jews, and any who were at all religious, and thus used to thinking of God and His claims (*Acts* 16: 13; 17: 22–34).

(b) A clear order of priorities so far as spheres of witness in a community were concerned seems to have been followed:

(i) First, religious meeting places were a prime approach, and these were Jewish synagogues in the early years of gospel preaching (*Acts* 18: 4, 5; 19: 8);

(ii) Secondly, meeting halls were used when religious meeting places were not available (*Acts* 19: 9);

(iii) Thirdly, public places, such as markets, where people congregate, were resorted to where the opportunity presented itself (*Acts* 17: 17);

(iv) At the same time, and sometimes as an only possible means, the homes of believers and interested unbelievers were used (*Acts* 5: 42; 18: 7; 20: 20).

6. Missionary work couples church-planting with disciple-making.

(a) As men and women are brought

258

to faith and discipleship, they are to be gathered together regularly for instruction in the Word, fellowship and the breaking of bread (*Acts* 2: 42), and also for common action, where necessary (*Acts* 6: 2).

(b) Believers are to be taught to gather together on the Lord's day for the breaking of bread, and the ministry of the Word (*Acts* 20: 7–12).

(c) Believers are so to be gathered and integrated together that they know themselves to belong together (*Acts* 9: 2, 19, 26); they are to be instructed in brotherhood (*Acts* 9: 17; *I John* 3: 17, 18).

(d) Believers are to be taught the priority of prayer and the ministry of the Word (*Acts* 6: 4).

(e) Believers are to be taught concerning the type of men they are to call to serve as elders and deacons (*Acts* 6: 1–6; *I Tim.* 3: 1–13; *Tit.* 1: 5–9).

7. The key to world-evangelisation is witnessing churches.

(a) Believers are to be taught that whatever circumstances affect their lives, and wherever they may have to go, they are to preach the Word (*Acts* 8: 4).

(b) Once established, a church is to become a sending-church: for example, the church at Antioch (*Acts* 11: 20–30; 13: 1–3; 14: 26–28).

(c) The testimony of lip and the transformation of life of those who have newly experienced God's delivering power are two of the most powerful means of drawing attention to the gospel and of bringing people to faith (*Acts* 3: 9–16; 4: 4, 14; 9: 20, 21).

(d) Young churches are to be taught to shine in their communities, by the quality of their corporate life, like stars lighting up the sky, thus enabling them to offer effectively the message of life (*Phil.* 2: 15, 16).

(e) The transformation of lives through the gospel is a most powerful means of spreading the message of the gospel through the whole of an area, and beyond (*I Thess.* 1: 7–10).

8. Spiritual leaders are to be looked for and encouraged within the newly-emerging churches.

(a) It is to be expected that the Spirit will give gifts to a young church as to a more established church (*Acts* 13: 1–4).

(b) The lack of education men may have and their very ordinariness must not influence our assessment of what the Spirit can do through them—for example, Peter and John (*Acts* 4: 13).

(c) It is to be expected that the Holy Spirit will raise up in the young churches men and women of equal spiritual gifts to those who have brought the gospel to them (*Acts* 13: 1–4; 15: 35).

(d) The appointing authority of spiritual leaders—or better, the recognising body, for the Holy Spirit raises up spiritual leaders—is the church, not the missionaries (*II Cor.* 8: 19, 23).

9. Missionary advance must go hand in hand with church-consolidation.

(a) Sustained periods of teaching and preaching are to be the pattern of missionary work (*Acts* 18: 11; 19: 8–10).

(b) The aim of missions is to fully preach the gospel (*Rom.* 15: 19), to declare to new converts all that is profitable (*Acts* 20: 20), and to deliver to them the whole counsel of God (*Acts* 20: 27); this means their demands of the gospel (*I Thess.* 4: 1–8), and appreciating the tribulations which may well be before them as a consequence of faith in Christ and obedience to Him (*Acts* 14: 22).

(c) The work of missions is to build up babes in Christ to make them spiritual men (*I Cor.* 3: 1–3).

(d) The strengthening of young churches, therefore, is as necessary as starting work in new areas, and it may have a greater priority at times (*Acts* 18: 18–23; 14: 21–23).

(e) Believers are to be firmly established, and they are not to be left in an untaught state (*Acts* 8: 14–17); no effort is to be spared to this end (*I Thess.* 3: 1–3, 10).

(f) The task of missions is to see newly-founded churches governed by elders from among their own number (*Acts* 14: 23), and such spiritual leaders obviously profit from being called together and exhorted concerning their duties and warned of the dangers to which they may be prone (*Acts* 20: 17–35).

(g) Young churches need to be encouraged by visits for the purpose of edification (*Acts* 15: 36; 20: 2): they need to be stirred up by way of remembrance concerning truths they already know (*Rom.* 15: 15), and guided on important issues where more experienced Christians and churches have discovered the will of God (*Acts* 16: 4, 5).

10. **The proper relationship of missionary to local converts must be appreciated.**

(a) The relationship of missionaries to converts must be that of brethren (*Acts* 15: 36).

(b) Missionaries are to be in partnership with the Christians they see established as a fruit of their labours (*Acts* 13: 1–3; cf. 11: 25).

(c) Missionaries are directed by the Spirit through the united conviction of the church—whether the sending church or the receiving church (*Acts* 13: 1–4).

(d) Missionaries should be subject to the teaching, ministry and discipline of the local church, even if it is a newly-established church (*Acts* 13: 1.–4).

(e) Missionaries should teach converts, by example, to live according to the Scriptures (*I Cor.* 4: 6).

(f) Missionaries should reproduce themselves in the people among whom they serve so that they themselves can move on, knowing that the church will continue with a spiritual ministry (*Acts* 13: 1–4).

(g) The work of missions is not to make converts or churches dependent upon missionaries (*I Cor.* 3: 4, 5).

(h) Converts and churches should be taught to appreciate that the missionary's objective is not to bind them in allegiance to him but to Christ (*II Cor.* 11: 2).

11. **Literature has an important place in church consolidation.**

(a) Paul's letters in the New Testament bear witness to the place and importance of literature dealing with doctrine and conduct.

(b) Young Christians, particularly from heathen backgrounds, need literature to guide them (*Acts* 15: 20, 23–29).

49. HIDDEN FACTORS IN MISSIONARY ENTERPRISE

Question: What are the hidden factors we must take account of in missionary enterprise?

Answer: First, the Holy Spirit is the agent of God's new creation in Christ—the Church—and His power is essential. Secondly, we engage in a spiritual work when we engage in missionary work and our dependence upon God, expressed in prayer and the activity of faith, must be real.

1. The Holy Spirit is the Agent of God's new creation in Christ—the Church.

(a) The Holy Spirit's activity in God's new creation is all-important:

(i) He puts the redeemed in possession of the results of the Father's love and the mediation of Christ (*II Cor.* 3: 9; *John* 7: 38, 39);

(ii) Justification takes place through the name of the Lord Jesus and the Spirit of God (*I Cor.* 6: 11; *I Pet.* 1: 2);

(iii) Through the Spirit the redeemed are brought into the one body, the Church, this act being described as a baptism (*I Cor.* 12: 13);

(iv) The Spirit is the Author of the new birth (*John* 3: 5, 6).

(b) The Holy Spirit is directly associated with the extension of God's new creation—the Church (*Matt.* 28: 19; cf. *Acts* 1: 4, 8).

(i) He ensures that messengers are raised up and men sent forth to proclaim the gospel (*Matt.* 9: 38; cf. *Acts* 13: 2, 4; 16: 6, 7, 10; 20: 28);

(ii) He accompanies the preaching of the gospel with His power (*I Pet.* 1: 12);

(iii) He shows men their need of salvation by convincing them of sin (*John* 16: 8–11);

(iv) He bears witness to Christ (*John* 15: 26), and by His influence men are enabled to say "Jesus is Lord" (*I Cor.* 12: 3);

(v) For the care of the Church the Spirit raises up guardians or pastors (*Acts* 20: 28);

(vi) He allots varying gifts to Christians (*Rom.* 12: 6–8);

(vii) In each Christian the Spirit desires to manifest Himself in some particular way, for some useful purpose (*I Cor.* 12: 4–11);

(viii) The Spirit's purpose is to equip God's people for work in Christ's service, to the building up of the body of Christ (*Eph.* 4: 11–13).

(c) Not surprisingly the Lord Jesus, therefore, taught the apostles that they were dependent upon the Holy Spirit for the fulfilment of their commission (*Acts* 1: 4, 5).

(d) Missionary work should be marked by power (*Luke* 10: 17–19), and we need at every stage to acknowledge our dependence upon the Holy Spirit.

2. When we engage in the work of missions, we engage in a great spiritual battle.

(a) The work of missions is part of a great spiritual battle (*II Cor.* 10: 3, 4).

(b) Missionary work is in open conflict with the god of this world who has blinded the minds of unbelievers to keep them from seeing the light of the gospel of the glory of Christ (*II Cor.* 4: 4).

(c) Opposition and indifference, therefore, are not to take us by surprise (*Luke* 10: 10, 11; *II Cor.* 4: 3, 4).

3. Dependence upon God is to characterise missionary enterprise.

(a) It is to be clear to all that missions and missionaries depend upon God (*Luke* 10: 4).

(b) This fact is not to be interpreted, however, to the detriment of the responsibility of Christians to support missionary work: those who give themselves completely to the work of the gospel may live by the gospel (*I Cor.* 9: 1–18; *Luke* 10: 7).

(c) Furthermore, dependence upon God does not rule out the missionary being self-supporting where that would seem to be the more honourable thing to do (*Acts* 18: 3; 20: 34).

4. Our confidence in missionary work is in the Lord, not in the converts.

(a) God begins the good work in people's lives, and He will bring it to completion at the day of Jesus Christ (*Phil.* 1: 6).

(b) Missionaries may have confidence in God about their converts (*II Thess.* 3: 4).

5. The priority of prayer.

(a) Missionary endeavour is to be born in prayer, and carried through by prayer (*Acts* 4: 23–31).

(b) Paul's prayers for the churches indicate the priority he himself gave to it in his endeavours (*Eph.* 1: 16–23; 3: 14–21; *Phil.* 1: 3–11; *Col.* 1: 9–12).

6. Missionary work involves acting according to faith.

(a) We are called to work, believing that the Lord Himself will work with us (*Luke* 10: 1; *Matt.* 28: 20; *Mark* 16: 20).

(b) The assurance we have, by faith, that God's purposes shall be fulfilled gives us the necessary grace to persevere (*Acts* 18: 9–11).

7. Missionary work is momentous.

(a) The kingdom of God comes near men and women by means of missionary endeavour (*Luke* 10: 9–11).

(b) The response men and women give to the missionary representatives of Christ is the response they give to Christ himself (*Luke* 10: 16).

50. SUPPORTING MISSIONS

Question: How are we to support missionary work?

Answer: We are to support missionary work wholeheartedly and generously, by finance and prayer, as part of our worship of God.

1. Some preliminary considerations.

(a) Giving people the gospel means giving them our very selves in service—there is no room for half-heartedness (*I Thess.* 2: 8).

(b) Christians in churches which have been brought into being and blessed through the gospel should provide the wherewithal for others to labour in new and emerging churches (*II Cor.* 11: 8).

(c) Those who come to faith are to be taught to have a sense of responsibility for one another in every way, both spiritually and materially (*Acts* 4: 32–37).

(d) Missionary service should not be a burden to those who are served (*I Thess.* 2: 9; *II Thess.* 3: 7–9).

(e) Missionaries have a right to be supported (*I Cor.* 9: 4–14): those who proclaim the gospel should get their living by the gospel, according to the Lord's command (*I Cor.* 9: 14).

(f) A basic principle of missions is that it is more blessed to give than to receive (*Acts* 20: 35).

(g) The whole of the local church is involved in the sending forth of a missionary, under the direction of the Holy Spirit (*Acts* 13: 1–4).

(h) God's people should be encouraged to have a sense of responsibility and of partnership in missionary enterprise (*Phil.* 1: 3–5; 4: 15).

(i) A truly worshipping church is a missionary-minded church (*Acts* 13: 2).

(j) A missionary-minded church happily sees its most gifted members sent forth as missionaries (*Acts* 13: 1–4).

2. Supporting missions by finance.

(a) The tribes, in the Old Testament period, were required to give from their inheritance a certain portion for the use of those who were set apart for God's service (*Josh.* 21; cf. *I Cor.* 9: 13, 14; *Gal.* 6: 6).

(b) Giving is part of our honouring God and fearing His name (*Mal.* 1: 6–8).

(c) Our giving proves the reality of our faith (*II Cor.* 9: 13).

(d) Giving is part and parcel of our confession of the gospel of Christ (*II Cor.* 9: 13).

(e) Giving is to be by all (*I Cor.* 16: 2), by tithes and by offerings (*Mal.* 3: 10).

(f) To share what we have is a spiritual sacrifice pleasing to God (*Heb.* 13: 16); there is a fellowship of giving and receiving (*Phil.* 4: 15).

(g) We should so give that there is an abundance in God's house (*Mal.* 3: 10).

(h) When it comes to giving, it is best to say little, and do much (*Mal.* 1: 14).

(i) Giving is part of our missionary partnership (*Phil.* 4: 15), and properly used it brings thanksgiving to God (*II Cor.* 9: 12).

(j) Giving should be regular and systematic (*I Cor.* 16: 2), according to how we have decided for ourselves (*II Cor.* 9: 7) and promised (*II Cor.* 9: 5); our giving is to be cheerful (*II Cor.* 9: 7), loving (*I Cor.* 13: 3), according to our ability (*Acts* 11: 29), and in proportion to our prosperity (*I Cor.* 16: 2).

(k) Our giving should be in the light of God's inexpressible gift to us (*II Cor.* 9: 15).

(l) The more God enriches us, the more scope we should find for generous giving (*II Cor.* 9: 11); our gifts should not be exactions but a bounty (*II Cor.* 9: 5).

(m) The Lord watches the giving of His people, and He does not despise any gift: the value of the gift is in proportion to what a person has left, and what it has cost them to give (*Mark* 12: 41–44; *Luke* 21: 1–4).

(n) Giving is not to be influenced by the difficulties of the times: the difficulties serve to provide an even greater opportunity of proving God (*Mal.* 3: 10).

(o) We are foolish if we say we cannot afford to give and to be generous (*Prov.* 22: 9; cf. *Deut.* 15: 9, 10; *II Cor.* 9: 7, 8; *Prov.* 19: 17; 28: 27).

(p) When we fail to give, we work hard with little profit; we eat, but never have enough; we drink, but we are always thirsty; we clothe ourselves, but we are never warm; we earn a wage but it goes nowhere (*Hag.* 1: 6).

(q) Generous giving to meet the needs of others brings blessing from God (*Prov.* 22: 9; *Hag.* 1: 5, 7, 9–11).

(r) As we meet the needs of others God will meet ours (*Mal.* 3: 11; *II Cor.* 9: 8, 9, 10; *Phil.* 4: 19).

(s) Sparse sowing means sparse reaping, and bountiful sowing means bountiful reaping in the sphere of giving, both for the work at home and the work abroad (*II Cor.* 9: 6).

(t) In distributing our money set apart for others, we need to recognise that we do not always know who needs help most, but others do: we should happily leave the distribution to such as know the needs (*Acts* 4: 34–37; cf. *Acts* 5: 1–11; *I Cor.* 16: 1–4).

3. Supporting missions by prayer.

(a) Missionary concern is seen in prayer to God (*Rom.* 10: 1).

(b) We should begin by praying for governments and world leaders, that they may be enabled to maintain peace and order so that the preaching of the gospel may go forward, according to God's pattern and will (*I Tim.* 2: 1–4).

(c) Paul's requests for prayer guide us in the kind of petitions we should bring to God on behalf of missionaries:

(i) Deliverance from malicious unbelievers (*Rom.* 15: 30, 31);

(ii) Acceptance with God's people (*II Cor.* 1: 11; *Rom.* 15: 31).

(iii) Health of mind and body (*Rom.* 15: 32; *II Cor.* 1: 8–11).

(iv) The ability to speak the right words boldly at the moment of opportunity (*Eph.* 6: 19);

(v) The turning of untoward circumstances to good (*Phil.* 1: 19);

(vi) God-given opportunities for preaching Christ (*Col.* 4: 3);

(vii) Progress in the establishment of the church through the Word (*II Thess.* 3: 1).

(d) Paul's prayers for the young churches guide us in the kind of petitions we should bring to God on behalf of our Christian brethren among whom and alongside whom our missionaries work (*Eph.* 1: 16–23; 3: 14–21; *Phil.* 1: 3–11; *Col.* 1: 9–12).

(e) Our support by prayer should be unceasing (*Eph.* 1: 16).